The Rise & Fall of America's Greatest High-Performance Automobile Dealer

LOST MUSCLE CAR Dealerships

DUNCAN BROWN

CarTech®

CarTech®

CarTech®, Inc.
6118 Main Street
North Branch, MN 55056
Phone: 651-277-1200 or 800-551-4754
Fax: 651-277-1203
www.cartechbooks.com

© 2019 by Duncan Brown

All rights reserved. No part of this publication may be reproduced or utilized in any form or by any means, electronic or mechanical, including photocopying, recording, or by any information storage and retrieval system, without prior permission from the Publisher. All text, photographs, and artwork are the property of the Author unless otherwise noted or credited.

No portion of this book may be reproduced, transferred, stored, or otherwise used in any manner for purposes of training any artificial intelligence technology or system to generate text, illustrations, diagrams, charts, designs or other works or materials.

The information in this work is true and complete to the best of our knowledge. However, all information is presented without any guarantee on the part of the Author or Publisher, who also disclaim any liability incurred in connection with the use of the information and any implied warranties of merchantability or fitness for a particular purpose. Readers are responsible for taking suitable and appropriate safety measures when performing any of the operations or activities described in this work.

All trademarks, trade names, model names and numbers, and other product designations referred to herein are the property of their respective owners and are used solely for identification purposes. This work is a publication of CarTech, Inc. and has not been licensed, approved, sponsored, or endorsed by any other person or entity. The Publisher is not associated with any product, service, or vendor mentioned in this book and does not endorse the products or services of any vendor mentioned in this book.

Edit by Wes Eisenschenk
Layout by Monica Seiberlich

ISBN 978-1-61325-910-8
Item No. CT644C

Library of Congress Cataloging-in-Publication Data Available

Written, edited, designed, and printed in the U.S.A.

CarTech books may be purchased at a discounted rate in bulk for resale, events, corporate gifts, or educational purposes. Special editions may also be created to specification. For details, contact Special Sales at 6118 Main Street, North Branch, MN 55056 or by email at sales@cartechbooks.com.

Publisher's Note: *In reporting history, the images required to tell the tale will vary greatly in quality, especially by modern photographic standards. While some images in this volume are not up to those digital standards, we have included them, as we feel they are an important element in telling the story.*

TABLE OF CONTENTS

Acknowledgments 6
Introduction 7

Chapter 1   Clippinger Chevrolet and Russ Davis Ford 10
Chapter 2   Dana Chevrolet 19
Chapter 3   Yeakel Plymouth Center 32
Chapter 4   Albertson Brothers Oldsmobile 47
Chapter 5   Reynolds Buick GMC 54
Chapter 6   Melrose Motors 65
Chapter 7   Conroy Pontiac Buick Versus Mander Chevrolet Oldsmobile 70
Chapter 8   Cliff Bristow Motors 85
Chapter 9   Dale Chevrolet 89
Chapter 10 White Bear Dodge 95
Chapter 11 Mr. Norm's Grand Spaulding Dodge 105
Chapter 12 Nickey Chevrolet Sales 119
Chapter 13 Fred Gibb Chevrolet 130
Chapter 14 Royal Pontiac 145
Chapter 15 Bill Knafel Pontiac 159
Chapter 16 Bill Allen Chevrolet 168
Chapter 17 Yenko Chevrolet 174

Index 190

ACKNOWLEDGMENTS

Very special thanks to a great collaborator, my editor Wes Eisenschenk. His guidance, excellent suggestions, and contacts made this book possible.

CarTech supported this book through multiple changes of direction, which also tested the patience of design and copyeditors faced with last-minute layout juggling. Thank you!

Special thanks to my mother, for developing my reading, writing, and art. Thanks to my dad, for my first camera. Liddel Lisa Minella solved an avalanche of crazy computer issues.

Bob McClurg provided access to his archive of excellent photos, including this book's main cover image.

George Pappas turned this book around at a critical point with a treasure trove of intriguing photos and stories, and great encouragement.

Don Reynolds took time from running his busy dealership to assist in any way he could.

Father Jim Perkl provided a motherlode of vintage images. He also blessed my car for my road trip!

Nancy Gibb went above and beyond to ensure this book had a wonderful array of images from her family's dealership.

Living in your car gets tedious! Hosts on the road included Mark and Ginnie Hassett; Bill and Sue Liddy; Derek, Tara, and Pearl McCulloch; Liddel Lisa, Javen, and Devin Minella; Bill and Patti Nawrot; and Jim Wangers.

Thanks to Richard Adair, Gene Adams, Alameda County Courthouse, Alameda Public Library, Bob Allen, Joel Altman, Dave Anderson, Rod Arnzen, Jason Ball, Ken Barnhart, Dave Beem, Bellingham Public Library, Robert "442" Bescott, Thomas Bettencourt, Billy Bissonet, Allen Booth, Mark Brailey, Adam Brandes, Tim Brown, Mel Browning, Tim Burgess, Robert Carrothers, Tom Carter, Jim Cecil, Chicago Public Library, Rob Clary and Tom Clary, Patrick Comey, Pat Conroy, Tim Costello at MCA, Garth "Maximus" Cox, Laurie Craig, Dennis Cumby, Scott Dahlberg, Dean and Helen Darnell, Roger Day, Terry Denomme at Bone Stock, Detroit Public Library, Dave Fillion, David Garton, Bill Glowacki, Google Earth, Dave Govett, Cam Grant, Merle Green Jr., D. Hardy, Mark Hassett, Mark Hassett Jr., Historical Society of Seattle and King County, Bob Hoogstra Van Hurst, Cam Hutchins and Paul Hutchins, Iliana at Milwaukee County Historical, Frank Isaak, Jamie Jarvis, Jill at The Winking Judge Pub, Tim Johnson, Don Keefe, Mr. Norm Kraus, David Lambdin, Al Leibof, Library of Congress, Los Angeles Public Library, Spence Lyon, Manhattan Beach Public Library, Kathleen Marks, Bob McClurg, Tom McEwan, Mecum Auto Auctions, Andy Meyer and Dick Meyer, Douglas Morton, Skip Murphy, Annie and Rick Nelson, Newspapers.com, Dave Nicholas, Oakland Public Library, Oakland City Hall, Olympia Public Library, Rollie and Cheryl Paulsgrove, Bob Peck, John Politzer, Portland Public Library, Don Powell, Hayden Proffitt, John Quesnel, Rachel at Missouri State Historical Society, R. E. Olds Transportation Museum, Carlos Rivera, Michelle Roberts, Al Rogers, San Francisco Public Library, Denny Sanders, Dave Savage, Pat Sawyer Family, Dr. Eric M. Schiffer, Ken and Becky Schoentaler, Milt Schornack, Marty Schorr, Seattle Public Library, Keith Seymore, J Scott Shannon of Covina Past blog, Greg Sharp, Wayne and Shiela at NHRA Museum, Russell Small, Russell Stidham, Steve Strand, Mike Strickler, UCLA Library Special Collections copyright law specialists, Sandy Vandeberg, Mike Vercheak, Jim Wangers, Washington State Historical Society, Washington State Library, Jeanne Weise, Michael White, Todd R. Wingerter, and Robert Yeakel.

Introduction

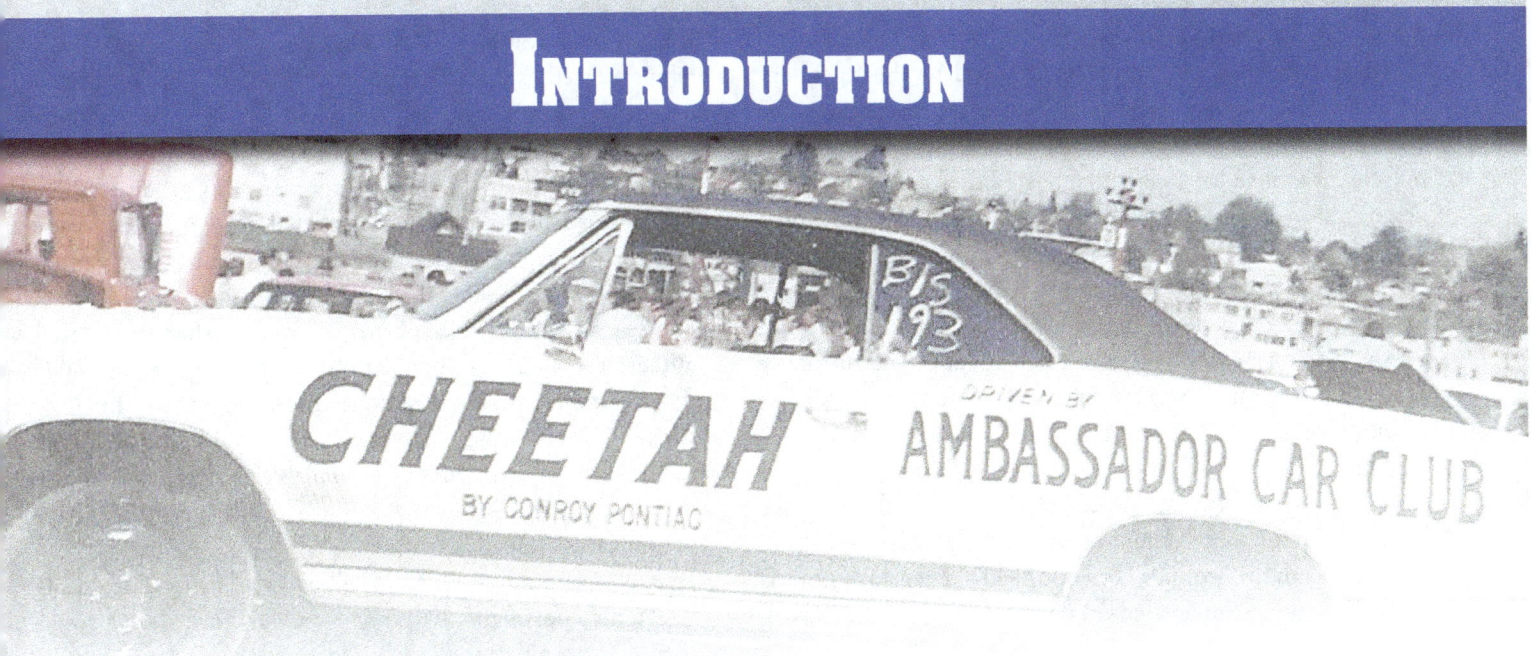

The years 1964 to 1970 are considered to be the golden era of high-volume domestic muscle cars. A majority of dealerships in the 1960s reluctantly sold muscle cars, and many of them shied away from even a whiff of performance. However, there were many dealerships that embraced the factory muscle car marketing and amped it to the tune of squealing tires, no-holds-barred thrills, speed, and raw savage power. Some dealerships even usurped the factory limits with engine swaps and high-performance enhancements. Other dealers may not have produced their own dealer specials, but they sold a lot of muscle cars because they were passionate about them. They offered dyno tune-ups, car club meeting spots, and speed parts.

A ridiculous number of V-8 big-block cars were sold as muscle car mania gripped nearly everyone below the age of 30 (and a lot of people over 30). Car dealers today still sell some muscle cars but not like the 1960s' tsunami of horsepower that was hitting the streets. In our small, modern muscle market, the high-volume muscle dealers that survive have shrunk back to regular dealerships and are now just as "lost" as the dealers that are physically wiped out of existence without any trace. Many former muscle car dealers now sell SUVs and trucks only.

Writing this book involved a lot of talking, research, and endless nights roaming through dozens of cities trying to follow the ghosts of cruising and street racing. Not much was left to find. The remnants of glorious old steel and glass dealerships have been mostly replaced by fast-food places. The few dealerships still standing suffer the modern affliction of plastic-cladded surfaces, just as car engines now have plastic engine covers.

Defining a Muscle Car Dealership

The dealerships I've included in this book specialized in excitement. I've considered any business that spent money to plunge into the risky wild waters of performance, which means I traveled farther afield with some lesser brands. The famous well-known dealers are in here, but I also included relatively obscure dealers.

Jim Wangers was an ad man at McManus, which handled marketing for the Pontiac Motor Division. Jim's dedication to Pontiac image building during the peak of 1960s Pontiac Performance continued during the aftermath of Pontiac at car shows and in books and magazines. He created the ultimate version of a muscle car dealership when he leveraged factory support to transform Royal Pontiac in Royal Oak, Michigan, into a complete performance dealership. This makes him the ultimate person to consult when defining what "makes" a muscle car dealership.

Jim defines a muscle car dealer as *only* a dealership that aggressively marketed, stocked, tuned, and raced muscle cars; had a deep inventory of speed parts; and had fanatics in the sales department and mechanics that could supertune. The dealership existed solely to offer performance.

If we strictly adhere to Jim's definition of a muscle car dealership, only a few true muscle car dealers existed during the 1960s. If we open up the floodgates the other way, it could be argued that *every* dealer probably sold at least a few muscle cars. We can't count every dealership that ever sold a muscle car, and if we restrict the field to just the highest peak dealers, we miss out on some pretty cool dealerships.

Racing Sponsorship Dealerships

Few people in the 1960s could travel to the legendary dealerships to buy a muscle machine. Most muscle car hunters were restricted to local dealers. Those in the market for a muscle car looked for a place that hosted the local car club or a performance clinic. Seeing a dealership's name on a sponsored drag car at the weekend races was a potent hint that suggested this place would speak the lingo and have the goods.

Jim Wangers believes that a dealership that puts its name on the side of a race car is not automatically a performance dealership. He said, "So they have a racing car? Big deal. It's an empty gesture! Most of those places were full of hopeless clowns!

"You walk into one of these dealerships with their race car sitting in the showroom, but no one there knows a 4-speed from a hole in the ground!" he continued. "Their inventory is a *joke*! Nothing but loaded-down, option-heavy slugs with 323 open rear ends!"

Jim concedes that many "sponsorship dealers" may have had someone sympathetic to performance on staff, but he insists that the dealership itself was rarely capable of capitalizing on the exposure racing provided. Other major players from back in the day agree with Jim.

Hayden Proffitt drove race cars for all the major manufacturers during the 1960s, and he stated to me flatly that he usually had nothing to do with the dealerships that sponsored him. He said, "They never gave me a penny. The dealers who sponsored a car were just a front for the factory."

Tom "the Mongoose" McEwen went further in racing than many others partly because he was a highly successful promoter as well as a good driver. Tom told me that he had extremely minimal involvement with any of the dealerships that put their names on his cars. When I asked him about some of his sponsors, he admitted, "I don't remember having much to do with them. It's kind of hazy."

Often a driver approached a dealer for a few bucks to sponsor a car and that was as far as the dealership ever went. However, the dealerships soon noted the influx of sales when a car with its name on it won at the strip, and they quickly educated themselves about this new market.

Engine-Swapping Dealerships

Cars driven on the street were more important than the cars a dealership sponsored on the racetrack. That dealer's drag racers may get buyers in the dealership door, but a new muscle car absolutely had to put a buyer's friends, brothers-in-law, or neighbor down the street into the weeds.

Whenever legendary muscle car dealerships are listed, Ford and Chrysler fans become slightly disappointed by the massive number of GM dealers that appear. This occurs because more GM cars were sold in the 1960s, meaning that more GM dealerships existed as a starting point. Also, GM vehicles needed engine swappers *more* than Ford and Chrysler dealers, which is a compliment to the Blue Oval and Mopar camps.

The avalanche of engine swappers in the GM dealerships evolved due to GM's corporate insistence on a 400-ci engine limit for GM intermediate and pony car muscle machines during the 1960s. General Motors held its cubic inches back because it was hovering at 60-percent market share and feared antitrust action. The automaker did whatever it could to mollify government hostility toward the corporation. Luckily, full-size GM cars and Corvettes were immune to these limits. Those monster engines were available as crated motors for transplantation or through wily use of the Central Office Production Order (COPO) system.

Anyone could buy a 428 Shelby out of many Ford dealers. At the end of the 1960s, any regular Ford dealer could order a Mustang stuffed with a factory 428 Cobra Jet (CJ). When the Mustang CJ hit the strips, it was hailed as the fastest passenger sedan of 1968½. The CJ was a bone-stock factory machine. Suddenly, years of Ford Total Performance on the racetrack was translated to the showroom floor.

Affordable Daily Driver Muscle Car

Even a basic prepackaged factory muscle car with a bare-bones order sheet stretched most budgets to the limit. The masses with limited cash revered the muscle car dealers that gained their reputations by catering to the "small guys."

White Bear Dodge became the world's largest Dodge dealer by adhering to a slim profit margin made possible through volume turnover of a massive inventory. A budget muscle driver could get a 383 Dodge Challenger 4-speed with marginal cash outlay. White Bear Dodge had hordes of buyers in brand-new muscle on a used-car budget due to owner Jerry Perkl's perspective of "Let's make deals. Let's sell these cars!"

The mega motor dealer swappers put some fabulously crazy machines on the roads, but they were rare. Mr. Norm's Grand Spaulding and Tasca Ford dumped an insane amount of heavy iron into the streets using the volume approach. Bob Yeakel did everything big. Bob's "More is better" approach funneled a lot of hot Plymouths into the world.

The Parts Palaces

The typical muscle car fan was making payments on a bare-bones muscle car and had to tweak it gradually over time in small steps. The average owner suffering stoplight whippings in a stock 396 325-hp Chevelle SS or Mustang GT390 improved the car in tiny increments.

Racing is hard on drivelines, and parts departments

often picked up a lot of money stocking replacement heads and pistons. Missed shifts bent valves. Over-revving toasted transmissions and clutches. Oversize maximum-traction aftermarket tires frequently broke rear ends. So, the muscle car specialists raked in "hidden" revenue via the speed parts department.

Many muscle car dealerships from the era did very strong business selling short-blocks, cranks, heads, cams, pistons, and so on. Some muscle car buyers were seriously involved in major teardowns, yanking out stock engines and building serious engines. If a 383 blew up, the owner might decide to build a 440 instead of spending nearly as much on that shot 383.

Reynolds Buick established the first Hooker Header distributorship when Gary Hooker began selling his aftermarket headers through the parts department. *Hot Rod* magazine listed the part numbers that were available at Reynolds to hop up Buicks.

Berger Chevrolet featured its parts guru, Jim Luikens, in print ads promoting its high-performance inventory. Mr. Norm's took out full-page ads listing go-fast parts in car magazines. Both places sold parts through mail order as well.

Choosing "Lost" Dealerships

By the late 1960s, a "tuff" image was part of the muscle car formula. A lot of people who bought these cars spent their time cruising and hanging out, not tinkering or waiting in line to run at a drag strip. At the end of 1969, General Motors had 14,000 dealerships and Ford had 6,000. Add in Lincoln-Mercury, Chrysler, and AMC, and that is an insane number of dealers! For every dealer that made some effort to specialize in muscle cars, there were hundreds if not thousands more that wouldn't touch performance with a 10-foot pole.

Some readers will throw this book at the wall and demand to know why I am clogging up the works with offbeat muscle dealers. Readers who challenge the inclusion of some lesser players will have a perfectly legitimate point. However, these dealer specials fit in with the cool muscle image machines.

After all of the statistics and facts are sifted, documented, and digested, the real point is that the golden era of muscle cars was a fun one. The owners and cars had attitude, and that excitement gave dying dealerships a second life, allowing dealers to really run with the muscle movement. The rare dealers that exploited the performance angle were pioneers who deserve remembrance, which is why they are included in this book.

CHAPTER 1
CLIPPINGER CHEVROLET AND RUSS DAVIS FORD

Clippinger Chevrolet
Location: Covina, California
Years in Operation: 1921–circa 2005
Founder(s): Isaiah Hale Clippinger
Current Status: Overflow lot

Russ Davis Ford
Location: Covina, California
Years in Operation: 1925–1972
Founder(s): Russell W. Davis
Current Status: Vacant

Clippinger Chevrolet

Since 1921, I. H. Clippinger and his son, N. H. Clippinger, along with their experienced, friendly staff of 97, have been serving the Covina area in the sales of Chevrolet Cars, trucks, Corvettes, Corvairs and "OK" used cars and trucks. Open seven days a week plus weekday nights. Citrus at San Bernardino Road, 1 mile north of the San Bernardino Freeway, EDgewood 9-7776.

Clippinger Chevrolet's original building is shown in this promotional photograph. The Clippinger Chevrolet sign atop the building is typical of signage from the early 1960s. When Clippinger built its new premises in 1967, the sign became simpler and less ornate. (Photo Courtesy J Scott Shannon, Covina Past Blog)

Fortuitous dealer locations sometimes resulted in some healthy competition between adjacent dealerships during the muscle car era. Yeakel Plymouth and Sachs & Sons were across the street from one another, which incited each dealership to display hotter and more outrageous cars on the lots and to field wilder machines at the strip under their sponsorships. Up north in Canada, Mander Chevrolet Oldsmobile and Conroy Pontiac Buick pushed one another to new heights of dealer specialty cars.

Covina, California, a suburb of Los Angeles, retains a small-town feel. Good neighborly respect meant that the rivalry between Clippinger Chevrolet and Russ Davis Ford was muted somewhat by goodwill from both sides of San Bernardino Road, where the dealers faced one another.

Clippinger Chevrolet

Late 1960s advertising proclaimed that Clippinger Chevrolet was California's oldest Chevy dealership. The dealership was located in West Covina, California, and held honors for the most Corvettes sold by a single individual. That individual was Bob Wingate, who was lionized as the single biggest individual volume Corvette salesman in all of the United States.

Founder Isaiah Hale Clippinger was born on October 4, 1877, in Iowa and began his auto career in 1917. Hale established Clippinger Chevrolet at 7th and Central in Los Angeles in 1921. He moved the dealership from downtown Los Angeles to 137 W. San Bernardino Road in Covina in 1929.

10   Lost Muscle Car Dealerships

The Clippinger neon sign still stands at the corner of Citrus in Covina. This dealership was state of the art in 1967. Now, the lot serves as temporary overflow parking for foreign dealerships.

Hale's son Norman H. Clippinger (born January 14, 1913) became vice president of the dealership beginning in 1933. In the 1940s, Hale bought back the first car he ever sold (a 1921 Chevy) to display as an advertising gimmick and a good luck talisman. Soon, high-performance cars proved to be luckier!

Russ Davis Ford

Russ Davis Ford was a successful Covina Ford dealer housed at various Citrus Street locations. In the 1940s, Russ Davis Ford moved directly across from the Clippinger Chevrolet lot. The new Russ Davis location at 116 San Bernardino served as a constant reminder to both dealerships about their immediate competition.

Russell W. Davis was born around 1899 in Quincy, Illinois. His family moved to Seattle, Washington, when he was nine. They quickly headed south to sunny California, where his father, Henry S. Davis, was a school superintendent.

Russell began college at the University of California in Los Angeles (UCLA), but he had to leave school for officer training for World War II. After the war, he began working at Los Angeles Gas and Electric. He soon left there and found his true calling as a Ford salesman in Los Angeles dealerships.

Russell and Ira E. Escobar partnered in their own El Segundo Ford agency at the start of 1925. In October 1925, Russell branched out on his own when he bought the Pottinger auto business. The Pottinger garage was in the Weegar Building at 320 North Citrus Road at School Street, Covina. Russ renamed the business R. W. Davis Ford Garage.

Russell wed Dorothy N. Newberry. Their son, Richard R. Davis, was born in 1931. Richard would later prove to be a very important part of Russell's success in the muscle car era.

Russell's Ford franchise did well enough to warrant a move in 1930 to a larger location on 543 North Citrus at Geneva Place. The prestigious Lincoln lineup was added to the roster. A satellite location in Baldwin Park was also opened in the 1930s.

Russell added 2,500 extra square feet of service area soon after getting settled in on San Bernardino Road. By the mid-1950s, the R. W. Ford franchise was the Valley's largest volume Ford dealership and was now known as Russ Davis Ford.

The archetypal, deep-rooted battle was already being fought between the two blockbuster brands of Ford and Chevy long before the muscle era amped up the energy. Adherents of either brand could become rabidly intense about brand loyalty. The small-town atmosphere of Covina fostered civil and positive relations between Russ Davis Ford and Clippinger Chevrolet, but there is no question that the muscle car era prompted a bit of an extra spur. The sales race resulted in better inventory and bolder moves from both sides of the street.

Russell Davis had pointed out the technical and high-performance features of his Ford models as far back as the 1930s with the Ford V-8. In the 1950s, as Ford gradually backed away from the Thunderbird two-seat concept and went to the "personal car" version, Chevy pounded racecourses with Corvettes. In the later 1950s, this disparity between the Chevy and Ford performance scene set up Clippinger with an edge over Russ Davis.

Today, Clippinger's empty lot contains only its futuristic 1960s lights. The style reminds me of the version of the future shown in the *The Jetsons* cartoon from the early 1960s.

Chapter 1: Clippinger Chevrolet and Russ Davis Ford   11

Clippinger performance salesman Harry Edison (left) stands with his Camaro and a long line of Camaros he intends to sell. Bob Wingate (right) leans on his personal Corvette. Note that not just Bob's Corvette but also those behind it are outfitted with aftermarket mag wheels and raised white letter wide ovals. (Photo Courtesy J. Scott Shannon, Covina Past blog)

Clippinger Salespersonnel

Clippinger had some hotshot salesmen who funneled the factory performance into sales. Soon after beginning work at Clippinger in 1955, Clarence "Willie" Willison achieved top sales of Chevrolets for the entire state of California. Willie averaged more than 500 cars per month during the 1960s and 1970s. Willie had two car carriers reserved for his exclusive use just to keep up with his sales volume. Many of those cars were high-performance Camaros and Chevelles. Willie remained at Clippinger until his death at the age of 89 on his birthday, April 1, 2005.

Clippinger offered numerous new Camaros in all colors. They were equipped with rarely found top dog 396 375-hp engines, close-ratio 4-speeds, and Posi-Traction. Camaro Z28s and 427 Corvettes were also listed. Salesman Harry Edison sold many of Clippinger's Camaros. Customers were assured that the Vettes had been dyno checked.

Bob Wingate

Corvettes were the exclusive territory of Bob Wingate. Bob started at Clippinger in 1955. He quickly focused on muscle cars. Bob raised eyebrows by buying up stagnant 1962 Corvettes that were a hard sell when the radical new 1963 model glittered on the horizon. He bought unsold 1962 Vettes from other dealers and reinvoiced them through Clippinger. This amped Clippinger's tally of Vettes and broadened Bob's quota capacity to order the new 1963 models. Bob sold all those 1962s and obtained more than 100 new 1963 Corvettes because of this inventive move. He continued to build on his success and was soon getting factory assistance.

GM's Corvette national sales promotion manager Joe Pike asked Bob to guide Corvette clubs through start-up procedures in the Western zone of the United States for 1964. Chevy provided Bob with a Corvette to drive courtesy of the factory. Bob also assisted with the local Clippinger Corvair,

Clippinger Chevrolet's high-performance car offerings stretch back as far as the eye can see. Bob Wingate's 1967 Corvette 427 435-hp screamer parked at the front of the line has a white stripe that runs down the middle of the car, which made him a distinctive sight at car club gatherings. Note that Bob's Vette and the next in line have custom six-pod rear taillights. Normal 1967 Vettes have four taillights. (Photo Courtesy J. Scott Shannon, Covina Past blog)

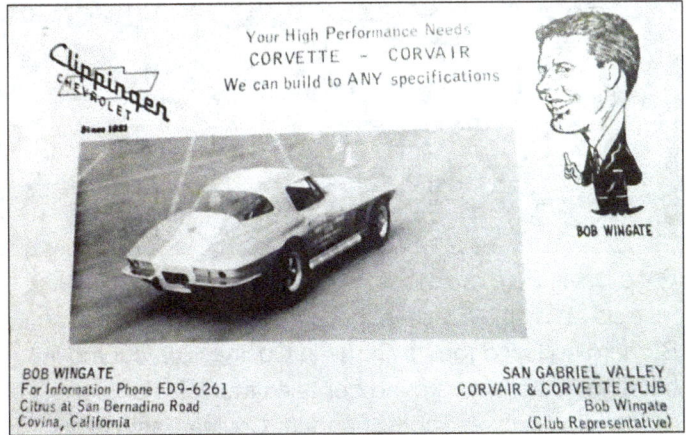

The caricature of Bob Wingate that appears in this promo item would actually mean something to most Corvette people. Bob's face was instantly recognizable to Vette people due to his constant appearances at all the Corvette events and attendance at the drag strips.

Corvette, and Camaro club, which met at the Covina Public Library. The proliferation of Corvette clubs in California led to the formation of the Western States Corvette Council (WSCC) in January 1966 with Bob Wingate as president. The WSCC coordinated the activities of the 40-plus clubs. Clippinger also hosted the National Vintage Chevrolet show on the Clippinger premises.

In 1966, Bob Wingate sold more than 150 cars (mostly Corvettes) and was awarded a special factory custom Corvette in appreciation. Normally these types of cars were strictly built for executives. Some sources refer to Bob's car as a Factory Shop Order (FSO). Bob's Vette was very special and gives some indication of how much of a stir he caused with his Corvette promotional activity.

Bob's first factory reward 1967 Vette was basically a show car. When executives from General Motors saw it, they suggested a toned-down car that was more in keeping with what was actually available to customers. Bob's second factory special car was a 1967 Greenwood Green 427 435-hp Vette with a wide-ratio 4-speed with 3.55:1 rear axle and side pipes. It had a white stripe over the top of the car, six taillights, fender flares to house American Racing mags, a removed front bumper, and a custom interior.

Bob immediately had this Vette lettered with Clippinger sponsorship and raced it at the strip as well as bringing it to car events. He kept it for a year until his next new factory special car arrived: a 1968 L89 convertible. The 1968 Corvette was forced into production even though the car wasn't ready. For the first few months of production, only convertibles were being built while engineers worked out the T-top solution for the coupes.

Bob hated convertibles, but he made do with it for a few months while the factory sorted out the T-top issues. As soon as 1968 coupes were built, Bob received another 1968 factory special Corvette. This time it was a coupe with 17-inch American Racing wheels.

Bob Wingate's final factory special Corvette was a 1970 convertible with the fabulous high-winding LT1 350 motor.

Clippinger Chevrolet's high-performance car salesmen stand with exciting offerings that stretch back as far as the eye can see. Harry Edison (left) had a niche sales area that featured 375-hp Camaros, while Corvettes were a Wingate exclusive. Note that the first five Camaros are SS and RS (hidden headlight) models. (Photo Courtesy J. Scott Shannon, Covina Past blog)

James Garner's A.I.R. Corvette L88s weren't ordered through Clippinger Chevrolet, but the order was put together by Clippinger's super salesman Bob Wingate. Garner displayed two of the L88 cars in the Clippinger showroom and gave this picture to Bob Wingate in appreciation for getting the cars pushed through the pipeline. (Photo Courtesy George Pappas)

Garner's A.I.R. Corvettes

James Garner was a popular film star and became a partner in American International Racers (A.I.R.), using his name to help the racers secure funding. He ordered three 1968 Corvette L88s with assistance from Bob Wingate. The cars were not bought from Clippinger Chevrolet; they were actually slated to be delivered through Fred Gledhill Chevrolet. However, due to Bob's reputation as "Mr. Corvette," he was able to ensure the order forms Garner sent in were correct.

After they competed in the February 1968 Daytona race, two of the Garner racers were displayed in the Clippinger showroom. The display was Garner's thank-you to Wingate for getting the order started and sourcing needed speed parts. Having the Garner cars in the showroom drew performance nuts and movie fans alike.

These were not the only L88 cars that Wingate was involved with. Wingate ordered about 8 to 10 Corvette L88 cars into Clippinger over the years. Clippinger's slogan "First In High Performance Cars" was painted on its sponsored cars and summed up

The Clippinger building still has most of its glass remaining where the sales offices and showroom faced the street. This is where the Garner A.I.R. cars were displayed 50 years ago. To the right is the service entrance.

Russ Davis Ford is seen here at night with the new 1960 models on display. This is the front of the lot where San Bernardino Road meets Citrus in Covina. The curved lit building in the background contains the sales offices. (Photo Courtesy J. Scott Shannon, Covina Past blog)

the enthusiasm here. The dealership also did well with Camaro sales and led California in Yenko distribution along with Washburn Chevrolet. These two dealers were the first two California dealers to bring in the Yenko Corvair "Stingers."

Gas Ronda and Russ Davis Ford

While performance was literally exploding right across the street, Russ Davis grasped the opportunity that the exciting new Mustang provided. He sponsored the Russ Davis Ford Mustang-Falcon Owners Club, which held rallies and other events.

Things really came together when Russ Davis's son Richard returned to civilian life after serving in the US Air Force in the Korean War. Richard became heavily involved in the family business and convinced Russell that they should sponsor popular drag racer Gas Ronda. There is no doubt that the action across the street at Clippinger helped inspire Russ to agree to the plan.

Cobra Jets

Ford finally got with it and listened to *Hot Rod* readers and Tasca Ford and built a Mustang 428 Cobra Jet. In late

This night photo of Russ Davis Ford was also taken of the 1960 models. It shows the length of the display lot stretching along San Bernardino Road. This view is west of the photo that showed the curved sales office area on Citrus. (Photo Courtesy J. Scott Shannon, Covina Past blog)

Gaspar "Gas" Ronda

Gaspar Ronda was born on August 25, 1926, in Hollister, California. After serving in the US Navy in World War II, Gas ran two dance schools in San Francisco and Oakland. Bill Waters Ford at 9600 East 14th, Oakland, was Gas's first drag racing sponsor with a 1962 Galaxie 406.

Gas relocated to Los Angeles and became a car salesman while racing his 1963 Ford Galaxie 427. This car was sponsored by George Newtell's Downtown Ford at 1900 S. Figueroa.

Gas changed dealerships for the last time when he became a salesman at Russ Davis Ford. He was now racing a factory Thunderbolt 1964 Fairlane 427 lightweight. Russ Davis later sponsored Gas in a 1965 A/FX Mustang drag car. The Ford factory sent 11 Mustang fastbacks (missing the 289 engines) to Holman-Moody, where they were built to compete in A/FX class. Top racers were allowed to choose their cars according to their ranking. Gas Ronda got one of the five best cars with the exotic 427 SOHC engine. His Poppy Red Mustang set a new A/FX class record at Winternationals AHRA World Finals.

Gas posted a 9.25-second 156.79-mph run to win top fuel stock eliminator in the AHRA July 1966 race with his factory Mustang. Gas spent two years driving Funny Car Mustangs before stepping back to campaign the potent Super Stock Mustang Cobra Jet in early 1968.

Russ Davis took delivery of this 1968 Mustang 428 Cobra Jet, which is one of the last 18 in the run of the first factory 50 built to qualify for drag racing. The CJ is a lightweight seam sealer and sound deadener delete car.

Amazingly, the Russ Davis 428 Cobra Jet was street driven. More than a few people had their doors blown off by this beast. Engine failure sidelined the car. It was parked in Jim Heidenreich's backyard around the time of the insurance sticker expiration date. Note the Russ Davis license frame and original California black plates.

David and Patty Garton rescued the Russ Davis 1968 Cobra Jet. After his death in 2008, Jim Heidenreich's car collection in his Glendale, California, backyard included this CJ. Also hidden under tarps was a 1970 Boss 429 that Jim had purchased new from Russ Davis Ford. (Photo Courtesy David Garton)

The heart of the Russ Davis Cobra Jet is a monster motor that is easily accessible because the hood hinges were replaced with four pins to hold it in place. Phil Glass signed the inner fender. Phil is the original owner, and as a friend of Gas Ronda, he got one of the lightweights. After racing it, Phil sold it to Jim Heidenreich.

The Russ Davis Cobra Jet received this sticker on the oil pan after competing in the NHRA Springnationals 1969. The sticker has remained intact because the Cobra Jet has a mere 178 miles on it.

The remnants of a motto painted on the glass of the Russ Davis building references the old days of service. It is likely this was put in place by Ray Andrews Ford or Clippinger Pre-Owned Auto Center after Russ Davis had vacated the lot.

1967, Ford built 50 Cobra Jet Mustangs to qualify it for drag racing in NHRA stock class.

This reversion to stock class certainly helped Russ Davis Ford sell cars once customers could actually order a Mustang Cobra Jet at the dealership through Gas Ronda himself. In fact, Russ Davis Ford was allocated 6 of the new 1968 Wimbledon White 428 Cobra Jet Mustangs built in that first run of 50 race cars. Only heavy-hitting dealers such as Tasca Ford and Paul Harvey Ford got more CJs than Russ Davis.

Modern collectors refer to this first run of 50 factory 1968 Mustang Cobra Jet 428s as the "135 series Cobra Jets" because the first three digits of their unit numbers are 135. David and Patty Garton rescued the Cobra Jet with VIN 8F02R135045. It is an original paint car that spent its life in a backyard very close to the Russ Davis dealership after a blown engine sidelined it.

The Cobra Jet name had an enduring identity with both 428 and 429 versions powering all sorts of monster machines over the next few years. When Ford finally got everything in place, the muscle car era was on the wane. Ford always had great image cars and now it had the power, too. Russ Davis Ford sold all sorts of insane beasts before the end of the muscle era.

The end of the 1960s saw the start of the coming Pro Stock racing movement. Despite the Cobra Jet accruing both street and strip success, Ford didn't fully embrace stock classes again. The automaker really should have rode the wave of racers who were shying away from nitro-fueled cars to return to the roots of stock class. Instead, it continued to campaign Funny Cars, which proved to be tragic for Gas Ronda.

Gas's return to Funny Cars with a 1969 Mustang ended in disaster when his engine blew up. Gas was severely burned

The main offices of the former Russ Davis lot circle around this front display area that features the 1960s-themed angled support posts for the canopy. Note that the building was repainted by Clippinger when they took over this building as a used car lot.

Clippinger's new 1967 building sketch places its neon sign farther north up the side of the right corner of the lot. The sign was actually erected right on the corner of the intersection. The blank buildings and lot on the bottom of this image on the opposite side of the street belong to Russ Davis Ford.

Russ Davis Ford is long gone now, but the sign proclaims that it is open. The main doors open in front of that sign. We are standing close to Citrus at the far west corner of the building in this photo. The glassed-in offices curve around to the right.

in 1970 and underwent a long recovery period. By the time Gas was up and around again, the movement toward Pro Stock was gaining a lot of strength. If Pro Stock had come sooner, Gas would likely have enjoyed an injury-free career.

Clippinger Chevrolet Expands

All the racing action going on across the street certainly kept Clippinger Chevrolet on its toes. Having two major dealerships in one block brought in a lot of traffic to both dealerships. Clippinger was doing so well that in the spring of 1966 the father/son team embarked on a massive upgrade to the dealership. Work was completed in early 1967 on a brand-new, 70,000-square-foot building that took up the whole block when the parking display area was added. The new premises had 96 service stalls, 35 salesmen offices, and a 16,000-square-foot parts department.

The new building also included a dynamometer, which was handy for performance tuning. Mention of the dyno was made in advertisements in 1967, which stated that Clippinger had a complete high-performance department.

Having a dyno on-site made Clippinger a go-to dealer for performance tuning. A huge parts department also enabled the dealership to sell new cars with customer-specified add-ons, which were rolled into the monthly payments through GMAC.

Founder Hale Clippinger literally worked up until the day he died. He passed away in his sleep on Monday, October 6, 1969, two days after his 92nd birthday. His son Norman H. Clippinger took over the dealership at age 56.

Russ Davis Ford Fades Out

Gas Ronda's accident set back morale at Russ Davis Ford. At the same time, muscle car sales were dropping and the dealership itself was in transition. As late as January 1971, Russ Davis still stocked very impressive muscle cars. A single newspaper listing included a 1970 Boss 429 4-speed, a 1970 Mach 1 428 drag pack 4-speed, and a 1970 Boss 302.

Around the end of 1972, Russ Davis Ford was taken over and renamed Ray Andrews Ford. This brand lasted through the 2000s, after Ray Andrews Jr. carried on with the business.

When Ray Andrews Ford closed, Clippinger Chevrolet ran the facility as a used-car outlet. Despite being re-signed as Clippinger Pre-Owned Auto Center, the front door under the 116 number address has a clear sticker that says "Blue Oval Certified" with the Ford logo below it. This is the only remnant of Russ Davis still on the buildings. Today, this dealership lot is vacant.

Clippinger's service waiting area and cashier office were on the north edge of the building past the showroom. A sign high up on the wall welcomed customers to "the Clippinger Family."

The empty lot of Russ Davis Ford looking east along West San Bernardino Road toward Citrus. This lot once was bursting with new Cobra Jets, Boss, Mach 1 cars, and other exciting used muscle car trade-ins.

The Demise of Clippinger Chevrolet

During the mid-1980s, Clippinger Chevrolet was headed by Norm Clippinger's son. When Norm's son died, Norm (who was then in his 70s) came back to run the dealership once again. In 1999, he sold the dealership to Dighton America Inc., which was owned by Ziad Alhassen. Norm Clippinger died on January 22, 2003, shortly after he turned 90.

Clippinger Chevrolet relocated to a new dealer row right along I-10 at 1900 East Garvey Avenue South, West Covina, in 2005. After a short time, the location closed and was briefly occupied by Hummer. By 2012, the Hummer dealer was closed and the property was up for sale.

The 1967 state-of-the-art Clippinger dealership in Covina is currently being used as an overflow storage lot for local dealerships. The vacant former locations of Clippinger Chrysler Jeep (298 N. Azusa Avenue) and Clippinger Chevrolet-Oldsmobile (137 W. San Bernardino Road) were placed in auction.

Wesley Willison, the grandson of sales wizard Willie, mounted a campaign in 2007 to save the 60-year-old neon Clippinger Chevrolet Sign that still stands above the 1967 mega dealership building.

A brand-new building at 1900 East Garvey Avenue South hosted Clippinger Chevrolet for a brief stint shortly after Norman Clippinger sold it. The building is now vacant.

CHAPTER 2
DANA CHEVROLET

> **Dana Chevrolet**
> Location: South Gate, California
> Years in Operation: 1966–1971
> Founder(s): Paul Dombroski and Peyton Cramer
> Current Status: South-Lyn Auto Sales

Dana Chevrolet was a high-performance center back in the 1960s that reused the existing structure of a prior dealership. Inside was another story. The former Simpson Buick building was re-engineered to prep race cars and the lot was infused with high-performance goodies. (Photo Courtesy Dave Fillion Collection)

Dana Chevrolet shares fame with Nickey Chevrolet for being the earliest dealerships to create Chevrolet Camaro 427 conversion cars. Both dealerships also operated under similar partner dynamics. Each dealership had a behind-the-scenes, virtually invisible partner watching finances while the other partner courted the press with racing exploits.

Mild and Wild Dana Locations

Dana exploded onto the scene from nowhere specifically for the muscle car era, and it just as suddenly vaporized again. The reason for Dana being a flash in the pan was the unsustainable volatile balance between the two owners of Dana Chevrolet. Like Dr. Jekyll and Mr. Hyde, Dana had two very different personalities driving the dealership.

Dr. Jekyll was Paul Dombroski. He was a respected car dealer with a carefully established conservative image. This enabled him to gain access to the required capital through the banks.

Mr. Hyde was Peyton Cramer. He was a major player in the Shelby American organization. That high-performance connection caused banks to reject his loan applications.

Dana Chevrolet's "regular car" showroom was located at 8730 Long Beach Boulevard at the intersection of Laurel Place in South Gate, California. This dealership was formerly the location of Enoch Chevrolet. Ted Enoch has been a Chevy dealer for 31 years when he retired and sold the business to George E. Fuller and George F. Cashman in 1953. The Enoch run ended in June 1966.

When Paul and Peyton took over the dealership, they chose the name Dana Chevrolet after an avenue in Ohio that was known for the local street drag racing scene of Peyton's youth. Dana emerged onto the scene and quickly established a presence in the West Coast muscle car scene by operating five different locations with vastly contrasting showrooms.

The Dana Chevrolet Hi-Performance Center facility was located down the street at 9735 Long Beach Boulevard at the intersection of Indiana Avenue in South Gate, California. This dealership was the former location of one of the Simpson Buick Co. lots, which had occupied the spot since the 1950s.

Partnership of Opposites

Dana Chevrolet Inc. and Dana Chevrolet Hi-Performance Center were reflective of the personalities of the two owners and also the sole domain of each. Paul Dombroski watched over the regular showroom at 8730 Long Beach, selling normal cars to normal people. The regular Dana showroom

Enoch Chevrolet was located at 8730 Long Beach Blvd at Laurel Place in South Gate, California. This mid-1960s photo of the dealership shows Enoch just prior to Dana Chevrolet's takeover of the location. The building structure was retained when this became the "bread and butter" location of Dana in 1966. (Photo Courtesy Dave Fillion Collection)

took in the trade-ins and made "bread and butter" sales under Paul's direction.

Peyton Cramer rebuilt and branded the 9735 Long Beach location as a no-compromises, high-performance palace. Mundane matters such as financing or regular transportation sales were shunted off to Paul's location. Peyton ensured nothing ordinary ever set tire within the confines of Dana's

Paul Dombroski ran the regular dealership outlet of Dana Chevrolet, providing the respectable front that obtained financing for the franchise. Paul developed the former Enoch Chevrolet dealership to become a customer-oriented building.

performance outlet. Corvettes and other hot cars were sold and serviced alongside seemingly relentless full-scale race car preparation.

Peyton seized on performance as a conduit to visibility and sales. He generated all the excitement and media attention at the Dana operations. The mismatched pair of Peyton and Paul co-owned Dana from 1966 to 1968. Paul became sole owner from 1968 until 1971.

Paul Dombroski

Paul Francis Dombroski was born on October 10, 1930, in East Springfield, Pennsylvania, and went to school in Ohio. After two years in the army, Paul entered the car business with a Mercedes-Jeep dealership in Huntington Park, California. He was the established dealer who furnished the base capital and dealership experience for Dana Chevrolet.

Peyton Cramer

Peyton Cramer had zero experience running a dealership but plenty of experience managing large operations. He also had ample knowledge about directing racing activities and performance sales.

In the early 1960s, Peyton was working at Ford Motor Com-

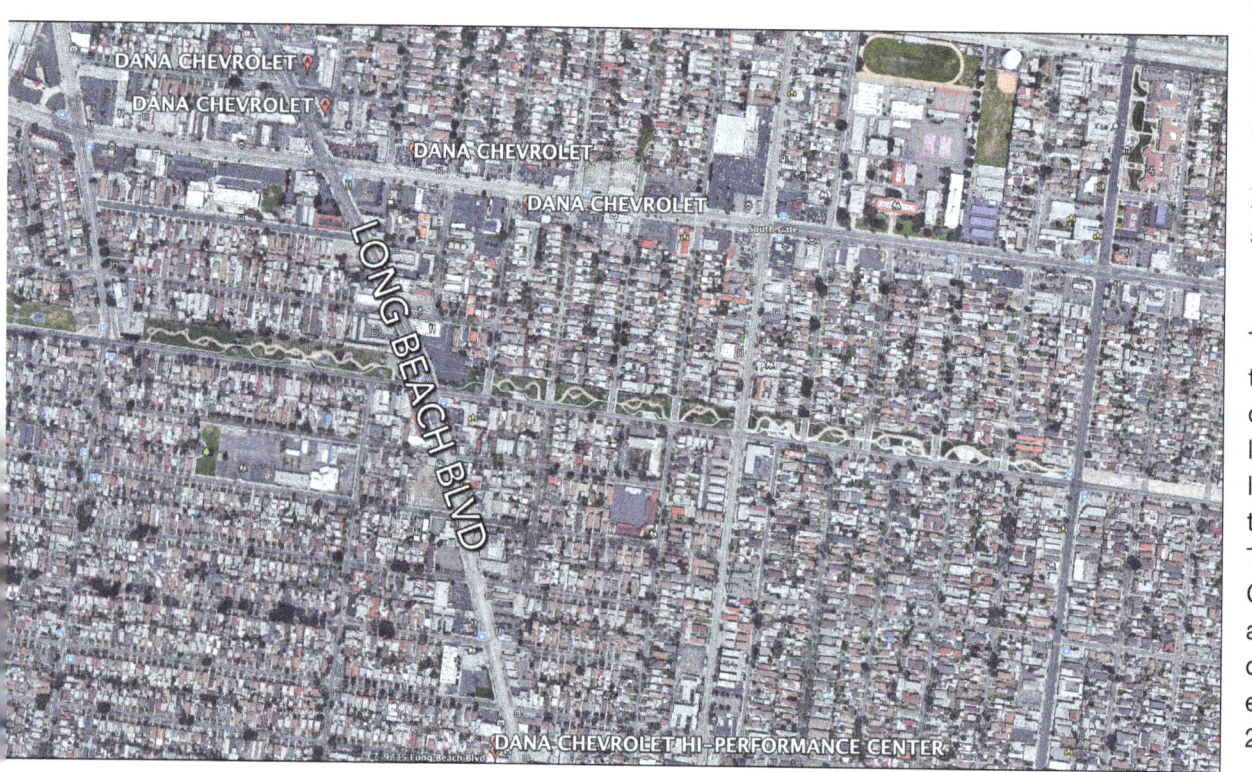

This map illustrates the close proximity of the "regular" Dana location to the used lots operating under the Dana umbrella. The Hi-Performance Center was located about 0.7 mile south of the "regular" dealership. (Map data © 2019 Google)

Peyton Cramer ran the high-performance outlet of Dana Chevrolet. He gutted the former Simpson Buick building to develop a space to prep race cars and complete high-performance work on customer vehicles.

pany. His career at Ford became exciting when his management acumen was tapped to help run the Shelby American operation. Carroll Shelby was excellent at building Mustang GT350s and Shelby Cobras but murky with management. Ford sent Peyton to California to get things organized. He eventually became general manager at Shelby.

In mid-1965, Peyton shifted from Shelby general manager to setting up European Shelby dealerships. In 1966, with Shelby car building being farmed out to the Ford factory, the Shelby operations were going to slow down. Peyton decided this was the time to strike out on his own.

Dana Chevrolet Franchise

Peyton couldn't secure a Ford franchise despite his Shelby experience, but he did receive some interest from Chevrolet. However, he needed an established dealer to back him up in his ambition to open a dealership.

Paul Dombroski was acquainted with Peyton's wife, and the two discussed the business proposition. Paul enabled Peyton to get a bank loan. The official Dana Chevrolet partnership was set up with Paul as president and Peyton as vice president and treasurer.

The partners received their Chevrolet franchise on August 11, 1966. Paul immediately set out to modernize and remodel the decades-old dealership. Paul's approach was in keeping with his long-standing customer-oriented process. He said, "We intend to have one of the most up-to-date and progressive dealerships in Los Angeles, and to make shopping for an automobile a pleasure, not a pain."

In contrast to Paul's customer-oriented renovation to the action at the Hi-Performance location, Peyton ripped the floor out and had it repoured to ensure it was perfectly level. This move improved the precision of high-performance car building destined to take place in this spot.

On August 18, 1966, an *L.A. Times* advertisement appeared soliciting salesmen for the new Dana dealership. Applicants were told to see Mr. Berry or Mr. Kymes. Right from the start, Peyton was fully immersed in building up the dealership as a performance mecca and insulated from daily matters.

Dana advertised its new high-performance center.

Camaro Headquarters

The approximate first day of business at Dana Chevrolet Inc. was August 23, 1966. It had two used fleet vehicle dealership facilities at 8806 Long Beach Boulevard and 2955 E. Firestone Boulevard that were also acquired as a result of the Enoch Chevrolet acquisition.

Dana began advertising itself as "Your New Camaro Headquarters." The dealership also stocked an assortment of 4-speed and automatic 1966 Impalas in a range of colors. They quickly blew out in October that year.

Interestingly, Peyton's connection to Carroll Shelby resulted in the "enemy" brand of Ford being included in the inventory. This was usually unthinkable back in the days of strong brand loyalty, but Peyton liked anything fast. Dana Chevrolet ordered in a brand-new GT350 in September 1966 and also had a used 1963 Shelby Cobra Roadster for sale.

Dana Personnel

From the very start, the Dana Hi-Performance Center was never an ordinary dealership. Dana employed famous racer Dick Guldstrand as chief engineer. Aside from setting up the race cars, Dick's presence on the Dana premises served as a promotional tool all on its own. Dick drew in curious crowds eager to watch the famous

This early Dana advertisement relies heavily on the Hi-Performance Center's offerings to define its market. A Corvette picture catches reader's attention, but the Dana 427 Camaro prominently promoted in the ad is not pictured, possibly because it was still being sorted out at this point. (Photo Courtesy Dave Fillion Collection)

Chapter 2: Dana Chevrolet

Dick Guldstrand

Richard "Dick" Herman Guldstrand was born in Los Angeles on December 1, 1927, to an engineer father and vaudeville mother. Dick tinkered with cars and was a hot rodder as a teen. He also demonstrated his mother's knack for showmanship during the Korean War when he was assigned to the USO as a singer. An electrical engineering degree from UCLA got him into an aeronautics company.

Dick "threw it all away" to race Corvettes under sponsorship of Los Angeles–area Chevrolet dealerships. He made it onto Roger Penske's team in SCCA racing. Dick not only raced and won often in Corvettes in the 1960s but he also had a knack for understanding the intricacies of the big-block Chevy engines and was skilled in chassis engineering.

racer prep race cars. Of course, the street cars prepped for customers also benefitted from Dick's race-proven experience.

Peyton Cramer had a ready-made, tried-and-true team available to follow Dick Guldstrand's program. When Ford diverted production of Shelby cars to its factory plants, Shelby's workers were left idle. Peyton scooped up most of the former employees from Shelby American to carry on in the same mode over at Dana Chevrolet.

One particularly notable addition to Peyton's team was Don McCain. Don was a former Shelby West Coast representative who was running the Mel Burns Ford Performance Center. He fervently supported the concept of street super-

Dana Camaro Fiberglass Hood

In the 1960s, the optional Dana hood was a way to get some weight off the front end while creating a distinctive look for the Dana Camaro. Now, these hoods with the dual square functional air intakes serve as evidence in the unravelling of the origins of Dana 427 Camaros.

A limited number of the very early 1968 Nickey Chevrolet/Bill Thomas Camaros sold in the later part of 1967 and released into the West Coast market were equipped with the same hood that was synonymous with Dana Chevrolet. This was not the norm, as the Nickey Chevrolet Camaros were already being outfitted and campaigned with the Nickey Stinger hood to set them apart from the Dana 427 Camaros. The optional Dana hood links the activities of Bill Thomas to Dana.

The hoods were built by Berry Plasti-Glass, which was located at 2460 Lemon Avenue, Signal Hill, California, about 7 miles from the first Dana location. Berry Plasti-Glass was owned by Richard Berry with son Richard L. Berry as vice president. Berry Plasti-Glass rose to success when Carroll Shelby hired the company to build the Ford GT40, GT40 Mark II, GT40 Mark IIA, and GT40 Mark IV fiberglass body parts.

Berry Plasti-Glass was well-established in the automotive scene, supplying plexiglass dragster windows, lightweight hoods, racing seats, fenders, and other intricate automotive components. It was also instrumental in the development of various fiberglass components for the 1965–1967 Shelby GT350 Mustangs. Peyton Cramer had established a close working relationship with Richard Berry during this campaign, and this relationship influenced the development of what is to be known today as the Dana hood.

Peyton was instrumental in the development and was the conduit through whom those hoods appeared on Dana Camaro 427 cars in May 1967. He was clearly inspired to create a super 427 Camaro based on his experience with Carroll Shelby, who developed super Mustangs with his Shelby GT350. Carroll went all out for the GT500 with a 428 engine, which probably prompted the Dana 427 route. The Shelby influence is very clear in Dana's use of a unique fiberglass hood.

Berry Plasti-Glass was a father/son team that rose to prominence through its work for Shelby American, which explains the GT40 pictured in this ad. Shelby American alumni Peyton Cramer sourced Berry for the optional hood available on the Dana Camaro. Back in the day, Los Angeles Camaro owners mimicked the Dana Camaro 427 look by installing one of these Berry hoods. (Photo Courtesy Dave Fillion Collection)

cars, and in February 1967 he joined the Dana team as a sales manager. He began to actively campaign the 427 Camaro on the drag strips and continued to be an integral force behind further development of the Dana Camaro.

Over the next few years, Dana Chevrolet specialized in Corvette sales and service while also unleashing 1967, 1968, and 1969 Camaros packed with 427 engines and chassis upgrades that made them into savage muscle cars that could tear up just about anything else on the road. They also stocked and sold 427 Impalas and small-block Camaros with any hopped-up add-ons.

1967 Camaro 427 Conversions

Dana Chevrolet is best remembered for engine transplant 427 Camaros built for 1967 through 1969 model years. The majority of the 1967 Dana Camaros came in "base" SS 350 form, packing a 1966 Corvette L72 427 engine rated at 425 hp hooked up to Muncie 4-speed transmission and 3.55:1 axle. A Dana Camaro was upgraded with a heavy-duty radiator, headers, metallic brakes, and a heavy-duty clutch and pressure plate. It also included NHRA-approved safety scatter shields.

Dana had access to other crate engines too. A customer willing to pay an extra $150 could up the ante with an L71 Tri-Power 427 435-hp engine. Dana would even go right up to the L88 427 engine.

Eye appeal was enhanced with a custom steering wheel, chrome Edelbrock scripted valve covers, and a Stelling & Hellings air cleaner. Dana added a Stewart Warner 8,500-rpm electric tachometer, and a Stewart Warner 0–100-psi oil pressure gauge, a Stewart Warner 0–250°F water temperature gauge.

The Dana Camaros weren't nose heavy or ungainly. For an additional $125, customers could add a lightweight fiberglass competition-style hood with functional air intakes. Even with a heavier stock steel hood, quick-response steering, heavy-duty suspension, Traction Masters bars, and F70-14 wide track tires on 6-inch-wide wheels made the 427 Camaros handle.

Who Did It First?

Bill Thomas and Dick Guldstrand are suggested as some of the earliest guys to transplant a 427. There is a suggestion that Bill sparked the Dana project. The threads connecting the key figures are there, but untangling them without documentation remains elusive work for historians. What is known for certain is that Peyton Cramer was a strong believer in the 427 Camaro. Large signs at the Dana Hi-Performance Center highlighted the fact that this lot was the "Home of the Dana Camaro."

Dana Offers Super Drag/Road Camaro

SOUTH GATE, Calif., Nov. 7—Southern California's Dana Chevrolet is first on the scene to offer a super Camaro.

Two versions will be sold, one for the street, one for the drag strip.

Dana's road car offers a lengthy list of handling and performance options including: heavy duty suspension, heavy duty clutch and pressure plate, NHRA-approved scattershield, four-wheel metallic brakes, Muncie four-speed transmission, positraction, 3:55 to 1 ring and pinion, 9000rpm tach and 385hp, 427CID engine.

This November 7, 1966, article about the new Dana Super Camaro 427 gets most of the facts right. However, it underrates the engine at a "mere" 385 hp when it was really a 425-hp beast. (Photo Courtesy Dave Fillion Collection)

The Dana dealership at the 8730 location was up and running in late August 1966. Development of the 427 Camaro began immediately after the debut of the Camaro platform from General Motors. Two versions of the first 427 Dana Camaro were underway, as indicated in an article dated November 7, 1966. Based on the publication date, it's conceivable that the 427 Dana supercars were available as early as mid- to late-October 1966.

Other dealerships also recognized the marketing potential and were putting a 427 engine into a Camaro early in the production run. One way to determine how early these conversions were made is the fact that both Dana and Nickey were using a Camaro SS 350 as their donor platforms. The 396 375-hp Camaro was the ideal candidate for conversion, but at the time of these early 427 conversions, the 396 wasn't available. The 396 325-hp platform became available in late 1966 or early 1967; the 375-hp version didn't appear until March 1967.

Bill Thomas Race Cars was located at 502 East Juliana, Anaheim, California, in the fall of 1966, which was about 25 miles east of Berry Plasti-Glass. Bill Thomas was an unofficial factory representative for Chevrolet racing (Chevy was not racing, if anyone asked). Bill Thomas Race Cars hooked up with Nickey Chevrolet in Chicago and established a West Coast distribution deal. The relationship continued until the end of 1967. Bill was given a surreptitious request by Chevy engineering's product performance leader Vince Piggins to get the Camaro beefed up.

The commonality between the Dana Camaros and the Nickey Chevrolet Camaros built by Dick Harrell is unmistakable. The time frames are very close as well. The article "First Test Anywhere of Nickey 427 Camaro" appeared in a magazine with an early publication date of January 1967. Cover dates are advanced later than genuine newsstand printing dates. Once you count back for the lead time to write the story, the date of actual Nickey conversion was about the same as when Dana is believed to have converted Camaros to 427 power.

Mysterious First Camaro 427 Candidates

When trying to track the early Dana Camaro conversions,

The 427 Dana Camaro and Hi-Performance Corvettes continue to dominate SoCal. That tiny air cleaner just makes that mondo monster 427 motor seem all the more menacing when stuffed into a Camaro. The 1967 Dana Camaro 427 prototype car can be identified by the Bardhal sticker placed on the radiator support. (Photo Courtesy Dave Fillion Collection)

Dana license frames didn't distinguish between their two radically different locations. Without much space to write a message, they kept it simple. (Photo Courtesy Steve Strand)

the waters are somewhat murky, so try to bear with the intricate details.

Hot Rod magazine presented research on an old racer unearthed in 2015 that was purportedly the source car for the first Dana Camaro conversion (DC1). Its contender for the honor was a 1967 Camaro sold through Brown & Hoeye Chevrolet in Mesa, Arizona. The car was a Sierra Fawn 1967 Camaro 327 Powerglide built on November 26, 1966. It was repainted black early in the game. The platform (small-block Powerglide) and time frame suggests this may be a one-off customer project racer sold through Dana, but it didn't fit the parameters of the usual Dana package conversion cars.

The theory presented was that the engine was swapped at Shelby's Arizona facilities in December 1966, which contradicts the known fact that at least one location of Dana Chevrolet was already up and running by this time. Peyton Cramer was directing Dana racing action and preparing his Hi-Performance dealership in South Gate. It was also known that the Shelby operations had gone into standstill mode in August 1966 due to his creation being moved to be built on a Ford assembly line. There was no need for Peyton or his Dana staff to travel to Arizona to use Shelby's facilities or to borrow Shelby's staff in Arizona to do the job. A conversion could be done at the "normal" Dana dealership or one of the two used car locations if needed.

Dana Camaro conversions were known to be a package built using a Camaro SS 350 4-speed platform as a starting point, not a 327 automatic platform. Why go to the extra work of switching out pedals to build a 4-speed car when you can simply order a SS 350 to start with and also get the heavy-duty components (suspension, transmission, axle, etc.) already on the car?

The answer lies with Dana Chevrolet Inc. acquiring its franchise date in August 1966. With Dana emerging onto the scene in late August, the 1967 Camaro production campaign was in full swing with other dealerships placing orders and standing in line to get their hands on what was to be GM's answer to the rival Ford Mustang. Peyton's desire to campaign the 427 Camaro led Dana to acquire other Camaros from the network of dealerships. By then, Dana had already established its position in the 427 Camaro race and brought its car to the market in mid- to late-October 1966.

Even after Dana Chevrolet was in the swing of ordering Camaros directly from the factory, it continued to transfer Camaros from other dealerships to fulfill the explosive appetite. Peyton's established relationship within the dealership network enabled him to acquire early production 327 Camaros, and it is believed that the Arizona car is a result of this transaction. The Camaro's origin and historical facts have been endorsed by the original owner of the car. The Arizona Camaro went on to be raced extensively until the 1980s, when it was parked. The car has been revived and is now out racing again.

The Bardahl Car

The general consensus is that one of the earliest Dana Camaro package conversions was a white 1967 Camaro SS 350 converted to 427 power. This early car was built as a specific Dana Camaro according to the packaging formula laid out for a Dana Camaro.

This car has been nicknamed the *Bardahl Car* because it was destined to go to the Bardahl Oil Company to test lubricants at speed. Bardahl loaded the Camaro from the factory with vinyl roof, tinted glass, Rally Sport package, custom interior, etc. The "Bardahl Camaro" Dana package was the base 427 Dana conversion.

The Bardahl Camaro was used for photo shoots and testing in *Camaro* magazine, *Car Life* magazine, and *Motor Trend* magazine. Photo and story lead-ins could be as early as December 1966, and no later than winter 1967. The Dana Bardahl car was first seen in *Camaro*, which was likely released in late 1966 or early 1967.

The April 1967 issue of *Car Life* tested the Dana 427 "Bardahl Camaro." The writers were not impressed with the rear braking lockup caused by extra upfront weight of the 427. The proportioning valve was set up for the 350. When *Car & Driver* tested a Nickey/Bill Thomas 427 Camaro, it also encountered early rear wheel lockup because of excess weight up front.

Car Life also criticized the Dana Camaro's suspension, which was Chevy heavy-duty SS stuff, plus Traction Masters, which prevented spring wind up. The *Car Life* assessment dovetailed with the later *Motor Trend* test regarding lack of traction hindering acceleration runs on street tires. *Car Life* saw a top speed of 130 mph and got 14.2 at 102 mph on the quarter with a non-Posi 3.55:1 axle. Chassis tweaking could take 2 full seconds off without doing anything else to the car.

The thing people forget when wondering why Chevy bent the rules to let the Corvette get the monster 427 was that the chassis was better suited to handling the power. Corvette's chief engineer Zora Arkus-Duntov was opposed to big engines in his Corvette. But when a big-block was plunked into a Corvette, nearly 50-50 weight balance was still possible because the engine was mounted rearward. This is particularly noticeable in 1968 and later "Shark" Corvettes. You are sitting beside the transmission in those cars. Vettes also had four-wheel disc brakes. When COPO ZL1 Camaros were built, the light aluminum 427 solved a lot of the handling issues.

Pictures of the *Car Life* test car indicate that the Bardahl Camaro didn't have the optional lightweight fiberglass Dana hood with functional air intakes, which was produced and sold to Dana, as the hood development was not completed until May 1967 and later offered to the public in October 1967 by Berry Plasti-Glass. The Dana hood was on the Bardahl Camaro when *Motor Trend* got it. Shaving some weight off the front end may have contributed to positive reviews from *Motor Trend*. This also smacks of the Peyton Cramer touch, having learned this trick from Carroll Shelby on his GT350 and GT500s with their unique lightweight front ends.

Motor Trend's July 1967 test of the Bardahl Camaro noted that Peyton Cramer was duplicating his former employer (Carroll Shelby) by offering a super pony car for the same $3,995 base price as a Shelby Mustang GT350. Shelby's big-block monster 428 version of the Mustang, named GT500, was more expensive.

Part of the trick with Dana's pricing was that the customer received a credit for the yanked 350 engine, which was a saleable performance piece that had just debuted as an exclusive powerplant for the 1967 SS Camaro.

The *Motor Trend* test Camaro overwhelmed the street tires in quarter-mile tests. First gear couldn't be used on the F70-14 tires because the 3.73:1 rear axle put the rear end around and torched the tires. Incredibly, quarter-mile times of 14.2 at 105 mph were clocked using either second or third gear to start. Top speed on this Dana test car was 130 mph. Note that top speed and quarter-mile ET were the same as the car when tested by *Car Life* with a 3.55 rear end.

When Goodyear slicks were filling the rear wheel well, the Camaro ripped off a quarter-mile in 13.3 at 107 mph. Uncorking the headers dropped times into the high 12s. This was all with the basic car! If you wanted to go faster, there were packaged options available.

Customers spending more money could have Dana tweak the platform with an optional engine upgrade to the 3x2-barrel 435-hp V-8 ($150) in addition to Stage I ($235) and Stage II ($275) suspension upgrades for street use, and a Stage III ($2,000) package intended for all-out drag racing. These packages may have been devised to address the criticisms leveled in the *Car Life* test. Dick Guldstrand put years of racing experience into these performance packages.

Authenticating the Dana 427 Camaro

Dana cars are difficult to authenticate because most of the Camaro owners did not have the foresight to understand the importance of paperwork retention. The dealership paperwork was discarded when Paul dissolved the dealership. How many Camaros were converted in total is unknown. It is also unknown how many cars were created according to the Dana package prior to and after the April 1967 *Car Life* publication test.

Both Dana and Nickey definitely beat heavyweight Yenko Chevrolet to the punch when it came to churning out 427 Camaros. Of course, once Don Yenko got into Camaro 427 conversion, he eclipsed everyone else in sheer volume and visibility of his supercars by developing a dealer network to sell his creations all over the United States.

The Dana Camaro was a complete dealer supercar package. Aside from ready-to-go Dana 427 Camaros, customers could bring in their car to have a Hurst shifter installed or an engine swap. These were not being sold as complete Dana supercar packages.

Other Dana High-Performance Vehicles

The Dana Hi-Performance Center began running ads in January 1967. It was running full swing prior to the Le Mans race in June 1967. The Corvettes raced in Le Mans were prepared in the Dana Hi-Performance Center. Assuming that the cars were converted in the newly completed Hi-Performance Center facility, this would push the date of conversion to as early as January 1967.

Aside from Camaros, the Hi-Performance location converted Chevelles and specialized in Corvette sales and service. Forgotten in the modern era, Dana also stocked a lot of big-block Impalas, which were popular.

Another very cool vehicle Chevrolet produced was the El Camino, which managed to merge the great looks of a car with the utility of a truck. Unlike today's SUVs and pickups, which are huge, incredibly ugly monstrosities, the El Camino was

Connecting to Enthusiasts

Dana made an effort to connect with enthusiasts by hosting a sports car club meeting for the "Early Times Club" on March 7, 1967, at the Hi-Performance premises. Dana Hi-Performance Center also hosted the California Corvette Association meetings. On March 8, 1967, Dana hosted the technical inspection for the Willows Spring race as well.

well proportioned and sleek looking. An El Camino delivered through Dana Chevrolet remained in mostly as-delivered condition with some performance upgrades made at the dealership.

Dana Chevrolet offered minor to full engine modifications to satisfy the appetite of a thrill-seeking customer. Dana would tweak your car with a dyno tune or some bolt-on parts from its vast parts inventory, or it could go all the way to engine swaps and race prep if you wanted to go those routes.

The parts department was well stocked with Chevrolet high-performance parts. Inventory was augmented with aftermarket pieces as well. A February 11, 1967, ad stated Dana's position: "The only exclusive Hi-Performance Chevrolet Center in California. Specialists in Corvettes and 396 Camaros. Hi-Performance parts and service. Huge inventory. Immediate delivery."

A father's day ad noted that the Dana inventory was chock-full of 4-speed Vettes, Camaros, and Chevelle SSs. It stated that Dana Hi-Performance paid top dollar for used Corvettes and 4-speed sports cars. Dana also advertised in the Hot Rods section of the *L.A. Times* newspaper that they had a big selection of 4-speed high-performance V-8s on hand. Of course, there were also Pontiac GTOs in the used inventory.

A June 23, 1967, ad announced that the Hi-Performance Center had more than 20 Vettes in stock and that they were *all* 4-speed cars. They didn't even bother buying automatic cars!

Early 1967 non–SS 350 Dana conversion raced at Lions Drag Strip in Wilmington, California. (Photo Courtesy Dave Fillion Collection)

Unique Dana "Yenko Stinger"

Dana was also a distributor for the Yenko Corvair Stingers. On October 13, 1967, Dana sold a Dana COPO

This 1967 Corvair Monza is beefed up with a Yenko-specific COPO order. Three of these COPO Corvairs were sent directly from final assembly to Dana Chevrolet. Dana was to complete the cars as Yenko Stingers to save Don Yenko shipping cost to the West Coast. Dana and Yenko's partnership dissolved before the Corvairs showed up. Dana sold them "as is." (Photo Courtesy Sandy Vandeberg)

The COPO order applied to this 1967 Corvair provided high-performance rear axle and hubcap delete in anticipation of custom wheel installation. The most essential part of the 1967 COPO Corvair package was the 140-ci 160-hp engine. The 140-ci engine was no longer available in Corvairs but served as the basis for the various stages of Stinger powerplants. The COPO order got this engine installed. (Photo Courtesy Sandy Vandeberg)

This November 29, 1966, article charts the progress Dana made after the November 7 announcement that it had a 427 Camaro built. By carrying the Yenko Corvair Stinger, Dana was poised to tap into the Yenko distribution system with its new Dana Camaro. It never actually happened. (Photo Courtesy Dave Fillion Collection)

Corvair. This was a Yenko Stinger minus the identifying Yenko badging. This rarity is of interest to the Yenko collectors because it seems to be a one-off oddity.

Yenko supplied Dana with regularly badged Yenko Stingers and the two super dealers briefly teamed up to promote "Super Camaros." An article dated November 29, 1966, proves that the two dealerships at the very least intended to produce 427 Camaros in a partnership. Whether they actually built any cars in partnership is not known.

Don Yenko was soon using the services of Dick Harrell's shop to build 427 Camaros for sale through his Yenko network. Dick Harrell influenced more 427 dealer conversion Camaros than anyone else. Dana Chevrolet announced a reciprocating distribution agreement with Yenko Sportscars.

Dana Chevrolet Racing

In November 1966, Paul Dombroski, president of Dana Chevrolet, announced the dealership would sponsor Chuck Parson's McLaren-Chevy for remaining races in Canadian-American Fall Series. The announcement also indicated

The Dana racing jacket in orange matches the color of the Dana Camaro 396 drag racing promotional car. Note that Dana had retained brand consistency with its distinctive logo, which was used on the license frames and in ads. With his background at Shelby American, it's no surprise that Peyton Cramer was keenly enthusiastic about road racing. He chose a road racer for the logo on the patch sewn on the jacket's heart. These racing jackets were worn by the Dana Chevrolet Racing Team during the Lola and USRRC Maclaren racing campaign. (Photos Courtesy Dave Fillion Collection)

the company's participation in future racing programs under direction of partner and vice president Peyton Cramer.

Dick Guldstrand prepped two 1967 Camaro SS 350 cars for Trans Am racing by switching them out to Z28 configuration. He gave the white car to Tom Lynch to campaign; Dick drove the blue car himself.

Dana also cosponsored a 1967 Corvette L88 427 race car for the 24 Hours of Le Mans in France. Sunray Oil, which also sponsored Don Yenko, was the main sponsor for this car. Dick Guldstrand and Bob Bondurant shared the driving. Unfortunately, the Corvette didn't finish the race. Dick was miffed because Chevrolet refused to allow him to prep the car at all. It had to be bone stock except for race safety items and lettering. The failed wrist pin in the engine that shut them down was an item that would have been rectified during Dick's routine engine prep.

Bob Bondurant returned to pilot a McLaren for the Dana team along with Peter Revson in the 1967 Can Am races. Bob was replaced by Lothar Motschenbacher when he had a major crash in June 1967 at Watkins Glen.

A Dana 1968 Chevrolet Camaro was drag raced to raise the profile of the dealership. Dale Armstrong performed driving duties. When Dale came to work at the Dana Chevrolet Hi-Performance Center, the dealership's involvement in the racing scene began to lose traction.

Peyton Versus Paul

Interviews with Peyton Cramer reveal his patient, long-range vision. The Dana racing team was plagued with bad luck and broken parts, but Peyton focused on the glacial progress they were making throughout the year. His years of engineering and experience racing allowed him to take a long-range view of things.

Peyton firmly believed that even though the racing hadn't paid off immediately, over time it was good for business. He strongly believed that raising your profile was essential and racing was an excellent medium to do so. Setbacks and money hemorrhages that would fluster lesser mortals didn't seem to make a dent in his optimism about the progress his Dana team was making.

Sadly, Peyton's approach didn't work out for his partner, Paul, who felt he was left in the shadows and that racing was costing too much money. Another blow came in late October 1967 when Dick Guldstrand decided to part ways with Dana Chevrolet Hi-Performance Center to pursue a business opportunity. He opened his own shop: Dick Guldstrand's American International Racing Corporation in Culver City, California. Dick was instrumental to the success of the Trans-Am Camaros, Lolas, and US Road Racing Championship (USRRC) McLaren.

Dana Partnership Dissolves

Paul appreciated the "draw" that performance gave the dealership, but he was a traditional dealer prior to this and grew tired of how expensive racing was. It may have seemed to him that Peyton was out having fun and getting interviewed by the news media while he was in the trenches every day taking care of business.

With the writing on the wall and an already strained relationship with Paul, Peyton decided to leave in February 1968. Paul bought out Peyton's share in the dealership. Before he left, Peyton sold his racing inventory to Carroll Shelby. His Dana employees who were ex Shelby workers also returned to Shelby American.

No matter who was right or wrong, Peyton or Paul, enthusiasts benefitted with the hot iron processed through

The 1968 Camarao *The Canuck*

Dale Armstrong convinced Paul to donate the 1968 Camaro and he would finance the engine build. Dale raced the orange 1968 sponsored Camaro under his nickname *The Canuck* in Super Stock/C class.

Strangely, Dale's 1968 Camaro was not a 427 conversion car. Dale chose to build a 396 375-hp that was a rare aluminum head version. Dale did it up with L88 rods, camshaft, and intake manifold. Doug's Headers and an M-22 4-speed rounded out the package. Dale recalled that his best ET was 10.61 seconds at 128 mph.

Dale ran the car until the end of 1968, when he left Dana. With Paul not wanting the car, Dale obtained ownership and the orange 1968 396 Dana Camaro sat at a friend's service station lot for a while until it was purchased by Jim Bowers. Dale agreed to run the car at the 1969 AHRA Winternationals in Phoenix, where it set the record at 11.31 seconds at 118 mph.

Dale Armstrong moved on from Dana and won 12 National Hot Rod Association (NHRA) and 12 International Hot Rod Association (IHRA) events in 1970 with the Pro Comp title in 1975. He continued to participate in racing by becoming Kenny Bernstein's crew chief and was inducted into numerous halls of fame. Dale died on November 28, 2014, at the age of 73.

This 1968 Camaro RS/SS was converted from 350 4-speed status into a 427 monster by Dana Chevrolet. In 1969, second owner Bertwin Nakamura shipped the car to Honolulu, Hawaii, where he raced it until 1971. After storing it until 2007, he sold it with only 1,700 miles but suffering rust from the salt air. The car currently resides in the Charley Lilliard Collection. (Photo Courtesy Bob McClurg)

The big-block 427 in the Hawaiian 1968 Dana Camaro has a fly eye air cleaner atop the Holley carburetor. Absence of power assist for steering or brakes provides less weight and slightly better access to the engine, which fills the engine compartment. Note the Mickey Thompson finned valve covers. The headers are a tight fit. (Photo Courtesy Bob McClurg)

Dana Chevrolet. The Dana Chevrolet Hi-Performance Center continued to crank out high-performance muscle cars despite losing Dick Guldstrand and Peyton Cramer. The incredible appetite for Novas, Impalas, Corvairs, Chevelles, Corvettes, and Camaros continued. These cars continued receiving anything from small modifications to full-blown engine and performance package upgrades.

During 1968, Paul withdrew from the racing side of performance, but he kept selling the "Mr. Hyde" potions available at the Hi-Performance laboratory. Through the efforts of sales manager Ron Byrum and the strong momentum established by Peyton Cramer, the wave of muscle cars continued selling through the hot lot.

The Hi-Performance location continued to advertise choice stuff, such as a Chevy II with mags, slicks, and 4-speed or a batch of Corvettes. An April 12, 1969, advertisement stated that Dana had 22 new Camaro Z28s in stock in all colors. Dana's goal was to sell half that inventory of Z28s over

The interior of the Hawaiian 1968 Dana Camaro RS/SS 427 features a Hurst T-handle shifter and Sun Super tachometer mounted on the steering column. What may surprise people expecting a "stripper" is that the original owner went for houndstooth seats, radio, and weight adding console. The bulky box between the seats is a "reverse loading" 8-track player. You had to put your 8-track into it by feel. (Photo Courtesy Bob McClurg)

The first owner of the Hawaiian 1968 Dana Camaro RS/SS 427 ordered the optional hood made by Berry Plasti-Glass. Note the mesh on the rear air extractors. Both front intakes and rear extractors used this mesh to keep gunk out of the engine bay. The front intakes delivered cool air to the carburetor while the rear extractors cooled the engine and reduced underhood pressure. Two hood pins hold down the lightweight hood. (Photo Courtesy Bob McClurg)

The Hawaiian 1968 Dana Camaro has red line tires mounted on wide mags to improve handling and appearance. No dog dish or steelies on Dana 427s! The yellow traction bars at the rear wheels ensured the fat tires got that power to the ground. The original owner ordered a vinyl top to augment all the brightwork trim that came with the RS package. (Photo Courtesy Bob McClurg)

the weekend. The ad also noted a plethora of SS cars, Chevelles, Camaros, and Novas and some with 427s installed.

One thing that is sometimes forgotten is that aside from the "Dr. Jekyll" regular transportation cars being sold through Paul's location and the "Mr. Hyde" rip-snorting killer package cars coming out of Peyton's Hi-Performance location, there were many middle cars.

Not everyone could afford a 427 Dana Camaro or a big-block Corvette. Some documented Dana cars are hot little pieces that were inexpensive and yet well optioned. Small-block cars with good suspension upgrades and some tuning work came out of Dana that could hold their own against a standard big-block muscle car sold off a regular dealer lot.

There are also cars now forgotten or undocumented that benefited from gradual improvements. When a customer had money, he or she might improve a car step by step. These forgotten cars that came through the Dana pipeline were high performance but low profile. For example, in 1968, Paul oversaw an extremely interesting 1969 Camaro project. Robert Watts from Flagstaff, Arizona, crossed the state line to have Dana convert his new Camaro to a 427 L88. He had a Doug Nash 5-speed hooked up to the car in an era where 4-speeds were the norm.

Closing Down Dana Chevrolet

In June 1969, Paul consolidated his operations and closed Dana's Hi-Performance Center. He moved the remaining high-performance inventory to Dana Chevrolet Inc. (located at 8730 Long Beach Boulevard), where he continued to campaign the heavily optioned Corvettes, Chevelles, Camaros, Novas, and Impalas.

In late 1971, due to continued EPA restrictions and pressures, Dana Chevrolet Inc. closed its operation at 8730 Long Beach Boulevard and fleet vehicle location at 3052 E. Firestone Boulevard. Paul sold his controlling interests and remaining inventory to Cormier Chevrolet.

Today, the Dana Chevrolet Inc. dealership at 8730 Long Beach has been demolished. The lot was subdivided in order to lease out portions to various automotive-related business, such as repair shops, used car sales, and car insurance offices.

The Dana Hi-Performance Center became home to a motorcycle dealership, South-Lyn Honda Suzuki. The South-Lyn grand opening was in July 1970. Following the motorcycle dealer's close-out sale in 1990, the lot was occupied by South-Lyn Auto Repair. Today, the former Dana Hi-Performance Center lot is currently the location of South-Lyn Auto Sales. An old Camaro from the 1970s and a fuselage Road Runner have been sitting on the lot for decades, keeping that old Dana vibe alive!

The "normal" Dana Chevrolet lot at 8730 Long Beach Boulevard in South Gate was renumbered 8738 Long Beach Boulevard and retains much of the original layout. It is now Luiggi's Auto Sales and transmission shop. Luiggi's also rents out space to various other auto-related businesses.

The barbershop is attached to the former Dana Hi-Performance building. The barbershop likely inhabits a former automotive service building or office. The for lease space is part of the old Dana layout.

South-Lyn Auto Sales has retained most of the original Dana Hi-Performance lot and building layout. Current South-Lyn staff state that the interior of the building hasn't changed from the Dana days.

The Post-Dana Years

In February 1968, Carroll Shelby bought the former Dana Chevrolet Lola racer and, under Peyton Cramer's guidance, entered it in the US Road Racing Championship (USRRC). Peyton's racing action seemed to seamlessly carry forth despite the rift with Paul and the loss of the Dana dealership. Nothing and nobody could ruffle Peyton Cramer.

Peyton went on to form a slew of Torrance, California–area dealerships: Peyton Cramer Ford, Peyton Cramer Lincoln Mercury, and Peyton Cramer Jaguar. He also built up Mazda and Infinity franchises. Peyton successfully ran all these dealerships but didn't use performance as his niche angle for any of them. When the muscle car era died off, Peyton adapted to the new world around him. AutoNation bought out the Cramer franchises and he retired in the 1990s.

After selling the Dana dealerships, Paul Dombroski moved to Temecula, California, and switched careers. He

To the right of the canvas tent, the South-Lyn offices are now in the original main sales office used by Dana Hi-Performance.

spent the rest of his life training horses. Paul died on August 18, 2011, at the age of 80.

Dick Guldstrand moved his hot rod shop from Culver City to Burbank in 2000 and continued to work and interact with Corvette clubs up to the end. Dick died on September 2, 2015, at the age of 87.

Sundown at South-Lyn Auto Sales shows that this lot is mostly unchanged from the days when it was Dana Chevrolet Hi-Performance Center. In the twilight zone before night, it is possible to imagine this lot has high-performance Chevys parked there instead of modern imports.

CHAPTER 3
Yeakel Plymouth Center

Yeakel Plymouth Center
Location: Downey, California
Years in Operation: 1958–circa 1970s
Founder(s): Robert Arthur Yeakel
Current Status: McDonald's restaurant

Yeakel Plymouth Center is shown right around the turning point of the muscle era. Both Yeakel and its friendly rival Sachs & Sons (which was across the street) were chasing the zenith of the muscle car era with the hottest factory cars and only the slightest slowdown in volume sales.

Yeakel Plymouth Center in Downey, California, owes its prominent racing and high-performance sales reputation to two men: Bob Yeakel and Lou Baney. These two characters had slightly different agendas, but unexpected circumstances thrust them and Yeakel Plymouth Center into muscle car prominence.

Bob Yeakel

Robert Arthur Yeakel was born in Illinois on October 22, 1919, to Carl Frederick Yeakel and Ida Maude Yeakel (nee Turreff). Bob was the second youngest in the large family. His brothers were Edward, Frank, Jack, George, Carl, Harry, Philip, Fred, and Warren. They had one sister, Ellen. But Bob stood out from his siblings in his short, action-filled life.

Bob's entrepreneurial roots stretch back to his great-grandfather Philip Yeakel, who used his brewery experience growing up in Germany to open the first Alton, Illinois, brewery in 1842. When Philip died in 1854 at age 51, Bob's grandfather George carried on the family business until 1872, when he passed away at age 38.

Bob's father, Carl, was born on April 2, 1871, and was the youngest son. Carl became a popular Alton insurance broker who parlayed the family fortune into real estate. Around 1921, he moved the family to California. The youngest of the clan, Warren, was a newborn at the time and stayed behind with his uncle and aunt, which made Bob the youngest of the Yeakels in Los Angeles.

In early 1927, Carl suffered severe shock in a car accident. His health dissolved, causing his early death on May 8, which

Bob Yeakel was president of Yeakel Brothers Automobiles. This was Bob's first car lot, which sold used cars. Bob only had $500 when he established this lot in 1946 on 239 South Vermont at 3rd Street. (Photo Courtesy Yeakel Family Archives)

Bob Yeakel and his dog Casey are seen here on the lot of one of his early dealerships. (Photo Courtesy Yeakel Family Archives)

Bob drove his rocket car as a publicity stunt to draw attention to his Cadillac dealership in 1947. It was a premonition of the future. Bob had no idea that he would become a franchised dealer of Oldsmobile Rockets in the next decade and rocket himself to stardom.

spelled disaster for Bob. Bob and two of his brothers were placed in a Los Angeles orphanage, where Bob lived for the next five years.

Bob emerged from the orphanage burning with ambition. By 1940, he was 20 years old and had completed high school. He married California-born telephone operator Jeanne B., who was also 20 years old.

Bob was an insurance salesman making good money. His powerful sales personality had already carried him ahead of his older brothers in salary and prospects. His 22-year-old brother Harry was a vacuum repairman while 26-year-old brother Edward was an order clerk. But they all had another plan.

The Lucky Dutchman

Bob drove a truck for Douglas Aircraft and juggled various other enterprises while establishing himself in the car business. With $500 working capital, Bob and his brothers started their first car lot in 1946 with Bob as president.

Bob nicknamed himself "the Lucky Dutchman" and proved it by taking that $500 stake and shooting above his competitors, piling victory upon victory. Bob's car lot scored sales right away. Part of the secret to his success was his talent for drawing attention to his dealerships and himself.

One example of this talent occurred in 1947, when Bob and his team modified a regular car chassis and added a 15-foot propane power tube down the middle, creating a running jet-propulsion car. Bob invited the press to Rosamond Lake, California, on January 7. When they all gathered, Bob wore an asbestos suit while he drove the car. He told the press, "We learned what we wanted to know—that the darned thing would run."

Bob was noted as a "dynamo" always interested in promotion. Well before the television advertising wars between Southern California dealers caught on, Bob was exploiting television to increase his exposure exponentially. He

Bob Yeakel's Rocket Cars

Bob briefly owned a radical custom Manta Ray car that had rocket themes in its design. Glen Hire and Vernon Antoine of Whittier, California, built the car after being inspired by the XP-8 Le Sabre concept car. Hire and Antoine were aircraft designers at North American, and they used their technical skills to create something radical out of a 1951 Studebaker Commander. Bob had to own that car, of course, having built his own rocket car.

sponsored late-night movies on television in the early 1950s. When an entertainment columnist complained about too many heavy-handed used car commercials intruding into the movie flow, Bob took note. The next movie he sponsored merely had brief flashes of his "City of Cars" address without any talking. At the end of the film, a few cars were shown. In August 1953, the newspaper printed a retraction of their prior criticism.

The main Yeakel Cadillac agency was located at 4610 Crenshaw. The original building with the narrow pillar extended up above the building to display the business name is intact. Now the name on the sign belongs to a bodyshop called Pacific Elite.

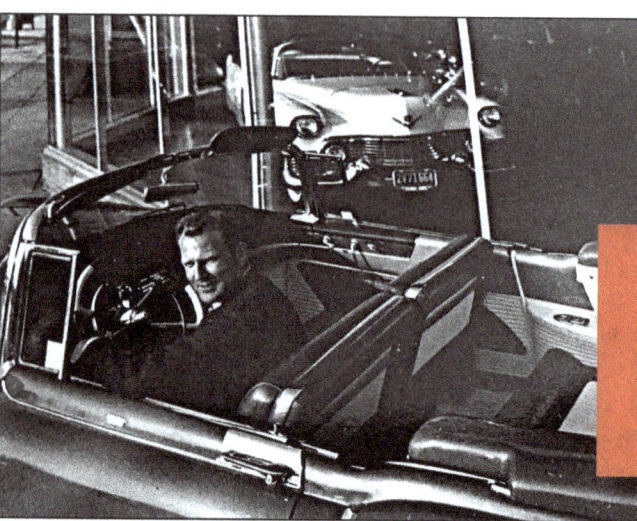

Bob's son Dugan E. Yeakel was born a few years later on August 10, 1943. Remembering his orphanage experiences and his large family growing up, Bob and Jeanne adopted five children. Bob's reach seemed to be all-encompassing and universal in scope, radiating out into a variety of endeavors. His energy exploded like fireworks splashing across the sky. He was interested in real estate, radio, movies, television, and politics.

Yeakel Brothers Cadillac

Yeakel Brothers Cadillac was located at 4610 Crenshaw Blvd, Los Angeles. It had another lot at 3838 Crenshaw at one time and later added a lot at 4740 Firestone. The Yeakel dealerships became quite successful.

Bob hired Lou Baney to manage the Cadillac agency, freeing Bob to delve into multiple other projects. Lou was expansive in his reach, just like Bob; however, all of his activities were centered on high-performance cars. Lou lived to race. That passion colored the activities of all the Yeakel agencies in the coming years.

Bob Yeakel's nephew Fred Yeakel started working in the Cadillac dealership in the 1950s at age 14. Fred recalls that the Cadillac shop had a dynamometer as early as 1955, which was really something in that era. Of course, that was a direct result of Lou Baney coming onboard.

Lou Baney

After Frank Baney immigrated to the United States, he married Rose Serio (born in Connecticut) and had three children. Lou Baney was born on February 29, 1920, in New York. He was the second born and the only son. He was named for his grandfather, who came to live with the family in Los Angeles in his later years.

Lou built his first hot rod at age 19 and raced it extensively as a member of the L.A. Gophers car club and later the Culver City Screwdrivers car club. Lou was involved in dry lakebed racing and drag strip racing. He also served as president of the Russetta Timing Association. Lou raced both El Mirage and Bonneville. In 1949, he set a record of 143.12 mph while driving in C Coupe Class.

Bob Yeakel pilots a Cadillac convertible through the lot of his Cadillac agency. Note the large crest on the hood of the Cadillac in the showroom and the Cadillac crest on the door of Bob's car. The crest of Cadillac was tied to an excellent reputation for quality. Unknown to wealthy customers, the Cadillac engines were prized by drag racers. (Photo Courtesy Yeakel Family Archives)

Lou Baney is the big, square-bodied man in the middle of the picture. He was managing the Yeakel Plymouth Center when this picture was taken in 1958. On his left is Bernie Freeman. Seated on the right is Plymouth Area Manager Bob Fischer.

Bob Yeakel shows off details of a new Oldsmobile engine to Los Angeles Rams football team members at his new Oldsmobile dealership in 1955. This was Bob's first Oldsmobile lot at 215 S. Western. Bob had already recruited Rams star end Tom Fears as a publicity agent for the new dealership. Tom's cronies from the Rams are seen to the right.

Lou worked as an engine builder at Ansen Automotive. At age 20, Lou was living near Ansen Automotive. According to the 1940 census, he was a service station operator. Until the early 1950s, Lou owned a Golden Eagle gas station that became a Saturday-night gathering place for hot rodders. The Lou Baney station at 52nd and Normandie attracted many rods to its speed shop.

Lou's shop acquired the nickname Hot Rod Heaven because of his reputation as an engine builder for cars and speedboats. Building reliable boat engines is much more challenging than car engines because boats run full throttle continuously when in operation. Lou's engine expertise was extensive enough that he mentored legendary mechanic Ed Pink in the late 1940s. Pink went on to great fame as a Hemi engine builder for the top drag racers of the 1960s.

In 1951, Lou married Millie, which may have induced him to seek more stable work. He closed his shop and became the general manger at Yeakel Cadillac. Of course, Lou hadn't stopped being a hot rod guy. Yeakel sponsored Lou's blue fenderless 1929 drag roadster. It also was fortuitous for Lou that Cadillac engines were prized by racers. He had access to parts, and soon racers flocked to Yeakel.

Yeakel Cadillac also sponsored a Cadillac-powered fuel dragster overseen by Lou. His entourage of racers and hot rodders congregated in the service area of the Cadillac shop, much like the old days at his speed shop.

Wilshire Oldsmobile

Bob Yeakel cosponsored a Mobil Gas Economy Run winner in April 1955, which infers Bob had already been granted an Oldsmobile franchise. Paola Motors and Bob's Wilshire Motors sponsored Woody Bell in a 1956 Olds 88 (which won C class) and a 1956 Olds 98 (which won D class). Link Paola, one of Paola Motors' owners, later drove a 1958 Olds 88 in the Mobil Economy Run under Bob's sponsorship.

In May 1955, Bob made it official when he placed an announcement in the papers stating that he was now an authorized Oldsmobile dealership. He said that his methods were going to stay the same: volume sales that enabled him to offer bargain prices.

Bob was congratulated in the June 12 newspapers for his Wilshire Oldsmobile opening weekend at 215 S. Western Ave. This location was formerly owned by W. A. Stillwell. Bob's brothers Harry and Jack stayed behind to run Yeakel Cadillac.

Rocket to Stardom

One normal dealership grand opening weekend wasn't enough for Bob. He made sure everyone knew he was carrying Oldsmobile by kicking things off with a TV special. He introduced the Oldsmobile lineup to the dealership on July 2, 1955. The introductory show went over so well that Bob decided to run a TV show every weekend.

The *Rocket to Stardom* amateur talent contest drove the Oldsmobile dealership to top sales for Southern California.

Bob Yeakel's immensely popular television show *Rocket to Stardom* featured a picture of him framed in a TV set, which also is vaguely reminiscent of a space helmet worn by an astronaut shooting off into space. It took Bob a few days to adjust to normal daytime functioning after hosting the marathon around-the-clock television show on weekends.

The title *Rocket to Stardom* referenced the Oldsmobile rocket motif, but it also dovetailed nicely with Bob's earlier rocket car promotion.

The Yeakel Olds live show aired on weekends. The show was a marathon telecast that started at 11:30 a.m. on Saturday and paused at 5:30 p.m. The talent contest resumed at 11:00 p.m. Saturday night and carried on through the night until 11:30 a.m. Sunday. The show also flipped back and forth between channels during the air time!

Mistakes were broadcast as they happened. The show was filmed from the dealership itself and hosted by Bob and Bob's older sister Ellen "Betty" Giroux.

The Smothers Brothers got their start on this TV show. Other famous performers, including Lenny Bruce and Phil Spector, infiltrated the ranks of amateurs seeking their moment in the spotlight. There was a fascination with the amateur foul-ups of contestants that would be channeled intentionally two decades later by Chuck Barris with *The Gong Show*.

Potential customers could phone into the show to have salesmen evaluate their trade-ins right on the air. A *Billboard* magazine article from July 16, 1956, assessed the results of Bob's show one year later. Bob had become the biggest Oldsmobile dealership in Southern California (SoCal) within three months of starting his television show. SoCal is a massive market. Some of the competing Olds dealers had taken decades to build up to their current status, and Bob blew them all away in three months. Bob Yeakel ran advertisements stating that Yeakel was the world's largest Oldsmobile dealership.

Once success hit Bob Yeakel's Wilshire Oldsmobile, he relocated to larger premises at 690 S. Western Avenue, Los Angeles, where it remained during the 1960s. The dealership was not actually located on Wilshire but a bit south at 7th and

Bob Yeakel was so successful that he moved his Wilshire Oldsmobile dealership to a larger location. Advertising gave directions to the new dealership by using the long-standing Wiltern Theatre as a reference point. The Wiltern still stands today. This photo is taken standing beside a three-story parkade that may have once been the site of the Yeakel midget racetrack behind the dealership.

The parkade seen here is directly behind the Wiltern Theatre and is most likely the spot where customers of Bob Yeakel Oldsmobile could try taking a spin on the "Vest Pocket Rockets" racetrack. The Ralphs building in the background is the former Wilshire Oldsmobile agency.

South Western Avenue behind the Wiltern Theatre, which sat on the 3900 block of Wilshire Boulevard. The former dealership is the current location of a Ralphs supermarket.

Dealer advertisements at the Olds agency invited the whole family down for free driving instruction in the "Vest Pocket Rockets," which is a nickname for the Midget racers Yeakel kept on a racetrack behind the dealership. The *Pocket Rocket* term ties into the Oldsmobile division's use of the Rocket theme for cars and engines.

Oldsmobile played up the rocket angle because it tied in nicely with the emerging space race between the United States and the Soviet Union. Obviously the Midget racing theme was endorsed by Lou Baney, who was keen for any racing-related action. Any gimmick to get a potential buyer's family into the dealership was appealing to Bob.

Bob's brothers were then running the Yeakel Brothers Cadillac location on Firestone Boulevard, South Gate. They lost the lease in October 1956 and blew out their inventory through Bob's Oldsmobile location.

A New Gimmick

Appreciative of how effective television was, Bob expanded his vision. He decided to run for mayor of Los Angeles, despite having no government experience or connections. He ran as an independent on a platform as a "family man." Many cynics doubted that Bob would make even a small dent in the political world. Bob was already running his dealership with the family angle. His financing was based on the individual. He stated in ads that he understood the financial pressures family heads faced and his goal was to get every family man into an Oldsmobile. One of his taglines was: "We bank on the individual not his bank."

Bob had already become president of the Automobile Association of California, so he had some working knowledge of political positions. He sent 72 family members as well as an unrelated Yeakel clan out to solicit votes for him.

The April 2, 1957, election saw the incumbent Republican mayor, Norris Poulson, re-elected. What shocked everyone and received mention in the papers was that Bob Yeakel finished second in the race while the three other candidates trailed so far behind their effect was insignificant. Norris scored 311,970 votes to Bob's impressive 114,306 votes.

Media Mastery

Bob Yeakel had clearly achieved full mastery of television in the late 1950s, many years before the California "TV Car Dealer Wars" occurred. Ralph Williams Ford in Encino didn't start with hyper commercials until the 1960s. Williams later hired Chick Lambert, who was former spokesperson for Brand Motors Ford City (which was later run by Lou Baney). Lou had clearly learned from watching Bob Yeakel's use of television for sales.

But there is a big difference between Bob Yeakel's television persona and that of the later TV car dealers. Bob was sincere about giving people a chance on his talent show. He was certainly aware that many people watched the show with the same mixture of fascination and horror that a witness to a slow-motion train wreck has, but he was unfailingly supportive of his contestants.

The later car dealers commercials were relentlessly zany and wild. Chick Lambert's ads introduced himself as sales manager and pointed out his dog Storm. Cal Worthington spoofed Chick in his commercials with various "dogs" named "Spot" that ranged from hippos to apes. The rivalry between Williams and Worthington inspired some funny scenes in the film *Used Cars*.

Bob didn't limit his interest in media to television. He also had a bit role in a black-and-white film released in December 1957 called *Man on the Prowl*. In the film, Mala Powers stars as a woman stalked by a psycho played by James Best. Best's character is an employee of a car dealership. Bob Yeakel's dealership was used for shooting the film, and Bob played himself as the president of the dealership.

Bob didn't sit pat after his foray into politics and film. He was president of the California Automobile Dealers Association, but he was still restless. He needed something new, so he followed in his father's footsteps and delved into real estate development in Los Angeles and Palm Springs. Bob's interest in television and film inspired him to invest in media as well. He was the central figure in a syndicate that bought the radio station KRKD at a cost of $1.2 million.

Soon, Bob's personal fortune became immense. He built a palatial mansion on Lido Isle (just off Newport Beach) and owned a 110-foot yacht that he named *The Lucky Dutchman*. He didn't forget his experience at the orphanage, and he frequently took orphans out for rides on the yacht.

Yeakel Plymouth Center

Bob was always trying to break new ground. In 1957, the newspaper reported on the innovative setup on his Oldsmobile lot. He lined the cars up by color combinations (some were two tone or solid colors) and assigned a number for each car. When a customer selected a color that appealed to them in the showroom books, it was easy to find that exact color out on the lot using the number code.

Bob's energy was unstoppable. He felt that there was untapped potential in Long Beach, so he opened Yeakel Plymouth Center on May 24, 1958. Yeakel Plymouth Center was located at 711 N. Long Beach Boulevard in Downey, California. Bob left his brothers Phil and Frank in charge of Bob Yeakel's Wilshire Oldsmobile while he pioneered new territories.

Bob brought general manager Lou Baney with him to get things running at the Plymouth enterprise. The timing was fortuitous for Lou. As the 1950s wound down, many racers were discovering the Chrysler Hemi engine. The Hemi was starting to overtake the formerly very popular Oldsmobile and Cadillac V-8 engines. Lou was suddenly involved with Chrysler right at the dawn of the approaching Mopar Hemi drag strip dominance.

Lou was enjoying the performance potential of the new dealership offerings while Bob was pleased with how well the new enterprise caught on. The Plymouth dealership was flourishing with a second location at 9250 Lakewood Boulevard in Downey. Business was so good that operations were moved to a new larger location that opened on March 15, 1960, at 9249 Firestone in Downey.

An ad placed for salespersonnel on September 21, 1960, showed the manic excitement igniting the Yeakel Plymouth dealership with: "We will give 5 absolutely top salesmen the best-selling position in the country . . . if you want to work with champs instead of also rans . . . More floor play than Disneyland . . . A million dollar advertising budget . . . $1,000.00 per month guarantee . . ."

Another ad for salespersonnel began with a giant: "HELP!" The ad went on to state that Yeakel Plymouth's new agency (9249 Firestone) was the largest in the world with 300 buyers on the lot daily. Yeakel had a television campaign 10 times bigger than any other dealer had ever dared try before.

Bob's empire was poised to reach out in infinite directions. Then it all ended. On November 3, 1960, during rush hour, Bob Yeakel was piloting his small Comanche plane above the San Bernardino Freeway (now the I-10) through intermittent rain on his way to his Indian Wells home. The plane was barely aloft and hit the power lines outside Pomona, causing a large blackout in San Dimas. One hour and six minutes later, a witness observed the plane seemingly without power gliding into an attempted landing. It hit high-tension wires that started sparking. The plane crashed in a brilliant flash of light, exploding alongside the highway near the Archibald offramp, about 25 miles southeast of Los Angeles.

A witness described the plane plummeting "like a shooting star." Projectile fragments of the plane hit four cars, destroying three of them and killing 48-year-old Sonora, Mexico, resident Jose Castanda. Bob's business associate and friend, Joseph D. Taylor (48) of Newport Beach, died in the plane along with Bob and his adopted sons Robert A. Yeakel Jr. (14) and Kenneth R. Yeakel (24).

New Leadership for the Yeakel Empire

Bob was the driving force behind the Yeakel empire, and once he was gone, most of his dealerships started to wither and fade away. A 1964 advertisement announced that Bob Yeakel's Wilshire Oldsmobile dealership was now renamed simply Wilshire Oldsmobile. Bob's brothers got into various legal scrapes later in the 1960s related to cliched dealership fast-talking escapades.

In sales terms, the Olds dealership languished without Bob's dynamic force behind it, but Yeakel Plymouth Center actually blossomed during the 1960s. Following Bob's sudden death, his widow put Lou Baney in charge of the dealership. It was the right time in drag racing history to be a Chrysler dealership. Part of the continued Yeakel Plymouth success story was also due to a change in tactics.

With Bob Yeakel, everything had to be done on a grand scale. His brothers were less daring and didn't invest as much in advertising or inventory, preferring to be more cautious. This slowed the Bob Yeakel juggernaut somewhat and clamped down total sales. Bob was always a volume man, and his success to a large degree depended on him thinking big and acting large in all ways. Bob never reined himself in. The mammoth operation he established relied on that gush of energy and money to keep it whirring along.

When Lou Baney took over Yeakel Plymouth, he immediately scaled back spending where possible. A May 22, 1966, decision by the Public Utilities Commission rejected Lou's bid for a refund. He backdated his claim to the origin of excessive phone service instigated when the dealership was opened. Bob had demanded an outrageously prodigal phone switchboard service be installed at opening. Monthly service costs averaged a whopping $19,608 during the first eight months of operation. That is gigantic spending even in modern money, but absolutely astonishing in 1960s dollars.

Lou immediately eliminated 52 phones from the dealership and cut trunk lines. He made further cuts over the years until he eventually got the phone bill down to $145.30 per month. If Bob was still alive, the dealership could probably have supported his colossal vision. Bob would have continued with his advertising budget of 10 times more than anyone had ever dreamed of, and with his fiery optimism wedded to the continuous expansion of business in the 1960s, he would have done just fine. Bob's personality would have meshed with the 1960s boom times.

Bob's excess translated into a golden lining for a racer. He had inflated his empire to such an extent that the dealership

Lou Baney was busy campaigning a fuel dragster as well as this Super Stock Plymouth Belvedere 413 out of the booming Yeakel Plymouth Center. The next iteration of the Super Stock Plymouths coming through Yeakel would be painted black with the trademark "612" number signifying that Hayden Proffitt was driving. (Photo Courtesy Tim Burges)

The heart of the Yeakel Super Stock Plymouth Belvedere is the amazing 413 with cross-ram dual quads. (Photo Courtesy Tim Burges)

had money to fund Lou's quest for drag strip supremacy. As if it was planned, the Yeakel Plymouth Center was built close to the long-established Sachs & Sons dealership, which sponsored some heavy-duty Ford racers. A friendly rivalry between the two dealers appealed to Lou's sense of competition. Already the motivating force behind Yeakel's racing, Lou stepped up sponsorship and lured some very famous drag racers into the Yeakel agency.

Sachs & Sons

Leonard W. Sachs was born around 1870 in Missouri. Leonard established Sachs & Sons Ford on Crawford Street in the Los Angeles suburb of Downey around 1933 with his sons Wayne T. and Ray as partners.

Sachs switched to a Lincoln-Mercury franchise in the 1940s. Sachs & Sons Lincoln-Mercury moved to 9515 Lakewood Boulevard in Downey in the 1950s and remained there until its closure in 1985.

Leonard's daughter Helen E. became president of the dealership on November 25, 1959. The new company was legally known as Sachs & Sons and Helen Sachs Inc. Helen and service manager Keith Swanson were made keenly aware of performance when Yeakel Plymouth set up shop across the street.

Sachs Sponsors Jack Chrisman's Super Cyclone

As if on cue, Mercury suddenly immersed itself into performance. Mercury dove into stock car racing and followed this with a hill climb victory at Pikes Peak in a Mercury Marauder.

Next up, Mercury used dealership sponsorship as a cover to provide Comet 427 factory drag cars to racers. Ronnie Sox, Bill Shrewsbury, Jack Chrisman, and Hayden Proffitt (former Yeakel driver) all received Comet Caliente AF/X coupes. Don Nicholson received a Comet wagon.

Sachs & Sons served as a front for the factory when it sponsored Jack Chrisman's *Super Cyclone* 1964 Mercury Comet S/FX drag car. Mercury subcontractor Bill Stroppe (through Stroppe and Associates) built the car. The car still wasn't wild enough for Jack, who stuffed the Comet with a supercharged 427 run on nitro. The NHRA decided the car was more of a dragster than anything else. Jack's high-profile Comet certainly roused Lou Baney to push for even deeper racing action over at Yeakel.

In the later years, Sachs & Sons remained receptive to performance when it became an official distributor for Delorean Motor Cars (DMC), which sadly proved to be a short-lived venture.

In 1986, Joe Cram Lincoln-Mercury took over the Sachs lot. It was followed by Pacific Lincoln-Mercury, and then Downey Lincoln-Mercury. Pacific Autobody, and later Advantage Rent A Car, and then Neighborhood Car Rental occupied the lot in later years. The former Sachs & Sons lot is now home to a Planet Fitness.

The Yeakel Racing Program

Racing shone a light on the Yeakel Plymouth lot packed with hard-hitting iron. Instead of relying on bombastic bargains based on massive volume sales, Lou was getting his business via high-performance specialization.

Lou's first priority was to get a Hemi dragster onto the strip. Now that he was running a Chrysler dealership, he had a ready-made rationale for switching to the Hemi. Teams were actually running Hemis with stock heads and cranks in dragster competition and winning.

Drag racing certainly helped boost the dealership's profile. Lou ensured there were tons of hard-running muscle cars on the lot and that the cars were tuned right by the dealership. The SoCal cruising lifestyle put 20,000 miles on a California car on an annual basis. Constant upgrading of a car and thrashed parts all added up to a lot of money being spent on maintenance and parts, and most of that cash went through the parts and service departments of muscle car dealerships such as Yeakel Plymouth.

Bruce Morgan

Bruce Morgan was a truck driver from San Gabriel, California, who made history when he won B/S Stock in the 1961 NRHA finals without any sponsorship. Bruce raced a 1957 Bel Air Sports Coupe 283 fuelie off the lot from Colliau Chevrolet. The Chevy was a dealer demo showing 2,000 miles. Bruce ratcheted up the miles quickly! He drove the Bel Air all over the country to races. He switched out his 3.55:1 gears when he arrived at the track, where he ran 4.56:1.

Bruce maintained an impressive record, which attracted some help from "Dyno" Don Nicholson. After winning Top Stock Eliminator in 1961, Bruce raced his first prize: a new white Pontiac Catalina Super Duty 398 painted up with red Hurst Corporation lettering. After blowing the engine, Bruce campaigned a 1956 Corvette until Lou Baney signed him on to drive SS/A for Yeakel.

Insurance Versus the Muscle Car

Back in the 1960s, everyone wanted to own a muscle car. Street racing, cruising, and sanctioned drag racing was a massive social force. The Baby Boomers were still young enough to be unencumbered by mortgages and kids. Urban sprawl hadn't completely taken over and land was still cheap, which allowed drag strips to remain profitable and isolated from suburban development.

A whole separate culture soon sprang into being. Street racers were very skilled drivers, and high-speed experience made them less likely to misjudge the limits of their cars. But if you constantly push to the maximum, situations will arise where accidents occur. These experienced racers also died in races.

While Lou Baney was focused on ramping up the racing program under the Yeakel Plymouth banner, another Yeakel family member was also fervently chasing performance on the street with catastrophic results. Bob's nephew Steve Yeakel got into hot cars and landed in as much trouble as possible.

For every fortunate kid who avoided disaster on the streets, there had to be someone who took a hit to contribute to the grim statistics that insurance companies liked to use as a justification for the suppression of muscle cars. In 1962, the person behind the statistic was Steve Yeakel.

Bob Yeakel's brother Ed Yeakel lived in the upscale area of Manhattan Beach, California. Ed's son Stephen "Steve" Alan Yeakel was born in 1945. Steve was a typical kid from the area. The kids had a bit of money and hot new cars. Steve was out cruising on the night of July 12, 1962, and like so many California kids that night, he was out racing with about five other cars. Steve was piloting his friend Ken Grave's 1962 Chevy 409, which had run a very respectable 106 mph at the strip. The area near the airport had some good stretches for racing.

Steve was racing another car past the El Segundo police station, which invariably attracted the cops. Sergeant Andy De Jong gave chase. Before engaging in a chase with the cops, Steve dropped off his 21-year-old passenger, Llewellyn (Butch) Bartholomew, in front of El Segundo High School.

A second cop car piloted by Harold De Witt joined the chase. Police pursuit stayed on Steve's tail along Main Street, across Imperial Highway, and onto Pershing. One of the racers turned east. The police stayed with Steve and chased the Chevy 409 at 110 mph (or 115 mph according to other estimates) until it all ended on Pershing Drive near the end of the south runway of the airport.

Steve lost control on a tight turn and swerved into the southbound lane, where he hit a compact car head on. Sources believe it was a Corvair. Police stated that the front wheels of the compact "sports car" were rammed back within 5 feet of the rear tires. The driver of the compact car, Thomas C. Clement of El Segundo, died in the flaming wreckage at 12:40 a.m. He was 19 years old. Police were able to drag Steve out of the 409, which turned into a fireball. He died two hours later at Daniel Freeman Hospital.

Police chases and hard running resulted in fall-out in the form of broken frames, transmission mounts, and sway bars. Some chases ended with engine bay fires or torn off exhaust systems. Steve Yeakel may have crashed simply as a consequence of trying to take a turn too fast; but it is also highly likely he may have broken something in his steering or suspension. Driving 110 mph on roads not designed for this speed destroys parts.

Another possible factor leading to Steve's crash is that the 409 Steve was driving clocked 106 mph down the quarter-mile at the drag strip. That kind of ET is associated with a car set up with a loose front end and soft shocks for weight transfer. Good launching chassis prep work is a disaster waiting to happen during precise high speed turns.

Insurance companies pointed at Steve Yeakel's accident as an example of why they needed to prohibit youthful males from insuring muscle machines. Muscle car owners who occasionally died in a flaming wreck added fuel to the insurance companies' mission to price insurance out of reach for young kids and to demonize muscle machines. Meanwhile popular culture openly celebrated the Southern California cruising and street racing scene. Good clean fun or awful tragedy all depended on the roll of the dice.

Ironically, the second driver signed on at Yeakel, Hayden Proffitt, had also campaigned Pontiacs and Chevys prior to his Yeakel gig. Plymouth and Yeakel focused all their efforts on Hayden in mid-1964 and didn't renew Bruce's contract. Bruce didn't follow up on other offers as a driver and faded back into his day job.

Hayden Proffitt

Back at the Yeakel Plymouth Center, Lou sponsored safe, legitimate racing at the drag strip. Despite the original safety purpose of the National Hot Rod Association (NHRA), plenty of drivers died on sanctioned drag strips. Lou kept at sponsored racing despite the dangers, and he bagged a real winner when he sponsored Hayden Proffitt.

While racing for Chevy, Hayden had rejected overtures from Chrysler to race for them. He bluntly informed

Hayden Proffitt prepped and drove this 1963 Plymouth 426 Wedge under Yeakel Plymouth sponsorship. This photo was taken on May 26, 1963, in Half Moon Bay, California. Hayden tackled the *Melrose Missile IV* on that day. Note Hayden painted 1962 Mr. Stock Eliminator on his roof C panel. Hayden won the NHRA Finals driving a Chevy 409. (Photo Courtesy Thomas Bettencourt)

Yeakel Plymouth sponsored this 1963 Plymouth driven by Bruce Morgan. This shot was taken March 10, 1963, in Fremont, California. Soon the effects of GM's total racing ban would take effect and Hayden Proffitt would become Yeakel's prep man and driver. (Photo Courtesy Thomas Bettencourt)

The starting line at Lions Drag Strip in 1963 features Fred Sanders in the foreground driving the red Al Roberts Plymouth S/SA versus the white Yeakel Plymouth Center Super Stock driven by Bruce Morgan. (Photo Courtesy Denny Sanders)

Hayden Proffitt's Beginnings

Hayden Proffitt was born on June 4, 1928, in Texas. After serving in the Merchant Marine, Hayden raced the circle tracks in Houston. When he moved to California at the end of the 1940s, he was drawn to the California drag racing craze and soon became well known at Santa Ana Raceway. Hayden raced a variety of Chevys during the 1950s and produced a virtual fleet of cars that he tuned and prepped for competition.

Hayden caught the eye of Mickey Thompson, who hired him from 1960 to 1961 to test parts and different setups for Pontiac SD 389s and 421s. Hayden's winning record in the Pontiacs led Chevrolet to sponsor him in a 1962 Bel Air that was run out of Cone Chevrolet with a Bill Thomas–built 409 under the hood. Hayden set up the car. The red Chevy had both their names on it. That would be enough to make many racers think twice when lined up against that Bel Air!

Hayden's 612 number traces back to the day he won an event in a car numbered 612. The win caught the attention of a bug spray company coincidentally named 612. The company paid Hayden a small fee over the years to keep the number 612 on his subsequent cars.

Chapter 3: Yeakel Plymouth Center

factory reps that their cars were "too ugly" for him to be seen in. The early Chrysler cars of the 1960s were indeed awkward and strange-looking cars. The 1964 ones were not much of an improvement, but Hayden had to pretend the looks had been fixed for the 1964 model year when General Motors pulled out of racing and he was left without sponsorship.

Hayden was offered a factory Plymouth race car for a token $1.00 fee if he could find a dealership to paint its name on the side of the car as a "front" for the factory. Lou Baney was thrilled to get involved. Hayden took delivery of a 1964 Belvedere hardtop in November 1963, painted "Yeakel Plymouth Center" and his trademark 612 number on the car, set it up in his well-equipped shop with help from his mechanic Les Shockley, and went racing for Yeakel Plymouth.

Yeakel Plymouth Versus Milne Brothers Plymouth

Hayden Proffitt quickly entered into races against another local Plymouth high-performance dealer named Milne Brothers' World of Wheels. The Milne Brothers were located at 1951 East Colorado Boulevard in Pasadena.

The dealership was established in 1939 by Jack and Cordy Milne with a $4,000 investment from motorcycle racing winnings. Jack was born on June 14, 1907, in Buffalo, New York. Cordy was born on April 14, 1914, in Michigan. The brothers grew up in Pasadena, California. In the 1930s, Jack sold his service station and invested the money in a motorcycle racing team he formed with Cordy.

The brothers placed highly in various races and toured extensively. After adventures racing the world, they came back to California and established the Milne Brothers' World of Wheels. The dealership carried bicycles, motorcycles, and various sporty foreign cars as well as Plymouths.

Given their racing heritage, it was only natural for the Milne brothers to sponsor a Super Stock Plymouth drag car. The Milne Plymouth was driven by Bill Hanyan, who was from Glendora, California. In February 1963, the 1962 Milne Plymouth captured the Super Stock automatic championship with a quarter-mile time of 12.30 seconds at 115.38 mph.

Yeakel Plymouth Center's Plymouth (driven by Hayden Proffitt) took on the Milne Brothers' Plymouth on April 21, 1963, at the Kingdon racetrack. At this point, Milne was ranked fourth in Super Stock. Yeakel and Milne squared off against one another again at Kingdon in the spring of 1964 for another match race. Hayden shut down the Milne car.

In Milne's 1964 advertisement, the dealership billed its Plymouth location as the "Headquarters for 426 Super Stocks!"

Milne Brothers Plymouth was one of the dealers supporting this performance ad put together from Plymouth when the division was riding high in early 1964.

Milne Brothers Plymouth took out this large ad touting their extensive credentials as a performance place. The image quality is murky, but there is a small photo of their main dealership in the top of this ad.

The Milne Brothers trailered in this deadly duet to Kingdon in March 1964 to do battle with Yeakel in particular. Hayden Proffitt drove the Yeakel car that shut down the Milne Brothers in the match race. (Photo Courtesy Thomas Bettencourt)

Jack teamed up with Harry Oxley as owners of Costa Mesa International Speedway Inc. This put Jack in company with Coletti Chrysler and Alan Green Chevrolet, whose owners also branched out into racetrack ownership.

The Milne Brothers dealership morphed into California's largest Jeep dealership as the 1960s muscle car mania drew to a close. Cordy Milne died on October 15, 1978. Jack carried on. When Chrysler acquired AMC and Renault, Milne expanded to distribute these franchises during the 1980s. Jack Milne died on December 15, 1995.

The former Milne Plymouth lot was torn down and replaced with a Domino's Pizza and a Taco Bell.

Hayden's Proffitt's Plethora of Plymouths

Hayden captured the AHRA Winternationals championship in his A Class Plymouth. Hayden recalls that Plymouth didn't have the most money of the sponsors he'd had over the years, but he was treated really well. Plymouth was also pushing the edge constantly. These 1964 Max Wedge cars were technically referred to as 426-III engines, which distinguished them from the 1963 426-II design. Plymouth continuously engineered more power (mainly headwork) and reliability into this already killer engine nicknamed "the Orange Monster."

A few months after getting his first car, Plymouth sent Hayden a new one for the start of 1964. This Max Wedge car was a factory lightweight Savoy sedan. Plymouth wasn't sleeping at night! The factory competition in "stock" cars was intense.

Hayden's lightweight stock car only came with the higher 12.5:1 compression ratio version of the 426. The hood, air scoop, front fenders, bumpers, and bumper supports were aluminum. It also had an aluminum radiator, support, air deflector, stone shield, and hood lock brace. The lightweight carpet lacked underlay. There was no sound deadener and the battery was relocated to the trunk.

In the summer of 1964, a truck pulled up in front of Hayden's speed shop. The truck had driven straight through from Detroit, Michigan, to deliver his new Hemi. The 1964 Hemi was the first time Chrysler had revived the Hemi head design since the 1958 392-ci version that was still powering top fuel dragsters in 1964. After the 426 Hemi knocked everyone over with a sweeping 1-2-3 win at NASCAR Daytona 500 in February 1964, Chrysler began adapting the engine for drag racing.

Hayden's 1964 Hemi car was the ultimate drag racer. The potent Hemi heads were combined with the gargantuan cubic displacement of the 426 block and all the chassis tricks learned with the Wedge cars. Hayden unloaded his car from the truck and ran a 11.90 quarter-mile in it without touching it. After Hayden worked a few of his tricks on the chassis, he took it out to the strip and ran 11.66 on its second day in his possession.

Hayden Proffitt recorded a 11.61-second 126.4-mph quarter-mile run on June 28, 1964, at Lions Drag Strip. It was still behind Dyno Don's winning Super Stock AFX Comet, which posted a scorching 11.27 at 124.67. The Hemi cars quickly dominated drag racing and Yeakel Plymouth had its dealership name painted on one. But that wasn't all Yeakel had going on.

Yeakel Sponsorships

Yeakel wasn't just fronting for the factory drag program that Hayden was doing so well with. It also sponsored 66-year-old Van Nuys garage owner Norm Thatcher in the

Hayden Proffitt brought two of his 1964 Plymouth 426 Wedge Yeakel-sponsored cars to Kingdon dragstrip near Lodi, California, on March 15, 1964. This is Hayden's driver, which beat the Plymouth of local rivals the Milne Brothers in a race that day. (Photo Courtesy Thomas Bettencourt)

This is the second 1964 Plymouth 426 Wedge-powered Yeakel-sponsored car that Hayden Proffitt brought to Kingdon dragstrip on March 15, 1964. Hayden prepped this car for driver Roger Caster. When Hayden and Roger went head to head that day, Hayden won. No need for Roger to feel bad: Hayden also blew the doors off the *Melrose Missile* that day. (Photo Courtesy Thomas Bettencourt)

1963 Bonneville speed week B Production class. Bonneville salt flat racing was very close to Lou Baney's heart because of his early start racing on dry lake beds. Norm's 172-mph run of 1963 was overshadowed by his 205.55-mph run in 1965 with a 1964 Plymouth Sport Fury.

Lou had his hand everywhere in racing, but he channeled it into promoting the Yeakel name. Lou coined the term "The Yeakel 426 Club" to refer to the potent presence of the Hemi on the strips. He had Plymouths all over the place lettered with the Yeakel name, but he also had his own personal car out there with Yeakel lettering.

Lou intently campaigned his own dragster under Yeakel sponsorship. Jim Ward was the first driver of the Yeakel fuel dragster named the *Yeakel Plymouth Special*. The body was a Woody Gilmore chassis with a 392 Chrysler Hemi engine built by Vince Rossi and John Garrison. Because the dragster was actually owned by Lou Baney, he kept himself perpetually in debt. Lou didn't care. He kept it running on the strip constantly.

Tom "the Mongoose" McEwen

The second driver of the *Yeakel Plymouth Special* was flamboyant showman driver Tom "the Mongoose" McEwen. Tom was born in Pensacola, Florida, on January 14, 1937. His dad was a navy test pilot who died in a test crash. Tom's mother, Sybil, took him and his younger brother Richard to Long Beach, California, to live with her mother and sister.

Tom and Lou Baney knew each other from way back. Tom had formed the drag racing driver's union United Drag Racers Association (UDRA) with Douglas Kruse in 1963. The idea was to improve prizes awarded to competitors. Lou was interested and sympathetic. In 1965, Lou became president of the UDRA. Having once run a drag strip (he co-owned Saugus Speedway) as well as running race teams that always lost money, it seemed Lou had the perspective to unite the two sides of the story.

Lou made a valiant attempt to mollify both the drag strip owners and drivers. But he was unable to accomplish the task. He let Tom McEwen step in and try to sort it out. Tom became president on December 4, 1965, but he was also unable to create any satisfactory understanding between the two sides. Part of the problem was simply that Tom couldn't unite the drivers. Many drivers were still pretty rebellious maverick types.

Tom "the Mongoose" McEwen's nickname came about as a promotional gimmick to portray Tom as the ultimate

A wheelie blows Tom McEwen's run during qualifying at Beeline Dragway for the 1965 AHRA Winternationals. Popular driver Tom "the Mongoose" McEwen continued to drive this car for Lou Baney once it was given a Ford cammer, rebodied, and renamed the *Brand Motors Special*. (Photo Courtesy Paul Hutchins)

Tom "the Mongoose" McEwen in 1965. Tom drove the *Yeakel Plymouth Special* fuel dragster for Lou Baney. When Lou made the switch to Ford, Tom stuck with it. However, he was gone after the Ford 427 SOHC rubbed him the wrong way. Lou inadvertently started the famous Snake versus Mongoose rivalry when he hired Don "the Snake" Prudhomme to take over for Tom.

Yeakel Plymouth Center was torn down and now nothing remains. In place of the high-performance Plymouth center, there is now a McDonald's.

nemesis for Don "the Snake" Prudhomme. Don was younger (born in 1941), had also grown up in SoCal, and was an excellent driver. His nickname referenced either his lightning quick reflexes or the weaving pattern he left on the strip by pushing his rides to the outer limits; it depends on who you ask.

The occasional match races between the Mongoose and the Snake captured the crowds and kept interest high during 1964 and 1965, when Tom was driving the *Yeakel Plymouth Special*. Drag racers and spectators of the time vividly noted the contrast in personality between the racers. Don was a consummate professional, utterly focused on the task at hand, and came off as distant or moody. He *had* to win. If he lost a race, he was pissed off and retreated from the world. Tom would lose a race and be shooting the breeze, entertaining his friends with stories immediately after getting out of the car. This personality contrast worked well for the promotional aspect of match racing.

Only a natural showman like Tom could keep spectator interest high. Of course, he also had to win, which he did frequently enough. Tom admits that the Snake held the lion's share of victories in their pairings.

Tom had a great series of races during the 1964 AHRA Winternationals. It looked like the *Yeakel Plymouth Special* was going to win the event, but he lost to John Mulligan in the finals when his throttle pedal broke at the starting line.

Tom also got Yeakel Plymouth's help to build a Funny Car named *Hemi Cuda* (predating the factory production Hemi`Cuda by many years). The car was officially sponsored by the Southern California Plymouth Dealers Association with Chrysler Corporation. The bodywork on the car caused an unexpected accident. The car flew into the air. Tom killed the engine and pulled the parachute. The car glided down, landing on its roof, where it zoomed to the end of the strip before flipping again. Luckily Tom was uninjured.

Lou Baney Leaves Yeakel

While Lou was running the Yeakel agency, he also purchased his own dealership. Baney Chrysler-Plymouth was located at 3443 West 43rd Street, Los Angeles. Lou ran his dealership from 1964 until 1966. In 1966, Lou made an abrupt switch from Yeakel and his own Chrysler dealership to run Brand Motors Ford City on Crenshaw at 28th.

At the same time, Lou yanked the Hemi from his dragster and procured one of the rare Ford 427 SOHC "Cammer" motors. He had Ed Pink build his Ford SOHC and renamed his dragster the *Brand Motors Special*. It was supposedly one of only three in the entire United States running a Ford motor.

Tom McEwen followed Lou to Brand Motors as his driver, getting the *Brand Motors Special* dragster out on the strip in September 1966. Tom was shaking down the new dragster, which was having problems. Mistakenly believing Tom was at fault, Lou replaced him with driver Kelly Brown. Things became intense in a hurry when Lou brought in Don "the Snake" Prudhomme shortly after. Of all the drivers he could have chosen, there was no one else that could have stung Tom more. The promotional rivalry between the Mongoose and the Snake became a fiery passion for Tom. It was real now.

Lou's dragster then pulled in another big name. Carroll Shelby came onboard with Lou to help develop the SOHC dragster, which was renamed the *Super Snake*. Without realizing the implications of his move, Lou Baney set in motion the future of drag racing. Lou's driver switch ignited an obsessive need in Tom McEwen to beat Don Prudhomme. On July 1, 1967, the Snake and the Mongoose faced each other for a best of three at Irwindale. Don was piloting the *Brand Motors Special* and Tom was running Chrysler power in Don Johnson's dragster. September 23, 1971, found the duo battling it out again at Irwindale for another best of three.

The old Yeakel Cadillac agency lot as it appears today. Note the old architectural style of the building despite modern additions. The curved leading edge combined with the center sign pillar was a popular way to create a noticeable and pleasing building.

Lou Baney stayed the Ford course despite the issues plaguing the SOHC. He eventually went on to work with Foulger Ford. In the 1970s, Lou become managing director of the Specialty Equipment Manufacturers Association (SEMA) at a very difficult time for performance. The EPA was cracking down on aftermarket speed equipment and tampering with cars was forbidden. Lou embraced the challenges of trying to get good-running, fuel-efficient high-performance equipment into production that conformed with the tightening emission controls.

On September 27, 1993, Lou Baney died of heart failure at age 73 in Palm Springs.

The End of Yeakel Plymouth Center

Muscle car fans recall that Yeakel was still on top of its game in 1970 with an array of Superbirds and Duster 340s, highlighting a lot full of potent muscle machines. Meanwhile, the other Yeakel lots were sinking into total obscurity.

Today, the Yeakel Plymouth Center lot is the site of a McDonald's restaurant. The Yeakel Cadillac lot on Crenshaw is now an auto body repair shop. The Yeakel Oldsmobile lot is a Ralphs Pharmacy.

The old Yeakel dragster was found and restored by Lou's son Frank Baney. Bob Yeakel's son Dugan George Yeakel signed a release for his family name to be used on the dragster. Thus the two sons of the two major forces behind the Yeakel empire collaborated to revive the dragster. It was restored to 1960s paint job and condition with a 392 engine.

The Yeakel Oldsmobile building now housing Ralphs still has the scalloped sides of the original building. The building in the background to the left is the Wiltern Theatre.

CHAPTER 4
ALBERTSON BROTHERS OLDSMOBILE

Albertson Brothers Oldsmobile
Location: Los Angeles, California
Years in Operation: 1948–2007
Founder(s): Wilson Henry "Lou" Albertson and his brother Myron Charles Albertson Jr.
Current Status: Mall complex

The winning cars appear with the winning team on the Albertson Oldsmobile lot in 1960. Standing left to right are: Lou Albertson, Leonard Harris, and Phil McNabb. Kneeling in front are Gene Adams and Ronnie Scrima. If you look closely at the license frame on the car to the right, you can see the rocket logo Albertson Brothers Oldsmobile used on its dealer plates. (Photo Courtesy Gene Adams)

Albertson Brothers Oldsmobile nurtured a secret fraternity of performance nuts within its ranks that burst into the public eye in 1960. The dealership was further carried along by a wave of excitement garnered by the emergence of a natural-born racer named Leonard Harris, who took it to NHRA Championship status overnight.

Albertson's "Rocket Ride" to fame crashed to Earth after a few short months. It continued to support performance in a subtle fashion for many years after subsuming back into regular dealership status again. The parts department, which was the heart of that flash of brilliance in 1960, carried on with underground performance right through the muscle car era.

Albertson's History

Albertson Brothers Oldsmobile was established in 1948 by Wilson Henry "Lou" Albertson and Myron Albertson. The Albertson brothers' association with car dealerships traces all the way back to their grandfather, Edgar Albertson, who was a Foster Steamer dealer in 1902. The Foster Automobile Manufacturing Company of Rochester, New York, produced cars until 1903.

Albertson Brothers Oldsmobile had license frames with blank inner plates that featured a mini rocket. The actual frames were generic. Most dealerships had their frames made by the same manufacturers and followed the same format as each other.

Chapter 4: Albertson Brothers Oldsmobile   47

Edgar's son Myron Charles Albertson Sr. was born in West Elkton, Ohio, on February 23, 1881. He worked with his father in the steamer business. This experience led to Myron establishing a Dodge dealership in Santa Monica, California.

Lou Wilson and with his brother Myron Jr. followed the family tradition. A few years after the death of their father on December 26, 1945, the brothers established the Albertson Oldsmobile Inc. dealership in Culver City. It was located on 4114 Sepulveda Boulevard at the corner of Washington. Albertson's GM dealer code number was 24 016.

After being open less than a year, flourishing sales incited the brothers to invest in a state-of-the-art new dealership. The grand opening of the new facilities on November 20, 1949, included an antique phonograph player blasting the 1905 song "In My Merry Oldsmobile."

The new dealership covered 35,000 square feet, including the used car lot and parking area. The glassed-in showroom and service departments consumed 15,000 square feet. The facilities included cutting-edge technology for the time, such as dustproof air-filtered paint booths, a body shop, modern wheel alignment equipment, and so on. The parts department wasn't singled out as being particularly important in articles touting the virtues of the new dealership. Soon, the interest in Oldsmobile performance at a grassroots level pushed that parts department into a position of great significance for Albertson Brothers.

Albertson Brothers Oldsmobile promoted itself as "the home of the famous Red Rocket." A large genuine rocket ship was painted red and planted on the Albertson car lot, towering above the dealership. The rocket gimmick was an inspired bit of association on the part of the Albertson Brothers. Not only did the rocket stand out and draw attention to the dealership but it was also an appropriate tie-in to the entire advertising imagery of the Oldsmobile Division.

The Albertson Oldsmobile dealership wasn't too concerned about performance because Olds sales were rolling along just fine, selling "bread-and-butter" cars to regular customers. But the growing hot rod culture of Southern California was percolating, and the parts department at Albertson was starting to reflect this interest in the Rocket engine.

Tragedy Strikes

Lou Albertson was married to Beverly Farish Boswell. Together, they had three kids: Bruce, Muriel, and Carol. In 1951, Myron Albertson vanished while on vacation with Dr. John Sneadaker of Los Angeles. The two men were reported missing October 19, after they tried to fly out of Idaho's Middle fork of the Salmon River in stormy weather. Two years later on November 4, 1953, their bodies were found in Idaho Hills, 30 miles east of Cascade, Idaho. Their plane apparently banked too low and crashed into a heavy stand of jack pine trees. This tragedy resulted in the dealership becoming Lou's sole responsibility.

Street Rocket Performance

Although Lou Albertson was selling regular Oldsmobiles, he was aware of the halo effect of the performance image bestowed upon the entire Oldsmobile lineup courtesy of the success of the Olds 88 in NASCAR races. The street scene also took note of the Olds 88. In 1951, the song "Rocket 88" tied the engine name and car name together and cemented the public's perception of the Oldsmobile cars as "Rockets."

Oldsmobile picked up the excitement and named an experimental 1956 show car "the Golden Rocket." The show

Oldsmobile Racing

The Rocket name originated back in 1949 as the name of an excellent performing Oldsmobile engine. The new Oldsmobile overhead valve V-8 called "the Rocket Eight" was available in the large Oldsmobile 98 and also in the smaller, lighter Oldsmobile 88. The Oldsmobile logo was a rocket and its cars were referred to as Rockets in advertising and sales literature. In the late 1950s, Oldsmobile designers incorporated chrome rockets and rocket-style tail fins and rear taillights.

The Olds 88 became an unbeatable NASCAR racer during the 1949–1951 races due to the combination of V-8 power and a light body. An 88 also won the 1950 Carrera Panamericana race. However, the Oldsmobile lock on the competition eroded as Hudson started winning at NASCAR. Soon, Chrysler came on very strong with a series of Hemi V-8 engines.

From an official standpoint, the Chrysler 300 series of cars were the dominant performance racers in the later 1950s, but the street scene saw limited Hemi action. The availability of the Hemi was minimal due to higher expense and rarity. The Olds engine could be easily hopped up and was plentiful in junkyards. By contrast, the Chrysler Hemi was a harder-to-find engine, although it was faster and tougher out of the box.

Lou Albertson is pictured in 1956 at the 11th annual Southern California Motor Car Dealers conference and golf tournament in Palm Springs, California. Lou was president of the Southern California Motor Car Association.

car name inspired the entire 1957 line of Oldsmobile production cars to be named the Golden Rockets.

The Olds rocket imagery was cutting edge at a time of futuristic visions and a massive space program in the United States. As the 1950s unreeled, the space race between the United States and the Soviet Union kicked into high gear. The Oldsmobile Division and Ford's Mercury Division both benefitted from their ready-made connection to the exciting new frontiers opening up with the Mercury series of rocket missions.

Back down on Earth, Oldsmobile performance was still strong among street racers. The Rocket Olds engines powered many dragsters. The Ford V-8 didn't get overhead valves until 1954, and Chevrolet and Pontiac didn't get V-8s until 1955. The head start Cadillac and Olds had (both divisions debuted the overhead valve V-8 at the same time) gave racers a long learning curve to suss out the engine as well as time to develop aftermarket parts and experiment with factory parts.

Given a choice between an Olds or Cadillac OHV V-8, many racers opted for the less-expensive more readily available Olds engine. Cadillacs had lower production numbers and typically received less wear and tear, so they were less frequently encountered in junkyards than Olds motors.

Albertson's Spectacular Race Team

The racers' need for parts boosted the Albertson Brothers Oldsmobile revenue. The parts department also served as a gathering center for Olds faithful. Racers congregated in Albertson's parts department and forged friendships. Race teams were created right there at the counter.

Leonard Harris

Leonard Harris was a regular at Albertson's parts counter. He was a local racer and Oldsmobile fan. Leonard was born in California on December 4, 1932, and attended Venice High School. He wasn't known as a car guy back then. Leonard was famous with his classmates for winning two national championships on the rings in gymnastics. He is cited for his appearance in the 1948 championships when he was 16. Although Leonard was only 5 feet, 6 inches tall, he made an impression due to his powerful upper body combined with a very likeable personality.

After high school, Leonard purchased a Seaside service station in Playa del Rey, California. The Seaside Oil Company was based out of Santa Barbara and had a few franchises operating during the 1950s and 1960s. The Seaside stations were phased out in 1973. Philips bought out the Seaside company and rebranded the remaining stations as Philips stations.

Leonard was known to be a good mechanic and driver. On his off time from his gas station, he raced his street 1956 Oldsmobile. After racking up too many tickets, drag strip racing became the logical next step. Leonard needed parts to keep his car in top shape as things were worn out or rendered obsolete by new high-performance items. Leonard's constant presence at the Albertson Brothers Oldsmobile parts counter led to his meeting Gene Adams.

Gene Adams

Gene was an Oldsmobile racer and engine builder who had just returned to California from the army. Gene lived about 1.5 miles from the Albertson Brothers Oldsmobile dealership, and he bought his factory parts there. Gene worked for Hilborn, which helped him out with injectors. Gene also happened to have an Olds engine that was sidelined while a dragster project was being sorted out.

Gene Adams was introduced to Leonard Harris through Don Farr in the Albertson Brothers Oldsmobile parts department. The timing was just right. Gene lent his 407-ci Olds motor to Leonard for a Fiat-bodied project racer named *Lil Red Rocket*. That was the first racer with Albertson Olds lettering on it. The car was painted blue with a small red rocket painted on the door to tie in with the Red Rocket on the Albertson lot.

Gene observed Leonard applying his athleticism to racing and recognized true greatness. Leonard's superb coordination and strength made him a very smooth, expert driver. He could transition from clutch braking to acceleration without going up in smoke, and he was very consistent in his driving. Leonard is one of the first drag racers to slip the clutch effectively to enhance his traction and times. Gene snagged Leonard for his driver when his dragster project was ready to go.

Lou Albertson Officially Sponsors Racing

Leonard and Gene needed some help with the dragster. Engle Cams and Gene's employer, Hilborn, helped them out quite a bit, but regular racing requires cash flow. The pair

The first Albertson Brothers Oldsmobile dragster had a red rocket painted on the door. The name *Lil Red Rocket* also tied in to the Albertson lot. This Fiat-bodied dragster had a 407 Olds powering it down the quarter. (Photo Courtesy Greg Sharp)

decided to enlist the help of their friend Don Farr, who was the Albertson Brothers Oldsmobile parts department manager. Don had a good reputation as a helpful and knowledgeable guy, and he had influence within the dealership.

At Leonard's urging, Don and Albertson's general sales manager Phil McNabb ganged up on Lou Albertson and convinced him to sponsor the dragster. Some extra exposure for the dealership wouldn't hurt business. Lou had observed that the parts department was doing well because of the high-performance guys. Olds engines were still very popular on the street and at the drag strips. The people who bought parts attended races and would be exposed to Albertson's name through this sponsorship.

The new dragster chassis was owned by Ron Scrima. Gene owned and built the Olds engine. They painted the dragster blue and added Albertson Olds lettering. Leonard Harris went on to break NHRA records with a blazing streak of wins in a short, glorious six-month period beginning on April 24, 1960.

On its first time out at the San Fernando strip, the dragster broke the existing Top Eliminator strip record (set by Tommy Ivo) with a 9.30-second run at 163.33 mph. Leonard's auspicious start continued with new records until the 407 engine blew on May 15. Gene built a new 462-ci Olds engine for the dragster. It ran 9.08 seconds at 163.33 mph on May 21 at Lions Drag Strip.

Albertson Olds didn't just sign off on sponsorship and forget the racing team. Gene recalls that general manager Phil McNabb attended most of the dragster's local races at Lions Drag Strip in Long Beach. Phil brought his kids along to witness the consistent winning record unfolding throughout the summer.

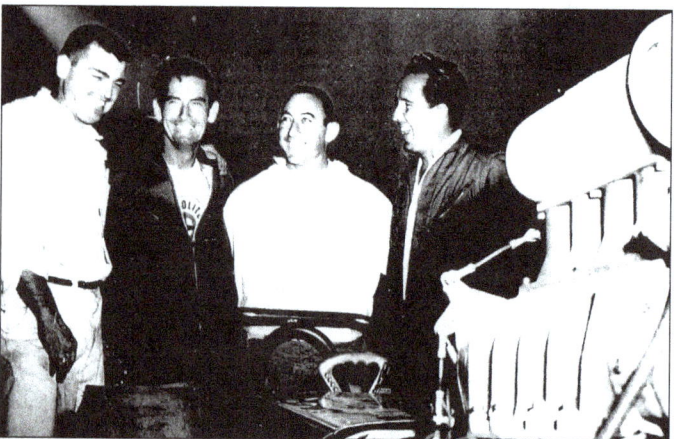

The tower of power jutting above the frame of the second Albertson Oldsmobile dragster looms large in the foreground of this picture of the race crew. (Photo Courtesy Gene Adams)

The second Albertson Oldsmobile dragster blocked the driver's head with the high intake. Leonard leaned his head left to see around the top of the engine. (Photo Courtesy Gene Adams)

50   Lost Muscle Car Dealerships

The Albertson crew with a super stock and two dragsters. Gene Adams has his back to the camera, kneeling close to the engine he built. Across from him is part owner of the dragster, Ronnie Scrima. Standing at far left is Lou Albertson. Middle is driver Leonard Harris. Sales manager Phil McNabb stands right. (Photo Courtesy Gene Adams)

Leonard Harris charged out of the hole in Detroit at the NHRA Nationals. Note that even for the biggest event of the season a flag man turns the cars loose. The Christmas trees haven't become part of the system yet. (Photo Courtesy Gene Adams)

The winners! Albertson Olds won gas dragster class at the 1960 NHRA Nationals. Left to right are: Don Garner (Champion Spark Plug Racing director), Ronnie Scrima, Leonard Harris, Gene Adams, Vern Tomlinson, Harold "Stump" Davis. (Photo Courtesy Gene Adams, and Joe Gutherkz)

Albertson Olds also helped the team by supplying new factory heads, blocks, and cranks. The dealership was proud of the crew's accomplishments. Gene Adams did a lot of work on the heads of the Olds motors to make them competitive, such as installing offset spacers to allow larger valves to be used. Gene also incorporated some aftermarket racing parts.

The 1960 NHRA Nationals

After a terrific win record, Lou Albertson believed it was worthwhile for the team to travel to the NHRA Nationals in Detroit over Labor Day. Gene recalls that Albertson Olds came through with traveling expenses for the team. The Albertson team won the 1960 NHRA Nationals in the gas dragster class on September 5, 1960, with a run of 9.25 seconds at 167.49 mph.

Leonard's athleticism earned him praise. His calmness under fire combined with strength and coordination helped him balance the tightrope act of controlling a primitive dragster through the length of a strip. He was able to launch without losing traction through very skilled use of the clutch. Leonard was in his element on a slippery track. While the other drivers went up in smoke and lost valuable ET time trying to get hooked up, Leonard's precise launches won race after race.

By September, it was almost routine for the Albertson Olds to win Top Eliminator at Lions every week. By now, the car was in the 8.90s and usually crossing the finish line a bit over 171 mph. Incredibly, the car won Top Eliminator 12

The Albertson Olds crew celebrate winning NHRA Nationals. From left to right are: Harold "Stump" Davis, Ronnie Scrima, Leonard Harris, Bob D'Oliva (*Motor Life* low ET trophy presenter), Vern Tomlinson, and Gene Adams. In this image, Harris's torso clearly reflects his years of gymnastic ring work. (Photo Courtesy Gene Adams)

times in a row at Lions. The team also netted 22 Top Eliminator wins out of 30 races ran in the prior six months at various strips. The phenomenal winning streak enhanced the action at the parts department of Albertson Olds.

The End of the Albertson Sponsorship

On October 22, 1960, Leonard was scheduled to take on Jack Chrisman's *Twin Bears* dual-engine dragster in a match race. This was a much-hyped and anticipated contest. However, one of the dual engines broke in the Chrisman dragster, resulting in the match race being canceled. With nothing else to do, the Albertson team decided to compete in the general racing.

The Albertson Olds dragster successfully made a qualifying run but in the pits Gene discovered water pouring out of one of the spark plug holes. The dragster was trailered. Another team had a Chrysler-powered dragster that was having handling issues and Leonard was asked if he was interested in shaking it out for them. Leonard did a qualifying run and noted that the car wanted to pull to the left, but no one thought too much of it. When Leonard made a second run, the car veered off the end of the track and crashed into a chain link fence, killing Leonard. Many drivers noted that Leonard Harris's driving talent would have taken him to the big time if not for being killed at the young age of 27.

The shocking accident resulted in Albertson Olds pulling out of sponsoring race cars. Lou Albertson was personally horrified by the tragic accident. He also considered the effect this could have on his dealership and was concerned about the possibility of being sued in the future if other accidents occurred. Ron Scrima was completely demoralized by the tragedy and sold his share of the dragster.

Racer Tom "the Mongoose" McEwen bought the chassis from Ron Scrima to become part owner of the dragster. Tom recalled this time as a bittersweet turning point in his career. Tom really liked Leonard Harris and felt bad that he was launching the next phase of his career off this tragic development, but it was time for him to move into the big time with dragsters.

Tom began the learning curve of piloting a finicky dragster. He went on to fame as "the Mongoose" in later years, but in the early days of his dragster racing, he was frequently tongue lashed by Gene Adams. Gene was frustrated by Tom's heavy-handed launches; he had been spoiled by the finely tuned work of Leonard Harris.

Albertson's Parts Department

Despite swearing off racing sponsorship, Albertson Oldsmobile remained a strong parts supplier for racers both on street and strip through the years. As the 1960s unfolded, the demand for Olds power on the drag strip started to diminish in the face of Chrysler's indomitable Hemi.

Just as the Oldsmobile motor was fading out in dragsters, the Albertson Olds dealership experienced a second wave of Oldsmobile performance enthusiasm when the Oldsmobile 442 came on strong. Oldsmobile had fielded some performance-oriented cars, such as the full-size Starfire and the Jetfire supercharged version of the compact F-85.

The midyear release of the 1964 Olds 442 answered the Pontiac GTO with a quickly cobbled together copycat that relied on a police spec small-block 330 engine with 4-barrel carburetor, 4-speed manual transmission, and dual exhaust (hence the name 442). From the very start, a lot of attention was paid to the 442 suspension and handling in an attempt to create a fully balanced muscle car.

Even the first year 442 for model year 1964 created minor ripples and barely received any notice on street or strip. The 1965 version of the 442 changed things because it now had a 400 motor and was an official muscle car.

The first model year of the 442 registered barely a blip on the sales radar compared to the Pontiac GTO, which had a big 389 engine, a huge head start, and tons of "Tiger" charisma momentum built up in the promotion and advertising of early Pontiac performance. Unlike Chrysler's extremely potent performance products of the time, which were basically invisible on the street, the GTO package came complete with racy appearance and tons of youth image.

1965 Oldsmobile Racers Take Notice

Oldsmobile kept the 442 name for 1965 despite making a 3-speed manual shift and an automatic transmission available. The 442 now had its own big-block 400 engine, allowing the 442 moniker to be revised to stand for 400 (4), 4-barrel (4), and dual exhaust (2).

The 1965 442 enjoyed improved sales over the introductory 1964 version. California dealers started sponsoring the 442 on drag strips. When guys on the street became interested, Albertson Olds started selling 442s off the lot at a brisk pace. These new 442 owners also needed parts. When a 442 guy came into the dealership, Don Farr's vast experience with racers in the parts department would steer them to the exact parts needed to make an Olds engine run well and reliably.

Albertson's parts guys also understood linkage issues involved with swapping in a tri-carb setup. The heads, intake, and carbs were available over the counter as a popular swap, but you needed to know how to set up the triple carburetors. Very few Olds triple carb cars were built, meaning fewer mechanics had experience with them.

Despite a flurry of dealerships flocking to sponsor 442s, Albertson didn't sponsor any. Lou Albertson was done with racing. But Albertson Olds was an invaluable resource for performance people. The feedback from the racers hanging out buying parts meant that Albertson's parts guys knew what cam worked best in an Olds 400/425. They could get you a 425 short-block that dropped right into a 442. Guys also bought complete engine assemblies and dumped them into Cutlasses or F-85s.

The Olds 425 block was very popular as a drop in for Cutlass or 442s. When General Motors let loose with the big engines in 1970, guys routinely stuffed their cars with the Olds 455. These blocks were readily available through the Albertson Olds parts department.

Dealership Takeover

On July 24, 1969, Lou Albertson died at age 54. The dealership continued under the ownership of his son, Bruce Albertson Sr.

By the 1990s, the generic compact cars produced by General Motors prevented any divisions from really putting their unique stamp on the styling. Albertson stayed the course and remained loyal Oldsmobile suppliers as General Motors lost its grip.

In later years, the Albertson Oldsmobile dealership added a Chevrolet franchise to buoy sales and was renamed Albertson Brothers Oldsmobile Chevrolet. Bruce Albertson kept the lot up to date with extensive remodeling done by the architectural firm Southern California Builders.

As the dealership tried to diversify and compete in the import-heavy California market, the franchise lineup expanded to become Albertson Brothers Oldsmobile Chevrolet Geo. After Oldsmobile was discontinued in 2004, Albertson hung on for a scant few years as Albertson Chevrolet before closing in 2007.

Bruce Albertson went on to become a recording engineer at Clear Lake Audio. The dealership's location is now a mall complex named Culver Crossroads.

The former Alberston lot on the corner was torn down and replaced with a strip mall. This view shows both corners of the new building on the intersection of Sepulveda Boulevard and Washington in Culver City.

CHAPTER 5
REYNOLDS BUICK GMC

Reynolds Buick GMC
Location: West Covina, California
Years in Operation: 1915–Present
Founder(s): Irven G. Reynolds
Current Status: Open, phone number: 626-384-4448

This period postcard show the 1964 purpose-built showroom at 345 N. Citrus Avenue. The main showroom remains here to this day with some renovations. North (right) of the showroom stands a smaller building for the truck lot. The city limit sign between Covina and West Covina is posted between the truck lot and the glass showroom. (Photo Courtesy Don Reynolds)

Reynolds Buick was the Buick version of Ace Wilson's Royal Pontiac dealership. On the surface, Reynolds fits into the mold of the hyper-popular Royal Pontiac formula. Reynolds sponsored racing and enjoyed many wins, just as Royal did. Reynolds stocked its parts department with speed parts and enjoyed brisk sales, as Royal did. Reynolds had a pipeline to the latest factory performance developments and tested new engineering hardware, just as Royal did. However, performance at Reynolds happened "the Buick way," which was very different from the norm during the 1960s muscle car craze.

The Performance Era

Unlike Royal Pontiac, which rode the landslide excitement of massive performance marketing from Pontiac Motor Division, the Buick approach was all stealth. Pontiac was in your face with Tri-Power 4-speed "Tigers" while Buick did muscle cars its own way, engineering cars around stock exhaust with quiet mufflers and automatic transmissions. Buick didn't base its work on 4-speeds, exotic factory experimental aluminum-bodied cars, or altered wheelbase racers. Instead, it focused on being fast bone stock off the showroom floor with closed exhaust.

Pontiac's high-performance saturation media exposure included radio songs, television tie-ins, and massive magazine coverage. Even the Ford and the Mopar guys knew about Royal. However, Buick performance was almost an underground cult in the 1960s. Reynolds fit well into the offbeat Buick Motor Division sleeper approach. At first, Reynolds was only known as "The Fastest Buick Dealer" among the Buick faithful.

Hot Rod magazine back in 1965 was one of the earliest publications to discern the performance virtues of Buick's new Gran Sport intermediate GTO clone. The general masses were continuously in shock when Reynolds' Buicks won races. Most people didn't even know what an Invicta was until the trophy was handed out. It wasn't until the 1970s Stage 1 versus Hemi feuds and evil-looking 1980s Darth Vader Grand Nationals that Buick performance filtered down to the general public.

According to most Buick enthusiasts, 1970 was the ultimate muscle car year. That year, Buick got the jump on Pontiac. Buick Motor Division had been primarily selling large luxury cars and only entered the muscle car fray because Pontiac had broken the trail.

Performance-oriented division head John DeLorean departed Pontiac for the 1970 model year, leaving a vacuum into which formerly staid Buick rammed a Stage 1 455 engine that eclipsed Pontiac's hastily developed and compromised 455. Pontiac returned with a vengeance in 1971 with a round port 455 HO, but by then compression was lowered across the board.

At the peak of the muscle car wars, Buick tuned its 1970 Stage 1 455 blockbuster muscle machine for ideal showroom floor performance with a closed exhaust, an air conditioner, and a full gamut of comfort and convenience power accessories. Even the radical striped and winged GSX had typical Buick luxury built into it. The GS and GSX only needed gas to go fast. They also handled really well.

Reynolds Buick's Beginning

Irven Gibbs Reynolds was born on January 17, 1890, in Carrollton, Missouri. His family moved to Covina, California, in 1905. Covina was east of downtown Los Angeles with an economy based on orange groves. Irven graduated from the University of California at Berkeley (UCB) in 1912.

Irven entered the car business in 1915, using a rented desk in "Daddy Weber's" local Covina gas station. Irven's distributor agreement with the massive Howard Automotive Company in Los Angeles and excellent rapport with his employees and customers resulted in quick expansion. His first dealership building opened at the corner of Citrus and Badillo in 1922. In 1923, Irven added a GMC truck franchise and also held a Pontiac franchise until at least 1940.

Irven's son Irven Gibbs "Pete" Reynolds Jr. was born on April 2, 1926, in Covina, California. Pete served in World War II in the US Navy, graduated from UCB in 1950, and then started working at Reynolds Buick.

When Irven retired in 1958, Pete took over Reynolds Buick and used the same ethics taught to him by his father. Buick Motor Division sales were based on service, quality, restrained style, and luxury; it was "one step below Cadillac" and marketed to an upscale, refined audience. Reynolds Buick followed this approach until the fateful day when Pete met Buick technical instructor Bill W. Trevor at the GM Training Center at 1105 Riverside Drive in Burbank, California.

Reynolds' Racing History

Bill introduced Pete to "Pop" Lennie D. Kennedy, who drove a truck for a living. But his real passion was drag racing Buicks. Bill and Pop sparked a change of emphasis at the dealership from typical Buick quality/luxury to seemingly incongruous excitement and performance.

At that time, Buicks were not on anyone's performance radar, with the exception of true believer Pop Kennedy. Pop was an absolute Buick zealot. He liked to prove that a showroom stock Buick would beat any other showroom stock car. Buick had an edge off the line using high–torque motors coupled to high–stall speed automatic transmissions. These cars launched out aggressively in an era where most automatics were derisively named "slushboxes" because of their delayed shifts, slippage, and slow acceleration.

Pop was atypical in his fervent Buick philosophy, and he himself was an anomaly in the drag racing world. As his name infers, Pop was not a teenage hot rod kid with greased-back hair. Pop's insurance policy dated January 7, 1967, states that he was 57 years old, placing his birth in 1909 or 1910. Despite his age, many witnesses remarked that Pop had the best eyesight and quickest reflexes they had ever seen. The combination of a "senior citizen" racer driving an automatic transmission "senior citizen" plush Buick and winning races against stick shift kids in hot cars was mind blowing at the time.

The Reynolds Buick champion racing driver was 60 years old when the muscle car era peaked in 1970! Reynolds' winning Buicks ran in stock classes using automatics in an era of 4-speed reverence. Their wins and class records perplexed all competitors who believed "Buicks don't run."

1959 Invicta

Pete Reynolds bucked the popular trends when he broke out of the staid Buick image and sponsored Pop Kennedy at drag strips. Pop drove a red 1959 Buick Invicta with an engine built by Jim Bell that was soon known as "the Winningnest Buick of all time." With milled heads and a 4.44:1 axle ratio,

Buick Philosophy

As the 1960s began, most performance cars paired the top engines with full-size bodies packing lots of weight and expense. The budget-priced intermediate-size Pontiac GTO was still several years away. All the racers were campaigning in full-size cars.

The weight savings game from the factory was starting to get serious, but Buick wasn't offering aluminum parts or drilling out the frames. The Buick philosophy was that you shouldn't have to touch its cars to perform. It is interesting to note that years later, the absolute beast of all Buicks, the 1970 GS Stage 1, was engineered for maximum performance with quiet street mufflers in place.

Reynolds Buick sponsored this 1959 Buick Invicta. Driver Pop Kennedy is behind the wheel while engine builder Jim Bell squats beside the car. (Photo Courtesy Don Reynolds)

the basically stock Invicta surprised many and was known as a sleeper.

Pop believed in strictly stock cars and wanted to win fairly. His engine builder, Jim Bell, had some initial trouble convincing Pop that running headers instead of stock exhaust manifolds wasn't cheating. Pop raced heavy Buicks, relying on the drivetrain to get him down the strip first.

Reynolds wins NHRA Back to Back

In 1961, the Reynolds 1959 Invicta was sold off as a used car to engine builder Jim Bell and replaced with a Rio Red 1961 Invicta set up with 4.44:1 axle, milled heads, headers, and Casler slicks. Jim worked his magic on that 1961 Invicta, and Pop's reflexes never wavered. The Invicta won 38 consecutive races between May 21 and September 10, 1961.

Pop drove the Invicta to Indianapolis and won the NHRA 1961 National Championship D-Stock Automatic Class with a 15.19-second run at 92.21 mph. The excitement of the win translated to an elevated awareness of Reynolds Buick, which had a display of trophies filling the showroom. The

Retired Reynolds Buick founder Irven Reynolds shared the excitement with his son Pete Reynolds and driver Pop Kennedy. The three men are posed with the trophy and 1961 Invicta after winning the 1961 Indy Nationals. (Photo Courtesy Don Reynolds)

Pop Kennedy poses in the Reynolds Buick dealership with the 1961 Invicta, his trophy, and the tool set he won at the 1961 Indy Nationals. Note that the dealer name in shoe polish has been cleaned off the car. (Photo Courtesy Don Reynolds)

The second car that Reynolds Buick sponsored was this 1961 Invicta, which has the dealership name lettered on the car with shoe polish. Driver Pop Kennedy poses with the trophy. (Photo Courtesy Don Reynolds)

In 1962, driver Pop Kennedy and dealership principle Pete Reynolds pose with the 1961 Invicta following Pop's second consecutive win at the Indy Nationals. The lettering on the car is now professionally painted and no longer done with shoe polish! (Photo Courtesy Don Reynolds)

enhanced sales ensured that the racing sponsorship carried on.

Pop Kennedy took the 1961 Invicta back to Indianapolis the following year and won the 1962 NHRA Nationals again in D-Stock Automatic with 15.85 at 93.20 mph. *Hot Rod* magazine carried a picture of Pop launching against a Pontiac in the November 1962 issue summary of the finals.

Reynolds' 50th Anniversary

Reynolds racing sponsorship went in hiatus for a few years while Pete coordinated construction of a new dealership. In 1964, the dealership moved from Covina to a new purpose-built glassed-in modern building at 345 N. Citrus Avenue, West Covina, California.

Pete ordered a fleet of 50 gold Buicks to celebrate Reynolds' new location and upcoming 50th anniversary in busi-

Buick Skylark Gran Sport

The 1965 Buick Skylark Gran Sport intermediate-size muscle car was the Buick Motor Division version of the Pontiac GTO. Pontiac released the Pontiac Tempest GTO option as a 1964 model and officially started the muscle car era. Back then, the big engine/intermediate cars were commonly known as "supercars."

Pontiac flouted the GM 330 engine limit for an intermediate car and dropped a 389 into the lightweight GTO. Pontiac sweetened the recipe by adding imagery (round racing gauges, bucket seats, and fake hood scoops) and economy (a mere $295 for the option) to create an exciting "factory hot rod" that youthful buyers could appreciate and afford. Pontiac's performance marketing barraged their fans with "Wide Track" and "Tiger" slogans that equated with exciting cars.

Buick had previously made slight inroads into performance with the Wildcat, which was an executive hot rod. The Wildcat failed to combat Pontiac's full-size Grand Prix sales winner and became passé in light of Buick's greatest accomplishment of the 1960s: the stunningly beautiful Buick Riviera. The 1963 Riviera was an understated exercise in grace and excellent design that killed the Wildcat sales. Everyone wanted a Riviera, which was a personal luxury car, not a performance concept.

For the 1965 model year, the Gran Sport option was added to the Riviera in an attempt to match the full-size Pontiac Grand Prix and Pontiac 2+2. When it came time for Buick to release its own GTO clone, it tied it in with the Riviera performance option and named the new intermediate-size muscle car the Skylark Gran Sport. Buick's Skylark Gran Sport was a subdued version of the GTO visually and in marketing approach.

Buick's Skylark Gran Sport failed to sell as many units as the other GM GTO clones. The Chevrolet Chevelle SS and Oldsmobile 442 didn't do as well as the GTO but posted respectable sales. The Gran Sport was hindered by a sedate image, higher cost, and a perception that the "Nailhead 401" Buick engine was not a performer.

High-Stall Automatic Transmission

As if tacitly acknowledging a dearth of power, Buick didn't offer the Hurst shifter for the first two years of Gran Sport

The Tiger Gold first 1965 Gran Sport race car is shown with Pete and Pop. The car hasn't been lettered yet but has Casler slicks mounted to the rear Buick mag-style wheels. Note the temporary dealer tag instead of a license plate. (Photo Courtesy Don Reynolds)

Chapter 5: Reynolds Buick GMC   57

Bill Trevor (right) wears a Buick ball cap as he accepts a trophy on behalf of Pop. The joke is that Pop rarely posed with the track event presenters because he was hurrying to collect his winnings! Note that the first 1965 Gran Sport racer has been lettered. (Photo Courtesy Don Reynolds)

production. Drivers interpreted this as Buick not deeming a heavy-duty shifter necessary for a lower-horsepower engine. But Buick wasn't heavily into the 4-speed craze of the era and oriented its cars around good automatic transmissions. Zone technical advisor Bill Trevor was known in drag circles for preferring Buicks to have well-silenced mufflers. He was keenly aware of the Buick image and doing things the Buick way.

Where the Buick shone was the same place Pop Kennedy worked his magic at the drag strip: Buicks had a great high-stall automatic transmission. The variable stator vanes in the transmission provided much greater latitude than the mere two or three forward speeds suggested. Combined with freight train torque from the Nailhead, an automatic Gran Sport hurtled off the line with great launches. *Hot Rod* magazine noted three-car-length leads at launch from a Gran Sport automatic.

The Gran Sport had less racy bodylines than the Pontiac GTO and a typical passenger car strip speedometer layout instead of the racing round gauges of the GTO. The Gran Sport was more expensive than a GTO. Buick performance marketing was meager compared to the media blitz at Pontiac. Kids read horsepower figures and left with the impression that Buicks were slower than the Pontiac Tigers. All these details were demerits against Buick in the eyes of the youthful muscle car buyers.

The Gran Sport was a thoroughly developed muscle car built using a convertible frame to increase rigidity in a structure beefed up with a heavy-duty driveline. The Nailhead 401 provided ample torque. High-end horsepower was slightly compromised, but off-the-line torque can win many short distance stop light drag races. That essential HP figure was what diminished the car in the eyes of potential buyers.

Buick's Nailhead 401

The Nailhead 401 engine (named "400" because of GM's engine limit for intermediates) used valve designs that trace back to the 1950s. The first Buick V-8s replaced an inline-8 and needed to be quite narrow to fit in the same underhood space. This forced engineers to work with small valves (hence the *nailhead* slur). The engineers compensated for the small intake and exhaust valve openings with greater duration and lift, which created the unique Buick "rumpety rump" idle and tremendous torque.

Anyone who has owned high-mileage 1960s GM cars from the various divisions can attest that Oldsmobile and Buick engines last longer than Chevrolet or Pontiac engines. This isn't just a side effect of older conservative owners not abusing the cars. Buick and Olds factories enforced higher quality control and installed more expensive internal parts, resulting in smoother-running engines across the board. Olds and Buick used expensive bearings in assembly. Buick tested and ensured that cylinder pressures were equal in all the V-8s they assembled. This was just part of the quality image Buick Motor Division was selling.

Chevy or Pontiac motors often vary from car to car. My Chevy and Pontiac motors tended to develop issues after the first 100,000-mile mark was passed. They used oil and went out of tune due to timing chain wear. Bearing issues plague high-mile Pontiacs. However, I have owned Buicks and Oldsmobiles with ridiculously high mileage that didn't burn oil, ran smoothly, and pulled surprisingly strongly. The Oldsmobile small-blocks were good for about 110 mph while Buicks really did run 120 mph. Many Buick collectors confirm that every 350-ci Skylark in the late 1960s will run an honest 120 mph top end.

But what about the racers who wanted a hot-looking, fast, inexpensive car? The GTO was their answer. Kids didn't want to pay extra for Buick's invisible features of durability and balance. Guys seeking a "mature" balanced GM muscle car were drawn to the Olds 442 with its front and rear sway bar, high-horsepower rating, and slightly lower price than Buick. Olds also incorporated the 4-speed concept right into the name of the car: 4-barrel, 4-speed, 2 exhausts. When automatics became available on 442s, the name was amended to mean 400 engine, 4-barrel, 2 exhaust, but the idea that an Olds 442 has a 4-speed persisted in the minds of enthusiasts.

ness. The anniversary cars were painted Pontiac's Tiger Gold by special order. Pete's son Don recalls Pete stating that all 50 Tiger Gold cars were 1965 Buick Skylark Gran Sports. Pete Reynolds chose the new intermediate Skylark Gran Sport for his anniversary statement at a time when they were midyear new releases. An open house celebration was held June 4–6, 1965, between 9 a.m. and 6 p.m. each day.

"Buick Sunday"

Reynolds Buick sponsored Pop in an automatic transmission 1965 Skylark Gran Sport. Pete's secret weapons of Pop and engine prep man Jim Bell ensured that Reynolds won. Pop Kennedy's Buick Gran Sport was painted Pontiac's Tiger Gold to match the other 50 Gran Sports gathered for the dealership anniversary. The Reynolds 1967 and 1968 Gran Sport drag cars sponsored by Reynolds retained the Anniversary Gold paint.

The first 1965 Gran Sport racer lived for a mere three months but made its mark in that span. Stock book entry number 181 from January 11, 1965, lists the pertinent details of the racer. Model number 4427 indicates a new midyear Gran Sport Pillared Coupe. The car is summarized as "Pete's Demo." This car made an immediate splash when it became one of the six Buicks to win their classes on Sunday, February 21, 1965, at San Fernando Dragway.

The sweep of the races was known in Buick circles as "Buick Sunday." Roland C. Withers, Buick's general sales manager, was inspired to report on the victories in a letter sent out to all Buick dealers.

Pop Kennedy won B-Stock in the brand-new 1965 Reynolds Buick Gran Sport, covering the quarter-mile in 14.04 seconds at 101.81 mph. The May 1965 issue of *Hot Rod* mentions that this car ran 104.46 mph in 13.42 seconds with open headers.

Reynolds also sponsored another winner: the 1964 Special 300-ci V-8 driven by Gil Labarge. This car won class D-Stock with 14.76 at 97 mph. The old Reynolds 1961 Invicta (the 1961–1962 NHRA class winner) was entered by a private party who won Class F with 14.5 at 95 mph.

Boulevard Buick of Long Beach, California, won C-Stock in a 1965 Gran Sport convertible with 14.56 at 88 mph. E-Stock was won by Bill Murphy Buick of Culver City, California, in a Riviera with 14.88 at 92.75 mph. K-Stock was won by Ted Baker Buick out of Fillmore, California, in a V-6 Skylark coupe with 16.18 at 86.16 mph. Buick Motor Division took out an ad in the *L.A. Times* to crow a bit about the landslide wins.

Reynolds' Buick Gran Sport

A May 1965 *Hot Rod* article about the 1965 Gran Sport summarized the procedures Jim Bell used to prep Pop Kennedy's car. The *Hot Rod* writer was astounded at how little modification was needed to make the car race ready. The 401 was disassembled and checked for factory clearances with a deck height of 0.030 inch. Combustion chambers were measured out to 123 cc and a valve job was done. Hooker headers and 3-inch collectors replaced the stock manifolds. Posi-Traction axles ran 4.30:1 gears. Slicks were Casler recaps. Delco air shocks aided right-side traction on launch. That was it. Not too far a deviation from Pop's revered "showroom stock" status.

Pete Reynolds didn't restrict his performance activities to racing sponsorship. The *Hot Rod* magazine's article on blueprinting the Buick motor gave the part number of an ideal camshaft to use, which also noted they were for sale in the Reynolds Buick parts department. Don Reynolds recalls that his father established the first header distributorship with Gary Hooker. Pete's diary log indicates that he made a deal with Gary on March 17, 1965.

Shown here are two of the winning racers from February 21, 1965, aka Buick Sunday. Pop Kennedy poses with the Reynolds 1965 Gran Sport (left). The Boulevard Buick convertible on the right was driven by Ralph Bergeron. (Photo Courtesy Don Reynolds)

The rolled 1965 Gran Sport drag racer has the hood lying on top of the crushed roof to facilitate easy removal of the drivetrain. The car sits up high in front without the weight of the 401 engine and transmission in the car. (Photo Courtesy Don Reynolds)

The second Reynolds 1965 Gran Sport drag racer was Arctic White repainted Tiger Gold to match the first racer. The second racer had a red interior and used white Buick steel wheels on the rear instead of the Buick mag-style wheels used on all four corners of the first racer. (Photo Courtesy Don Reynolds)

In the mid-1960s, Hooker Headers was still just a small-time operation. Don recalls that several times Pete remarked to him that Reynolds Buick did very well with high-performance parts sales, which centered around Hooker Headers. Gary Hooker's close association with Reynolds is evident in an October 1965 *Hot Rod* article about rear axle switches. The car Gary was working on in the article had a Reynolds Buick license frame.

On April 3, Pete drove the winning 1965 Gran Sport over to Gary Hooker's shop in Pomona, California. Gary wanted to see the Reynolds race car because he was also racing a 1965 Gran Sport, but his was a 4-speed. The tremendous torque of the Nailhead 401 caused drivetrain breakage and hassles. The Buick torque was better matched to an automatic. He was curious to examine Pete's automatic Gran Sport.

Pete was driving on Casler slicks on his return trip when he was caught in a rainstorm. Casler tires provide excellent traction on racetracks but are treacherous on wet surfaces. The lack of wet traction caused a rollover that crushed the roof. Pete came away unscathed, but his wife, Caroline, banned him from driving the racer again.

Reynolds' 1965 Gran Sport Drag Car Number 2

On April 5, the drivetrain from the rolled 1965 Gran Sport Reynolds racer was transplanted into a new 1965 Arctic White Gran Sport with a red interior. The new racer was bought April 4, 1965, off another dealer in San Bernardino. This Gran Sport was originally shipped March 9, 1965. The VIN 44275Z115997 indicates a 1965 Buick Skylark V-8 built in the Fremont, California, final assembly plant.

The new Gran Sport was quickly painted Tiger Gold and became Reynolds' 1965 Gran Sport racer *Car Two*. The June 18, 1965, *National Dragster* reported on the Palmdale, California, races June 11–12, 1965, where Pop drove *Car Two* to Top Stock with 13.45 at 104.8 mph.

Coverage of the second Gran Sport racer in the May 1966 issue of *Drag Strip* magazine (formerly known as *Modern Rod*) described it much the way *Hot Rod* magazine described the first 1965 racing car the year prior. *Car Two* was basically stock with Header Hookers and rear Delco heavy-duty shocks, just like the first car.

Some extra details on *Car Two* included 90/10 shocks up front. The Buick Super Turbine 300 automatic transmission in *Car Two* was not column shifted. It had a shifter poking up through a hole cut in the carpet. Idiot lights were replaced with warning gauges. The most noticeable change was that the second car didn't mount Casler slicks on the Buick-styled wheels. Instead *Car Two* had 8.50x14 Goodyear Blue Streak cheaters mounted on plain white painted stock Buick wheels. The article reports a best run of 12.88 at 108.78 mph.

When Buick Motor Division introduced the all-new 1967 Buick GS 400, Reynolds upgraded the racer. Pop Kennedy bought the 1965 racing car as his personal driver on January 7, 1967. Pop held on to it for several years.

The GS 400

The new 1967 Buick Gran Sport was now called GS 400. The Buick name abbreviated Gran Sport to GS and included the engine size the same way that Chevrolet did with the Chevelle SS 396. Buick expressing the name the "Chevy way" is likely just a coincidence. GS 400 was meant to draw attention to the 400 ci because it was a brand-new engine.

Buick released a new 400 engine in 1967 to replace the old Nailhead 401. The new 400 had large valves, hot cam,

Reynolds' 1965 Opel Kadett

Reynolds also had another drag strip winner of a much different stripe! Reynolds sponsored a 1965 Opel Kadett that beat Volkswagens on the strip. One of the winning quarter-mile times took an agonizingly long 19.09 seconds at 69.01 mph. Reynolds salesman Ed Dilliard was the driver and caused a bit of conversation when he folded his 6-foot 7-inch frame into the micro Opel!

All 6 feet, 7 inches of Ed Dilliard somehow fit into this Reynolds Buick–sponsored 1965 Opel drag racer when he drove it to several victories. Note that the Reynolds signage behind the car reflects this new franchise as Buick-Opel-GMC. (Photo Courtesy Don Reynolds)

and streamlined manifolds, which produced more top-end horsepower, bringing Buick in line with the engine formats used by competitors. The Reynolds race team found the new 400 engine responded well to mods but had a propensity for blowing up quite frequently due to oiling issues on the rear bearings. Pete Reynolds and Bill Thomas at the Buick Tech Center helped Pop by replacing his blown engines numerous times.

Although Pop Kennedy and Jim Bell contended with engines that blew regularly, the payoff was getting the Reynolds 1967 Gran Sport down the quarter-mile in a blazing 12.10 seconds at 111 mph. That new 400 was a stormer.

Reynolds Upgrades in 1968

Reynolds Buick usually kept a racer for a couple of years, but the 1968 GS 400 debuted a brand-new streamlined body-

Pop Kennedy poses with Tiger Gold Gran Sport racers number 2, 3, and 4. The 1967 racer is at left and the 1968 on the right. Hidden behind Pop and the trophies is the second 1965 drag racer. The first 1965 racer was totaled. (Photo Courtesy Don Reynolds)

Pop Kennedy with the 1968 Reynolds GS 400 racer. In mid-1969, this car became a test mule car for the new 455 Stage 1 and Stage 2 engine. (Photo Courtesy Don Reynolds)

style that allowed larger rear tires that were helpful at launch. Reynolds made the jump to the 1968 model for this reason.

The 1968 GS 400 racer proved to be quite interesting. Dennis Manner in Buick Engineering used the drag car as a test mule for various Stage 1 parts under development. By this time, Buick was really getting it together with performance development. Race car testing aided development of parts essential to the Buick masterpiece 455 Stage 1 and Stage 2 engines.

The 1968 GS 400 racing car was logged as car number 226 in the inventory bible on January 4, 1968. Unlike most Skylarks and Gran Sports shipped to California, this car wasn't built in the Fremont final assembly plant. The VIN 46378H126648 contains an H, which indicates the Flint, Michigan, final assembly plant.

According to the 1968 inventory bible, Reynolds sold about 609 new 1968 model Buicks. This jibes with long-term salesman Spence Lyon's memory that Pete Reynolds used to say, "If we sell 60 new cars a month, the dealership pays for itself."

Of the 1968 new cars sold, 50 were Buick Skylark Custom two-door hardtops and 3 were GS 400 two-door hardtops. The fourth GS 400 listed in Reynolds' inventory was Pop's race car. These figures illustrate the low-profile sales of the GS 400. Pontiac GTO sales had dropped since the peak in 1966, but GTO was still selling like crazy in 1968 with 87,000 sold. The Chevelle SS 396 was creeping up on GTO sales with 57,000 SS cars sold and 5,000 El Camino SSs. The new upstart Plymouth Road Runner sold 44,000 cars in its debut year for 1968. Established GM division muscle cars sold less than the Plymouth Bargain Bird with Olds 442 selling 33,000 and Buick GS 400 only moving 13,000.

Part of the low total for GS 400 can be blamed on the bleed-out of sales to 10,000 GS 350s, but the primary reason is that Buick was still a sleeper during the muscle era. With approximately 2,000 Buick dealers, only five or six GS 400s could expect to be sold at any given location per year. When the rarely seen GS 400 won at the drags, it caused a lot of surprise.

All the manufacturers had figured out that muscle car youth sales were critical to their bottom line. Even Buick was getting wild with speed, although within the context of preserving its reserved image. The restraint ended in 1970. Goaded by in-your-face cars such as the GTO Judge, Mach 1, Boss 302, Road Runner triple carbureted 440 with liftoff fiberglass hood, the Superbird, and other wild cars, mild-mannered Buick responded.

Buick Releases the GSX

In 1970, Buick trumped just about everyone when it released one of the pinnacle muscle cars of all time: the 1970 GSX. The GSX combined a potent 455 with scoops, stripes, and spoilers. The GS that the GSX was based on weighed less because it didn't have the spoilers. But it was available with the same optional 455 Stage 1 motor as the GSX.

Reynolds dropped the gold paint tradition when it sponsored Pop in a white 1970 Buick GS 455 Stage 1. This was already a tough car, but the Reynolds racer was switched to Stage 2 engine parts and the tall Stage 2 hood scoop that rose

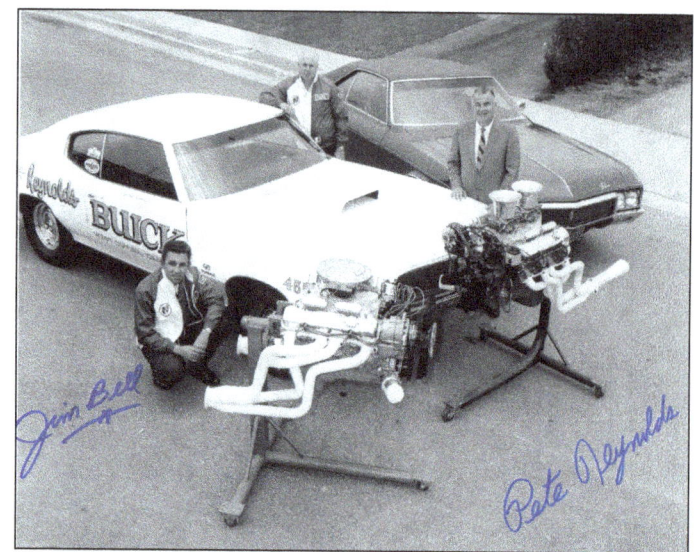

Jim Bell squats in front with two of the engines he built. Pop Kennedy stands in the middle with the 1970 GS 455 Stage 2 drag racer. Pete Reynolds is at the right with a stock 1970 Riviera behind him. (Photo Courtesy Don Reynolds)

The 1970 GS 455 Reynolds racer at the dragstrip with Motor Wheel Corporation's alloy Spyder wheels. The GS 455 looks better with the plain aluminum mags, but the Spyder wheels were strong and provided large brake cooling slots. (Photo Courtesy Don Reynolds)

above the dead air zone on the hood achieved a true ram air effect. Dennis Manner in powertrain development at Buick was refining incredible parts and fielding them via the Reynolds race program.

Buick had built a showroom stock car that could roast well-prepped race cars. After Jim Bell tweaked the 455 with Stage 2 parts, the Reynolds race car was poised to clean house. Great disappointment ensued when the car was refactored into a different power weight ratio by the NHRA. At this point, the new 1970 racer was taken away from stock parameters and the stops were pulled out. The Stage 2 eventually ran 10.70 ETs.

During their racing partnership, tuner/engine builder Jim Bell and driver Pop Kennedy had retained a strong friendship. When Jim was overwhelmed by his duties in his performance shop, he teamed up with Pop Kennedy to divide the labor. Together they formed a high-performance development team named Kennedy-Bell.

Pop Kennedy Retires

Pop Kennedy lost most of the use of his left side from strokes, which affected his launch technique. The muscle car era was collapsing, and small-guy drag racing was gradually diminishing. All these factors plus the move away from showroom stock state of tune were contributing factors to Pop retiring from driving in 1972.

When Pop retired from race driving in 1972, the name of the company he founded with Jim Bell was changed to Kenne Bell. Reynolds Buick sold Pop the 1970 GS race car. The racer was found and restored by Guy Parquette of Mosinee, Wisconsin.

Reynolds Continues Racing Sponsorships

Reynolds drag racing subsided with Pop's retirement, but Reynolds continued to sponsor track racing cars. One of its drivers was Arlene Hiss, a teacher who raced on weekends.

The 1970 GS 455 Stage 2 launches at the dragstrip. The driver wearing glasses is clearly not Pop Kennedy. Note how the rear tires have grown again since the 1968 racer. The 1970 GS wheel wells were opened up higher on the bodyline than in 1968–1969. (Photo Courtesy Don Reynolds)

Reynolds sponsored her white Opel 1900, which won SCCA Showroom Stock Championship. Arlene later became the first woman to race an Indy car in USAC in Phoenix on March 14, 1976. She finished the race but reverted to USAC Stock Cars.

Buick still sold some exciting cars. It sold a replica 1975 mega motor Indy 500 Pace car. The Buick engineers experimented with turbos and paced Indy in 1976 in a V-6 turbo. Eventually the turbo work made Buick top dog of the GM divisions when muscle car revival G-Body cars came out in the 1980s. The Grand National went faster than everyone with an automatic transmission.

Arlene Hiss stands with her champion Reynolds-sponsored Opel in the mid-1970s. Note the Venus glyph on the side of her car, indicating that she was one of the rare female drivers on the circuit. Letterhead that she sent also used this glyph as her signature. (Photo Courtesy Don Reynolds)

Two generations of Reynolds Buick relive racing history. Don Reynolds sits in for Pop Kennedy behind the wheel while Pete Reynolds resumes his place at the front of the car just as he appeared in a period photo from the 1960s. The tribute car is a re-creation of the second 1965 Gran Sport with the white painted steel wheels in rear and a red interior. (Photo Courtesy Don Reynolds)

Reynolds had some Grand National fun cars pass through, but what kept the dealership healthy was decades of GMC experience that enabled the dealership to become a sales leader in that emerging market.

Reynolds Buick Today

When the muscle car era faded, Pete Reynolds didn't fold up. Instead, he adapted to the new trends. When the vehicle landscape shifted to motorhomes in the 1970s, Reynolds responded with alacrity. Although Irven had retired in 1958, he shared the excitement of his son Pete's success in the muscle car era. Several photos feature the two generations posing with a winning Reynolds' race car. Irven died on February 28, 1981, at 91 years old.

Pete's son Don Reynolds was born on August 11, 1965, shortly after the 50th anniversary open house at the new Reynolds showroom. Don began washing cars in the dealership during junior high. After graduation from California Polytechnic State University in 1988, he began full-time work at the dealership. He took over the dealership in 1999, making him the third generation of Reynolds helming the business.

Don and Pete hosted large gatherings of Buick faithful on dealership anniversaries. They welcomed guests who brought a replica 1965 Gran Sport racer (done up with the painted white steel rear wheels of *Car Two*) and the actual 1970 GS 455 racer, which was perfectly restored. Pete died in his sleep at age 90 on December 26, 2016.

Reynolds Buick sales swelled due to high performance for a decade despite the fact that Buick wasn't the obvious brand of choice during the muscle car era. Unlike Royal Pontiac and most of the dealerships from the muscle era, Reynolds Buick is still a successful business to this day. Don Reynolds has preserved all the documents and photos from the lengthy dealership history and is supportive of the new trend toward history and nostalgia in the muscle car hobby.

The 1970 GS 455 Stage 2 race car returns to Reynolds Buick for the 95th Anniversary celebration after a thorough restoration by the new owner Guy Parquette. Guy brought the car in all the way from Mosinee, Wisconsin. Pete and Don presented Guy with the original dealership paperwork that came with his car. (Photo Courtesy Don Reynolds)

CHAPTER 6
MELROSE MOTORS

Melrose Motors
Location: Oakland, California
Years in Operation: 1952–2006
Founder(s): James Di Bari and possibly Dominick Vallerga
Current Status: Vacant

The 1965 altered wheelbase Hemi Plymouth Melrose Missile VI sits on its own open-air hauler at the track. Many dealerships of this era towed their race cars behind another car or a pickup truck. Jim Di Bari spared no expense on equipment. Charlie was still doing some of the strip driving but Cecil Yother had replaced driver Tommy Grove. (Photo Courtesy Richard Adair)

Not everyone needed to live in Los Angeles to stay competitive. Despite being a substantial drive north of the major L.A. drag strips, Melrose Motors from Oakland, California, did well with various incarnations of its *Melrose Missile*. It even won some championships.

The Beginning of Melrose Motors

Melrose Motors Inc. was a Chrysler Plymouth dealer originally established in 1929. It began as a service station at East 14th Street and 45th Avenue. James Di Bari and possibly Dominick Vallerga owned the business in the 1940s.

James "Jim" Di Bari was born circa 1910 in New York. He married Margaret (born circa 1913 in New Jersey). A few years after the birth of their son, Charles Di Bari, in 1935, the family moved from Patterson, New Jersey, to sunny California.

In 1946, Jim became a Kaiser Frazier dealer. He instantly became the biggest Kaiser Frazier dealer in Northern California and opened a larger space across the street from his first location at 4431 East 14th. The road was renamed International Boulevard in 1996, which further obscures the original locations from current discovery.

Jim and his partner Henry Vallerga (son of Dominick Vallerga) added a Plymouth DeSoto franchise in June 1952. When DeSoto died off, Jim's proven track record awarded him expanded franchises. Jim then added Chrysler and Imperial products.

Melrose Enters Racing

Soon, Jim Di Bari became the sole owner and president of Melrose Motors. He then brought his son, Charlie, in as vice president. Jim listened to Charlie, who connected the dealership to the youth muscle car movement.

Melrose Motors was doing just fine in the 1960s, having won the Chrysler Quality Dealer award three times already with a booming location. The Melrose Auto Service portion of the business was an official state light and brake station during the 1960s. Melrose had 37 factory-trained mechanics and 4 apprentices on duty. It didn't really need performance to amp up business, but Jim appreciated publicity, which is how Charlie got Jim interested in drag racing.

Jim Di Bari's flair for promotion was demonstrated at new car unveilings, where he went way further than any other car dealer. Back in the 1950s and 1960s, dealerships papered over

On May 26, 1963, Melrose Motors brought its *Melrose Missile III* an hour's drive south to the drag strip in Half Moon Bay, California. Both Tommy Grove and Charlie Di Bari are listed as drivers on the roof C pillar on this version of the *Missile*. Note the lettering along the base of the car references Melrose winning the 1963 NHRA Winternationals Super Stock. (Photo Courtesy Thomas Bettencourt)

their windows and hid the new cars from view until the release date, which typically took place in mid-September. While other dealers were content to serve some refreshments and mingle, Jim served refreshments, gave away a TV prize, and had the whole show set off by a marching band. In 1954, Jim displayed the new cars on a revolving turntable. He was a guy who loved to do things big, and as such, he was ripe for the picking when it came to drag sponsorship! Jim's son knew how to appeal to him.

Charlie convinced his father that racing would be great promotion for the dealership. He had managed to score the second of 200 built factory 413 race cars. The first went to the Golden Commandos.

Melrose Motors was conveniently housing a rabid performance nut in their ranks. Tommy Grove was a 28-year-old mechanic working in the dealership. He had experience driving a dragster as well as Super Stocks. Charlie enlisted Tommy's help to get the 413 prepped. Jim reluctantly advanced money for blueprinting and headers.

Melrose Missiles

Tommy Grove began driving for Melrose Motors in June 1962. He was both mechanic and driver, and he was thoroughly expert at both tasks. When the car immediately won its class, Jim was ecstatic—as much for the promotional value of racing as for the sheer excitement and fun of it. Once Jim was in, he was all in. He bought a second car so that the team would never be out of the running if there were technical difficulties.

Melrose sponsored Tommy in a series of cars all named the *Melrose Missile*. The *Missile* appeared first in Max Wedge and later in Hemi form. The *Melrose Missile* name had addendum numbers to distinguish various versions campaigned. The first *Melrose Missile* in 1962 was packed with a potent 413 engine and managed to cut mid-12s at 115 mph. Charlie also managed to convince his father to let him drive a pushbutton automatic 1963 Plymouth Savoy 426 Wedge that was a twin to Tom's stick shift racer.

The stick shift *Melrose Missile III* won the 1963 NHRA Super Stock Winternationals championship with Tommy driving. The Missile posted 12.37 seconds at 114.94 mph.

In the summer of 1963, the *Melrose Missile III* set a new NHRA Super Stock record with a 12-flat 118.26 mph at Half Moon Bay. The *Missile* was powered through a pair of 4-barrels on top of a 426 Max Wedge engine. It was lightened with an aluminum front end, including factory aluminum hood scoops.

Tommy won Mr. Top Stock Eliminator in February 1964 at the 4th Annual Winternationals in Pomona, California, with an 11.63 elapsed quarter-mile time at 124.13 mph. This fifth version of the racer was named *Melrose Missile V*.

Jim Di Bari in 1960 when he was owner and president of Melrose Motors in Oakland, California. Jim's son, Charlie, was poised to infect Jim with racing madness, which would take hold of him for the entire decade of the 1960s.

The *Melrose Missile III* was the third version of the popular series of Plymouth drag cars launched from the Melrose Motors launching pad. The hood scoops are factory items made from aluminum. Current owner Bob Mosher restored the *Melrose Missile III*.

The *Melrose Missile III* was powered by a Max Wedge 426 engine with foam seals on the dual quads to gulp cool air from the scoops. Despite having a completely stock interior with working window cranks, full carpeting, and seats, the car was able to cut a 12-flat quarter-mile with this potent engine.

Note the clean transition from header tubes to collector used for the *Melrose Missile III*. Many drag cars were utilitarian and wouldn't bother to hide the weld seams between tubes and collector. Nice detail work appears all over this car. Bob Mosher (Mosher's Muscle Car Motors) restored the *Melrose Missile III* in 1990.

On December 8, 1963, Melrose Motors was back at Half Moon Bay, California. This version of the Melrose drag car was named *Melrose Missile IV* and was running an automatic transmission. The Melrose team cars were frequently switched out from manual to automatic when circumstance demanded it. Tommy Grove could do the swap in no time flat. (Photo Courtesy Thomas Bettencourt)

Chapter 6: Melrose Motors   67

Tommy Grove and Ford

Tommy Grove caused some furor at the Chrysler factory by running a Ford Dana rear end in his cars for the sake of durability. Chrysler put a Mopar number on a Dana axle soon after this to validate the use of the axles. This may have been a sign of Ford coming into Tom's life.

In February 1965, He switched over to Ford sponsorship. Tommy campaigned a Ford Mustang AF/X under Broadway Motors sponsorship. He then moved on to Funny Cars, including an SOHC. The Cammer engine was rarely seen on the drag strips.

By March 1964, when this photo was taken, Melrose had a *Melrose Missile V* ready to rumble. This version of the *Missile* is a 4-speed car. The *Missile* is at the Kingdon drag strip near Lodi, California, where Melrose ran against big names such as Hayden Proffitt and Gas Ronda. (Photo Courtesy Thomas Bettencourt)

Tommy's fame was a draw for performance nuts who came to the dealership to get their cars sorted out. As icing on the cake, Melrose Motors had an in-house dynamometer. Getting the winning tuner to tweak your car on a dyno could make you king of the street.

Like many competitive dealerships, Melrose entered the Mobil Economy run and of course decided to enter a 1964 Plymouth Savoy to match its race car. The Mobil entry was driven by Bob Cahill (Royal Oak, Michigan).

Racing Continues

After Tommy departed from Melrose sponsorship, the dealership didn't stop racing. Jim, Charlie, and the staff were addicted, and from a business standpoint, racing was justified. Melrose was now *the* go-to place in the Bay Area for hot cars. The dealership was specializing in high-performance vehicles, and it didn't make sense to stem the flow of sales.

The muscle car era was just heating up, and the street Hemi was on the horizon. The dealership was selling some interesting high-performance cars, including the Chrysler 300 and Plymouth GTX, at good prices because they had high volume and lower margins.

Melrose Motors brought Cecil Yother in to take over the driving duties for the *Melrose Missiles*. Cecil did well with various *Missiles*, including a 1965 Hemi altered wheelbase car.

The 1966 version of the *Melrose Missile VII* was memorable because it cut weight by chopping the roof off! In the spring of 1968, Cecil was running a Barracuda Funny Car under the *Melrose Missile* name. This seemed a strange choice because the dealership was selling Road Runners like gangbusters. But in the elite, specialized world of NHRA competition, it was necessary to seek out a potential opening and squeeze every drop out of your ride.

Many top racers were going to lighter and lighter platforms to stay competitive. Cecil was running injectors, but he didn't take the next step to running nitro. Too many drivers were burned or killed when engines blew up. Eventually, he wasn't able to stay competitive, so Cecil Yother quit while he was ahead and still intact.

The Bay Area Road Runner Specialist

Regular Plymouth dealers were suddenly rolling in extra revenue when the 1968 Road Runner took off with the youth market. It was like the first two years of the Pontiac GTO all over again. There were some remarkable similarities between the cars, too. The first 1964–1965 GTO was a bare-bones, affordable, light muscle car with a big 389 topped by the heads off the 421. The initial 1968 Plymouth Road Runner was even more spartan than the GTO ever was. The Road Runner was first released as a post coupe only. The engine was a 383 with the big 440 cam and a better carburetor bolted on. It sold like crazy.

Jim Di Bari made a sudden switch to become a Ford franchise in September 1971, just in time for the 1972 new model releases. Jim was still the face of the dealership in advertising, but his son Charlie was an important partner in the business.

Because Melrose Motors was already an established performance dealer, it got the jump on everyone else when the Road Runner craze hit. Jim Di Bari ran a joke ad showing the Road Runner beating a demoralized turkey in a race during the Thanksgiving holiday of 1968. The price for a Road Runner was no joke though: a mere $2,799. This price held fast a year later in fall 1969 for a new 1970 Road Runner from Melrose.

Charlie realized he only needed to order five cars in a particular color to get some radical paintjobs in special paint colors. To set apart his dealership's Road Runners from the siege of others out there, he ordered batches of five Road Runners painted in various vibrant colors. Charlie sold them out instantly and restocked with other interesting colors.

Charlie is pretty sure the factory took note of this trend and that his ordering technique played into the development of Chrysler's High Impact colors for the 1969 model year. He claims credit for jumpstarting the wild colors soon to be an industry standard for muscle cars. However, the Southern California regional manager for Plymouth L.A. dealers was playing with colors also and started shaking up the color charts in the fall of 1968. California seems to have played a role in nationwide adoption of wild colors for 1969.

AMC soon had "Big Bad" color schemes. Pontiac went totally over the top with Carousel Red (really a neon orange known in Chevy parlance as Hugger Orange) as the identifying color for the 1969 GTO Judge. The Judge was developed as an answer to the Road Runner.

In the winter of 1971, Melrose Motors was pondering a switch to Ford. Jim was blowing out new 1970 Road Runners still in stock for a mere $2,599. Some of the more expensive new cars on the lot were being slashed by $1,500 off the original price.

Melrose Motors Becomes Melrose Ford

Melrose Motors switched to being a Ford franchise in time for the introduction of the 1972 models. On September 1, 1971, Jim Di Bari relocated the dealership down the street to the former Ramsey Ford location at 3050 East 14th.

Melrose continued its high-performance angle with Ford cars, but soon found it was promoting Pintos as the muscle car era dried up.

Jim held out against "urban flight" by staying in the city. He was fighting against the tide at a time when the area was degenerating, making business increasingly harder to maintain. At one point, Jim placed a bid to provide the city cars. His quote was rejected because his total was slightly higher than a competitor who had relocated to the suburbs. Jim argued to have his moderate bid accepted over the lowest bidder by pointing out that he and his son paid a lot of taxes and invested a lot of money in the Oakland dealership.

The End of Melrose

Eventually, Jim succumbed to the forces that drove out other businesses. The location at 3050 International Boulevard (which used to be known as East 14th Street) was Melrose Ford's last. This area is now run down. A real estate listing from 2006, when the newly vacated dealership property was put up for sale, states that the building is about 28,500 square feet and the paved lot is around 32,400 square feet.

The renumbering of the street has obscured the exact location of the original Melrose Motors. On the odd-numbered side of the street, a NAPA location is numbered 4425 and claims to have been there since 1957. Immediately beside it, old house fronts are numbered 4471.

CHAPTER 7
Conroy Pontiac Buick Versus Mander Chevrolet Oldsmobile

Conroy Pontiac Buick
Location: West Vancouver, British Columbia, Canada
Years in Operation: 1963–1971
Founder(s): William F. "Bill" Conroy
Current Status: Skyscraper complex

Mander Chevrolet Oldsmobile
Location: North Vancouver, British Columbia, Canada
Years in Operation: 1963–1969
Founder(s): James Orland Mander
Current Status: Mini mall

The Mander Chevrolet Oldsmobile lot at 845 Marine Drive, North Vancouver, drew in a lot of performance buffs with its sponsored race car prominently displayed. This 1967 Camaro Z28 was the second car that Laurie Craig raced under Mander sponsorship. (Photo Courtesy Laurie Craig)

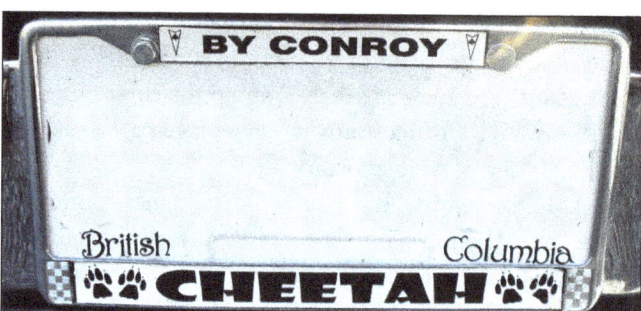

This Conroy Pontiac Buick license frame identifies its signature Cheetah car as "By Conroy." The Conroy dealer conversion Cheetah was a unique creation; the dealer even copyrighted the name in Canada.

Bill Conroy Ltd., popularly known as Conroy Pontiac Buick, was known by the slogan "white glove service" but is now remembered as the source of hot muscle cars and dealer conversion supercars. In the 1960s, the dealership was losing sales to Mander Chevrolet Oldsmobile, the "Total Performance Car Center" that was located down the street in North Vancouver. Mander experienced sales success due to a strong emphasis on performance cars and started to ride the wave of muscle car mania that gripped North America in the 1960s. This resulted in a Canadian dealership rivalry like no other.

Conroy Pontiac Buick

William F. "Bill" Conroy was born in Edmonton, Alberta, on October 18, 1914. Bill served in World War II and was also the mayor of St. Paul, Alberta. He owned a GM dealership in St. Paul, which he sold prior to his move to West Vancouver, British Columbia, Canada.

In 1963, Bill bought the prior Roger Motors Pontiac Buick lot at 680 Marine Drive S.E. in West Vancouver. He established Conroy Pontiac Buick there. The Conroy lot was situated on First Nation–owned land that was leased out across from Park Royal. But, Conroy found it had other competition: Mander Chevrolet.

Mander Chevrolet

James Orland Mander was born on September 29, 1923, in Moose Jaw, Saskatchewan. After a stint in the Royal Canadian Mounted Police followed by service in World War II, he opened James Mander Motors in North Vancouver, British Columbia. In December 1962, he switched from Ford to General Motors. Mander Motors was originally located at 1160 Marine Drive, North Vancouver, with T. F. Roote as secretary treasurer.

James Mander was a car enthusiast who filled his inventory with the right stuff. In August 1963, Mander conducted a huge blow-out sale prior to the business expanding and moving to a brand-new location at 845 Marine Drive in North Vancouver. This change in location brought them closer down the street toward the newly established Conroy Pontiac Buick.

Mander had been hosting the Corvette Club on its premises since 1964. It was the top Corvette dealer in the Lower Mainland area partly due to the discount offered to Corvette Club members. Mander was stocking and selling Vettes and hot muscle cars like crazy.

By 1966, the new Mander lot had 500 cars on the premises and was billed as British Columbia's largest used GM dealer. Mander even had its own test track for customers to try

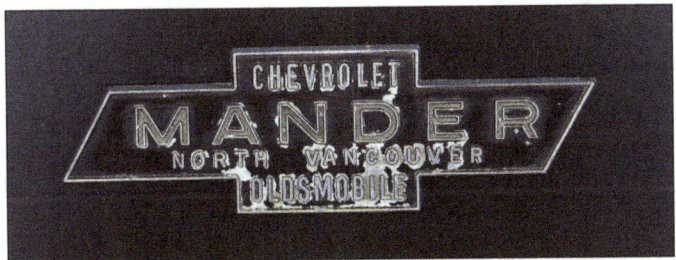

This original Mander Chevrolet Oldsmobile dealer emblem was used during the muscle car era. Prior to this, a silver script of the full James Mander name was used for the dealer logo.

The right place and the right time! The original owner of this Tropic Turquoise 1966 Chevelle Malibu SS traded it in after less than a year of ownership because it had "too much power." Frank Isaak was standing on the Mander lot at the instant she pulled in and scooped it up. Frank still owns it to this day.

Mander's big lot at 845 Marine Drive lit up at night. Note the classic 1960s showroom design, which is all glass, allowing passing cars to see the display cars from a distance. A huge lot sat to the left of the showroom with a test track in back.

Frank Isaak's 1966 Chevelle was ordered by Mander with the 360-hp 396, which was the most powerful advertised version of this motor built on the Oshawa, Ontario, assembly line. Few people knew that it was possible to special order an L78 375-hp version.

Frank Isaak's 1966 Mander Chevelle SS sports new slot mags parked with his buddies in attendance on the fence in 1967. Note the chrome exhaust extensions. Frank sits at the far right.

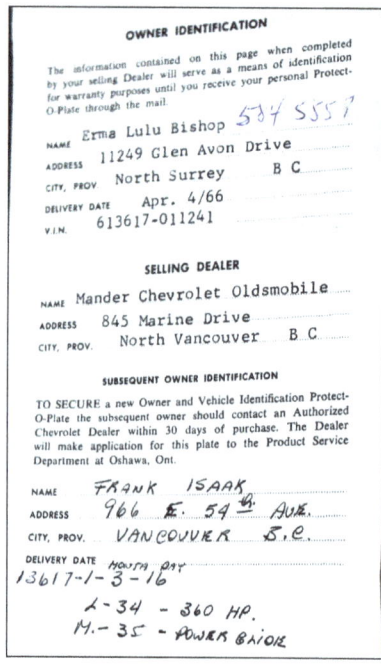

Erma Lula bought the Mander 1966 Chevelle SS new on April 4, 1966. Less than a year later, Frank Isaak became the proud new owner. Back in the day, Frank made notations about the engine and the power brakes. The SS also came with a console-shifted 2-speed Powerglide automatic transmission and rear speaker for the radio.

out cars. A May 1966 advertisement from Mander Chevrolet Oldsmobile offered all its salesmen's demonstrator cars for sale. Owner Jim Mander was driving a 1966 Delta four-door hardtop, but some of his salesmen had sportier two-door cars such as a 1966 Chevelle, a 1966 Corvair Corsa, and a 1966 Chevy II SS.

Mander Goes Racing

In the summer of 1965, Mission Raceway opened in downtown Mission, British Columbia. The track brought the muscle car movement to life. Mander Chevrolet had two drag racing employees actively campaigning cars here.

Mander gained great publicity when it agreed to sponsor racer Laurie Craig in a Riverside Red 1964 Chevrolet Corvette coupe. Ironically, the Vette that Mander sponsored didn't come through the Mander dealership. Laurie's Corvette was originally ordered through Dueck Chevrolet Oldsmobile in Vancouver. The Vette was built September 19, 1963, in St. Louis final assembly with 327 365-hp engine, M21 4-speed, 4.56:1 axle, and J65 big brakes.

When the potent Vette showed up at Dueck, the eager buyer had to cancel out due to a sudden attack of marriage. His girlfriend had just gotten pregnant. Laurie Craig stepped into the void and snapped up the unsold Vette. Laurie envisioned this Vette as an ideal daily driver that was also up to the task of racing. Laurie was running Marinview Service in Burnaby, British Columbia, which was a used car dealership and repair shop.

Laurie and his red Vette plunged into road racing, hill climbs, and Gymkhana. Mander Chevrolet Oldsmobile sponsored the car, but it wasn't an arduous cost/benefit balance: the Corvette was initially raced in bone-stock dealer floor condition, including the tires! Laurie Craig's sole concession to prep work was to add a roll bar and tires in 1965 while decimating the sports production class.

Stirling Moss was in town at the Westwood Race Track in Coquitlam, British Columbia, in May 1965. Laurie was

Laurie Craig

Laurie had specifically moved from his birth home in New Zealand to Canada to get into racing. His early years were packed with experience in pit crews for heavyweights such as Carroll Shelby and Stirling Moss.

Laurie Craig bought his red 1964 Corvette from Dueck Chevrolet Oldsmobile in Vancouver but received sponsorship from Mander Chevrolet Oldsmobile in North Vancouver. Mander linked Laurie's race-proven winning with its performance reputation in this ad. (Photo Courtesy David Lambdin)

Laurie Craig won the 1965 Okanagan Hill Climb with a 1:28.2 time in his 1964 Corvette while under Mander Chevrolet Oldsmobile sponsorship. Laurie's Vette is a bone-stock street car with whitewall showroom tires. The sole prep work visible to the car is the removal of the hubcaps. This annual contest later became the Knox Mountain Hill climb. (Photo Courtesy David Lambdin)

Stirling's old crewman, and he gave Stirling the keys to run a few laps in the Vette. Thus, the Mander car was briefly helmed by Stirling Moss!

Players Pacific Championship

Laurie won the May 15, 1966, Players Pacific Championship at Westwood, defeating exotic race cars and world-class drivers while fighting pouring rain. This was the biggest event of the season, and Laurie was the first Canadian in history to win this race. His win generated terrific publicity for Mander.

Laurie and Mander continued their sponsorship deal when Laurie ordered a black with white stripe 1967 Camaro Z28 through Mander. This was the first Z28 to make it into Canada. Laurie was on location when his new Z28 was unloaded off the train in the Burnaby railcars. A roll bar and race-spec seat belts were installed as soon as the car made it to the shop.

Laurie Craig campaigned his new 1967 Camaro Z28 in Trans Am and Player's events, but the Mander performance era was coming to a close. Laurie continued running various updated Camaro race cars until the 1980s.

Conroy Imports

In the 1960s, Conroy Buick Pontiac struck back at Mander by stocking hot cars as well, including Acadian 327s and Beaumont SDs with 327s. The SD stands for Sport Deluxe, and when equipped with the 396 Chevy big-block, it was a Canadian equivalent of a GTO. Other typical offerings included low-production cars such as a 1965 Regal Red Sport Deluxe two-door hardtop with black interior and L74 327 and a 1965 Satin Silver metallic Sport Deluxe two-door hardtop with black buckets and L79 327 M20 4-speed. These cars constituted a nice first shot across the bow toward Mander. But Mander was slaughtering Conroy with Corvettes, Chevelle SSs, and Oldsmobile 442s.

Conroy didn't sell a lot of Buick Gran Sports because of the high cost. The dealership did sell a decent number of Canadian-made Pontiac Parisiennes, Beaumont SDs, and Acadians in the early 1960s. It also imported Pontiac GTOs, which amped the excitement significantly. The GTO was *the* muscle car to own in 1965.

Conroy sales manager Michael Carmichael was displeased with the GTO's high cost, which cut into his margin.

Laurie Craig pilots his second Mander Chevrolet Oldsmobile–sponsored race car. After several years with his red 1964 Vette, Laurie raced this black 1967 Camaro Z28 under Mander's auspices. (Photo Courtesy Laurie Craig)

Chapter 7: Conroy Pontiac Buick Versus Mander Chevrolet Oldsmobile

My Old Car

Laurie Craig's old Vette was sold off the Mander used lot and eventually wound up in Anchorage, Alaska. David and Stephanie Lambdin of Sitka bought Laurie's old Vette in 2012 without any knowledge of its famous Mander racing past. Dave wanted the Vette solely to relive the excitement of his youth in Alexandria, Louisiana. Dave remembered the old days behind the wheel of his Daytona Blue 1963 Corvette street and strip racing in C Sports Production class.

Interestingly, 1966 was Dave's big racing year. He won the US Southern Regional Drag Racing championship the same year that Laurie Craig won the Players up north. After finally getting another Corvette in 2012, Dave began researching the history of his car. The research process that led to the discovery that they owned the Mander Vette and the journey to allow Laurie to drive his old car again is documented in the couple's book *My Old Car*.

The problem with the GTO was that the duties and tariffs involved with importing the car exaggerated the cost for the buyer in Canada. By doing in-house work, Conroy could build a muscle car at a cost that undercut or equaled the Mander goodies. Michael Carmichael devised a plan to get the Conroy name out there to performance buffs with a complete muscle car he named the Cheetah.

The Canadian Cheetah

Instead of spending the extra money otherwise lost on tariffs and duties for a GTO, the same money could be spent upgrading a Beaumont SD into a top performance car. Michael could create a comparable supercar on a level with the GTO or even better for the same money or less by customizing a Beaumont base vehicle.

In 1965, Conroy's dealer supercar conversion, the Cheetah, was announced. The Conroy Cheetahs were Canadian-built Pontiac Beaumont Sport Deluxes with dealer performance upgrades. They were not in any way related to the 1964 Bill Thomas Cheetah race cars. The name is coincidental.

In 1966, the Cheetah began with an order for a Beaumont SD with L34 396 engine, M20 wide-ratio 4-speed, 12-bolt Posi-Traction rear axle, metallic brake lining, and heavy-duty suspension. Usually the cars were ordered with high-content options of vinyl roof, bucket seats with headrests, and consoles.

Once the Beaumont arrived on the Conroy lot, practical and visual improvements included stripes on the cars. Buick mag-style wheels were added along with chrome dual sport mirrors and Cheetah identification. Approximately 10 Cheetahs packed the potent L72 427-ci engine.

Michael Carmichael trademarked the Cheetah name for the Canadian market on February 17, 1965. The name was officially registered to Bill Conroy Ltd. on October 29, 1965.

Conroy's 1967 Cheetah came with the SD body length stripes. Most of the Cheetahs were ordered with vinyl tops. Conroy added Buick mags or Ansen mag wheels.

Conroy Pontiac Buick installed dual chrome racing mirrors to the Cheetah. Aside from the practical enhancement of driving awareness, these bullet-shaped mirrors made the cars look really hot.

Cheetah identification piled on top of the already potent SD identifier let others on the street know this was a fast car. SD stands for Sport Deluxe and was the Canadian Pontiac equivalent to the GTO.

Canadian Beaumont Sport Deluxe

Some readers may be asking "What is a Beaumont?" Answer: a Canadian-only version of the US-built Pontiac Tempest/LeMans. The Beaumont used a Chevelle body with Pontiac-themed taillight panel, front lights, grille, dash, steering column, horn button, and trim. The Beaumont Sport Deluxe was a Canadian-built equivalent to the Pontiac GTO.

To add to the confusion, the Beaumonts were marketed as stand-alone models and didn't have the name Pontiac on the cars, the advertising literature, or the owner's manual. Hard-core believers argue to this day about whether or not they are Pontiac Beaumonts or just plain Beaumonts. The "plain Beaumont" crowd argues that they are not Pontiacs at all.

I'm stepping in here to declare that it is "safe" to refer to them as Pontiacs. They were only sold through Pontiac dealerships and the VIN number "7" correlates with all other Canadian Pontiacs. Beaumonts didn't hide their Pontiac heritage; the cars used a hybrid Canadian maple leaf/Pontiac logo on the trim.

A Unique Canadian Pontiac Lineup

The Beaumont nameplate came about primarily due to import rules, high tariffs, and low-volume Canadian car sales (when compared to US production numbers). In 1965, Canadian new car sales totaled 708,716 (including overseas exported vehicles). This is less than 10 percent of US sales for 1965, which were 9,322,000.

In 1966, Canada managed 694,820 sales with slightly less at 642,498 in 1967. It was a good year in 1968 with 737,605 cars, and 1969 jumped to 756,015. Truck sales were usually 130,000 to 150,000 units.

To give an idea of how these smaller sales numbers affected the situation, the Canadian GM franchises lacked a sufficient population of buyers to support stand-alone brand-name dealerships. Pontiac-exclusive dealers were unheard of in Canada. Canadian franchises cut the GM line in half. If you were a dealer principle in Canada, General Motors either gave you a Chevrolet Oldsmobile Cadillac franchise or a Pontiac Buick GMC franchise.

Low Volume Sales Collude with Tariffs

The Chevy low-priced cars sold in sufficient volume to justify the Oshawa, Ontario, final assembly plant building Chevrolets in Canada. Not so for the Pontiacs. It was too expensive to tool up the factory in Canada for the smaller marketplace Pontiac accounted for. The only feasible way to supply the Canadian niche market for Pontiacs was to import them. The duties paid to bring in US-built Pontiacs inflated Pontiac out of the price slot between low-priced Chevrolet and higher-priced Oldsmobile.

Canadian Beaumont Sport Deluxe *continued*

Prior to model year 1970, Canadian Pontiac dealers were limited in the selection of imports due to tariffs. It was worthwhile to import the top US models, such as a loaded GTO convertible or Grand Prix, where price point wasn't the crucial issue. However, it didn't make sense to import low- and midrange Pontiac models such as the Tempest. Tariffs inflated the economical price of the Tempest to the level where the buyer may as well have moved up to a higher model.

Canadian Pontiac, Mercurys, and Dodges

How could Canadian dealers maintain good prices on low-end Pontiac models? The solution was to build Canadian Pontiacs in the Canadian GM plant in Oshawa on the Chevrolet assembly line. By using Chevrolet frames, mechanics, and body parts, and then adding in Pontiac-style noses, rear ends, and interiors, the Canadian Pontiacs became hybrids. It was easy to install a Pontiac dashboard and alter the fabric patterns inside to create a Pontiac look. Starting in 1937, Canadian Pontiacs were built in the Oshawa plant.

At the end of the 1960s, the Canadian equivalent to a top-line US Pontiac Bonneville was the Pontiac Parisienne, which was based on the Chevrolet Impala. The Canadian Pontiacs missed out on the "Wide Track" theme because the cars used Chevrolet mechanical parts. In the late 1960s, Canadian assembly lines substituted the wider track station wagon axle on Pontiacs to try to approximate the US Pontiac "Wide Track" style.

Mercury was the Ford equivalent of Pontiac. Ford Canada built Canadian-specific Mercury cars such as the Meteor. The US market adopted the name temporarily and suspended Canadian use of Meteor for two years, then the name returned to Canada.

Chrysler also created Canadian-only cars. Canadian-built Plymouths added Dodge interiors or noses to create a Canadian Dodge. The Canadian version of the Newport was named the Windsor in honor of the factory city in Canada where it was built: Windsor, Ontario. Only in Canada were the H code Swinger 340s built for two years following cessation of production in the United States in 1970. No one from the United States knew what these cars were!

1968 GM Service Bulletin

A GM service bulletin from 1968 emphasized to dealers that tourists visiting the United States in Canadian-built Pontiacs were to have their Protect-O-Plate warranties honored at Pontiac dealerships throughout the country. Any Chevrolet parts used were to be outsourced and billed back to General Motors.

This bulletin was in response to feedback that US Pontiac dealers were sending Canadian Pontiac owners to Chevrolet dealers. General Motors wanted to preserve the illusion of a Pontiac identity for these Canadian cars built using Chevrolet mechanicals.

Canadian Pontiacs benefitted from Chevrolet performance developments. Starting in 1958, Pontiacs offered good performance from the Chevy 348 engine. When the 409 became available, the Canadian Pontiacs could be ordered with this potent engine. Beaumont performance was mainly dependent on 396 350-hp engines. Starting in 1966, the 375-hp versions were technically orderable in Canada, but very few people knew this was possible. Most high-performance enthusiasts imported a US-built Chevrolet 375-hp car or purchased a crate engine.

Beaumonts: Pontiacs that Aren't Pontiacs!

The stand-alone Canadian Pontiacs debuted when a 1962 Chevy II was reimaged and named the Acadian. No mention of Pontiac contaminated the Acadian when it came off the Oshawa assembly line, but it was sold exclusively through Pontiac dealerships.

Acadian was supposedly not a Pontiac despite obvious Pontiac styling cues. The high trim level on the Acadian was named Beaumont, which was the first appearance of the name. The Acadian Beaumont Sport Deluxe was a Canadian equivalent of the US Chevy II Nova SS model. Conroy had plenty of these hard little runners on its lot.

The Beaumont name eventually migrated from the compact Chevy II body to the intermediate Chevelle body in 1964. The Canadian version of the US Pontiac Tempest/LeMans was a Pontiac-styled, Chevelle-based intermediate named Beaumont. The Acadian name shifted to Canso for the Canadian market had an equivalent model to the Pontiac GTO named the Beaumont Sport Deluxe (usually given the shorthand name Beaumont SD), which could be ordered with a 396-ci engine starting in 1966.

The intermediate-size Beaumont is not called a Pontiac, but it is a typical Canadian Pontiac with mostly Chevelle sheet metal and drivetrain spruced up with Pontiac dash and Pontiac-themed front and rear nose details. Although the body is a Chevelle, the Beaumont uses some unique Pontiac-styled parts that are different from either Chevelle or Tempest. The interior has some unique Canadian features to compliment the US-sourced Tempest dash.

Conroy copyrighted the Cheetah name and came up with specific logos for the body and engine.

George Pappas owns this 1967 Pontiac Beaumont SD Cheetah packing 427 ci shifted through a 4-speed. Conroy Pontiac Buick did the engine swap.

Conroy Pontiac Buick applied emblems to the Cheetah. The Conroy badges and 427 badges appear on the front fenders, the rear deck, and the glove box.

Conroy usually specified metallic brakes but without power assist. The reason was that the power brake booster interfered with engine swaps. This 427 Cheetah has manual brakes.

The 1967 Cheetah package added headrests to the seats. Conroy ordered most cars with great interiors: bucket seats, console, gauges, and 4-speeds.

Chapter 7: Conroy Pontiac Buick Versus Mander Chevrolet Oldsmobile   77

Conroy ran this 1969 Cheetah at the strip. Conroy decided to focus on a new class by choosing to prep this car as a 350 car. (Photo Courtesy George Pappas)

The Ambassadors Car Club was given this Beaumont Cheetah by Conroy to run in rallies and at the drag strip. (Photo Courtesy Don Powell)

The Cheetah name fit well with the Conroy Pontiac Buick inventory of Pontiacs (with the Tiger-themed Pontiac advertising) and Buick Wildcats.

The Cheetah was then personalized with Conroy stripes, tachometer, head restraints, mag wheels, and chrome dual mirrors. Some of them were fitted with headers, too. This was just the beginning. Soon engine swaps entered the picture.

The Cheetah through the Years

The 1965–1968 Cheetahs were built using Beaumont SDs as a base starting point. In 1969, the Cheetah was based on the low-budget post coupe. The model added a further twist that would confuse US residents a bit more: they had Buick mag wheels! This was easy for Conroy to do since it was a Pontiac Buick dealership. A customer could opt for upgrades to any aftermarket mags available from the extensive Conroy inventory.

Despite the greatness of the car, the expense of the Cheetah limited production to probably fewer than 5 cars in 1965. Only 12 Cheetahs were built for 1966, and approximately 15 per year in 1967 and 1968. For 1969, only 3 Cheetahs were built. Not more than 50 Cheetahs were built during its reign.

Cheetahs came with a plaque on the car declaring the Beaumont was a "Cheetah by Conroy Pontiac." Michael Carmichael had time to work out the program and modify a few small-block 1965 Beaumonts before the new crop of 1966 big-block Beaumonts became available in the fall of 1965.

The 1966 model Beaumonts were factory available with optional 396 engines. Of course, this was the starting point for any order placed from Conroy for a car that was destined to become a Cheetah. It is interesting to note that around the same time the new 1966 models were released, the Cheetah name was officially recognized by the trademark board.

Cheetah Drag Strip Debut

Michael Carmichael decided the best way to highlight his new creation was to sponsor a race team. In 1966, the Ambassadors Car Club was chosen to represent the dealership at Mission Raceway and Arlington Dragstrip in Washington State. The Ambassadors campaigned a pale yellow 1966 Beaumont Cheetah. Conroy gave the club free parts, provided access to its service bays to keep the car in top shape, and donated the dealership tow truck to flat tow the Cheetah to race events. The Ambassador's race driver, Don Powell, was running in the 13s most of the time in B stock class. Don's personal car was a US-built 1966 Chevelle SS 396 with a L72 427 425-hp crate engine.

The Cheetah that Conroy ran on the drag strip was a 396, but customers were hitting the streets with hotter versions of the Cheetahs! Many of the 396 cars were fitted with headers, so there were no slouches in the ranks, but where Michael Carmichael got it on was with the 427 Corvette engine. Conroy built about 10 Cheetah supercars running a transplanted L72 427 engine. Many of the 396 cars and all of the 427 cars were also augmented with aftermarket performance equipment.

Close to the end of the 1967 model year, five option-deleted Beaumont SD L34s were ordered. These cars were bench seat, floor-shifted strippers intended to reduce the cost of a Cheetah.

Mander's Counter Punch

Of course, Mander Chevrolet Oldsmobile couldn't allow this outrage to pass without retaliation. The Conroy Cheetah supercar demanded an answer, and it came pretty quickly. Mander advertised an over-the-top Mander supercar dealer conversion named the Super Hugger Camaro. The Mander Camaro had side exhausts, hood scoops, dual chrome racing mirrors, rear deck spoiler, rear fender

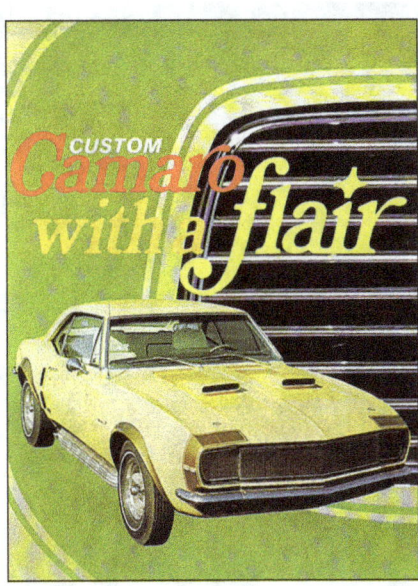

Mander's Super Hugger was the answer to Conroy's Beaumont Cheetahs. It is known that numerous engine swaps were performed on Camaros at Mander, but no surviving Super Huggers have surfaced to validate the actual building of any of these packaged dealer supercars.

The Mander answer to the Cheetah was a 427 engine swap into a 1967 Camaro with hood scoops, dual chrome racing mirrors, rear deck spoiler rear fender "air extractors," and wheel flares. This ad for a Camaro body kit from ATM Corporation Speed and Custom Division (1401 East Washington, Phoenix, Arizona) has identical mods as seen in the Mander ads for its Super Hugger. It is very likely Mander used the ATM body kit as part of its build process.

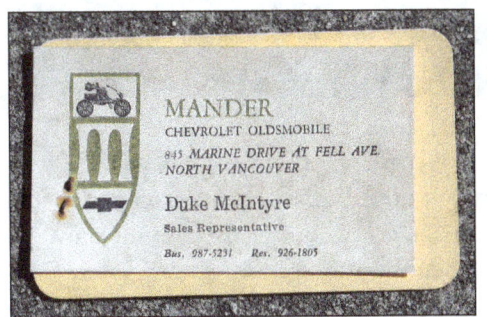

Duke McIntyre's business card from Mander Chevrolet Oldsmobile has Laurie Craig's Chevy shop business card stapled to the back. Laurie Craig's racing was sponsored by Mander. Laurie and his partner, Mike Conner, did supertuning, chassis prep, and custom racing engines in their shop at 69 McInnes Street, New Westminster, British Columbia.

"air extractors" and wheel flares, and mags. The bucket seats featured 427 emblems reminiscent of the SYC logo on the headrests of Yenko Camaros.

The Camaro had all the right performance equipment. The ad listed a 427 430-hp engine, close-ratio 4-speed, and a Posi-Traction rear axle with up to 4.88:1 ratios. The Super Hugger had heavy-duty radiator, alternator, starter, suspension, driveshaft, and axle. The most interesting point in the Super Hugger ad was the mention of a 5-year/50,000-mile warranty on the 427 engine.

The ad mentions Duke McIntyre and Neil Murphy as the contacts for the Super Hugger. Duke sold the Mander white 1967 Chevelle SS 396, and his business card attests to his performance specialty niche in the dealership.

Eastern Cheetah Theory

According to a theory that is prevalent in the Canadian Pontiac hobby, 46 Cheetahs were made in total. Supposedly, 25 of the cars were shipped out to St. Catherines, Ontario. The story is that Conroy had a main office there. The problem is that theory is wrong.

According to the "25 cars back east" theory, only 21 Cheetahs were British Columbia cars. The surviving Cheetahs that have turned up are mostly in British Columbia with a few in neighboring Alberta. No one from Ontario has any recollection of Cheetahs roaming the streets and no survivors have surfaced there.

The story that Cheetahs were gifted to high-ranking employees in a St. Catherines Conroy operation seems to have built itself on some mistaken rumor that has been passed along for decades now. This is a case where confusion through the years has linked an actual Conroy manufacturing business in St. Catherines with the unrelated Conroy dealership in West Vancouver. Michael Carmichael and the Conroy family emphatically stated that the Conroy Ontario business had no relation to Bill Conroy's dealership. The Conroy name is just a coincidence.

George Pappas's 1967 Cheetah 427

George Pappas is a long-term car collector who has seen and owned many muscle cars, including Canadian Pontiacs. When George was five, his dad, Mike, bought the first of five two-door cars from Jim Pattison Pontiac Buick on Main Street, Vancouver: a 1963 Parisienne. The second car was a 1968 Beaumont Deluxe. At that time, Mike's tenant owned a 1967 Beaumont Custom convertible. In his neighborhood growing up, George was familiar with three Cheetahs: 1966 Aztec Bronze, 1967 silver with black vinyl 427, and 1968 Cordova Maroon white vinyl 427 car.

Over the years, George has seen, owned, or tracked nearly every combination of big-engine Canadian Pontiacs offered through the 1960s. In the 1980s, he devised a system to document a car. This system was subsequently adopted by GM of Canada, providing a list of options along with GM certification of authenticity.

George owns an original 1967 Verde Green Beaumont SD Cheetah packing the L72 427 engine and dealer-installed headers. Michael Carmichael recalled that one 1966 Cheetah had a 427 with the rest built in 1967 and 1968. Three drivable Vancouver-area Cheetahs have appeared at car shows thus far; George's is the only 427. There are rumors of other surviving 396 and 427 cars on forums, but as yet none have been seen. Even back in 1967, when the muscle car era was in full swing, these rare cars piqued the imagination of many muscle car freaks.

Imagine the commotion a 427 Cheetah caused back in 1967! In Canada, most Chevelle and Beaumont enthusiasts didn't know you could order the 396 375-hp versions that were available to their US neighbors. The best you could get in a Chevelle SS 396 was a hydraulic lifter 350 300-hp job. Beaumonts were restricted to the same 350-hp ceiling. Just to rope in a 375-hp version of the 396, it was necessary to special order in a US-built car from final assembly across the border, which piled on duties and taxes.

Suddenly Conroy jumped not just over 396s with 325 and 350 hp but also shot up an additional 100+ hp with a 427. Add a dealer balance and blueprint plus headers and here comes more horsepower! That is serious action.

Mander Engine Swaps

Despite Mander's motto in a May 18, 1967, *Squamish Times* ad billing them as "the Performance Makers," no survivor Mander Super Hugger Camaros have appeared so far. Many Conroy Cheetahs are known and accounted for. However, Mander engine swap cars are known to exist and many are remembered dominating the streets. These big-block transplants are likely what Mander refers to in its 1967 performance makers boast.

This 1967 Provincial White Chevelle SS 396 350 hp was sold by Mander salesman Duke McIntyre on June 10, 1967. The Chevelle was a trade from Courtesy Chevrolet, in Burnaby, British Columbia. First owner Mel saw the car on the truck trailer and bought it before it was unloaded! He still owns the car today.

There is no doubt that engine swap cars came out of the Mander service bays on a regular basis, but the complete packaged Super Hugger Camaro would likely be built only if a customer order and deposit was received. At this point, Conroy was winning the muscle car war because it built the cars first and got the money later.

Mander funneled some nice cars through its doors, such as an Aztec Bronze metallic 1966 Chevelle Malibu SS 396 (L34) with black bucket interior, a Butternut Yellow Chevelle Malibu SS 396 with black bucket interior and M20 4-speed, and a 1968 Camaro RS convertible with L30 327. Many muscle dealer sales were of the garden-variety breed with the top stuff selling in smaller numbers.

Just by running that wild Super Hugger ad, Mander kept the pressure on Conroy, even while it sold regular 350-hp 396 cars. Just reading that ad made street enthusiasts drool. Now things were really crazy!

Conroy's Firebird Can Am

Conroy struck back at the pony car threat from Mander's Super Hugger by creating another high-profile, very unique dealer special car. Since Mander was purportedly fielding a super F-Body car, it made sense for Conroy to hit back with its own super F-Body.

The ATM Ad Conundrum

Modern internet ability to match up images has led enthusiasts to conclude that the photo of the Mander Super Hugger Camaro was likely nicked from a series of promotional shots for the catalog of ATM Corporation Speed and Custom Division in Phoenix, Arizona.

ATM created a kit that provided dual chrome racing mirrors and a flip-up gas cap augmented with bolt-on body parts: hood scoops, fender flares, side air extractors, and a rear deck spoiler. The ATM Camaro also had a roll bar, hood pins, and side exhaust topped off with mags. It seems most likely that Mander had a few ATM kits on hand and would only build a Super Hugger Camaro "on demand," which would explain not having its own photo of a completed car.

Mander may have intended to build its cars using the ATM kit, and that is why its photo looks like the ATM Camaro. The picture of the Mander Super Hugger Camaro is a different angle of the ATM Camaro done up with custom parts supplied by ATM. The Mander Super Hugger is posed with a Corvette, which doesn't appear in the ATM pictures.

There is serious doubt that any Mander Super Hugger Camaros were ever built in the visual style depicted in the ad. Mander may have simply used the ATM picture in the scramble to get a car built and airbrushed a Corvette in the background of the photo.

A give-away clue that the picture is likely an ATM picture and not a Mander original is that the Mander ad mentions "red stripe wide oval tires" when referencing the photo of the Super Hugger Camaro. Mander cars all had red stripe tires. The image Mander used was black and white, and a color image of the same car indicates that the car had white stripe tires.

The ad writer erroneously assumed the tires in the photo were red stripes. Black-and-white photos of red stripe tires cause the stripe to virtually vanish into the sidewall. If Mander built one of these cars, it is likely it would have taken its own promotion shots and that the tires would be red stripe tires in the picture.

Conroy had the new 1969 Pontiac Firebird Trans Am in stock, but it wanted to create a niche market item aimed at the high-winding sports car crowd. The Z28 and Boss 302 had plenty of street credibility, despite being technically sideways from the pure definition of muscle cars. Similar to Shelby cars, these cars were accepted as muscle cars despite smaller cubic inches.

This nice 1967 Chevelle Super Sport 396 was tweaked by Mander as part of the delivery service. Mander installed GM's 396 375-hp solid lifter camshaft to give the car some extra oomph. The SS was well preserved in a dry carport from 1980 to 2012, when the owner's widow sold the car to the current owner. (Photo Courtesy John Quesnel)

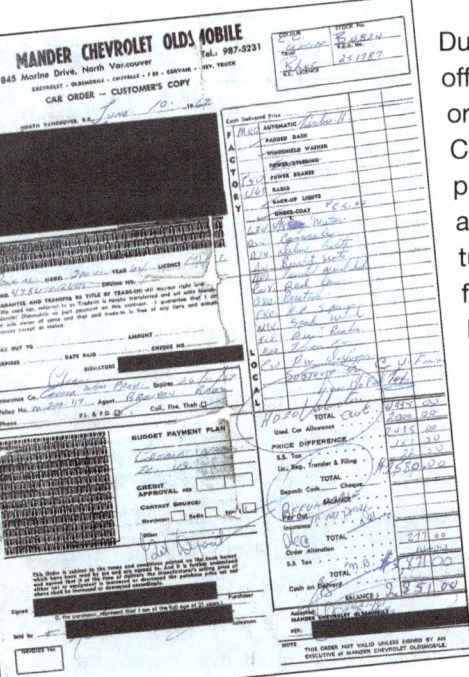

Duke McIntyre signed off on this Mander order for a 1967 Chevelle SS 396. The purchasers' name, address, and signature were removed for privacy reasons but otherwise the purchase order is intact. Note that McIntyre ensured that heavy-duty suspension and factory mags were included in the order aside from the usual console buckets and so forth.

Conroy had also investigated the unusual offbeat Firebird Sprint package, which Pontiac's general manager John DeLorean pushed to have built after upper GM management killed his two-seat Banshee project.

Conroy was channeling some of DeLorean's offbeat performance concepts when it created the rare dealer special "Can Am Firebirds" based on the Pontiac Trans Am racers. Conroy created eight Can Am Firebirds using a Z28 302 transplant that dovetails with a tactic that was used by racers back in the 1960s to get Pontiacs into the Trans America racing. There is speculation that Conroy built these cars for that purpose.

This 1968 Firebird Sprint with OHC 6-cylinder engine was very cutting edge for the time period. Conroy was actually aware of this unusual performance car and stocked its inventory with a few examples, such as this one with Rally II mags, bucket seats, hood tach, and heavy-duty performance suspension.

Conroy knew what Pontiac had with this 1968 Firebird Sprint OHC 6-cylinder. Unlike most pedestrian 6-cylinders built by domestic manufacturers in the 1960s, John DeLorean envisioned this as a competitor to the foreign import performance marques. Free-flowing manifolds, big V-8-style 4-barrel carb, and overhead camshaft coerced 215 hp out of this inline-6. In the lightweight Firebird, it actually performed quite well.

It is possible that Conroy's cars were used as the pretext to justify building Chevy-powered Firebirds for competition in Trans Am racing. It's also just as likely that racers simply stated that Firebirds were built in Oshawa and, like all other Canadian Pontiacs, used Chevy drivetrains. This fact was well known enough to get them through inspection without anyone checking to see if Firebirds were built in Canada (they weren't at this time).

Conroy built a small run of Can Am Firebirds and continued to create street-ready Cheetahs. An advertisement stating that there were "4 only" Can Am Firebirds available is somewhat murky with the message that they were subject to a three-week delivery. This suggests that like the Mander Super

Conroy's 1969 business was running full tilt with the new Pontiac Firebird Trans Am in stock and ready to move out.

Conroy advertised that four "Can Am" dealer special Firebirds were available. Note that the Cheetah-GTO-Judge triple punch is the opener on this advertisement. These were the headlining cars at the time.

Hugger these may have been "on demand" cars built when a deposit was received.

Mander and Conroy Race

Both Mander and Conroy were competing against each other at Mission Raceway with their dealer-sponsored drag cars. Mander's service manager Phil Hardy had two cars sponsored through Mander: a 1966 Chevelle 396 and a 1966 Nova L79. Mander also sponsored a black Camaro.

Conroy was still campaigning a Beaumont Cheetah through the Ambassadors Club, although it switched tactics for the 1969 season. The Conroy-sponsored Cheetah was based on a low-model post-1969 Beaumont with a mere 350 engine and automatic transmission.

The big-block Cheetahs ceased being built in 1969 when it became possible to order a 1969 Pontiac GTO built in the Canadian Oshawa final assembly plant. The Beaumont SD became superfluous. Aside from the 1969 Cheetah racer, there were two more 1969 Cheetahs built with 350 engines, but these cars had 4-speeds. All Cheetah customer cars were 4-speeds.

In 1970, Conroy brought in a Michigan-built Pepper Green 1970 GTO Judge Ram Air IV with M21 4-speed built April 20, 1970. Very few of the top-dog Ram Air IV GTOs appeared on any lots except at the absolute pinnacle performance palaces. The RA IV car demonstrates that Conroy was determined to keep up with Mander.

Dick Irwin didn't go half measure. Knowing that the Mander dealership he had bought was built on performance, he advertised the high-performance aspects of the dealership in this inclusive ad. (Photo Courtesy George Pappas)

Tim Johnson's restored 1969 COPO 427 4-speed Camaro was originally shipped to Dick Irwin Chevrolet Oldsmobile on July 3, 1969. Irwin had just taken over the legendary high-performance Mander Chevrelot Oldsmobile lot a few months earlier. Dick sold this Rally Green monster without realizing it was a COPO. When the owner blew the motor, a mechanic informed him it was not a 396!

Mander Chevrolet Oldsmobile Is Sold

James Mander sold his dealership at the start of 1969 while sales were still strong and muscle still ruled the streets. The Mander dealership was taken over by Dick Irwin, and performance was allowed to continue on the route already established. Despite a change of name from Mander to Dick Irwin, the rivalry with Conroy had not slacked off with the quality of the heavy iron coming through the lots.

Dick Irwin Chevrolet Oldsmobile Ltd was incorporated on February 7, 1969. A hilarious situation developed when a carrier unloaded some new cars into the newly named Dick Irwin lot in July 1969. The cars had been ordered by Mander and Irwin had no idea about their background. The cars were big-blocks, which was good news. The bad news was that the cars were a non SS 1969 Chevelle and a non SS 1969 Camaro. Irwin had a devil of a time selling a non SS car and the cars languished on the lot for a while.

When the cars finally sold, the salesmen had no idea that they had just sold two COPO 427 cars! The new owners had no clue either. The new COPO Camaro owner noted that it ran really hard for a "396" but didn't suspect what he had. It wasn't until he detonated a piston that the secret of the car was revealed. Once the engine was apart, the mechanic discovered

Tim Johnson's Rally Green 1969 COPO Camaro received the same cowl induction hood and L72 427 as the US versions of the COPO package. The build sheet mandated some extra protection antifreeze to deal with the Canadian winters. The order also thoughtfully included an engine block heater and rear window defroster. Irwin continued the Mander tradition of bolting on headers to most of its good inventory and rolling the price into the financing.

Dick Irwin took over the Mander lot in early 1969. The Dick Irwin logo always used whiteface on blue background but originally incorporated a stylized D and I. Later logos, such as this, include the information that Irwin was a GM dealership. An interesting coincidence is that Dick Irwin was a distant relative of Bill Conroy's!

that this engine was actually a 427! The Dick Irwin COPO Chevelle went through numerous owners with no one suspecting that it was a COPO car until collector George Pappas acquired it.

The 1969 COPO 427 Chevelle was painted Fathom Green. The car was built in mid-July at the Baltimore, Maryland, final assembly plant with black bench seat interior and M22 4-speed transmission. A 1970 Chevelle 454 LS6 also passed through the

A 1972 Buick Centurian convertible with top-dog 455 engine returns to the exact spot where it first sold. The front doors to this high-rise complex sit upon the site of the original Conroy Pontiac Buick dealership.

The first location of Mander Chevrolet Oldsmobile at 1160 Marine Drive, North Vancouver, was redeveloped into these condo buildings.

The second Mander Chevrolet Oldsmobile location at 845 Marine Drive, North Vancouver, was redeveloped into a mall with a dental practice on the ground floor. To the left, a giant parking lot bridges the gap between street and a Burger King. This parking area roughly correlates with Mander's old lot and test track.

lot. The Daytona Yellow special order paint car had an M22 and parchment interior and also originated at the Baltimore final assembly plant.

Royal Pontiac Buick Buys Conroy

Two years after Mander changed hands and became Dick Irwin, the Conroy dealership was sold to Michael Carmichael. In an interesting coincidence, Conroy was taken over and renamed Royal Pontiac Buick, which of course evokes the famous Ace Wilson's Royal Pontiac, the ultimate high-performance dealership central in all Pontiac legends. There was no connection between the legendary Michigan Royal Pontiac and this Royal Pontiac Buick agency. In fact, Ace Wilson's Royal Pontiac had been sold in 1969.

Royal Pontiac Buick Ltd. was incorporated on September 20, 1971. The Royal dealership continued to stock hot cars, but things were winding down in the muscle era by this time. As late as 1973, Royal billed the dealership as "the Performance Makers."

Royal came up with an innovative method for new car display. The hottest new cars were lined up right along the edge of the dealership adjacent to the sidewalk of Marine Drive. This section of Marine Drive leads to the Lion's Gate Bridge and is frequently backed up with cars attempting to merge down into one or two lanes when crossing the bridge. With nothing to do but sit stuck in traffic, drivers had plenty of time to study the cars offered for sale at Royal Pontiac Buick.

Royal Pontiac Buick Ltd was dissolved on February 20, 1981, when the land reverted to First Nation. Exempt from the prevailing West Vancouver building codes, the owners of the land replaced Royal Pontiac Buick with a leased skyscraper complex. The tower caused controversy by exceeding the height limits set by West Vancouver city planners. It seems this plot of land is always connected with excess in one way or another!

Bill Conroy died on April 8, 2001, in New Westminster, British Columbia, at age 86.

Dick Irwin Chevrolet Oldsmobile Winds Down

The original Dick Irwin incorporation dissolved on July 17, 1978, but the dealership carried on at the same location under a slightly new name. The dealership is listed as Dick Irwin Chev-Olds in an August 5, 1988, ad for vans in the *Richmond Review*. The Dick Irwin group sold the Chevy lot to Carter Chevrolet in the 1980s. The group currently owns a Mitsubishi dealer in North Vancouver as well as two other dealers in the lower mainland and one in Edmonton, Alberta.

The original Mander lot at 1160 Marine Drive was last used as a car lot by Autoway. The land was redeveloped into condos with stores on the ground floor and renumbered 1150 Marine Drive. The later 845 Marine location of Mander is now a mini mall with a dentist occupying the street frontage.

James Mander died on September 30, 2006, one day after his 83rd birthday. Today, Michael Carmichael is in an old age home and doesn't wish to talk about the old days. But plenty of people recall those glory years of the Conroy/Mander rivalry and the great cars that emerged from their battle.

CHAPTER 8
CLIFF BRISTOW MOTORS

Cliff Bristow Motors
Location: Three Hills, Alberta, Canada
Years in Operation: 1968–1972
Founder(s): Clifford David Bristow
Current Status: Unknown

Cliff Bristow's logo superimposes the GM logo on top of a maple leaf, which is the symbol for Canada. General Motors of Canada is actually a separate corporate entity from the US big brother, although cars were freely exchanged between the two.

Right in the middle of nowhere stood Cliff Bristow Motors, which is now referred to as the "Yenko of the North." Cliff Bristow Motors was located in Three Hills, Alberta, Canada, from 1968 until 1972. The dealership was formerly known as Three Hills Motors.

When Clifford David Bristow bought the Three Hills dealership, he named it Cliff Bristow Chevrolet Oldsmobile Pontiac Buick. Then all hell broke loose. The small-town little shop was immediately transformed into a "take-no-prisoners" full-scale performance dealership. Buyers would make the pilgrimage from as far away as Saskatchewan and British Columbia to view the hot muscle cars in the showroom.

Cliff Bristow's The Rat Patrol 427 Camaro

Local racer Dave Savage recalls the day when Clifford David Bristow first showed up on the Alberta muscle car scene in the mid-1960s. Dave was racing a 1965 Pontiac GTO at the Edmonton drag strip. Cliff was from up north and attracted some attention racing his Chrysler 300.

Cliff later campaigned a 1968 Camaro 427 named *The Rat Patrol*, which was prepped and driven by Rollie Johnston in Crossfields. The second version of *The Rat Patrol* was a 1970 Camaro packing a ZL1 427 aluminum-block engine that produced a best quarter-mile run of 10.4 at 138 mph.

The ZL1 engine came out of a LeMans Blue 1969 Camaro built in a small run of ZL1 cars. This particular 1969 Camaro (VIN 9N635720) was the 54th built ZL1 Camaro and had an automatic transmission. It was originally ordered through Stedelbauer Chevrolet Oldsmobile in Edmonton, Alberta. When the ZL1 showed up, the capped exhaust produced a lackluster test drive. The prospective buyer passed. GM's zone office connected Stedelbauer with Cliff, who made a fire sale deal to take the ZL1 for $5,500.

On May 9, 1969, Bristow Motors placed an ad in the *Calgary Herald* for "One Only" 1969 ZL1 Camaro all-aluminum factory-blueprinted 427 pegged at 600 hp. The Camaro had four-wheel disc brakes. He promised 10-day delivery.

When the car didn't sell, Clifford eventually pulled the engine and put it in his race car. He installed a 427 iron engine

1969
ONE ONLY
1969 ZL1-427 all aluminum Camaro, 600 h.p. Factory blue printed, fully equipped, 4 wheel disc brakes, 10 day delivery. Contact Cliff Bristow Motors in Three Hills, 443-5121.

It's amazing to look back and find that dealers had a very difficult time selling ZL1 Camaros. Cliff's ad didn't result in a sale, so he plucked the aluminum block out of the Camaro and stuffed it in his *The Rat Patrol* 1968 Camaro.

into the 1969 blue Camaro and sold it off the lot to a customer from Saskatchewan. The Camaro was a nice-looking car with VE3 front bumper, spoilers, console, and gauges.

Bristow Conversion Cars

Aside from a strong inventory of factory muscle, the Cliff Bristow dealership also offered dealer conversion packages. Bristow offered Stage 1, 2, and 3 packages.

British Columbia collector George Pappas owns a full race fuel Stage 3 1969 Nova 427 with 4-speed and factory 4.56:1 axle that was created by Bristow Motors. Dave Savage recalls a Bristow 427 Nova back in the day that was unbeatable in street racing. He's not certain as to what Stage package it was, but the car was a screamer.

In the fall of 1969, a Bristow ad for used cars contained a few regular transportation vehicles, but some heavyweights were mixed in there, including a 1967 Grand Parisienne two-door hardtop 396, a 1967 Sport Fury 383 two-door hardtop, and a 1966 Chev Impala two-door hardtop 427 425-hp 4-speed.

A Bristow 1969 GTO Judge

When it came time to buy a new performance car, there was nowhere else under consideration. Dave Savage bought a car from Bristow in February 1969. Although he would have preferred a Stage 3 car, Dave simply didn't have enough money to swing it. Instead, he special ordered a 1969 Pontiac GTO Judge. His first new car was silver with black buckets and no console. With a need for speed and lack of cash, the GTO had no options except the Judge package (which included Ram Air III 400), Posi-Traction axle, 4-speed transmission, hood tachometer, and AM radio.

Dave got the car for $4,000 (Canadian currency). No tax. No delivery. This was a great deal. He took the train up from Edmonton to pick up his Judge in April 1969. The drive home wasn't quite as fun as it could have been due to the weather still being pretty frigid. One year later, Dave was ready for another new car and wanted to jump all the way to the top.

Bristow Eliminator 1970 Chevelle LS6 cars

Now that the factory was putting 454s into Chevelles, there was no need for the Bristow 427 engine swaps. Of course, having a dealership bulk order a car properly can enhance the basic LS6 package.

In February 1970, Dave got a spec sheet for a Bristow Eliminator 1970 Chevelle LS6 with headers, Sun tach with gauges, and bench seat format 4-speed floor shifter. Dave envisioned his car as a blue car with a black bench interior. Dave's financial burden of a new mortgage forced him to back out of the deal. He still has that original Eliminator sheet.

In 1970, Bristow ordered a run of bare-bones bench seat 4-speed Chevelle 454 LS6 cars. It may have received the biggest single batch order of 1970 LS6 Chevelle 4-speeds ever delivered to an individual dealership. This bulk order of LS6 cars outstripped orders placed by large dealers in major metropolitan areas.

Bristow took delivery of the low-budget thumpers and judiciously spent the money saved on the order to enhance

The mouthwatering spec sheet for the Eliminators had a lot of guys daydreaming about the possibilities. Dave Savage was one of many dreamers from the era. He owned a 1969 GTO Judge and intended to move up to an Eliminator. He had his colors picked out, but his mortgage stopped him.

```
ELIMINATOR PACKAGES
           by
CLIFF BRISTOW MOTORS LTD.
    THREE HILLS, ALBERTA
     Phone - 443-5121

1970 CHEVELLE MALIBU 2 DR. H. T.        1970 CHEVY II 2 DR.
 450 hp - 454 engine                     450 hp - 454 engine
 SS package                              SS package
 M22 - H. D. 4-speed                     4-speed
 Positraction                            Positraction
 Dual exhausts                           Hurst competition plus shifter
 Headers                                 Radio
 Hurst competition plus shifter          Headers
 Radio                                   Sun super tach
 Sun super tach                          White stripe belted tires
 Power disc brakes                       7" wheel rims
 F70X14 belted white lettered tires      Super tuned
 Super sport wheels                      Ready to win price - $4,495.00
 Super tuned
 Ready to win price - $4,495.00

1970 CAMARO 2 DR. H. T.                  1970 CORVETTE CONVERTIBLE
 Complete 228 package                    300 hp - 350 engine
 Power disc brakes                       4-speed or hydro
 Special instrumentation                 Positraction
 Tachometer                              Tinted windows
 4-speed                                 Rally wheels
 Hurst shifter                           F70X15B belted tires
 Radio                                   Full price - $5,295.00
 Super tuned
 Ready to win price - $3,995.00
```

Lost Muscle Car Dealerships

This Cliff Bristow 1970 Chevelle SS 454 LS6 beast was delivered as an Eliminator Package. Besides go fast items such as headers and a Hurst competition plus shifter, Bristow made sure his cars looked fast as well. Despite the modern trend toward dog dish steelie restorations, many muscle machines were delivered with factory mags and raised white letter wide ovals, as was the case with this Bristow car. (Photo Courtesy Cam Hutchins)

the package. Bristow 454 cars came with two-spoke steering wheels, no console or buckets, no cowl induction, and no hood pins. The savings in the factory order could then be strategically applied to aftermarket additions.

Bristow power tuned the cars, added headers, and equipped the spartan screamers with a tachometer and gauges. A Hurst shifter was substituted for the long-arm stock bench seat unit provided by the factory.

Bristow 454 LS6 Novas

The availability of the 454 also inspired one of the hairiest dealer conversions imaginable. Bristow transplanted 454 LS6 engines into 1970 Novas! Aside from the monster cars, Bristow was also stocking factory stock scorchers such as Nova SS 396 cars packing L78s.

An October 1970 ad from Bristow listed a brand-new zero-miles 1969 Camaro packing a 454 for only $3,995 (Canadian). He also had some used goodies, including a 1970 Challenger R/T 383 4-speed for $3,495, a 1969 Hemi Super Bee 4-speed Posi-Traction with ET mags for $3,495, and a 1968 Impala SS 427 4-speed for $2,795.

Another interesting car imported from the United States

Part of the Bristow Eliminator package, as seen on this 1970 Chevelle SS 454 LS6, was the addition of headers. Headers improved power as well as dispensing with air injectors. The air pumps were mandated on the LS6 motors that used a big 850 Holley carburetor. Bristow dispensed with anything that slowed the car down.

Bristow ordered a plain bench seat and two-spoke steering wheel to save money that could then be rolled into speed-specific items, including a tachometer, gauges, and a Hurst shifter.

1972 454 NOVA?
NOW THAT'S PERFORMANCE!

- 450 HP - 454 Engine
- 850 Holley - Hi Rise Manifold
- Complete SS Package
- 4 Spd. & Positraction
- Headers
- Traction Bars & Sun Supertach
- The Ultimate Street Racer

FOR ONLY $4950.00

Contact:
CLIFF BRISTOW
PERFORMANCE MOTORS
THREE HILLS, ALBERTA
Phone 443-5121

Prices on 454 Camaros & Chevelles on Request

---

to the lot was a 1971 El Camino custom painted Burnt Orange Metallic with a 400-ci motor and M40. It was built in Maryland and shipped out on April 21, 1971.

Bristow continued to keep the faith during the muscle car decline. Cliff ran an ad in May 1971 offering some hot used items: a 1965 Corvette 327 365-hp 4-speed, a 1970 Nova 396 375-hp 4-speed, a 1969 Mustang 428 Cobra Jet, a 1970 Trans Am, and two 1964 Chev SSs.

In fall 1971, when the new 1972 models were released, Bristow ignored the supposed death of the muscle era by taking out a big ad titled: "1972 454 Nova? Now that's performance!"

This audacious ad appeared two years after factories dropped out of performance. Even stalwart Yenko Chevrolet had tried an under-the-radar car with the Yenko 350 Deuce for 1970. Two full model years down the road, Bristow was still dropping 454s into Novas! The 454 used in Bristow engine transplants was of course the LS6 450-hp version topped with an 850 Holley carb on a high-rise intake and equipped with headers. The Novas came with complete SS package, 4-speed, Posi-Traction, Sun Supertach, and traction bars.

Bristow Sells The Rat Patrol

Bristow advertised his race car, *The Rat Patrol*, for sale in April 1972 for half of the $15,000 invested. The 1971 680+-hp Camaro ran 10.13 at 135 mph. Bristow displayed the car in Sidorsky's furniture store in early April. Later, on April 22, 1972, at the Race Place, Bristow stated that his Camaro was the only Pro Stock race car in Western Canada.

Everyone else was cowed by the insurance crunch and rising gas prices. Even Yenko Chevrolet went to an insurance cheater 350 Nova for 1970 model year. Not Bristow. And of course you could have your Camaro or Chevelle 454 "on request."

Other cars were also on display with his Camaro. Bristow was joined by a raft of Corvettes from the members of "Corvettes Unlimited," which was the biggest Vette club in Calgary. The club was sponsored by Bristow Motors.

Bristow Fire and Bank Hassles

The Bristow dealership closed following a fire on May 29, 1972, that started around 2 a.m. Firefighters were able to pull 12 cars out of the dealership before it burned down. The fire interrupted anticipated weekend sales that were essential to keep General Motors Acceptance Corporation (GMAC) paid off. Without GMAC accounts in good standing, the dealership stood to lose the GM franchise.

A rare Canadian-built 1971 Monte Carlo from Bristow was restored from fire damage. It seems highly likely this car was one of the 12 pulled out of the fire.

Cliff and his wife, Sharon, were able to keep their loans floating with their local banker by making deposits and assigning assets to the bank. However, the bank head office shut things down despite the Bristows going to Calgary and pleading their case.

The Bristows were denied any leeway and their assets were forfeit. Cliff tried to keep the business afloat by canceling bank checks and directing customers to pay GMAC directly. This led to a court case in March 1974 in which Cliff was sentenced to a symbolic day in jail and a fine. The judge berated the bank for leaving Cliff between a rock and a hard place.

Cliff moved to Edmonton shortly thereafter, feeling bummed about the whole experience. But the legend of his dealership persists. Muscle car historians and collectors discovered Bristow cars and appreciated the concoctions that flowed out of Three Hills. Cliff Bristow was eventually bestowed with the title "The Yenko of the North."

Dave Savage followed the exploits of various Bristow cars in street races over the years. Eventually, he owned nine 454 LS6 cars in the 1970s and 1980s when they were just used cars. Dave stayed in touch with a local collector named Terry who owns an original paint Bristow red LS6. Finally in 2017, Dave found an original LS6 from that batch of cars special ordered for Bristow Motors. Dave finally made good on his initial intent to own one of these cars all these years later. He treated his find to a full restoration.

CHAPTER 9
DALE CHEVROLET

Dale Chevrolet
Location: Waukesha, Wisconsin
Years in Operation: 1945–1980
Founder(s): Elmer O. "Con" Dale
Current Status: Vacant

Dale Chevrolet used these "Deal with Dale" license plates as an attention getter.

During the 1960s, Wisconsin had a strong automotive presence. The state was associated with American Motors Corporation (AMC) due to the AMC Kenosha main plant dominating the downtown area along Lake Michigan. AMC also kept an old Nash body plant running in Milwaukee. The AMC proving grounds were in Burlington, Wisconsin.

Racers from Chicago would also drive roughly 60 miles north to Union Grove, Wisconsin, to Great Lakes Dragaway. Union Grove Pontiac was also nearby and worth a look. Dale Chevrolet's initial fame stemmed from stocking the largest selection of Corvettes in Wisconsin. At one point, it was rumored to be the largest Corvette dealer in the United States. Dale was also a COPO and Yenko distributor.

Milwaukee-Area Dealer

Elmer O. "Con" Dale was born around 1908 in North Dakota. His wife, Helen, was born around 1907 in Wisconsin. The Dale auto business traces back to the 1930s, when the Dale Tire Company was established at 225 Madison Street, Waukesha.

In January 1940, Con and Helen had a son, William. The family was living in Janesville, Wisconsin, and Con was a district manager for an automobile factory. He soon became CEO of Dale Tire Company and built up the business.

The Dale Chevrolet dealership was registered on July 24, 1945. It used dealer code 119 Zone 61. Zone 61 was used for the Milwaukee area.

Dale Chevrolet was located at 811 S. Barstow Street and 500 Line at Broadway during the 1940s and 1950s. The dealership advertised a "Free Scientific Motor Analysis" at its service center on 225 Madison Street. Madison Street became the main location in the 1960s with used car lots at North and Anne Streets and White Rock Street during the early 1960s.

Expanding Performance

In the 1960s, Con's son William took over the performance side of things and expanded the Dale reputation during the muscle car era. Con remained on-site in his office and was fully involved with the dealership during the performance era.

Bob Peck's 1972 Corvette owner's manual sits above an original Dale Chevrolet dealer emblem. Note that even with smaller chrome pieces, Dale preserved the continuity of its marketing by including the phrase "Deal with Dale," which was also splashed across the dealer plates. (Photo Courtesy Bob Peck)

Midnight Auto Parts

There is an aspect of the supercar era that is often forgotten. During muscle car mania, a lot of "Midnight Auto Parts" places were thriving. Nighttime theft plagued any high-performance dealership that wasn't in a city center. Yenko Chevrolet had thieves coming to the back of its dealership in rowboats. White Bear Dodge had to install a guard turret to watch its inventory during the night. Now that Dale was out of the populated downtown area, it too became a target. On February 10, 1966, the newspaper reported the theft of performance parts from some cars parked in the Dale dealership storage lot on Brookfield Avenue. It was one more reason Con wanted the city of Waukesha to annex the dealership.

William R. Dale was doing something right with his performance perspective because he was appointed vice president of the dealership during the 1960s. Muscle cars were driving the business forward, as was attested by a September 1965 advertisement pledging to add five to the sales staff. Dale Chevrolet described itself as the fastest-growing GM dealership in Wisconsin.

In 1966, the dealership had grown sufficiently to justify building new premises. In preparation for the move, a full-page ad in June 1965 promised to blow out *all* the trucks from the Dale truck lot. Dale simultaneously held a big sale on new and used cars at the other dealer locations in anticipation of the dealership move.

Dale Chevrolet relocated to a purpose-built location at 1543 E. Moreland Boulevard, which was located outside the Waukesha city limits on Highway 18 (aka Brookfield Ave) across from the proposed site of a new shopping mall. In a July 1965 application, Dale Chevrolet described the proposed new facility as a 70,000-square-foot dealership northeast of the city. It was estimated to cost about $750,000 to build the new dealership. Dale requested that the city annex the 13,299-acre site from the city of Pewaukee.

Corvettes, COPOs, and Dale Dusters

Dale ads placed during this time used an ignition key logo surrounding the details of the car for sale. The used cars advertised in the mid-1960s were invariably Corvettes, Impala Super Sports, and similar muscle cars.

Corvettes

Dale was known as one of the largest Corvette dealerships in the United States, so it only makes sense that it would receive a lot of used Corvette trade-ins. Dale also promoted its high-performance cars using the Corvette as the bar to measure from. When it stocked Camaro 427s, Dale promoted them as "the closest thing to a Corvette yet."

COPOs

Dale Chevrolet sold a Hugger Orange leftover 1969 COPO 427 ZL1 Camaro ordered by Gibb Chevrolet. Gibb set up the COPO deal by agreeing to an order of 50 1969 427 COPO Camaros, but the factory passed the development cost to the dealer, which inflated the price sky high. Gibb had trouble selling these expensive Camaros and only moved 13 of them. The leftover Camaros were dispersed to other dealerships, including Dale Chevrolet.

Aside from the exotic high end of the muscle scene, Dale also had a full house of "regular" 396 cars.

Dale Dusters

In 1968, Dale Chevrolet supposedly performed many in-house 427 engine swaps. Deciding to try some in-house supercar work again, Dale Chevrolet dreamed up the Dale Dusters, which were 427-equipped Camaros, Chevelles, and Novas. Evidence of their existence from ads and from promotional displays (i.e., on the Dale race car) suggest that they built some.

Although advertising implied that the dealership was turning out plentiful numbers of dealer big-block conversion

Dale Chevrolet sponsored this 1969 Camaro at the strip and used it as a billboard to promote the Dale high-performance center. The driver's door prominently broadcasts the availability of the "Dale Dusters." (Photo Courtesy Bob Peck)

1969 427 COPO Camaro

Dale Chevrolet stocked iron-block 427 COPO Camaros in 1969. James Schwalbach was at the dealership looking at new Corvettes in June 1969 and observed five Camaros being unloaded. The sinister exhaust tone prompted James to look closer at these factory 427 Camaros.

That day, he spontaneously became the owner of a Hugger Orange 1969 COPO Camaro 427 4-speed right off the delivery truck! The $3,900 window sticker rang in much cheaper than the new Corvettes James was looking at. A quick test drive sealed the deal. James recalled his new COPO Camaro running low 12s at 120 mph at Union Grove Raceway.

James sold the car in the early 1970s when he traded it in for a station wagon. The COPO Camaro was repainted custom black and ended up with a 396 engine at some point. The original Orange houndstooth interior was preserved during Sue Hamann's 30-plus years of ownership. When Sue died in 2009, Chad Slocum bought the COPO Camaro and discovered its history. Chad now shows his Camaro in "Day Two" condition.

This Dale advertisement strongly suggests that Dale Dusters were actually built. The wording of the ad includes the 427 Dusters as part of the on-site inventory of 40 Camaros.

Dale Chevrolet sold this Camaro Z28 with the rare four-wheel disc brake option. An indication of Dale's performance reputation is confirmed by its sale of yet another four-wheel disc Z28. (Photo Courtesy Bill Glowacki)

Dale Dusters, local muscle car hobbyist and researcher Bill Glowacki only knows of one definite 427 conversion.

Bill recalls the Dale lot back in the day. He said he was often, "Prowling through rows of Z28s, Chevelle SS, Corvettes, and around six to eight COPO Camaros including a ZL1 Fred Gibb return car. At least two of the Z28s were JL8 option cars." Later, Bill owned an Orange with Orange houndstooth Camaro Z28 with the rare JL8 four-wheel disc brake option that came from the Dale lot. Bill's buddy owned a matching Yellow with Yellow houndstooth Camaro Z28 that also came with the JL8 option. The Yellow Z28 was well optioned, which kept it sitting on the Dale lot for a year before it finally sold in April 1970.

This August 1969 advertisement lists the Dale inventory. It specifically includes Dale Dusters as a separate grouping in the various types of 60 Camaros they have available on the lot. The Chevelles listed do not have any COPO 427 cars or Dusters amongst the mix. This is a year-end sale and, of course, doesn't reflect cars that were in inventory and sold.

Where Are the Dale Dusters?

The Dale Dusters seem to have fallen through the cracks. Dale historian Bill Glowacki states that in all his years immersed in the muscle car hobby in the local area he only knows of one 427 Dale conversion: a 1968 Nova SS conversion to an L72 427 engine. The Ash Gold car was repainted red.

It is likely that the horrendous winters in Wisconsin ate up any Dale Dusters that were built and sold, just as none of the famous Magnum 400 cars from Knafel Pontiac have surfaced, though it's a known fact that 50 of those were built and sold.

It is also possible that the same thing happened with Dale Dusters that occurred in the case of many other dealer supercar projects that were launched late in the era. By 1969, insurance was becoming impossible for "regular" muscle machines, and a big-block swap-in high-profile dealer special would just be that much more unattainable. Several dealers, such as Mander in North Vancouver, British Columbia, have left tantalizing advertisements and urban legends where perhaps a pilot supercar may have been built but the project never made it into reality.

For certain, straight-up engine swap cars were being pumped through the Dale dealership for several years. A customer could purchase a 427 Nova or Camaro new from Dale by ordering a 396 375-hp factory car. Dale's performance mechanic Bernie Adams swapped in a 427 before delivery for a mere $600 surcharge. The reason the swaps were performed on 375-hp cars was to provide a good base-equipped platform for a 427 swap. The yanked high-horsepower 396 engine was an easy sell through the Dale performance parts counter.

Racing Sponsorship

In 1967, Schliepper's Speed Shop cosponsored the 1967 Dale race car. When performance cars sales fell off a cliff at Dale, the performance guys within the dealership migrated from Dale to keep the flame alive working for Schlieppers.

Ray Suminski's 1969 Camaro 427 4-speed race car had primary sponsorship from Buttitta's Speed Shop (which later became Mr. C's when John Chobanian took over) with help from Dale Chevrolet. Note the huge advertisement sign on the track for Jim Wanger's Chevrolet. When John DeLorean moved from Pontiac to run Chevrolet, Wangers acquired a dealership that he immediately turned into a high-performance palace. (Photo Courtesy Bill Glowacki)

Bill Glowacki recalls that Dale Chevrolet raced a Hugger Orange 1969 Camaro ZL1 that was the #7 car from Gibb. At the end of the race season, Dale sold the car with an L72 iron-block 427 installed. Through persistent research, Bill was able to locate the engine and car in 1981, but the asking price was out of his range. He passed the deal to Jim Price, who restored the car.

Dale Yenko Deuces

It was an exciting year at Dale when the dealership added a Yenko franchise in 1970 and several Yenko Deuces passed through the inventory. The Deuce was the Yenko stealth solution to the insurance prices. On paper, a Deuce was nothing but a 350 Nova.

But Yenko used COPO to load the Nova up with a LT1 350, which was definitely one of the best small-block performance engines of all time. Heavy-duty hardware backed it up, although the basic car was left plain. Once Yenko got

Dale Chevrolet staff were enthusiastic racers and campaigned this Funny Car with help from the dealership. (Photo Courtesy Tom Carter)

Dale widened the scope of its performance portfolio when it became a Yenko distributor. This 1970 Yenko Nova Deuce was sold through Dale Chevrolet. The Deuce was an innovative way to get a supercar past the insurance agents.

The Deuce's engine "only" displaced 350 ci, but the LT1 made every inch count for more than 1 hp. The bright wires leading upward from the firewall connect to the hood tachometer.

Note the Deuce's "strippo" rubber floor mat, two-spoke steering wheel, and bench seat. The stark interior was augmented by Yenko identification on the inner door panels and a switchover to a 4-speed-style floor shifter for the automatic transmission.

For customers who weren't satisfied with flying under the insurance radar in a Yenko Deuce Nova, Dale would take a 396 Nova and swap in a 427 engine. This Nova was purchased off the Dale lot with a dealer 427 and quickly accrued some owner-installed "Day Two" modifications. Dave sold the car in 1974 with more than 100,000 miles on the odometer. (Photo Courtesy Dave Eberhardy)

Yenko's crew pulled the column shift automatic lever off, leaving the attaching lump of steel on the steering column visible in the bottom right of this photo. Note that the shift quadrant below the speedometer didn't receive a block-off plate, although the red pointer has been removed.

Dale Chevrolet's purpose-built dealership at 1543 E. Moreland Boulevard was located approximately where this now-vacant building sits. The building served as a supermarket for several years after Dale Chevrolet closed.

the cars on-site, they were spruced up with stripes and badges and a quickie floor shift installation replaced the factory column shift for the automatic transmission. These Deuces were insurable and fooled many insurance agents.

There were no more advertisements in 1970 regarding the Dale Dusters. There are a few reasons for this. First, of course, the engine swap process was nullified in 1969 when Dale was able to obtain COPO 427 cars with the engine installed at the factory. Second, the insurance rates made these cars hard sells. Third, the 1970 model year Plymouth Duster was a runaway success, making continued use of the "Duster" name too confusing for a Chevy dealership.

The End of Dale Chevrolet

Dale Chevrolet moved out of the E. 1543 Moreland Boulevard location in 1975. The location was taken over by Edward Lynch, who established Lynch Chevrolet Inc. at this location on June 3, 1975.

This 1975 date tallies with problems incurred by the "Associates Inc." venture that Con Dale was involved in. He bought 1,600 acres of recreational development land in Buffalo County. The land deal placed a strain on the cash flow for the dealership. His son, William, and his wife, Helen, were also part of the project.

Some sources suggest Dale Chevrolet went out of business on December 17, 1980. The franchise was taken over by Boucher Chevrolet. As of 2017, Boucher states that it has been in business for "over 36 years," which tallies with the 1980 date.

Today, the ultra-modern Dale dealership location is a large shopping mall. The approximate spot where Dale was is vacant. A grocery store operated out of the building for many years. Now a used car agency occupies a corner unit in the building.

Dale Chevrolet's original location at 225 Madison was approximately where this condominium sits. To the left is a hospital, which may share some of the former Dale lot.

CHAPTER 10
WHITE BEAR DODGE

White Bear Dodge
Location: White Bear, Minnesota
Years in Operation: 1966–1980
Founder(s): Gerald "Jerry" L. Perkl
Current Status: Barnett White Bear Chrysler Jeep Dodge RAM

A winning race Hemi Dart is posed in front of the White Bear dealership in the fall of 1968. Note the clean late-1960s dealership design with canopy over the fully glassed in showroom. (Photo Courtesy Jim Perkl)

White Bear Dodge Inc. was located at 3430 Hwy 61 North, St. Paul, Minnesota. Jerry Perkl established the dealership in 1966. Jerry was into fast driving and exciting cars. He was the type to recognize the trends and get in on them quickly. His gigantic dealership allowed him to respond to a new craze in massive volume whereas smaller places would eventually get enough vehicles in stock just as the wave was receding.

Used Car Life

Jerry was born Gerald L. Perkl on July 18, 1934, in Forest Park, Illinois. Jerry's father, Bert A. Perkl, owned a used car dealership on 600 W. Lake Avenue, Minneapolis, Minnesota. When he was growing up, Jerry and his brother Robert spent a lot of time on used car lots. By the late 1970s, Bert was running Mid Lake Motors at 1401 E. Lake.

Bert was a laid-back guy. Once while waiting for his breakfast in a restaurant, he witnessed someone stealing his Cadillac from the lot. Bert said, "I'll deal with it after I finish breakfast." Bert had various paperwork and permits hassles with the city council regarding his final car lot. The whole thing culminated with him being fined and dragged into hearings. Bert was cavalier about things until the day he died on April 26, 1980, at age 72.

Roaring High-Volume Life

Bert's son Jerry, on the other hand, was a dynamo who diversified his energy into multiple schemes and innovations. Jerry was highly motivated to investigate the details of everything he was involved in. After graduation from De La Salle High School in Minneapolis, Jerry attended Dunwoody Institute. He began his working life creating architectural drawings. Almost immediately, Jerry burst out of that confining situation. He was eager to express his outgoing personality and indulge his love of cars.

Jerry worked his way up to become president of Holiday Oldsmobile at Ninth Street and First Avenue North in Minneapolis, Minnesota. He accomplished this before he was 30 years old. His success formula was "Let's make a deal." He relied on slim margins and volume turnover to keep cash flowing.

Jerry also truly enjoyed high-performance vehicles, which made riding the muscle car wave a cinch for him. Jerry took Holiday to sales success via a strong performance image boosted with drag racing sponsorship.

The Holiday Olds sponsorship on the 1966 *442 Much!* is hidden beneath the fender covers. Following a towing accident, the 442 was rebuilt as a 1967 model. Jim Lutz was the driver of this 3,020-pound all-steel altered-wheelbase 442. Myron Lundberg was the mechanic. The four-pin liftoff hood is removed in this picture for maintenance. The hood had a hole cut for the GMC supercharger that sat atop a stroked 482-ci Oldsmobile engine. (Photo Courtesy John Foster Jr. and Jim Cecil)

Holiday Olds 442 Volume Champs

Holiday Oldsmobile was an obscure Olds dealership in Minneapolis when Jerry arrived. By the time he got through with Holiday, it was the volume king of Oldsmobile 442s.

According to an article in the December 1966 issue of *Car Craft*, Holiday Olds ran a 1966 Olds 442 Funny Car named *442 Much!* It was campaigned by Jim Lutz and Myron Lundberg. To further consolidate its performance reputation, Holiday Olds sponsored a 1966 Olds 442 drag car named *The Conquistador*. The *Car Craft* article stated that Holiday Olds sold more 1965 Oldsmobile 442s than any other Oldsmobile dealer in the nation. Jerry kept things churning.

Holiday Oldsmobile's massive sales of 442s carried on unabated for the 1966 model year. Jerry's ability to sell 442s justified factory favoritism when allocation of the new 1966 W-30 cars was decided. The Oldsmobile factory designed the W-30 option specifically to take on the stock classes at the drag strip. Olds built slightly more than the necessary 50 cars for NHRA homologation on the factory line in June 1966. Jerry built Holiday Oldsmobile's performance reputation so high that the factory gave Holiday 12 of the 54 factory-built 1966 442 W-30 cars.

While Jerry Perkl was president of the Holiday Olds dealership, his son Jim clearly remembers his dad bringing home an Olds 442. Jim was too young to know if it was a W-30, but he recalls that Jerry really gave that 442 a workout while he had it.

White Bear Dodge

Aside from promoting Holiday Olds, Jerry was also president of the Minneapolis Automobile Dealers Association in 1966. As if there was no limit to what he wanted to accomplish, this was the same year Jerry set out to establish White Bear Dodge. Jerry used loans (and the sale of his wedding gifts!) to get White Bear Dodge off the ground.

Jerry Perkl's high-volume, low-margin approach was responsible for blowing out more high-performance 442s than anyone else in the United States when he was running Holiday Oldsmobile. Note the prominent "Red Cap Service" sign that refers to the second part of Jerry's success formula: fixing a car right the first time.

Jerry Perkl sold his wedding presents to scrape together the money needed to get White Bear Dodge off the ground. The dealership was built on former farmland just off famous Highway 61. This June 1967 photo documents the building progress. (Photo Courtesy Jim Perkl)

Jerry used his White Bear showroom to display the Batmobile from the TV show *Batman,* which was wildly popular with adults and kids alike. Batmobile custom builder George Barris was well known within hot rod circles. (Photo Courtesy Jim Perkl)

The Location

Jerry built White Bear on a tract of farmland along Highway 61. Jerry felt this stretch of Highway 61 could become a hub for auto dealerships. His success and example soon led to many dealers setting up in proximity to Jerry's Dodge dealership in the following years.

Highway 61 runs north following the Mississippi River from New Orleans right up to the Canadian border. Choosing such a heavily traveled highway was a smart move on Jerry's part. There was also a bit of mystique about this highway. Some blues songs and Bob Dylan's album *Highway 61 Revisited* popularized the route. Highway 61 wasn't hyped to the same level as Route 66, but it did have a feeling of long-term identity. Everyone knew where it was.

The Vehicles

Prior to setting up his Dodge dealership, Jerry researched Chrysler products. He liked the styling of GM products. The Chevelle SS 396, Pontiac GTO, and the Olds 442 were quick, but they were hampered by the GM 400-ci limit on intermediate cars. Chrysler always had heavy-hitting hardware and was finally getting styling on track. Jerry felt Dodge was poised to sell well in the muscle market with its 440 and 426 Hemi advantage.

How's this for the ultimate caricature of a heavy muscle car? The popular magazine *CARtoons* and some Mopar advertising of the time didn't even reach this level of exaggeration! (Photo Courtesy Jim Perkl)

Chapter 10: White Bear Dodge

Jerry bought himself a brand-new Dodge Charger while he was mulling over his new dealership concept. His new car attracted attention when it was in for service at the local Chrysler dealership. Jerry would come screaming in full bore. When it was ready to go, Jerry made a dramatic exit with squealing tires.

Skip Murphy had just started working at that Chrysler dealer in 1966, and he liked Jerry's youthful exuberance. Skip was born and raised in White Bear, Minnesota. The idea of working half a mile from home at the new White Bear Dodge dealership appealed to him. He struck up a friendship with Jerry, who hired him as his first employee. In fact, when White Bear Dodge first opened Skip was the *only* employee! Jerry and Skip washed and prepped all the incoming inventory themselves.

Jerry immediately applied much of the high-performance experience gained during his tenure at Holiday Oldsmobile to his new Dodge dealership. He ordered a lot of high-performance cars with total confidence that they were going to sell. At Holiday Olds, he filled the lot with 442s and word got out and the cars sold. He did the same thing at White Bear Dodge, only this time it was Chargers, Coronet R/Ts, and Darts. Once Jerry established White Bear Dodge, he expanded that high-performance success formula further.

Wild Promotional Gimmicks

Jerry ran an ad on July 25, 1967, that told the world he was here. It said: "Announcing the Twin Cities newest 'Good Guy' . . . White Bear Dodge (if you think Brand X was worried before you should see them now!)"

Jerry's other creative strategies included displaying the real Batmobile in the dealership during the mania for the popular TV show *Batman* (1966–1968). The Batmobile was a George Barris creation based on a Lincoln Futura show car. Kids loved it, and teens all knew Barris was the King of Customizers in California. This was a perfect draw to get the right audience into the White Bear Dodge showroom. Jerry had the place packed with the right stuff to tempt anyone who set foot on the lot.

White Bear periodically used caricatured car drawings in ads and promotional items. Jerry produced a coloring book full of car caricatures of all the popular performance vehicles from Dodge represented in whacky exaggerated "Day Two" status.

Jerry lit up the dealership at night with searchlights that shot into the sky for miles. He had freewheeling hubs attached to steel discs that replaced hubcaps on all the demo cars on the lot. Every demo car on the lot had a steel disc on each wheel that remained stationary while the wheels turned. The discs had the image of Yosemite Sam from the Bugs Bunny cartoons. Yosemite Sam was "blasting prices" down at White Bear Dodge!

This ad for White Bear emphasizes the high-performance slant as well as total size (now up to 10th largest Dodge dealership in the world). Note that the dealership also stocked high-performance parts for brands other than Mopar. (Photo Courtesy Jim Perkl)

Jerry Perkl in a rare moment behind his desk at White Bear Dodge in January 1968. Jerry was usually out promoting the dealership or on the floor making deals. (Photo Courtesy Jim Perkl)

Jerry's architectural and artistic background lent itself well to the advertisements. He did artwork for the White Bear ads. Some of the ads featured a cannon that had just fired: White Bear was blasting prices. The dealership was also all over radio and television advertising.

White Bear Blasts into Sales Stratosphere

Jerry and Skip Murphy had fun hyping the dealership. The duo attended any and all events in town. They were constantly networking and advertising the dealership. Skip described Jerry as always having his hand out to shake hands with his newest friend. Jerry liked everyone, and it went both ways. Jerry was present at absolutely any public event possible from sports games to auto shows to parades.

Jerry was deep in car culture. He was in demand as a judge for car shows due to his expertise with 1920s through 1940s cars. His personal collection of cars included vintage Packards, Bentleys, and Rolls-Royces.

White Bear Dodge took off immediately. Jerry quickly assembled a staff of salesmen who were energized by his Saturday-morning sales pep talks. Skip believes that Jerry could have become a motivational speaker. He had fun and sent his people out with a very positive attitude. He was everyone's friend and bought lunch for all the staff on Saturdays.

Everything Always in Stock!

Jerry also continued running on the narrow margins he worked with during his Holiday Olds days. He believed in making a deal. He didn't get bogged down at a sticking point on the price of anything. If the deal was slim this time or that time, it would even out in the end. No car was precious. Because he ordered in massive volume, no one got overly attached to the value of a car. Customers were irreplaceable and cars were interchangeable.

He said, "We can order a hundred more cars in just like this one and they'll be here tomorrow. This customer is only here once. We need to make a deal." Jerry made his customer the priority above price. He backed his sales with good service.

The usual dealer strategy in the 1960s was to stock the basic stuff and if a customer wanted a particular color or model, dealers would trade with other dealers to try and get that car. Jerry refused to trade cars with other dealers. Period. That car represented a customer he lost if he traded it out. Jerry believed the customer should come to him for the car they wanted. Jerry believed in having everything in stock that anyone could possibly want.

White Bear had 300 to 400 new muscle cars in stock all the time, and at the dealer peak it was as much as 500 cars! Another dealer might order 1 white Challenger 383, but Jerry ordered 10 of everything. He made sure to have every model, color, and drivetrain combination in stock. Jerry had so many cars on the property that he eventually needed fences and a turret for a night guard to watch over the inventory.

In 1968, Dodge had a great year. Chrysler Corporation overcome the awkward styling that had dogged its cars in the early 1960s. The Chryslers had always been fast and now they looked like it, too. The basic car shapes were all very good looking, even before vibrant colors, stripes, scoops, and spoilers were applied.

White Bear High-Performance Headquarters

Of course, a huge part of the White Bear success story traced back to the dealership's High-Performance

Jerry brought in the *Dodge Little Red Wagon* to the dealership for display. The popular exhibition drag strip wheelstanding pickup is sandwiched between a Charger R/T and a Super Bee. Note the Scat City cone atop the Charger. (Photo Courtesy Jim Perkl)

White Bear Dodge showcased one of Dick Landy's Coronet R/Ts parked out front in July 1968. Note the banner in background: "The Good Guys are Here." This was part of the "Dodge White Hat Good Guys" promotion evoking old Western films where the hero wore a white hat. (Photo Courtesy Jim Perkl)

Dick Landy

"Dandy" Dick Landy was born on March 15, 1937, in San Fernando, California. Once he started racing, he quickly got factory sponsorship. He is credited with kickstarting the Altered Wheelbase/Funny Car trend. He was a recognizable character with his unlit cigar and consistent winning streak. Skip remembers Dick's 1968 Hemi Dart racer on display in the dealership.

Jerry Perkl's wife, Ruth, and son, Jim, pose with the Daytona in the showroom where it was displayed to increase floor traffic. This photo was taken in the fall of 1969. (Photo Courtesy Jim Perkl)

Headquarters. White Bear Dodge was the only dealership in the area with an in-house dynamometer for performance tuning cars. White Bear also attracted a lot of racers with a well-stocked performance parts department that stayed open until 9 p.m. every day.

Jerry had some savvy, talented mechanics who looked after his personal cars (a Duesenberg open racer, a Dodge Daytona, etc.) and catered to the dealership's performance-minded customers.

The dealership got some attention when Jerry traveled to the West Coast and bought two of Dick Landy's race cars. He proceeded to sell them off the used car lot at White Bear Dodge.

White Bear had some Dodge Monacos and four-door Darts on-site ready to go, but about 80 percent of the inventory in 1969 was high-impact, colorful performance cars. Skip remembers that it was routine for salesmen to sell four or five cars each on Saturday. Selling seven or eight cars wasn't uncommon.

Customers were mainly youth who were active on the street and drag strips. They were tired of losing. Like the enthusiasts coming into the dealership in hordes, Skip and Jerry believed that the Mopars were the fastest cars for the money. An October 1969 advertisement for the dealership billed White Bear as not just a Mopar performance place but rather the "Performance Car Headquarters for the Northwest." The list of 17 high-performance used cars being blown out supports this claim. The list is impressive: four used Super Bees including a 6-pack 4-speed demo car, two Road Runners, a Coronet R/T, a Charger R/T 440, a Barracuda 340, three Camaros (one of which had a 427), a Firebird, a GTO, a Mustang Mach 1, a Cougar GT, and a 4-speed Javelin.

White Bear Dodge brought in two 1969 Dodge Daytonas. The foreground red with white interior Daytona was painted with the White Bear logo and offered up for testing by local newspaper writers. The Daytona in the background was also red, but with a black interior. Jerry and his son, Jim, pose with the cars. (Photo Courtesy Jim Perkl)

Ruth poses with a local hot rod that has been incorporated into a display using the Dodge merchandising items. The life-size cutout of Joe Higgins, who played the role of a stereotypical Southern sheriff in Dodge ads, is going to write you up a great deal instead of a ticket! (Photo Courtesy Jim Perkl)

In October 1969, Jerry also took delivery of two new 1969 Dodge Charger Daytona "wing" cars. He had one painted up with the White Bear Dodge logo and offered it to newspaper writers for testing.

As if two red Daytonas weren't enough promo, Jerry also sponsored a midnight TV show *Racing Scene* on channel 5 on Wednesday nights in 1969. This was the height of the muscle era, and Jerry was playing it hard. He also took advantage of all the Dodge merchandising gimmicks, displaying cones that said Scat Pack and window decorations. Jerry also displayed local hot rods as part of his rotating performance displays.

Expansion: Lotus and Rolls-Royce

Jerry's enthusiasm for performance also led him to bring in a Lotus franchise. Skip drove a black Lotus demo car for quite some time. Jerry drove "everything," but it was usually high-performance stuff. When the van craze hit, Jerry had a custom van converted to four-wheel drive and played with that for a while. Generally, he cut a swath through the high-performance iron on the lot and drove the cars fast and hard.

Another foreign franchise Jerry added to the mix was Rolls-Royce. When hockey star Bobby Hull signed a $1,000,000 deal on June 27, 1972, with the WHA, Jerry took the opportunity to promote his Rolls-Royce franchise. He drove Bobby from the Twin Cities airport to the signing in St. Paul in his vintage 1934 Rolls-Royce.

Want a Car?

Jerry worked hard to get White Bear Dodge's name out there. He managed to get his dealership name on park bench backs built during the 1976 US Centennial Celebration. You could sit on a bench covered in White Bear Dodge advertising while a bus rolled past with White Bear Dodge advertising covering the entire side of it. If you were listening to a portable transistor radio, which were popular at this time, chances were you would hear an advertisement for White Bear pretty frequently.

Because Jerry operated in large-volume, low-margin territory, he offered some great deals. A November 1970 advertisement offered blow-out sale prices on performance-oriented cars: a 1971 Demon for $2,295 and a 1971 Charger for $2,535. Jerry didn't let cars languish on the lot. He wasn't waiting for the right buyer for the right price. Jerry's mindset was, "We're here to sell some cars. Want a car?"

Skip recalls how easy it was to sell those cars. He said, "The factory kept hitting us with great new stuff. The Charger and Coronet R/Ts sold real well. Out comes the 440 Six Pack. *Boom!* We got a bunch and moved them out instantly. Then we stocked the Dart 440! Racers bought a lot of those. Then suddenly there is the new Challenger. *Boom-Boom!* It was a free-for-all!"

Of course, high-volume sales and low-margin pricing of the already bargain-priced Dodge high-performance cars

On June 27, 1972, hockey star Bobby Hull signed a million dollar deal with the WHA. Jerry drove him to the signing in his vintage 1934 Rolls-Royce. (Photo Courtesy Jim Perkl)

This nice Dodge Challenger R/T was originally sold through White Bear Dodge. (Photo Courtesy Scott Dahlberg)

An original dealer badge adorns this Dodge Challenger R/T. Note the very understated, tasteful layout of the badge. This emblem would also need to be used on top-of-the-line Monacos, so it didn't make sense to design a garish logo. (Photo Courtesy Scott Dahlberg)

Dodge cars scored the memorable name for this high-impact paint color: Plum Crazy. Plymouth had to settle for In-Violet, which is still cool. Note the wild-colored wall scheme that White Bear used to announce its performance status. The Challenger affirms its performance mentality. A hole was cut in the lift-off hood to clear the blower that was sticking up above fender level. (Photo Courtesy Jim Perkl)

played right into the hands of cash-strapped, performance-hungry youth. Someone going for a bare-bones 383 car could get a decent performer that looked great and barely cost more than a normal four-door used car.

Racing Sponsorship

White Bear Dodge raised awareness of its performance headquarters by sponsoring race driver Tom Hoover in a 1970 Dodge Challenger Funny Car. Jerry paid to have the body built in California. He hired mechanic Bill Schifsky to work on the Keith Black 426 Hemi that had supercharging and fuel injection. He asked Bill to help wring approximately 1,600 hp out of the engine.

After a few runs that didn't make the cut, Jerry quickly switched things up to a Ramchargers Hemi and manual-shift 2-speed. Jerry brought in a new mechanic, Bob Christianson, but nothing had changed yet. By the fall of 1970, Jerry had invested $40,000 in the Funny Car but failed to make a mark with it yet.

Note how psychedelic Jerry's posters became for White Bear Dodge. In tune with the times, this groovy poster had wavy lettering and borders as well as caricatured cars. White Bear was now the ninth largest dealership in the nation. Jerry had T-shirts, catalogs, and decals available. (Photo Courtesy Jim Perkl)

Tom Hoover's first foray into Funny Cars was with White Bear Dodge. Tom was obviously feeling a bit worried about the slow progress the White Bear car was making, according to an article at the time. It can be tedious sorting out the bugs.

The White Bear Challenger was finally coming together in the fall. A September 13, 1970, match race between Tom Hoover in the Double A Fuel Funny Car 1970 Challenger and the Crowe Knapp *Invader* Camaro driven by Gary Scow was close. Gary took the first run but red lighted the second one. The potential in Tom's car is inferred by a 7.60 at 194.36-mph quarter-mile run despite cool conditions inhibiting traction.

The car later ran a 7.28 at 206.8 mph in Rockford, Illinois, and began posting decent times as the season continued. Jerry noticed his sales improve once he had enough good runs to capture the attention of performance nuts. Guys swarmed over to his dealership from all over the state. Jerry still sold "bread and butter" cars but attributed his expansion in volume to muscle machines.

Winning 1971 Charger Funny Car

At the start of 1971, Jerry had a new AA Fuel Funny Car under preparation using the new 1971 Dodge Charger bodystyle. Tom Hoover won the AHRA Gateway Nationals that year driving the 1971 Dodge Charger Funny Car. The new aerodynamic body style boosted ETs. A return to a Keith Black Hemi helped matters too. Although the dealership had some great mechanics, Tom Hoover still relied on his father, George Hoover (who was a racer as well), to assist in prep of his cars.

After winning the Nationals, a 1/32nd-size model of the winning Charger was produced. This model further enhanced the White Bear reputation. Drivers all over the United States knew the name White Bear Dodge now.

Tom Hoover

Driver Tom Hoover had plenty of experience. His father, George, was a former racer. George and Tom's mother, Ruth, partnered with Tom to run a Dragmaster gas dragster in the summer of 1962. The Hoovers quickly jumped into Fuel competition. After switching to a Rod Stuckey fueler in 1964, Tom won the 1965 AHRA Winternationals. Next came a dragster named *The Fishbowl*. Tom ran both Chrysler Hemi and SOHC Ford engines in that car.

Time's a Changin'

As the 1970s descended into post-insurance crunch, deep emissions power cuts, and the obliteration of performance, a few bright spots appeared. Dodge found an interesting loophole with its creation of the 1978 Dodge Li'l Red Express Truck. Exempt from the same smog laws as cars, the pickup ran an unchoked 360 4-barrel engine derived from a police spec foundation right through high-riser chrome exhaust stacks free of catalytic converters. The performance was complemented with mag wheels and a hot rod–style paint scheme and woodwork.

Jerry Perkl's wife, Ruth, drove a 1978 Li'l Red Express for several years. She enjoyed blowing people's minds at the country club and blowing their doors off at the lights. She didn't switch up to a 1979 Li'l Red Express Truck because this model was slapped with emission controls.

Van Craze and Customs

In the later 1970s, Jerry was able to get in on the van craze too. Jerry had a shop in place to set up motorhomes. When that market crashed, he switched it up to customize vans. In March 1976, Jerry had 300 conversion vans in stock with custom lighting, carpeting, panels, mag wheels, bed conversion area, high-back swivel seats, and chrome dress up. Of course, larger engines with side exhausts and dyno super tunes were also available.

In 1977, White Bear Dodge was the largest Dodge dealership in the United States. In February, new car sales were about 270 vehicles. That is an impressive number when you consider that this is the slowest time of the year for car sales. It is certain that White Bear was averaging more than 300 new cars a month in the hot-selling periods. Skip recalls that the dealership moved well over 300 cars a month once you added in the used inventory.

A newspaper advertisement ran on October 31, 1977, played up White Bear's number-one spot. The ad stated that they were the "largest volume Dodge dealer in the world." White Bear had a surplus of trade-ins due to the massive sales of new vehicles and offered the trade-ins to the public at rock-bottom prices.

White Bear Crashes

Unfortunately, Jerry wasn't able to anticipate a confluence of changes that hit his large dealership harder than it would a smaller place. A giant has difficulty responding to sudden downturns in the business climate and soaring interest rates.

The first White Bear 1970 Challenger Funny Car encountered teething trouble. The second incarnation of the White Bear Funny Car was a 1971 Charger that hit the sweet spot, earning enough fame to warrant this scale model. (Photo Courtesy Jim Perkl)

On March 3, 1980, a newspaper article reported that the dealership was forced to close due to the massive overhead of a huge lot combined with a 20-percent drop in Chrysler sales in the zone. Jerry was paying 16.75-percent interest on his hefty new car inventory that wasn't selling. Unable to sustain $50,000 a month in interest charges on top of other operating costs that were soaring, he had no choice but to close.

A smaller dealer wouldn't have to fork out so much money to maintain unsold stock and might survive a short while during double-digit inflation and sales slowdowns. But having 400 cars on your lot is totally unsustainable when the perfect storm hits.

Jerry was disappointed at the loss of White Bear Dodge, but he was undaunted. He continued to work on other business concepts. He owned Savage Motors and Pine City Motors. He bought a shopping mall in Stillwater named Grand Garage and Gallery, which he revitalized. Jerry was working on a catalytic converter that used nonprecious metals to function (standard cats rely on platinum, iridium, and palladium).

Jerry and Skip Murphy lived in China for five years while they worked out the details of establishing an ice cream factory there. Skip came back to United States and was managing a few car dealerships, and he had Jerry stoked to get back into the car business. Sadly, Jerry died of a heart attack at home on June 30, 1991, at age 56.

Jerry tutored his son Jim Perkl in some of the tricks of high-performance driving. Today, Father Jim Perkl is asked to bless cars. Cars are an integral part of our lives getting us to work, school, the hospital to visit relatives, and so on. Father Jim sees the blessing of the car as blessing the person's ability to function well in life. After the blessing, Father Jim takes the cars for a spin around the block. Many are surprised to discover that he likes to drive really fast!

The former White Bear Dodge dealership lot is now occupied by Barnett White Bear Chrysler Jeep Dodge RAM.

Jerry put on a positive face while the whole world crashed around him. Note the lack of high-performance stuff on the lot. This was the dawn of the 1980s, when there was virtually nothing exciting on the lots anymore.

CHAPTER 11
MR. NORM'S GRAND SPAULDING DODGE

Mr. Norm's Grand Spaulding Dodge
Location: Chicago, Illinois
Years in Operation: 1962–1979
Founder(s): Norman "Mr. Norm" Kraus and Leonard Kraus
Current Status: Lumber yard

The Grand Spaulding Dodge showroom juts out to meet the sidewalk at the intersection of 3300 West Grand Avenue and Spaulding in Chicago, Illinois, in 1969. A customer's red Super Bee with the appropriate name *The Stinger* painted on the C-pillar has "Day Two" spring shackles and Moon stickers on the rear of the car. The blue Dodge Charger parked in front of the showroom still has the window sticker and no plates. The front end of a C2 Corvette is visible among the used cars lining Grand Avenue. (Photo Courtesy Mr. Norm Collection)

Right from the first day of opening, Grand Spaulding Dodge catered primarily to muscle car buyers. Not only did Norman "Mr. Norm" Kraus talk the lingo of his youthful performance-savvy customers, but he and his brother Leonard Kraus stocked the right cars at the right time. The dealership was awash in speed shop parts (Hemi engines, headers, mags, shifters, tachs) and had a Clayton chassis dynamometer on the premises to power tune every high-performance car before it rolled out of the dealership.

Grand Spaulding Dodge directly affected the cars that every Mopar fan drove in the 1960s. Mr. Norm worked with Gary Dyer, who ran the racing division, and Dennis Hirschbeck, the performance parts director, to create new high-performance muscle cars based upon modifications made in the Grand Spaulding dealership service bays. Dealers with this much influence were rare. Tasca Ford, well known for the high-performance Blue Oval offerings, enjoyed a significantly different relationship with Ford in creating new offerings.

Lucky Mr. Norm poses with Joan Parker, "the Dodge Fever Girl," at the Chicago Auto Show. Born on June 21, 1945, in New York, Joan competed in Miss America 1963, followed by a role in the 1966 *Batman* movie. Joan's beguiling blue eyes and bright personality were used to full advantage in Dodge television commercials from 1968 to 1970, which sparked a huge fan following. (Photo Courtesy Mr. Norm Collection)

The license frame for Grand Spaulding Dodge eventually included the phrase up top "Mr. Norm's" to tie into Norm Kraus's visibility as the "face of the dealership."

Dad's Gas Station

Harvey Kraus was born in Russia around 1905. His wife, Anna Kraus, was born around 1908, also in Russia. They immigrated to the United States, and around 1931, Leonard "Lenny" Kraus was born in Illinois. His younger brother Norman "Norm" Kraus was born in Des Moines, Iowa, about 1933.

At the time of the 1940 census, Harvey owned a gas station at the corner of Grand and Spaulding in Chicago. In 1948, Lenny and Norm began selling used cars out of this gas station. Harvey's gas station quickly filled up with used cars and overtook the service station business. Needing more space in 1951, the brothers were offered the lots next to the gas station, which they purchased, enabling them to expand the used car business.

The Mr. Norm Formula

Leonard "Lenny" Kraus was the president of the used car dealership, but he was virtually invisible. His younger brother Norman was the face of the dealership. Norm's image appeared in ads and his name became synonymous with the dealership. They ultimately became known in the industry as Mr. Outside and Mr. Inside.

The brothers' performance angle originated because Norm was savvy about anticipating emerging trends. When Norm was inundated with calls after listing a used V-8 stick shift 1956 Chevy Bel Air convertible, the brothers quickly focused exclusively on buying and selling high-performance cars.

The first part of the Mr. Norm formula was intentional: buy and sell big-engine four on the floor cars! However, the catchy nickname was completely accidental. The Mr. Norm nickname originated because newspapers often charged by the character for advertising text. The limited space resulted in car ads using abbreviations such as ps and pb to indicate "power steering" or "power brakes" or r+h to mean "radio and heater." Norman made the most of the ad space by eliminating his last name across the numerous sale ads. The "Mr. Norm" moniker stuck as a catchy nickname that became synonymous with Mopar performance.

Mr. Norm was perceived as a cool guy who related to the young drivers and tried to fulfill their needs. He became their go-to guy. It seems natural to assume he was some kind of car nut or racer, but he wasn't. Mr. Norm was an intelligent marketer and a savvy businessman who recognized the youth craving for performance and catered to it with strong advertising and networking. He absorbed feedback and molded the dealership to suit the market and even incited change within the executive ranks of Dodge.

The brothers' system worked flawlessly. Lenny bought the cars and Norm sold them. By specializing in performance V-8 stick shift cars, the brothers carved out a niche market for themselves. Beginning in 1961, Mr. Norm's ads stated that he was "the Hi Performance Car King." In an era of "slushbox" unresponsive automatic transmissions or "three on the tree" awkward column-shift manual cars, Norm quickly built a reputation for having a big selection of four on the floor cars that drivers wanted.

Dodge Woos the Kraus Brothers

The Kraus brothers caught the attention of factory representatives from Dodge, who urged them to buy into a franchise. The brothers resisted for a while. Their used car business had become the epicenter of high-performance in Chicago and was very successful. They weren't convinced that investing a lot of money in a new car franchise was the way to go.

In 1962, the Kraus brothers were shown photos on the new direction styling was taking at Dodge for the upcoming

Mr. Norm Persona

Image-seeking drivers were part of the sales formula in the muscle car dealerships. Sometimes a racer became associated with a dealership, which was the case with Parnelli Jones or Dick Harrell. Their popular personalities and racing reputations defined the dealer and drew attention. This is a clear-cut logical association. The Mr. Norm's name didn't follow this pattern.

Sometimes a flamboyant figure emerges as the "face of the dealership" without anyone exactly knowing the basis of his reputation. People speak knowingly, and no one wants to appear out of the loop and ask "Who is that?", so the reputation builds. For young drivers, it is important to be "hip," and knowing the right references is part of the game.

The name "Mr. Norm" evoked a gut reaction then, and it certainly does now. Mr. Norm became the face of high-performance Dodges across the nation, in no small part because of the tire-smoking cars he stocked that no other Dodge dealer would consider for inventory. Add his never-ending efforts to promote the dealership, the special high-performance models he created, and the success of his racing team, and you've got all of the elements it took to create a mystique that continues to resonate with Mopar enthusiasts.

1963 models that were designed under the direction of Elwood Engel. There was no doubt that hardcore serious hardware was being pumped out of the Mopar factories. With the new, improved styling, it looked like Dodge had a winner. The fall of 1962 saw the opening of Grand Spaulding Auto Sales under their father Harvey Kraus's name with the promise of building a showroom and service department in the spring of 1963.

Grand Spaulding Dodge was located at 3300 West Grand Avenue. The intersection the dealership straddled was West Grand at North Spaulding Avenue, which explains the dealership name. The emphasis on performance dictated the content of the new car inventory, which capitalized on the client base already established. Grand Spaulding Dodge immediately ordered truckloads of Max Wedge cars to launch the dealership. Those Maxies got the attention of high-performance enthusiasts and immediately set Grand Spaulding Dodge on the road to success.

Grand Spaulding Expansion

Grand Spaulding sold all the Max Wedge cars and quickly ordered another batch of heavy-hitting cars. By spring of 1963, the Kraus team replaced the gas station with a new car showroom. The service department was overwhelmed from the first day, so the brothers quickly contracted to expand it. The Kraus team worked like clockwork in its expansion. By early 1965, it was finished, providing an additional 44x95-foot extension to the original service department.

Mr. Norm's bore a lot of similarity to the nearby Nickey Chevrolet high-performance dealership. Performance sales made Nickey Chevrolet into the largest Chevrolet dealership in the United States in the 1960s. Mr. Norm's may have started about 20 years after Nickey, but the dealership leveraged high performance to work similar magic at Grand Spaulding, which became the number-one Dodge sales volume dealership in the United States in 1974.

Mr. Norm was making connections with the young drivers who came to the dealership and quickly realized the best way to reach his high-performance market was to hire performance enthusiasts for his sales force. Norm quickly built a team comprised of knowledgeable young muscle car guys selling the hot Mr. Norm cars to their peers. Mr. Norm also decided the best way to reach the people who were his primary clientele was through a club.

Mr. Norm's Sport Club

In 1963, Mr. Norm's Sport Club was formed with a newsletter carrying information for owners of Mr. Norm's cars. Every enthusiast who purchased a new or used high-performance car at Grand Spaulding automatically became a member of this club.

Perks

Mr. Norm's racing apparel was provided to all members of the Sport Club. The clothes created free advertising for the dealership, and there is no doubt that most of the members liked being part of something big.

Mr. Norm hosted club members at the dealership with free refreshments and live music. Norm cut a deal with a local Chicago band called the Buckinghams; all of its members owned cars from the dealership. The service department worked on the band members' cars for free in exchange for performances at the dealership. The band was gaining popularity on the radio and were the perfect draw for Mr. Norm's target audience.

Dean Darnell

In 1963, Dean Darnell was a 29-year-old street racer cruising in a hopped-up 1948 Plymouth. Dean lived 4 miles away from the Grand Spaulding dealership and would cruise by to see the new stuff on the lot. One day, one of the 1963 Max Wedge cars Mr. Norm ordered was sitting on the lot with the hood open to display dual quads. That glimpse burned itself into Dean's mind. He told himself, "That's going to be my car!"

Two days later on January 7, 1963, Dean drove out of Grand Spaulding Dodge in that black Max Wedge with red interior. He managed to swing the price of this ultra-fast brand-new car despite only working for moderate wages in an Admiral television factory. Mopars were cheap and Mr. Norm believed in blowing cars out in volume. Dean immediately took the car up to Western Avenue to street race it.

Dean won so many races that his wife, Helen, felt confident that he could outrun the cops! Normally when a police car hit the lights, Dean just pulled over and grabbed two or three dollars from his wallet. Back then, the Chicago police would pocket the money and admonish him to slow down and it was all over. This time his wife Helen said, "You can out run them in this car! Give me the money instead!"

Dean Darnell spotted this mean black 1963 Max Wedge car on Mr. Norm's lot. Mr. Norm's blew out cars in huge volume with thin margins, making it possible for young Dean to buy this major muscle machine on his Admiral TV factory wages.

Dean entered sanctioned drag racing with a 1968 GTX, but he hung on to his Max Wedge. At age 84, he still gets on it hard. We attracted some attention from the cops when we came screaming down a deserted road full on in his Max Wedge. Helen remarked, "Some things never change!"

When Dean Darnell first saw this 1963 Max Wedge on Mr. Norm's lot, the hood was open displaying the dual quads. Within days, the car was his. When you get past the double carbs, look at those incredible upward sweeping factory exhaust manifolds.

Dean Darnell's black Max Wedge's original red interior is still in good shape. The pushbuttons to the left of the steering column are for the transmission. The pushbuttons on the right are for the heater. To the right of the heater there is a red block-off plate because this was a radio delete car.

The Buckinghams

In late 1965, the Pulsations changed its name to the Buckinghams to cash in on the British music invasion. The name also referenced Chicago's Buckingham Fountain.

The group played at dealership parties and cut a record of the Mr. Norm's jingle "Get with the Go Group," which urged listeners to go down and see Mr. Norm.

Pop songs about cars were popular in the 1960s with Ronnie and the Daytonas (a studio band) hired by Jim Wangers to put out "Little GTO" and later Paul Revere and the Raiders recording a song for the 1969 Pontiac GTO Judge commercial.

The Buckinghams hit the big time in February 1967 with a hit song "Kind of a Drag." Seeing a pretty popular pop group for free filled up the dealership after hours and definitely led to increased sales. Mr. Norm also advertised his dealership on WLS, the mega-watt AM rock radio station, which got the message out across the country.

Where the muscle car audience really saw the benefit of Mr. Norm's Sport Club was that membership saved them money on parts. Racing was competitive, and no one considered his or her car "done" no matter how good it was. Hard driving breaks stuff, and increasing your performance takes money and parts. Any help there was a great inducement to make Mr. Norm's the go-to place for go-fast parts.

Club Member Cars

The club eventually increased deals to allow drivers to purchase cars at narrow dealer margins. Mr. Norm locked in the low price at $200 above invoice for club members. No one got favoritism in the pricing of a new Dodge at Grand Spaulding.

A "stock" Mr. Norm car was quicker than a regular showroom stock Dodge sold off the floor at a standard dealership.

The Grand Spaulding decklid emblem was a sticker featuring a snorting ram. The ram image was also used for the window stickers; one assured the buyer this car was dyno tuned and another validated membership in the Mr. Norm's Sport Club.

Mr. Norm's cars all had the carburetor re-jetted and distributor recurved for optimum performance using a dynamometer before the cars were sold. If a particular factory car came off the line running like a dog, the dyno tune could amp it up significantly. Even a car in ideal factory state would still see horsepower gains from the dyno work.

Mr. Norm's cars left the dealership with a Grand Spaulding Dodge emblem on the trunk lid, along with Dyno Tune and Sport Club stickers and license plate frames. This let the world know that you had a Mr. Norm's car. Your car didn't perform like an ordinary factory car if it said Mr. Norm on it. The word quickly got out that if you had a high-performance Dodge from Mr. Norm's, it had been precision power tuned on the Clayton dyno, and was not a car to be trifled with.

Owners proudly displayed a Mr. Norm sticker or Royal Pontiac badge in a fashion similar to the way gearheads advertised the hardware installed in their cars. In the 1960s, the rear quarter windows were plastered with stickers from STP, Thrush, Cragar, Hooker, Crane, and more. A Grand Spaulding Dodge dealer sticker carried serious weight on the street and the strip. That power tune was worth at least as much "found" horsepower as a set of headers on a car that started out in top shape.

The Mr. Norm power tune was probably worth all of the aftermarket pieces on a car that started in marginal tune when delivered from the factory. Of course, just bringing the car up to its full factory potential wasn't enough for some customers. With a well-stocked speed parts department, it was a snap for Mr. Norm's to load up a customer's new car with headers, gears, and mags. Mr. Norm could roll the upgrades into the regular financing, making it easy for customers.

The salesman were happy to assist a customer with performance and accessory enhancements. All of the salesmen were certain to discuss performance upgrades with the buyers, which resulted in a lot of red hot cars getting sold at Grand Spaulding.

Mr. Norm's club members also received an automatic free subscription to *Drag News,* where the owner could read about the latest victories of Mr. Norm's race team on the drag strip.

Grand Spaulding Racing Team

Norm liked hearing customers call into the dealership to report how they beat a particular car at the track. He wanted his customers to be winners. When his cars came out on top, so did he. That kind of success drove enthusiasts to Grand Spaulding because they wanted to own a winner too. Mr. Norm paid attention to what was happening out there with his customers and this helped him adapt to developing situations.

Mr. Norm stumbled upon racing just like he stumbled upon his name. Norm was not a drag strip guy at all, but he

The muscle car era was barely underway when Mr. Norm placed this ad in *Drag News* in mid-1964. However, his Grand Spaulding Dodge dealership was already bursting at the seams with performance parts, a high-performance club, and a car guaranteed to "run in the 11s—right off the showroom floor!" Note the wild Technicolor 1960s art work in this ad. The muscle car paint colors would soon catch up with this Pop art style. Mr. Norm would also buy a one-way ticket from anywhere in the country for potential buyers to come out and view a car. This sales technique was initiated at Nickey Chevrolet in Chicago. Mr. Norm picked up on it because he never missed a trick! (Photo Courtesy Mr. Norm Collection)

was open to any angle to promote the dealership. One day, a customer with a Max Wedge offered to paint the Grand Spaulding Dodge name on his car for his run at the Amphitheater in Chicago in exchange for spark plug wires and seat belts. The deluge of calls on Monday after the car won its class convinced Norm to immediately get involved in drag racing sponsorship. The Kraus brothers reasoned that if an independent racer could draw attention to the dealership, then a full-on effort from Mr. Norm's could spark gigantic interest.

The first Grand Spaulding Dodge racing team debuted in 1964. Mr. Norm began by campaigning both a Max Wedge and a Hemi car. Realizing that racing against and beating his own customers with a similar car was counterproductive, Norm switched it up for 1965. By racing in Factory Experimental, which evolved into the Funny Car class, Mr. Norm's received maximum exposure while simultaneously eliminating the issue of competing against his customers on the strip.

Altered Wheelbase

Mr. Norm's team quickly moved up into the rarefied air of superchargers and nitro. In 1965, the Mr. Norm's team began running an altered wheelbase Dodge Coronet powered by a blown and injected 426-ci Hemi. The car, driven by Gary Dyer, managed to set records from coast to coast, including an 8.63-second elapsed time at Long Beach, California. Dyer even beat Dodge's factory-backed Ramchargers at a famous match race at Ubly Dragstrip in Michigan.

Mr. Norm's race cars blasted out incredibly low ETs with the Coronet supercharged Hemi. Like other cars in the Factory Experimental class, Mr. Norm's race cars evolved into flip-top Funny Cars. Famous for racing a string of "Mr. Norm's SuperChargers" once the Challenger debuted, Norm had a new Funny Car built with a Challenger body. The race cars ran at events all across the country, were successful, attracted attention, and also gave validity to the tuning abilities of the Mr. Norm's staff.

Dealership Focus

Despite this exotic race program, Mr. Norm had a different focus for the dealership inventory. He wanted affordable, streetable cars to compete with GM and Ford products. His parts department was now one of the largest high-performance emporiums in the country and his chassis dyno was supplemented with a second unit to keep up with tuning demands.

Mr. Norm's driver Gary Dyer pilots the Grand Spaulding Coronet 426 Hemi ahead of Arnie Beswick in his 1964 *Mystery Tornado* GTO. Both cars are supercharged, but Mr. Norm's altered wheelbase is extremely radical. (Photo Courtesy Mr. Norm Collection)

Mr. Norm himself pilots the A/FX Grand Spaulding Dodge 1965 Coronet down the strip at the Great Lakes Dragaway in Union Grove, Wisconsin. Despite pulling air under the front tires, Norm isn't belted in nor is he wearing a helmet. This is a test run and not a race. (Photo Courtesy Mr. Norm Collection)

Grand Spaulding Dodge did so well racing that the dealership brought its 1965 Coronet altered wheelbase race car out West to Lions Drag Strip in Los Angeles, California. Dyer posted high 8-second runs in this car. (Photo Courtesy Mr. Norm Collection)

Mr. Norm wanted to move a lot of iron through his lot. He didn't believe the high-maintenance, prohibitively expensive solid lifter Hemi was the right approach for most of his customers. Instead of selling a few cars to a few people, Mr. Norm's philosophy was that an inexpensive hydraulic lifter performance engine in a light car was the way to get the attention and increase sales to the masses of Baby Boomers entering car-buying age. If Dodge wouldn't create the car, then Mr. Norm would do it himself!

The racetrack was a good promotional tool, but Mr. Norm was keenly aware that high-performance street cars mattered most to the customer. Dodge was missing the boat in his opinion. GM pony cars were being released with 396 375-hp solid lifter engines in the Camaro, and Pontiac had a nasty 400 HO in its Firebird. Ford finally got a 390 in its Mustang, although it was widely regarded as a stone. But wouldn't you rather own a 1967 Mustang GT390 than a Dart 273? The Dart looked really good with its 1967 redesign, but it was anything

Mr. Norm struts in striped pants while driver Gary Dyer is hidden in his fire suit behind the wheel of the blue Mr. Norm's 1970 Super Challenger Funny Car. This shakedown test occurred in May 1971 at Great Lakes Dragaway in Union Grove, Wisconsin. (Photo Courtesy Mr. Norm Collection)

Gary Dyer drove a 1966 "super" Charger Funny Car for Mr. Norm until the exciting new 1968 bodystyle came out. Mr. Norm's created this 1968 "Mini" Charger Funny Car. It is seen here at US 30 Dragstrip in Gary, Indiana. This area is now part of Hobart, Indiana. Note the Scat Pack Bee painted on the front fender of the Funny Car. This car only lasted a year before a new Mr. Norm's Charger Funny Car was built for 1969. (Photo Courtesy Mr. Norm Collection)

The Mr. Norm's prototype 1967 Dart GSS was run over the dyno drums with the new 383 in place. The Dart still had a dealer plate and factory hubcaps in place. Note that the Mr. Norm's dyno room has a prominent cartoon of a Ramchargers Funny Car with a fuel-injected Hemi. (Photo Courtesy Mr. Norm Collection)

but a high-performance car. The Mustang looked better and ran better than a Dart 273.

The Camaro and Firebird were being countered over at Plymouth with the 1967 Barracuda, which was a beautiful new design packed with a 383 to keep up with the pack. Chrysler had Plymouth covered but left Dodge without the big-block muscle in the A-Body platform. Dodge had nothing that Mr. Norm could sell in the compact high-performance category.

Because his dealership posted large volume sales, Norm was on the inside track at Dodge. He asked for a compact performance car, but the new 1967 model year Dart GT debuted with the largest engine as a small 273 V-8. Norm needed a Dart with some real horsepower to compete with a comparably priced Camaro or Mustang.

Mr. Norm's 383 Dart GSS

As soon as the first new Dart arrived, Norm instructed his parts and service guys to get a 375-hp 383, a 727 Torque-Flite, and an 8-3/4 rear end installed into the car. The whole job was done in a few days. Motor mounts were moved around and the front subframe was notched for clearance. The guys fitted it with a heat deflector for the steering box and it was ready to roll. Mr. Norm took it for a spin. He recalled, "It ran great, sounded great, and handled great."

Norm built one prototype. When the first of the production cars arrived, the original GTS badge was altered with the middle T replaced with an S for Grand Spaulding Special. It so happened his technical department only had a red *S* on hand, so they went with that.

Norm called the editor of *Car Craft* magazine to come to Chicago and test the new Dart GSS. Wanting a real world road test, Norm even invited several Sport Club members to put the big-block Dart through its paces on the streets of Chicago for the story. Everyone came away impressed with the performance of Mr. Norm's A-Body pocket rocket.

Once Mr. Norm had impressed the *Car Craft* writer, he called up Bob McCurry. Robert B. "Bob" McCurry Jr. was a Chrysler executive who was accessible and communicative with his dealerships. When Mr. Norm called up, Bob didn't hesitate. He said, "Bring it down to Detroit. I want to road test the car, and I want to show it to the engineers."

Norm recalled pulling up to the Chrysler headquarters in Highland Park, Michigan, in the Dart GSS. Bob came down in person and took the car out for a blast. Then he called the engineers down and said, "Look at what the kids from Chicago built."

The engineers said the reason they hadn't done it was the left exhaust manifold was too close to the steering box and would overheat it. Norm's techs had solved the problem with a simple heat shield. McCurry told his engineers that if Norm could do it, so could they. Needless to say, it got done ASAP. Bob McCurry told Norm that if he would order 50 of the 383 Darts, Dodge would build them. Norm didn't hesitate, and the rest is history. In fact, Norm promoted the 383 Dart so heavily that by the time they arrived, all of them were sold.

Mr. Norm Dealer Specials

Norm decided to create a new GSS model every year coupled with magazine coverage to keep attention focused and interest building. Keeping up with the constant upgrading of factory muscle machines in the late 1960s was a continuous pressure. Mr. Norm's competitor Royal Pontiac featured each new step in the performance race with magazine coverage. It kept the dealer before the public's eyes and also drove the performance to the cutting edge.

Dodge Dart GT

The Dodge Dart GT package came with a fantastic new engine from the factory for 1968. The Dart 340 was a terrific package. The small 340 was engineered from the ground up as nothing less than an all-out performance motor in every way. The little engine fit well in the engine compartment for ease of service and it flew. But in 1968, nearly everyone wanted a big-block muscle car, and Norm delivered. Mr. Norm would revisit the 340 in 1971 when the winds of change were blowing, but for now his eyes were on big-blocks.

By the time model year 1968 came up, the market was flooded with big-block installations in even the smallest cars. Mr. Norm could make his customers go faster by adding bigger cams, gears, and headers on B-Body Coronets or Chargers, but the step up to a Hemi was expensive and never a volume seller.

440 Dart

The 440 was a terrific performance engine in a midsize car, but Mr. Norm really saw the path to increased street and strip cred was with the compact A-Body Dart. After the success with the GSS 383 Dart in 1967, he stepped up his game and developed the GSS 440 Dart for 1968.

Just as he had done in the fall of 1966 with the then-new Dart, as soon as the first 1968 Dart arrived at Grand Spaulding Dodge in the fall of 1967, Norm had his resident race driver Gary Dyer and shop mechanic Rich Mouldry install a 440 in it. The RB big-block engine was a slightly tighter fit than the 383 B engine, but all in all, it was a simple conversion. Norm contacted Bob McCurry at Dodge. Initially, Dodge was too busy to handle the conversion, so Norm suggested that the initial production run be handled by Hurst Performance. After the first batch of 440 Darts was built by Hurst in 1968, the remainder of production was taken over by Dodge.

This Mr. Norm's dealer-special 1968 Grand Spaulding Special (GSS) Dart has a 440 engine crammed in the engine bay hooked to a Torque-Flite and 3.55:1 axle. Black cars look terrific with red stripes and red line tires. This car amplifies the great looks with full hub caps, console, and bucket seats.

Here is where it all happens in Mr. Norm's dealer special 1968 GSS. The 440 Magnum barely fits between the fenders. Note that Mr. Norm himself signed this car.

Mr. Norm proudly announced the 1968 Dart GSS 440 Magnum in this ad in *Drag News*. Mr. Norm promises every GSS is dyno tuned with carb re-jetted making them "ready to go." This theme is reinforced with the list of Hemis and 440s in stock for "immediate delivery." No weeks of waiting for your order to arrive was a great selling point for impatient youth. (Photo Courtesy Mr. Norm Collection)

When Dodge worked with Hurst Performance to build the drag race–only Super Stock LO23 Hemi Darts for the 1968 model year, they were ordered by Dodge dealerships all over the country. The goal was to get them into the hands of specific racers and dominate the NHRA SS/A and SS/AA classes. Needless to say, Mr. Norm wasn't about to miss out on selling Hemi Darts and ordered more of them than any dealer in the country. To be precise, he ordered 10 of the purpose-built race cars. As if that wasn't enough, six dealers ordered Hemi Darts and found that they couldn't sell them. One by one, they all called Mr. Norm and asked if he would buy the Darts. Deals were struck and Norm soon had 16 Hemi Darts. And yes, he promptly sold them all. Not only that, everyone who bought a Hemi Dart from Norm had them completely set up for NHRA competition. Such was the reputation of Mr. Norm and Grand Spaulding Dodge.

1969 Daytona

Mr. Norm ordered one of the early 1969 Daytonas. Norm's June 1969–built 440 Daytona was on the lot by August 1969.

The 1970 Challenger T/A was built to qualify the Dodge Challenger for Trans Am racing. This was a very radical street machine with larger rear tires than fronts and convoluted exhaust that created the impression of unmuffled straight outside pipes. On April 27, 1970, Chrysler sent Mr. Norm's advance shipping notice about this red example it ordered for the lot.

Here is the massive fresh-air induction Six Pack carburetor system dwarfing the 340 engine below it. This is a one-year-only factory triple deuce 340, but not the last time Mr. Norm stocked this combo. Later on, Mr. Norm's created its own dealer special 340 Six Pack Demons.

This was just about the most outrageous car from the muscle car era. But many of the 1969 and 1970 muscle cars were wild!

Mr. Norm aggressively promoted that "Wherever You Live, I'll Pay Your Fare From Anywhere" to come to Grand Spaulding Dodge in 1969.

The absolute peak of the Chrysler High Impact Colors was during 1970 and 1971, which also corresponds with the height of the muscle car phenomenon. Mr. Norm was a true believer in high performance and he realized early on that brightly colored cars would be popular with his customers. One look at the Grand Spaulding Dodge showroom and the traffic-stopping colors of the cars that comprised the front line were proof positive that bright colors increased sales.

Six Pack Demon Insurance Beaters

By the early 1970s, the insurance companies determined that performance cars and enthusiasts especially under the age of 21 were responsible for a disproportionate percentage of claims and lowered the boom with dramatically increased insurance premiums. Norm had everything in place with the right prices, but then sales came to a halt when it came time to insure a car. In particular, the rates were unaffordable for a big-block muscle car and hurt sales.

Mr. Norm immediately came out with an innovative, exciting answer to the big-block insurance dilemma. He created 1971 Demon GSS 340 Six Pack cars! The Dodge Demon 340 was a terrific car to start with; Mr. Norm just upped the ante by installing a three deuce intake system similar to those used on the 1970 Challenger T/A. It increased the performance of the Demon and added a mystique that other small-block performance cars lacked.

Demon was the second "me, too" car to come from the Dodge boys during the muscle car era. The first time top-dog Dodge was caught off guard by little brother Plymouth occurred back in 1968 when Plymouth knocked all of the muscle car offerings into the background with the Road Runner.

Runaway Road Runner sales prompted Dodge to release a Road Runner clone named the Super Bee. The Bee never caught on like the Road Runner, despite duplicating the bargain performance and cute character identity. History repeated itself when Plymouth once again scored a huge success with the Valiant Duster in 1970.

In 1971, Dodge got its own version of the Duster, which was named the Dodge Dart Demon. The Demon was based on the same 108-inch wheelbase as the Duster and, other than the front end cap and rear fascia, was essentially the same car. The rush to get the Demon into production cut corners. Critics noted that the Duster rear end had a different wheel well shape than the wheel wells in the front fenders of the Dart.

The Demon name only lasted two model years (1971 and 1972) before the name died in the fire of religious outrage. In 1973, the car was renamed the Dodge Dart Sport.

Demons and Dusters looked great, were lightweight, and were inexpensive. The 340 still had 10.5:1 compression for 1971 (General Motors dropped compression that year), a forged crank, a 0.455-inch-lift hydraulic cam, double-roller timing chain and sprockets, electronic ignition, a Carter ThermoQuad carb, and dual exhaust.

The 340 engine option added stripes, round gauges including a 150-mph speedometer, heavy-duty suspension, bigger brakes (drums all round) and tires, and a 3-speed manual floor shift. A 1971 Demon 340 tested in the April 1970 *Road Test*

Mr. Norm crouches beside a 1970 Super Bee that is about to be test driven by his drag racing driver Gary Dyer at the strip. The Super Bee sports factory raised white letter Polyglas tires. (Photo Courtesy Mr. Norm Collection)

In May 1971, Walter Miller of Canyon, Texas, got tired of being shut down by Mopars and sold his Chevelle SS 396. Walter bought this 1971 Demon GSS 340 Six Pack dealer special from Mr. Norm's through mail order.

Dig Mr. Norm's groovy Van Dyke beard and sideburns. White collars and skinny black ties were passé in 1970. Norm is pointing out details of a rare 1970 Challenger T/A. Behind him is a Charger. Note that Mr. Norm ordered his cars with mag wheels and raised white letter tires, not black walls with steelies and dog dishes. The office glass lettering lists reasons to join the Mr. Norm's Sport Club. Trophies and wall pictures chronicle Grand Spaulding's racing successes. (Photo Courtesy Mr. Norm Collection)

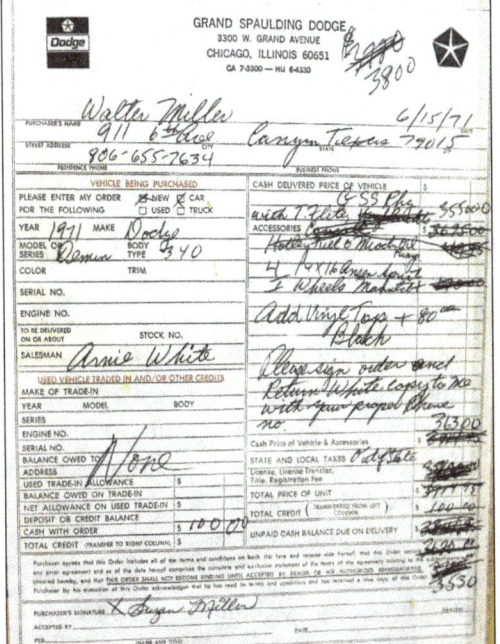

The original bill of sale for Walter Miller's 1971 Demon GSS is exempt from state tax because he bought it through mail order. Note that the high-performance manager Arnie White is listed as the salesman. Arnie rolled the cost of aftermarket Anson mag wheels into the final price of the car. With a huge inventory of performance parts, it was a snap to personalize a customer order like this.

The Mr. Norm's GSS package switched the intake to a high-rise unit that held three 2-barrel Holley carburetors. The camshaft, springs, and retainers were Crower items. The reinforcements went beyond the engine bay; heavy-duty rear suspension was supplemented with a traction bar.

Chapter 11: Mr. Norm's Grand Spaulding Dodge   115

Note that this 1972 Demon Mr. Norm's GSS is an early production car when Dodge still added the "Dart" nameplate to the rear decklid. Later cars were simply badged as Demons, and the Dart script was not installed. The sticker in the driver-side rear quarter window asserts that this car has been power tuned by Mr. Norm's. (Photo Courtesy Mecum Auctions)

1972 Demon 340 GSS Gets Supercharging

Mr. Norm instantly saw the solutions to any situation. When the compression ratio of the 1972 Demon 340 was dropped (and smaller valves were used), it looked like the end was in sight for performance. But Mr. Norm saw the lowered compression as an opportunity.

If you want to supercharge a car, you usually have to retrofit it with lower compression pistons. To Mr. Norm's mind, the factory had just prepped the 340 as the base for a Paxton supercharger. He immediately bolted one onto a Demon using 7 pounds of boost.

The 1972 Demon 340 GSS package included a special fresh-air intake setup with specific air filter. The engine received oversize hoses and pulleys, a special Holley fuel pump, and a fuel-pressure regulator. Things were toughened up with Crower aluminum valve spring retainers and a Milodon competition oil pump package.

Of course, the GSS went on the dyno to rework distributor advance curve and re-jet the carburetor. Mr. Norm's replaced the stock carburetor floats with hard epoxy-coated floats to withstand the supercharger's pressurized fuel charges. The 1972 GSS Demons came with factory Torque-Flite, Sure Grip 3.55:1 axles, and Wide Oval tires. Joe Oldham's test results on the Demon GSS came up with 13.92 ETs at 106 mph despite traction issues with the standard tires. Smart racers fixed that problem with a set of drag slicks and easily dropped deep into the 13-second bracket.

magazine ripped off 14.56 at 96 mph in the quarter-mile with a top end of 127 mph when Torque-Flite equipped.

When Mr. Norm got ahold of a Demon, he turned it into a GSS Six Pack by adding a high-rise 1970 Six Pack–style aluminum intake manifold with triple Holley 2-barrel carburetors and an aluminum Ford Tri-Power air cleaner. He also added competition-grade fuel and oil pumps and a high-capacity oil filter. Finned aluminum valve covers appear on many examples. Mr. Norm had Gary Dyer work up a performance protocol for the new Demon 340 that included a power tune on the Clayton rollers that got those triple carb cars sorted out for peak performance.

Insurance agents who used to be content merely slapping surcharges on recognizable muscle car names such as GTO or Road Runner were getting more detailed. Once they figured out that big-blocks could hide in regular name marques, buyers flocked to small-block powerhouses in small cars (Dusters and Novas). A small-block was immune to surcharges. Insurance agents responded by combing registration information for inflammatory equipment, such as 4-speeds.

The Demon 340 also contained another secret weapon as the early 1970s insurance backlash against muscle cars began to overwhelm potential buyers. Mr. Norm's ultimate stealth cars were 3-speed manual-shift 340 Demons. The 3-speed manual flew under the insurance radar but was still a good performer. The total irony here is that Mr. Norm started out in the performance game selling 4-speed used cars! But note that once the car was purchased and the insurance rate was assessed, it was an easy conversion to replace the 3-speed with a 4-speed with the insurance company none the wiser. One can only imagine how many Demons got this instant upgrade.

Any 1972 Petty Blue Demon is a real great looker. The Demon 340s were still scorchers in stock condition. Lightweight bodies allowed Demons to accelerate well despite factory detuning required for smog certification and low-lead gasoline use. When Grand Spaulding Dodge added a Paxton supercharger, it rightfully renamed this screamer a Mr. Norm GSS Demon. (Photo Courtesy Mecum Auctions)

A nice touch on the cover of the supercharger induction states that this is a Mr. Norm's Supercharged GSS. The Paxton superchargers were around as Ford aftermarket pieces as far back as the 1930s. Packard and Studebaker used Paxton superchargers as OEM and legitimized the company. Shelby American offered Paxton supercharger options and created widespread awareness of the brand. (Photo Courtesy Mecum Auctions)

Mr. Norm's Sales Ascend

Mr. Norm's stayed one step ahead of the muscle car movement until there was no market left to speak of. By 1972, Grand Spaulding was number three in Dodge sales, and by 1973, it reached number two for sales volume in the country.

In 1974, Grand Spaulding became the number-one volume seller of Dodges in the world even as the muscle car market completely evaporated. Grand Spaulding Dodge was now the fourth-largest dealership in the United States, earning $17 million per year. In public statements and ads soliciting salesmen, the dealership inventory was quoted at more than 700 cars and trucks.

Part of Grand Spaulding's continued volume success was due to fleet sales. Norm made huge inroads into the police car motor pool business. He supplied police cars to Mount Prospect, Buffalo Grove, the Chicago Police Department, and the state patrol. The dyno tuning provided an extra incentive for police to order Monaco 440 cars through Mr. Norm. In the end, having the lowest bids was what got him progressively larger orders.

But the lion's share of sales was attributed once more to Norm's savvy assessment of the marketplace. When the conversion van movement was picking up momentum, Norm bought vast quantities of vans. Norm recalls Bob McCurry asking him why he wanted to special order 500 vans to arrive just before summer. Bob had enough experience with Norm's prescient ways to trust that he was onto the next thing. Sure enough, Mr. Norm blew out all the vans when new van inventory for conversion companies dried up during factory assembly plant downtime for retooling during the summer months. Converters that traditionally built Chevrolets and Fords had nowhere else to turn if they wanted to keep their production lines going. They called Norm and bought Dodges, which was a win for Grand Spaulding Dodge and Chrysler.

Grand Spaulding in Buffalo Grove, Illinois

Grand Spaulding built a second location at 935 Dundee Road, Buffalo Grove, Illinois. The dealership was named Grand Spaulding Dodge of Buffalo Grove. Leonard Kraus was president of this location, just as he was of the original dealership.

Lenny was closely involved with the city in negotiating the zoning issues that cropped up while prepping this new dealership on 8 acres of property. The goal was to have the new dealership opened in September 1974, in time for the 1975 model introduction. By 1976, there were plans in the works to expand the Buffalo Grove location.

The End of Mr. Norm's

In 1977, Norm Kraus sold his interest in Grand Spaulding. During the recession of 1979, the dealership went out of business. The original Grand Spaulding dealership location is now the site of a lumber business. The Buffalo Grove location hosted a used Auto Superstore before closing. It is currently vacant.

This corner of Grand and Spaulding in Chicago, Illinois, gave Mr. Norm's Dodge dealership its official name. The basic structure of the building on the corner is intact, although all windows have been covered over.

This view from on top of a railway bridge covers the length of the former Grand Spaulding dealership at 3300 West Grand Avenue in Chicago. The empty lot in the foreground across the street from the Mr. Norm's buildings contains old cement foundations among the weeds.

This view from the front of the Mr. Norm's building on West Grand shows the basic structure of the building, which has been covered over and repurposed as a warehouse.

Norm continued to be active in automotive enthusiast circles and became a fixture at Mopar shows. Collector car shows created a large membership for the revival of the Mr. Norm's Sport Club in 1993. Today, Mr. Norm is a popular headliner at many nostalgic car shows.

When the new Dodge Challenger came out in 2008, Mr. Norm didn't miss a beat. He saw an instant opportunity to do the same thing he did at Grand Spaulding Dodge in the 1960s. Showing that he hasn't lost his touch for creating unique vehicles that capture the interest of Mopar enthusiasts, Norm worked with noted OEM Image vehicle builder Performance West Group to develop a variety of new Mr. Norm's GSS-branded packages for the reborn Challenger, which quickly expanded to include Chargers and Rams.

The Mr. Norm's GSS program picked up so much momentum nationally that in early 2015 a licensing agreement was consummated with Hurst to build limited-edition vehicles under the Hurst Heritage By GSS brand. This is a perfect example of history going full circle. In 1968, Hurst built the 440 GSS Darts for Mr. Norm and today, Norm is building modern muscle cars that continue the legacy of vehicles like the original Hurst Olds 442.

Mr. Norm displayed his new 2015 Challenger "The Mr. Norm's GSS Hall of Fame Edition" at the SEMA show to celebrate his induction into the Mopar Hall of Fame. Mr. Norm managed to find an exact duplicate of the Dodge Fever Girl's outfit and hired his own Dodge Girl Debbie to promote the car. The original Dodge Fever Girl, Joan Parker, was cured of her fever due to the heavy travel schedule involved back in 1970. Joan continued making TV appearances until the mid-1970s. Mr. Norm has never stopped. This GSS is just one of many special GSS editions he has unveiled. (Photo Courtesy Mr. Norm Collection)

CHAPTER 12
NICKEY CHEVROLET SALES

Nickey Chevrolet Sales
Location: Chicago, Illinois
Years in Operation: 1925–1977
Founder(s): Mr. Nickey
Current Status: Condominiums

Jim Jeffords pilots the Nickey Chevrolet sponsored *Purple People Eater* Corvette. Jim won the SCCA championship in 1958 and repeated the feat again in 1959. The later race car can be distinguished from this early version. The 1959 race car had the words *MK III* painted above the door. The *K* in *MK IIII* was reversed in keeping with the Nickey signage. (Photo Courtesy Dave Nicholas)

Nickey Chevrolet Sales Inc. was established by an actual person named Mr. Nickey. The Nickey dealership originated in 1925 in Chicago, Illinois, at 4120 Irving Park Road. Most accounts of the dealership history state that brothers Jack Stephani and Ed Stephani purchased the dealership and began running it after World War II. The date that the brothers purchased the dealership initially is not exactly established, but the end result is known: they created one of the most exciting performance dealerships of the 1960s. Nickey was the largest Chevy dealership in the world in 1967.

The Stephani Brothers

Edward "Ed" Joseph Stephani was born on January 21, 1910, in Berkeley, California, to Edward Ludwig Stephani and Cecelia Mryan Stephani. The family was in Chicago when Ed's younger brother John "Jack" F. Stephani was born. Jack was seven years younger than Ed, and their sister, Jean, arrived two years after Jack.

The family suffered a crisis when their father died at age 46 on October 13, 1933. When the family was enumerated in the 1940 census, the two brothers lived at 2929 Giddings Street, Chicago. Ed and Jack were supporting their widowed mother and younger sister through their roofing business.

Their mother died at age 51 on February 27, 1941. Soon after, the brothers went off to battle in World War II. When they returned, the action didn't stop.

Entering the Car Business

After the brothers returned from the war, they started working at Nickey Chevrolet. They soon began running the dealership and purchased it from Mr. Nickey. In the 1950s, a new highway went through the original dealership location. The dealership was relocated down the street to 4501 Irving Park Road.

Already the formula responsible for the success of the dealership had taken shape. Ed was president of the company and he controlled inventory, sales, and the books. Jack was secretary and treasurer, and he generated publicity.

The Stephani brothers were getting excited by high performance. Both were genuinely enthused by racing and

Chapter 12: Nickey Chevrolet Sales 119

Attention-Getting Ploys

In 1957, Jack noticed a backward letter in a Florida business sign and appreciated the attention-getting aspect of the ploy. He adopted the backward *K* in all the Nickey signs henceforth.

Jack was ready for people who came into the dealership to inform him about the mistake in his sign. When they did, he gave them gift certificates for an upside-down cake at a local bakery. Jack generated goodwill and got people into the dealership with that backward *K*.

Jack Stephani adopted the backward *K* in all the Nickey signs starting in 1957.

equally smitten with the promotional value. Their decision to begin sponsorship at the track was full bore and covered a wide variety of racing.

Nickey Chevrolet Race Team

In the era that Nickey Chevrolet sponsored a race team, it was traditional for race cars to be painted standard colors such as red, blue, white, or silver. Nickey Chevrolet bucked the trend and painted its Corvette purple and named it the *Purple People Eater* in honor of the popular Sheb Wooley song by the same name. The purple Nickey car stood out among the typical colored cars on the track. Putting the *K* in *MK 1* backward also created a further connection to the Nickey Chevrolet franchise.

The Nickey 1958 Corvette fuel-injected 4-speed car was blueprinted by Ronnie Kaplan and driven by Jim Jeffords. Nickey won the B stock SCCA championships in 1958. Famous driver Fred Lorenzon drove under Nickey sponsorship in stock car racing and won the championship in 1959 with a third version of the *Purple People Eater*.

A Scarab race car was also running under Nickey sponsorship. It was repainted purple and named *Nickey Nouse*.

Passion Reignites

After saturating the racing world with Nickey race cars, the stint was closed down when Ed reined Jack back in because of high operating costs. For a few years, Nickey Chevrolet was content to just sell cars, until the new 1963 Corvette reignited the passion for racing.

The 1963 Sting Ray blew everyone's minds when it came out. The beautiful design was visually ahead of its time. It was technically advanced for a domestic vehicle of the period with nearly ideal 50-50 weight distribution. The independent rear suspension and transverse rear spring was radical at the time.

Nickey sponsored a ZO6 Corvette in 1963 and 1964. Jerry Grant and codriver Skip Hudson won their class in the Sebring 12-hour endurance race of 1964. Nickey also owned a Cooper Monaco–bodied car with a Chevy driveline named *K-Choo*, which ran in 1963 and 1964 road races. A pit accident inspired Nickey Chevrolet to back out of car ownership and revert to sponsorship only.

The racing attracted attention to the dealership. A February 1, 1963, want ad for salespersonnel stated that Nickey had increased business by 100 percent since the prior year. Part of this could be attributed to the wide selection of 1963 Vettes on the lot that tied in with the racing exposure. In the listings, the dealership often highlighted the Corvair inventory as well. By the summer of 1963, the Nickey operation employed 120 people.

Nickey's Speedline Service

About 5 miles south of Nickey, heavy action was brewing at Mr. Norm's Grand Spaulding Dodge. News of Mr. Norm's new service department with dyno tuning and aftermarket speed parts spurred Nickey to enhance its street action with a new service center and speed shop.

The Nickey Automotive Discount Store had its grand opening in May 1964. Nickey promised the lowest prices on Goodyear tires (it was an authorized distributor) and other items. The Nickey speed shop also offered deals such as Hurst floor shift conversion kits. The kits were available for 3- and 4-speed applications. Nickey stocked brand-new 4-speed transmissions for $249.70 and had inventory to fit all 1957 to 1962 Chevrolets, including Corvettes.

Nickey experienced zoning hassles when it tried to use an off-site commercial building to stock overflow parts. A building initially constructed for business use had been caught in a rezoning crunch. The need for an entire overflow building illustrates the scope of inventory Nickey was developing.

Nickey's Speedline Service department opened in 1964. Cars were immediately assessed at the entrance and then shuttled through a long maintenance tunnel wide enough to accommodate three rows of cars.

when Nickey announced the grand opening of its state-of-the-art Speedline Service department. The Speedline Service department was a long tunnel that was wide enough to accommodate three rows of cars. Customers entered one end, where the car was immediately assessed using state-of-the-art electronic testing equipment.

The service department was open from 7 a.m. until midnight. Edward Stephani claimed this was the most modern and least expensive service department in all of the United States with a price guarantee. Combined with its discount store, it seemed everyone in Chicago would be using Nickey.

The master plan at Nickey was to have the best prices on maintenance items and speed equipment and then combine this with the best and most streamlined service center in Chicago.

Part two of the plan came into effect in October 1964

Nickey Speed Parts and Mail Order

Nickey Chevrolet's long history of sponsored Corvettes race cars translated into a growing demand for speed part inventory to back up the hot cars being purchased off the lot. As sales of speed parts escalated, the dealership adjusted to capitalize on the muscle car street scene.

"Hoss" Dan Blocker

Jack Stephani was friends with actor Dan Blocker, who portrayed Hoss on the popular television Western program *Bonanza*. Jack agreed to sponsor Dan Blocker's Genie racer named *Vinegaroon*. The car made the June 1966 cover of *Sports Car Graphic* with Dan posed on the *Bonanza* set in his costume.

The *Bonanza* TV show was sponsored by Chevrolet. The cast took part in tie-in advertising for Chevrolet, but Dan Blocker took it further. Dan was a walking advertisement for Chevrolet due to his interest in high performance. Dan's Chevy performance visibility was inflated further when he took possession of one of the 201 1965 Chevelle Z16 cars with 375-hp 396 engines. These were the first big-block Chevelles and included complete drivetrain upgrades. Unfortunately, the mass-production of SS 396 cars the following year came with 325-hp engines and few chassis upgrades in order to keep them affordable for the masses.

Nickey used the Chevrolet *Bonanza* advertisements provided to all Chevrolet dealerships but augmented that connection by featuring personal appearances from Dan at the dealership. A large ad on January 17, 1966, offered free tickets to see Dan and get free autographed pictures of him.

Another big ad on February 5, 1966, quoted Dan as saying it was nice meeting everyone in Chicago and promising to revisit the showroom soon. Nickey later listed used cars in April as "Hoss Cartwright Specials." The cars included a 1966 Chevrolet Super Sport and a 1966 Chevelle SS 396 4-speed.

There were often up to 400 used cars on the Nickey lot at any time. Many were given a Nickey 90-day 100-percent guarantee (even tires). In August 6, 1966, Dan Blocker's picture was used to promote "Nickey's close-out Bonanza sale." More than 1,000 new 1966 model cars were on the lot ready to be blown out before the new 1967 models arrived. Dan also returned in late October 1966 to stir up interest at the showroom.

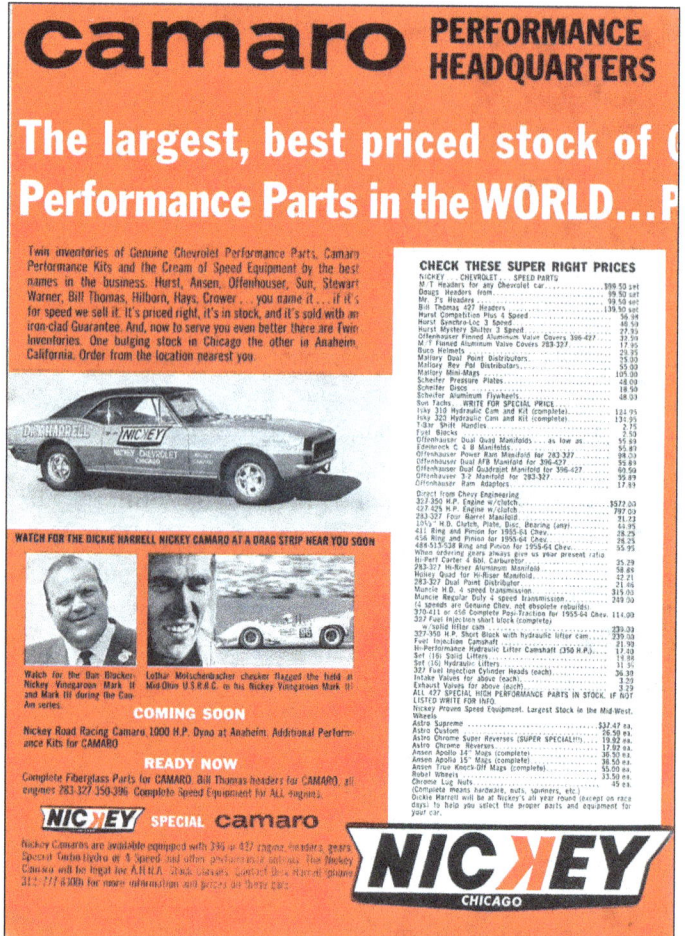

Nickey's speed shop advertised in enthusiast magazines to increase sales via mail order. Note the tie-ins with television star Dan Blocker (Jack befriended him) and drag star Dick Harrell.

Performance was selling well enough at Nickey to justify relocating its body shop off premises and converting the body shop space into a gigantic speed shop. Advertising in car magazines expanded the audience for parts to mail order as well.

By 1965, Nickey confidently stated that it had the largest stock of Chevrolet parts and aftermarket equipment in the world. It had tons of engines, transmissions, Hurst shifters, Astro wheels, and chrome accessories. The parts department was 20,000 square feet and had 140,000 parts on hand and ready to go. Later, Nickey speed catalogs upped the number to more than 200,000 parts!

Don Swiatek not only ran the speed shop but also was a performance consultant to new car buyers. A new car buyer was able to cherry-pick Chevrolet performance upgrade parts and even aftermarket items to bolster the new muscle car with the cost included in the financing at the end of the deal. Nickey sold entire engines and did engine transplants and other custom work according to customer demand. If it was done at the time of a new car sale, Nickey could wrap it into the financing.

A 1967 advertisement in November summarizes the frenzy at the speed shop by promising chrome reverse wheels for all US-built cars at the low cost of $17.95 each. Engines just out of Chevy engineering ran the gamut of 283 ci up to 427 ci, including Super Duty from $390 to $797. Bolt-on bars for 1955–1957 Chevys and Camaros, Firebirds, and Chevy IIs were only $39.95 a pair. Of course, the ad also mentioned an actual car for sale: a 1968 Nickey 427 Camaro all ready to go!

As an offshoot of the Goodyear distributorship, Nickey opened a location at 4201 N. Milwaukee Ave. The Nickey/Goodyear Tire Town and World of Wheels sold all performance wheels and tires, including Pirelli race tires. Nickey race-balanced wheels and tires on-site.

The Mobil Economy Runs

Aside from high-performance involvement, Nickey also entered the Mobil Economy Runs. Many race drivers tested their skills in this contest. A United States Auto Club mem-

Patricia "Pat" Sawyer drove the Nickey Chevrolet entry to victory in Class E of the 1965 Mobil Economy Run. Pat managed to squeeze 21.17 mpg out of her 1965 Chevrolet Biscayne 6-cylinder car over the 3,266 mile route from Los Angeles, California, to Times Square in New York, New York. (Photo Courtesy Pat Sawyer Family Archives)

Pat Sawyer pulls out of the Los Angeles starting line of the 1967 Mobil Economy Run behind the wheel of her Nickey Chevrolet–sponsored 1967 Camaro 6-cylinder. Prior to this run, Pat had racked up five Mobil victories, including consecutive victories for Nickey driving Biscaynes. (Photo Courtesy Pat Sawyer Family Archives)

Pat Sawyer pulls into Lake Tahoe during the 1967 Mobil Economy Run. The Sahara was a Las Vegas–style hotel opened in 1965. Note the snow in the background. Harsh weather made the Mobil runs severe in parts of the journey. This was Pat's final Mobil run. Her Nickey-sponsored Camaro arrived at the Detroit, Michigan, finish line last in class (8th), posting 22.36 mpg over 2,837.8 miles. (Photo Courtesy Pat Sawyer Family Archives)

ber rode shotgun in each car, watching drivers for full stops, no coasting, etc.

On April 11, 1965, the Nickey Biscayne 6-cylinder won at 21.17 mpg. The car was driven by widow Pat Sawyer and navigator daughter Pam. This run raised the minimum speed to 50 mph (from 45 mph minimum of the prior year) and expanded the distance to 3,266 miles from Los Angeles to New York.

The next year, Nickey entered three cars in the March 14, 1966, run from Los Angeles to Boston. More "real world" conditions on this run specified cars maintain a minimum average speed of 51 mph. To keep that average up, the cars generally had to cruise at 60–65 mph. The route also covered mountainous areas. All 57 cars in the event had automatic transmissions. Nickey's driver, Pat Sawyer, won her class once more in a 1966 Biscayne 6-cylinder (21.04 mpg). Nickey also entered a Chevy II and Chevelle SS 396 in the contest.

Dick Harrell, High-Performance Manager

In a small high-performance ad run by Nickey Chevrolet on June 19, 1966, the usual list of high-performance parts was supplemented by a brief but exciting message. Readers were informed that "Dickie Harrell will be available all year round to help you select the right equipment."

This little ad established that Nickey had hired famous racer "Mr. Chevrolet" Dick Harrell as its high-performance director. He had already been campaigning a drag car for Nickey in collaboration with Bill Thomas. Things went well, and soon Nickey hired Dick as much for the publicity as his expertise.

Nickey not only received some great publicity by hiring Dick but it soon became the recipient of an enduring legend when Dick created his "Super Camaro."

Nickey 427 Camaro

The first advertisement from Nickey regarding the 427 engine transplant Camaros appeared on November 13, 1966, in the *Chicago Tribune*. Nickey's ad in the newspaper section for Custom-Modified has the expected list of high-performance parts available in their speed shop but is headed off with mention of "High Performance Camaros Available (Up to 435 hp)."

In November 1966, *Car Craft* magazine sent Dick Scritchfield to Chicago to test drive the Nickey Camaro 427. The story appeared in the February 1967 issue. Having more than one complete car sorted out ready for sale and testing in November fits with the timeline of Harrell's recollections.

Dick commented that he and the Nickey shop got to work on the 427 program as soon as the first new Camaro came off the transport truck. Measurements were made of the engine bay immediately.

Based on the introduction date (cars were shipped in anticipation of that day), those first Camaros would have been unloaded in mid- to late-September or early October 1966 at the latest. It would take about a month to convert, test, and work out the bugs in the new car.

Bill Thomas in California was egged on by Vince Piggins to do something about the new Camaro and would likely have been looking into a 427 Camaro around the same time Dick was doing it. Dana Chevrolet also had approximately the same timeline.

There is suggestion that Bill Thomas's pre-existing relationship with Nickey (through mutual sponsorship deals in racing) influenced the Nickey move to build a 427 Camaro. If Bill did suggest the idea, it would have been at the same time Dick was out measuring the Camaro engine compartment.

The newspaper ad in November 1966 is the first dated mention of a dealer conversion 427 Camaro. The staggered cover dates on magazine tests can be extrapolated backward to derive a rough idea, but a newspaper ad occurs in real time. This doesn't settle the question unequivocally but suggests that credit for the first conversion should go to Dick Harrell.

Super Camaro

Dick casually summed up the Super Camaro by saying, "I thought the 427 would adapt well, so I tried it. It just fell in!" The Harrell version of the 1967 Camaro ignored the GM 400-ci limit on the new pony car.

When first released, the Camaro didn't even have the 396 available, but was held back to a ceiling of 350 ci. General Motors muzzled the pony cars with a horsepower-to-weight ratio that required a few less rated horsepower than the heavier intermediates. This rationale explained the upper limit of 350 ci being deemed adequate for the Camaro. Chevrolet made the new 350 engine an exclusive; it was available only in the Camaro as a way to make the SS 350 seem special. It was indeed a really nice engine, but even Ford was putting a 390 in the Mustang GT for 1967.

Nickey circumvented all of GM's limits by putting a 396 or 427 into a Camaro and selling it off the showroom floor.

Dick Harrell

Richard Melvern Harrell was born on October 4, 1932, in Phoenix, Arizona, to Joel and Mary Harrell. When his family was in New Mexico during his teen years, Dick began sprint car and stock car racing. After a stint as an aircraft mechanic in the army in Fort Sill, Oklahoma, he became an auto mechanic in Carlsbad, New Mexico.

Dick built and tuned his own race cars until 1961, when he attracted factory support. When Chevrolet ceased factory backing its racers, Harrell persisted and continued to win driving Chevrolets. By singlehandedly carrying on the Chevrolet banner in the 1963 AHRA Phoenix Winternationals and actually beating factory Mopar and Ford teams, Dick earned his nickname "Mr. Chevrolet."

When Nickey contacted him, Dick was maintaining a frantic travel schedule racing around the country. With Nickey and Bill Thomas sponsorship, Dick built a 427 injected Chevy II Funny Car that logged a significant portion of its track time doing wheelies; but it was still a winner. Dick's charisma and popularity with fans elevated Nickey's profile.

The Nickey racing experience led to a large, steady paycheck working at the dealership. His job as high-performance director enabled Dickie to juggle supporting his wife, Elaine, and two daughters while staying on the cutting edge of constantly escalating competition in the racing scene.

Nickey ordered 1967 SS Camaros with heavy-duty suspension and larger air-conditioner radiator, metallic brakes, 4-speed, and Posi-Traction. Dick Harrell and Nickey's service department swapped in either a 396 or 427.

In late 1966 to early 1967, the GM factory made the 396 available in the Camaro, allowing it to morph into a true muscle car, but this had little bearing on what was happening at Nickey Chevrolet. The 396 Nickey had solid lifters, a major cam, and 400 hp, taking it beyond the "regular" factory supercars of the day. Despite 396 or 427 status, the final car was a beast. The NHRA allowed the 396 to run but not the 427. If your car was prepped through Nickey, then the AHRA allowed it into Super Stock class.

In order to produce the Camaro 427, Nickey fiddled with fit and clearances for steering and the fan. They put a spacer in the front springs to restore the lost inch of height due to the 427 engine adding 90 pounds beyond the 350 engine. That extra 90 pounds could be shaved down when Nickey mounted headers instead of iron exhaust manifolds. Nickey added a traction bar to handle all the extra torque.

The *Car Craft* article from February 1967 described Dick's process with the 427 Camaro. In base form, the 427 was available with solid lifter or hydraulic (for street) cam, Holley 4-barrel, or 3x2-barrels or 2x4-barrels (with scooped fiberglass hood to clear it). Harrell modified the single-point distributor to spark properly at top RPM. The Camaro SS heavy-duty suspension was retained with slight mods to the rear to avoid spring hop. Factory metallic brakes and, amazingly, the stock shift linkage were also retained. These cars were also available with the automatic.

When *Car Craft* went to 4.56:1 axle and slicks, the base 4-barrel with 4-speed close-ratio Muncie blasted out an 11.9 at 114 mph. Dual quads dropped the time to 11.4 at 126 mph.

Nickey also sold Camaro packages for 350 or 396 cars: Stage I provided headers, 8,000-rpm tachometer, steering wheel, stripes, Nickey wheels, and underhood chrome. Stage II went to a radical cam, Hurst Shifter, and a heavy-duty clutch. Stage III used solid lifters, dual-quad manifolds, racing gears in a new differential, and Racemaster tires.

West Coast Nickey 427 Camaros

Nickey Chevrolet made a good connection to the huge California muscle car scene when it snagged a contract with Bill Thomas. Bill's career in California began as a dealership mechanic. His success at prepping dealer-sponsored race cars led to him opening his own speed shop at 502 East Juliana, Anaheim, California. Bill Thomas attracted factory attention and was contracted to conceive and prepare sporty Cheetahs for racing duty. This engineering and design experience and expertise fit into the plans at Nickey.

At first, Nickey's involvement with Bill Thomas centered on racing activity. Bill was an unofficial conduit for racers to get special Chevrolet speed equipment. The factory filtered it through Bill Thomas in order to disguise the automaker's continued involvement in racing. Nickey and Bill Thomas cosponsored Dick Harrell's Chevy II Funny Car, and one thing led to the next.

In 1966, Bill became Nickey's West Coast connection and distributor for parts and partner in developing dealer-special supercars. Bill Thomas Race Cars had an agreement with Nickey to build genuine "Nickey" cars at its shop following the formula set up by Dick Harrell's department at the Chicago dealership. Of course that is the official line. Each racer had his own techniques and preparation process. The Nickey/Bill Thomas Camaro 427 was one of the most memorable dealer-special cars of the 1960s.

The incredible news was that Nickey's Camaro 427 425-hp engine came with a warranty! Customers could specify stick or automatic and had a choice of axle ratios. They could also increase the engine rating to 450 hp with Nickey's dual-quad intake using a custom fiberglass hood for clearance. Cars were custom built to customer taste. Various rear ends, traction bars, cam grinds, and 4-speeds were on the list. Nickey even offered Cragar wheels with *Nickey* set in the caps.

Nickey Chevrolet also made it easy to get the car. The dealership paid any out-of-town customer's plane ticket to Chicago or Anaheim to pick up a car and drive it home.

To draw attention to the new Camaro, Nickey sponsored performance manager Dick Harrell in an NHRA drag Camaro. Dick was featured in a magazine article extolling the new dealer 427 Camaros to further publicize the conversion cars.

Nickey Copies Yenko

Don Yenko built 100 Corvair Stingers to qualify the car for racing, and he had a new problem once the SCCA approved the car. How does a small-town dealership sell 100 specialty cars? Don had a company named Span Inc. distribute them. Span was based out of Chicago and naturally tapped Nickey as a distributor of 25 of the Stingers. Nickey Chevrolet observed the process involved in getting dealer special cars sold across the country.

When Ed and Jack Stephani started selling their own dealer special car, they went a bit further by incorporating the parts catalog into the distributorship deal with Bill Thomas in California. Nickey Chevrolet maintained a huge, well-stocked parts department and spent money making sure people knew about it. In the April 1967 edition of *Hot Rod,* Nickey and Bill

Thomas Race Cars took out a full-page ad together. The ad listed parts, such as headers and wheels, as well as the capability to drive away in a 427 425-hp Camaro from the Chicago or Anaheim locations.

By the time that ad made it into print, the Anaheim connection was already severed. An argument between Bill Thomas and the Nickey organization in early 1967 rendered the West Coast racing connection dead in the water. No one knows the details, but it's easy to infer that Ed tried to scale back expenses just as he had at the start of the 1960s, when racing became too expensive. The deal between Nickey and Thomas to produce street cars survived the rift in the racing action.

Dick Harrell lost out in the fracas between Bill Thomas and Nickey Chevrolet. He moved on to a new racing sponsorship. Dick's main intention in life was to race, and once he wasn't racing for Nickey, he had to race for someone. When Don Yenko got wind of the Camaro 427 cars, he scooped up Dick to help Yenko Chevrolet pump out Super Camaros.

1968 Nickey/Thomas Camaros

In September 1967, Nickey offered a performance catalog for $1, which was refunded when you spent $5 or more in the speed shop. It was also selling the "Bill Thomas 396 Performance Handbook" for $4.95. A Butternut Yellow 1967 Camaro converted by Bill Thomas on behalf of Nickey on October 19, 1967, indicates that the relationship between the two companies was still holding up at this point despite no more racing collaboration.

Hot Rod magazine's issue in March 1968 ran a test on a red Nickey/Bill Thomas 1968 Camaro 427. This was a "basic" Nickey 4-barrel 427 configuration with Bill Thomas front roll bar, rear traction bars, and 3.73:1 axle. With a Bill Thomas 550 hydraulic cam, headers, and Scheifer clutch, it ran 12.50 at 113.21 mph with open headers on Casler slicks.

The June 1968 issue of *Popular Hot Rodding* tested the same Nickey/Bill Thomas 1968 Camaro 427 and agreed with *Hot Rod's* results: high 13s and low 14s on street tires due to traction issues. Open headers and slicks dropped times to 12.30 at 114 to 117 mph.

Although the car didn't get the L88, it was taken to a next performance level when Thomas converted it to solid lifter cam, dual Holley 4-barrels, racing clutch and flywheel, scattershield, and 4.56:1 axle. Times dropped to 11.43 at 124 mph on slicks. This was without the Bill Thomas blueprint or an L88, so this is not where a Phase III 427 Camaro would wind up. Another factor in times is that this crazy Camaro was using the stock Muncie factory shift linkage! For some reason, it wasn't swapped out for a Hurst.

What an amazing car! This Nickey/Bill Thomas Stage III Camaro RS/SS 427 dealer special car runs as good as it looks. (Photo Courtesy Rod Arnzen)

Car & Driver Super Camaro Test

The September 1967 *Car & Driver* issue printed a test of a 1967 Camaro 427 that was billed as a Nickey/Bill Thomas car. The lead-in time for articles combined with the extended cover date (versus actual newsstand distribution) places the time of this test as June 1967.

The car was picked up in California at Bill Thomas's shop from Bill Thomas's Camaro project manager Pierce Marshall. The red Camaro was built off a Camaro SS 350 platform, which suggests a fairly early conversion date. This demonstrator was likely also a test mule prototype prior to use for press testing. The 427 435-hp Corvette engine was topped with dual 4-barrel carburetors and fitted with headers. The car had the trademark Nickey chrome badges on the fenders.

Bill Thomas put a bigger front sway bar on the car and his own rear spring traction kit to deal with all that weight up front. The car was still nose heavy, but *Car & Driver* found the handling to be decent. The front weight messed up the proportioning valve in the brakes (*Car Life* complained about the same issue when it tested a Dana 427 Camaro), causing the rears to lock up early. *Car & Driver* assumed that changing to front disc brakes would solve the issue (Nickey ran all drums with metallic linings), but the Dana car had front discs and it didn't help.

The basic Nickey 427 Camaro cost $3,891, which was more than a Dana Camaro 427. However, the Nickey car came with dual 4-barrels while the Dana car was a single 4-barrel.

World's Largest Chevrolet Dealership

According to *Super Stock* magazine in March 1967, Nickey was the largest Chevy dealership in the world at that time. Ed and Jack Stephani retained their original partnership mode; outgoing Jack generated attention to the dealer while reserved Ed stayed in the shadows assessing the bottom line. Nickey vice president Al Seelig and parts manager Don Swiatek carried on with the Camaro 427 program.

A November 1967 ad stated that the 1968 Camaro 427 was ready for sale. The pattern with the new-model Camaro 427 followed the prior year, which took a month or two to get sorted out and ready after the release of the new model year cars. Nickey held back nothing and would put a crate motor L88 in your Camaro if you so specified.

Nickey also raised its profile by providing cars for contest winners at National Foods grocery store and for the annual Miss Photoflash contest. The dealership did this for several years running. In 1967, instead of an Impala or Chevy II, the National Foods weekly contest winner received a new 1967 Camaro.

Nickey once again entered the Mobile Economy Run on April 4, 1967. This time Nickey saturated the field with five entries (two were cosponsored): a Chevy II, a Chevelle, an Impala, and two Camaros, all factory stock. Nickey was really getting into this contest!

Nickey's focus on Camaro promotion is obvious. Nickey also sold Nova SS, Chevelle SS 396, and Impala SS, but its image builder was the Camaro SS. Today, many people forget that there was still interest in full-size muscle cars back in the 1960s, albeit this was fading away in the face of pony cars and intermediates.

Not many people have original photos of themselves taking delivery of their first car, let alone a car this rare and valuable. (Photo Courtesy Rod Arnzen)

Twin Holley gas guzzling carburetors sit atop the Stage III Nickey 427 powerplant. Wide open at full song, they helped propel the Camaro down the quarter-mile run. (Photo Courtesy Rod Arnzen)

More than 50 years later and not a metaphoric hair is out of place when it comes to the presentation of the driver's seat area. The only thing that has changed ever so slightly is the odometer reading. (Photo Courtesy Rod Arnzen)

Marie Strand was the winner of Miss Photoflash 1967. She received the keys to the new Camaro she is seated on. Nickey Chevrolet sales manager James Polera is handing off the Camaro on March 5, 1967.

This black 1968 Biscayne was bought new from Nickey Chevrolet in December 1967 with a L72 427 hooked up to a 4-speed and 4.56:1 Posi-Traction rear axle.

The black 1968 Biscayne's 427 engine was dressed up with Nickey identification. With only 6,000 original miles on the car, it was in fantastic condition when the second owner bought it in 1987. A repaint hid the Nickey heritage of this car until it was recognized at car shows. The extreme rarity and owner trail confirmed the stories.

Nickey's Downward Slide

Nickey stated that it had more than 700 new cars to choose from on the lot in November 1969. To get things moving, they repriced all the 1970s at the 1969 prices. The new cars Nickey listed were: 1970 Corvette, 1970 Nova SS 375 hp, 1970 Chevelle SS 396, and 1970 Camaro 375 hp. It seems the dealer wasn't going to bother with the 325- or 350-hp versions of the 396 at all!

This optimistic start to the 1970s didn't last. Despite having the high-water mark of amazing muscle cars on the market in 1970, industry sales across the country were down.

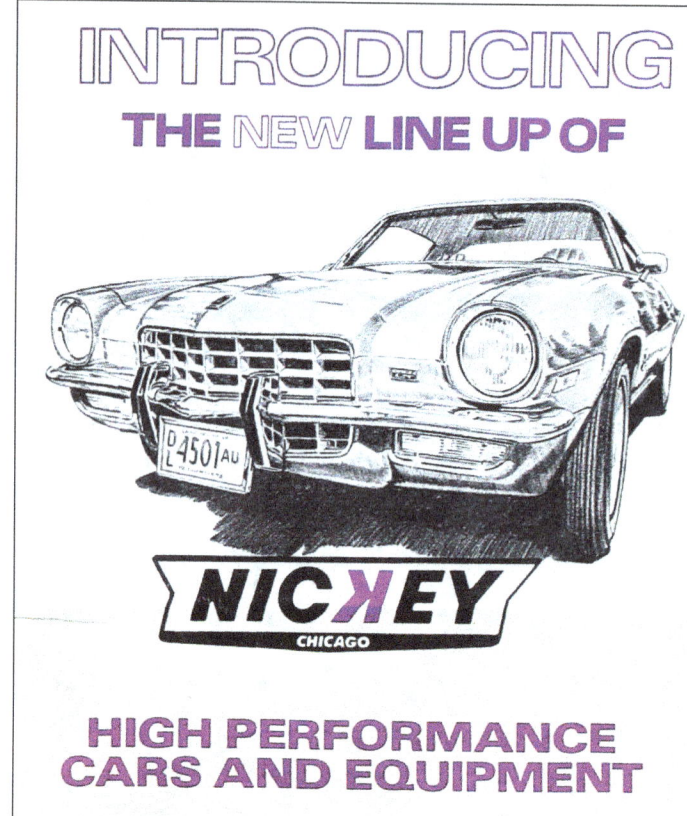

Nickey did so much volume performance parts sales that it was justified to spend significant money on the catalog. The Nickey catalog was printed on glossy paper and stapled.

A GM strike in the fall of 1970 didn't help, but the market for muscle was weakening anyway.

Nickey advertised that it had a dozen 1970 Corvettes available, some with 350 and some 454. Nickey continued with volume but the emphasis on performance faded as the 1970s kicked in with high insurance rates for muscle cars.

Nickey carried on with performance service, but the situation was coming apart. There were some amazing deals on used muscle cars as the market meandered downward. In January 1971, Rob Porter listed his used 1967 Nickey Camaro SS 427 425-hp Hurst 4-speed for a mere $1,900. A 1969½ Camaro Phase III was listed for only $2,650. This packed an L88 427 and 4.56:1 Posi-Traction. To put the incredible bargain of these prices on used Nickey monster muscle machines into perspective, a drafted soldier was selling his much tamer 1969 Camaro SS 350 3-speed with disc brakes for $2,100.

As another sign of the times, when Nickey supplied a prize car for a contest held at Goldblatt's Department store, it was a 1972 Vega, not a Camaro. Nickey was paying $100 more than book value when customers traded in any used intermediate or compact.

By 1973, Nickey was still claiming to be Chicago's oldest Chevrolet dealer, but it amended its status from world's largest to "one of the world's largest" Chevy dealers.

The End of an Era

Nickey didn't stop with monster motor swapping even when many other supercar dealers were scared off by the possibility of the EPA nailing them. In May 1973, *Hot Rod* magazine covered a 1973 Nickey L88 Nova that shouldn't have existed in the shutdown world of insurance squeeze and intense no-tampering laws regarding smog equipment. Nickey didn't take the smog stuff off; they just ripped out the whole engine. Problem solved! It's incredible that the story was published in a magazine and nothing happened to Nickey.

A magazine article triggered an investigation of Motion Performance, which suffered the wrath of the EPA in 1974. Jim Wangers was also crucified by the EPA in 1975 when his Chevy dealership in Milwaukee swapped out motors. Nickey would have certainly suffered the same fate if it didn't close down when it did.

Nickey continued to create monster motor specials up to the final instant. The last one created was a yellow 1974 Camaro LT Phase III with the wild 427 L88. The only problem was that in 1973, even Nickey with its massive parts palace couldn't source a complete L88. The team had to take a short-block and assemble it from replacement parts.

The yellow Camaro Phase III was originally delivered and converted in November 1973. It had a TH400 and a 3.23:1 rear ratio. The rear Cragars were 15s while the fronts were 14s. One month after that Camaro Phase III was completed, it was all over at Nickey.

Cash flow issues caused General Motors to shut down Nickey Chevrolet. At the end of 1973, the dealership was sold and became Keystone Chevrolet Co Inc. Keystone was later taken over by Lynch Chrysler Dodge Jeep.

Nickey Chicago

Edward Stephani sold his share of the company to Jack Stephani and became an automotive consultant in nonperformance avenues. Jack Stephani stayed the course of high performance despite the collapse of the muscle car movement.

Jack, his former parts manager Don Swiatek, and former Nickey vice president Al Seelig still owned the right to the Nickey name and had a performance heritage to tap into. They created a new speed shop named Nickey Chicago.

The momentum carried forward. Performance people didn't completely go away. The hard-core performance enthusiasts refused to cower before insurance companies and oil crisis doom and gloom. Those remaining performance people kept the Nickey speed shop alive for a few more years. The group also continued the lucrative Nickey car conversions. Nickey Chicago survived until 1977, when most people admitted that widespread performance was played out.

When performance finally came back with a vengeance in the new century, Nickey rose again in St. Charles, Illinois, as Nickey Chicago Inc. under the leadership of Stefano Bimbi. Stage I, II, and III conversions are being performed on the new factory Camaros as well as Vintage Continuation projects under the direction of former Nickey original parts manager Don Swiatek and racing crew chief and engineer Ronnie Kaplan.

The original Nickey building was torn down in the early 2000s and replaced with a condominium building.

The Nickey dealership of enduring muscle legend was built at 4501 West Irving Park Road. The block has now been renumbered with townhouses replacing the dealer block.

On the other side of Kilborn street, a fenced-in parking lot at the end of the 4400 block of West Irving Park Road may have once served as an overflow lot for the Nickey operations.

CHAPTER 13

FRED GIBB CHEVROLET

Fred Gibb Chevrolet
Location: La Harpe, Illinois
Years in Operation: 1963–1984
Founder(s): Fred Gibb Jr.
Current Status: Tire shop

Decades before Helen Gibb returned her 50th COPO Nova to the Gibb dealership building, this photo was taken of a Nova posed in roughly the same place when the dealership was still thriving. (Photo Courtesy Nancy Gibb)

Fred Gibb Chevrolet Inc. was located at Junction 9 & 94 in La Harpe, Illinois, during the performance years. Fred Gibb Jr. began his car career with a partner in 1946 when they started a Kaiser-Frazier dealership. In 1948, they added one more partner. The business later switched to a Chevrolet franchise and was eventually operated by Fred Gibb Jr. and his wife, Helen L. Gibb.

Fred Gibb may have been the first dealer principle to discover a way to play the Central Office Production Order (COPO) system, and he played the game long before dealers in the muscle car era used the system to defy the inside restrictions in the GM organization.

The original purpose-built Fred Gibb Chevrolet building at Junction 9 & 94 in La Harpe, Illinois, is still standing. After returning to a regular small-town Chevrolet dealership following the death of the muscle car era, Fred Gibb closed down in the 1980s. It's appropriate that the new tenants feature custom wheels in addition to the regular tire services. (Photo Courtesy Google Earth)

Fred and Helen Gibb

Fred Gibb Jr. was born on June 4, 1919, in Media, Illinois, to Fred Gibb Sr. and Grace Gibb. Fred Sr. was a farmer. Fred Jr. was the firstborn son and grew up on the farm. Fred's younger brother, Bryant John

Gibb, died in 1939 at age 16. Fred studied agriculture at the University of Illinois, but he didn't pursue farming. He ended up moving into town and marrying Helen Hartquist.

Helen was born on June 17, 1922, in Stronghurst, Illinois, to Edgar and Jessie Roberts Hartquist. She was valedictorian of her class. Fred and Helen's parents knew one another from farming, which led to the pair meeting and marrying.

North Side Motor Sales

In 1946, Fred Jr. and his partner Irvin Painter started a Kaiser-Frazier dealership. They did so well that local Chevy dealer Pop Cole came to them and said, "You guys are putting me out of business!"

The trio teamed up as North Side Motor Sales Inc. in 1948 on Main Street, La Harpe. The business prospered, and over time, Fred bought out his partners.

Fred Gibb Chevrolet Begins

Fred built a new dealership building in 1963. He was now operating a single Chevrolet franchise as Fred Gibb Chevrolet Inc. For those first few decades, La Harpe's Chevy dealership was indistinguishable from any other small farming town Chevrolet dealer when viewed from an outside perspective.

Fred Gibb may have been a small-time dealer, but his creative mind attracted the attention of the highest in the Chevy hierarchy. He first made some waves when he devised a very inventive way to boost his inventory using the COPO system.

COPO Chevrolets

Fred needed to get more cars to his customers at an economical price. He couldn't order in enough bare-bones cars until he hit on the solution: the COPO system. The Central Office Production Order was designed with fleets in mind. A phone company or police agency could specify special features or equipment particular to their needs and have a mass run built all identically for low cost. Fred ordered a bunch of COPO cars as taxis to get inexpensive cars into the hands of locals.

One day, Fred fielded a call from a GM executive who asked, "How many traffic lights and stop signs do you have in downtown La Harpe?"

Fred answered, "None. Well, we have a flashing yellow warning light at a school crossing."

"How many residents are in La Harpe?"

"Roughly 1,400 to 1,500."

"Ok, Fred. That's it! No more 'taxis' for La Harpe!"

Meeting Ed Cole, Pete Estes, and Vince Piggins

Every year, Fred and his family doctor went to the Dakotas pheasant hunting at a lodge owned by a local La Harpe resident. One year, Fred met Ed Cole, Pete Estes, and Vince Piggins there and became good friends with them. Ed, Pete, and Vince later went on to become key GM executives.

Like Fred, Ed Cole grew up on a farm. Ed was born on September 17, 1909, and by age 43 had become chief engineer at Chevrolet. Over the years of his friendship with Fred, he rose to be GM's president by 1967.

Elliot Marantette "Pete" Estes was born on January 7, 1916. Pete rose through Oldsmobile engineering with the Rocket V-8 to presidency of Pontiac Motor Division, which was pumping out performance in the 1960s. When he moved to Chevy, his right-hand man was Vince Piggins.

Vincent William Piggins was born on October 30, 1917. He kept Chevy competitive in racing despite a no-racing policy at General Motors. He was pals with Smokey Yunick, who was a master at bending rules. It must have rubbed off on Vince, who devised performance packages euphemistically labeled "off highway" or "heavy-duty." Vince pushed the 1964 Chevelle Z16 and later created the Z28. This all happened when Chevy was emphatically *not* racing!

At the time, there was no inkling that Fred's hunting buddies were going to open a path for him to burst out of his small Chevy dealership and unleash some of the wildest muscle cars of the 1960s.

Fred Gibb Chevrolet Starts Racing

In 1961, changes came to Fred Gibb Chevrolet. A new salesman named Herb Fox entered employment at Gibb. Herb was a young drag racer. He soon connected with the other speed freak working at Fred Gibb Chevrolet: service manager Ben Wright. Ben and Herb collaborated on a drag car.

In 1963, when the new building was constructed, Gibb began to sell more volume. Herb Fox became Gibb's best

An aerial view of the Fred Gibb dealership back in the day shows that the lot actually covered a reasonable acreage, despite being a small-town dealership. (Photo Courtesy Dennis Cumby)

Chapter 13: Fred Gibb Chevrolet 131

The new glassed-in Fred Gibb Chevrolet building and lot. To the left, a large "OK" sign carries the Chevrolet branded logo that assures customers of decent-quality used cars. (Photo Courtesy Nancy Gibb)

salesman. One day after work, Fred went to the races with Herb. He immediately became fascinated by the elements contributing to success on the track. Just as he carefully crafted a successful business, Fred applied the same approach to learning about racing.

Fred had already started stocking performance vehicles because Ed Cole had prodded him to purchase some of the stealth performance parts being offered by Chevrolet. Vince Piggins disguised these parts under bland names such as "off highway," but they were comprehensively engineered to blast the competition. Fred educated himself about the new parts, which laid the groundwork for his racing ventures.

Bob Lionberger worked his way through the dealership and saw the transformation take place. By the time Bob became Fred Gibb Chevrolet's parts manager (and Fred Gibb's son-in-law), the parts department was booming.

Bob observed that after Fred got into high-performance inventory, things went from very quiet to nonstop at the parts department. People would come from all over to buy carburetors, headers, camshafts, and wheels. Fred sold engines ranging from small-blocks to L88s. Gibb had bare short-blocks and completely assembled ready-to-bolt-in engines. All that parts department action was slowly working away at Fred's mind even before he took his first visit to a drag strip.

Racing Little Hoss

Fred Gibb Chevrolet sponsored a Red Plumb 1967 Camaro Z28 named *Little Hoss*. Vince and Pete made sure that Fred had cutting-edge parts in that car. The Z28's small 302 engine had a cross ram intake manifold that carried dual 4-barrels. That was a rare piece of equipment.

The Fred Gibb drag car *Little Hoss*, driven by Herb Fox, didn't lose any races in 1967 and set some AHRA records. In 1968, *Little Hoss* lost 3 races, but it won 30. Herb Fox won the 1968 AHRA Championship stock trophy. Most race teams take several years to inch their way up through the stiff professional competition. Cynics may point out that AHRA is easier to dominate than NHRA, but heavyweight experienced drag racers were running in AHRA in 1967.

Part of the credit for this amazing record right out of the starting gate lies in Herb Fox's driving skills and the lucky friendships Fred had formed at General Motors, which gave him access to the newest and best factory parts. Fred was also a

Herb Fox drives the Gibb 1967 Camaro Z28 to the win versus the Super Tang Mustang in Beardstown, Illinois. The Royal Plum Z28 was later repainted red to match the Dick Harrell race cars after Fred Gibb sponsored Dick. Later versions of the Z28 include the name Little Hoss on the fenders. (Photo Courtesy Nancy Gibb)

Herb Fox stands left with Little Hoss while Fred Gibb stands on the other side of the dealership-lettered utility box in front of the race trailer. Herb used the knockoff wheels from his personal driver Corvette to dress up the Camaro race car. Fred Gibb used Cragar mag wheels to dress up the trailer! (Photo Courtesy Nancy Gibb)

thorough and meticulous person who made certain things were done right. The final part of the magical record of *Little Hoss* was directly attributable to Dick Harrell, who also fortuitously appeared in Fred's life at exactly the right time.

Dick Harrell

Dick Harrell was a racer and tuner known as "Mr. Chevrolet." Harrell's legend as a racer and his nickname reflected his ability to win as a "little guy" racer when Chevrolet was no longer providing support to its racers. Dick created some very potent street muscle cars during his association first with Nickey Chevrolet and later Yenko Chevrolet.

In May or June 1967, Herb Fox had a chance encounter with Dick Harrell in East St. Louis that changed everything at Fred Gibb Chevrolet. Herb's wife, Isabel, was an avid baseball fan. On the way to a game, Herb got lost and wound up asking directions at Dick Harrell's high-performance shop. Once Herb saw two beastly big-block 1967 Camaros on the lot, he had a lot more on his mind than directions.

The Camaros had been treated to the Dick Harrell 427 conversion process. These were the first Dick Harrell Speed Shop 427 cars. Dick had been putting 427s in Camaros since fall 1966 on behalf of Nickey Chevrolet, but now he was doing work for Yenko on commission as well as producing his own stuff for customers.

In August 1967, Fred Gibb bought a couple of Harrell Camaro 427 cars for resale at the dealership. Both cars were not only 427s but featured dual quad carburetion. Dick's 427 engine conversion cars sold well and set the stage for more collaboration.

Dick Harrell blueprinted *Little Hoss*, incorporating internal engine mods as well as chassis engineering the car to launch properly. The prep work was top notch. Dick still worked on cars in his speed shop, which was an extension of his belief that the guys who went fastest at the races were the ones who wrenched on their own cars. *Little Hoss* embarked on a nonstop winning streak that validated Dick Harrell's philosophy and engaged Fred's attention. Fred was interested in Dick's take on the whole racing scene and wanted to work with him on other levels.

Racing Competition

Fred liked to analyze things and immersed himself in the minutia of the rules. When comparing drag racing classes and looking for an edge, his discussions with Dick Harrell soon focused on a golden opportunity Dick believed could close a gap in GM ranks at the strip. Dick's insights and experience finally had a direct connection to General Motors through the conduit of Fred Gibb. Together the two were destined to wring out the full potential of GM performance.

Ford and Chrysler were running wild, totally unanswered in automatic classes. The Chrysler Torque-Flite was so tough you could put it behind a Hemi and not worry. Ford had good luck with its C-6. General Motors finally had a fantastic transmission with the TH400, but it wasn't being used to its full potential yet. Chevy was absent in the automatic racing classes because its top engines weren't hooked up to automatic transmissions.

Typically, GM street cars had two different engines depending on automatic or manual applications. Combinations available for production sales dictated what could be run on the strip. A 396 375-hp engine wasn't available to customers in automatic form; hence, it wasn't eligible to run.

General Motors usually had two horsepower ratings for same displacement engines: one destined to go in an automatic car versus one going in a 4-speed. GM engines were produced with differences in camshaft specs, lifters, and sometimes valve size. Since Chevy didn't offer an automatic transmission

Matt Murphy (GMMG head) discovered and detailed this Fathom Blue 1968 COPO Nova SS 396 automatic before selling it to Helen Gibb, which brought it full circle back "home." Gibb Chevrolet originally sold the Nova in 1968 to a customer in Kansas City. This is the final Nova of the 50 produced under the COPO order. (Photo Courtesy Nancy Gibb)

Herb Fox was a hotshot salesman and weekend drag racer. Herb drove the Fred Gibb–sponsored Camaro *Little Hoss*.

with its Chevy II Nova SS 396 375-hp screamer, it was illegal for racing. If General Motors built a production automatic 375-hp Nova SS, then it would become legal to race that lightweight body and monster motor in automatic class.

Fred and Dick's Nova idea dovetailed perfectly with plans that Vince Piggins had in the works. Vince believed that the TH400 transmission was tough enough to bolt up to a 396 375-hp engine, but things were moving slowly at General Motors.

In order to get the automaker to do research and development on the combination, Fred had to take a big breath and sign for 50 cars. If Fred placed a COPO order for a run of 50 Nova SS 375-hp automatics, then the automaker could justify the development cost. Coincidentally, 50 cars was also the number needed to ensure that it was legal for racing.

Building COPO Novas

Fred was familiar with the COPO system from his early years, and he was confident he had a good customer base now that he was collaborating with well-connected racer Dick Harrell. Fred signed the order and GM engineers got to work tweaking the torque convertor in the TH400 to get it aligned with the 375-hp monster.

Fred's leap of faith not only got the Nova SS solid lifter automatic combination out into the world but also paved the way for automatic transmission solid lifter big-block Corvettes to be built in 1969. Chevy made 1969 model year 427 435-hp automatic Corvettes available, and even L88s were available with the automatic. Fred's future COPO Camaro was also available with an automatic due to the Nova engineering. In 1970, you could order a 454 LS6 rated at 450 hp from the factory with an automatic transmission. This all flowed out of that initial COPO Nova SS order placed by Fred.

This Tripoli Turqoise 1968 COPO Nova SS 396 was converted to 427 power by Dick Harrell in his performance shop. A quick glance only reveals a few obvious external clues to this car's potency: the Harrell-installed "Stinger Hood," 427 emblems beside the front turn lights, and red line tires.

Another ripple effect from Fred's COPO Nova SS order was a slight erosion of the rock solid bias against automatic transmissions inbred in high-performance nuts. By the late 1960s, the domestic Big Three manufacturers all had good quick, firm-shifting 3-speed automatics. Seeing one running at the strip had to have an effect on perception eventually.

When Hurst came out with its dual-gate automatic shifter (nicknamed His/Hers), it really seemed that 4-speeds were on the decline. But the hard-core drivers clung to the belief that "slushboxes" were no good. This belief persists to this day, where buyers will order a new Corvette, Mustang, or Challenger with a manual despite the automatic being faster.

1968 COPO Nova Delivers

Fred Gibb's run of 50 1968 COPO 9738 Chevy II Nova 396 375-hp automatic cars was ordered identically with a heavy-duty radiator and 4.10:1 Posi-Traction axles. Interiors were surprisingly unspartan. Instead of a bench seat and col-

A close look at the Nova reveals the hood pins and the plaque bolted onto the front of the hood proclaiming that Dick Harrell built this car. The Nova arrived at Fred Gibb Chevrolet on July 11, 1969, and was sold through Dick Harrell's Performance shop on January 2, 1969, to James R. Murowski in Topeka, Kansas.

The 50 Fred Gibb COPO Novas were ordered with nice interiors: three-spoke steering wheels, bucket seats, and a console with automatic floor shifter. These features dispelled the "stripper" image associated with Novas. This example has a block-off plate for the radio delete. Dick Harrell installed a tachometer on the steering column.

The heart of the Dick Harrell 1968 COPO Nova conversion is an L72 427 engine that has been worked and tweaked. Dick liked to redo the ignition and normally added headers, as he has done in this instance.

umn shift, the Gibb Novas came with bucket seats and console shift but no radios. In anticipation of mag wheel installation, the cars were delivered with plain steel wheels shod with red line tires. Power drum brakes create less drag, which is slightly better for racing. The blue cars received matching blue interiors while the other colors got black interiors.

The COPO 9738 Chevy II Novas ran quarter-mile times of 14.26 seconds at 101.46 mph as delivered. Dick Harrell had them down to 13.64 at 102.38 with a bit of finesse and slicks.

Dick raced one of the 396 Novas under Gibb sponsorship. He wasn't the only one out there flogging the cars. Fred Gibb sold off the whole run of Novas with little difficulty, some even going to out-of-state buyers.

A lot of the Nova SS cars were sold to the same people who had been patronizing Gibb's speed shop for the previous few years. The clientele of this small-town farming community Chevrolet dealership were now traveling in from miles around to get the top iron.

Despite all the excitement of racing and an influx of out-of-town customers, Fred Gibb Chevrolet remained a small-town dealership. The down-to-earth atmosphere was a welcome relief from big city, high-pressure "closers" or finance departments or other complexities. When Fred Gibb or Herb Fox made a sale, the customer dealt solely with one person during the transaction.

High-Performance Clinics

At this time, Mopar and Ford were holding high-performance clinics to sell their cars. Chevy could not officially finance these clinics, so Fred and Dick Harrell put on their own high-performance clinics. Fred footed the bill.

Fred was also paying out of pocket for the racing in the form of trucks, race car prep, and food and hotels on the road. Helen went on the road with the race team while Fred oversaw

The ZL1

The ZL1 was already a legend. The Chevrolet all-aluminum race engine was built to allow Jim Hall's Chaparral racing team to run a big-block without weight penalty in SCCA's Can-Am Challenge Cup racing. Vince Piggins kept Fred updated about ZL1 developments during the 1967 and 1968 race seasons.

With reliability established, the famous McLaren Racing team also converted to the ZL1 for the 1968 Can-Am season. Now Chevy's production engine group was considering the ZL1 as a production Corvette option. With the ZL1 engine destined to be a production item, it was fair game for a COPO catch.

The prior year, Don Yenko had tried and failed to convince General Motors to build him a COPO 427 iron-block Camaro out of a 396 375-hp base car. The automaker turned him down but did let him put together a 1968 COPO Camaro 396 with a 427 carburetor and "Sports Car Conversion" that had upgraded suspension and added a 140-mph speedometer. This made it easier for Don to turn the cars into 427 Camaros.

Don's strikeout with Chevy on his COPO 427 plan for 1968 wasn't because he didn't have pull with Chevrolet. Don received the first ever built 1967 L88 Corvette when he wanted to go racing with Sunray DX. Chevy engineering provided Don with purpose-built headers for that L88 and an "unavailable" special rear axle. General Motors was not willing to officially break the 400-ci barrier.

However, Vince Piggins envisioned this engine coming from nowhere and socking it to Ford and Mopar as a blindside drag strip lightning bolt. Putting the ZL1 engine into a Camaro would combine ultimate horsepower with an engine weight equal to a small-block iron Chevy V-8. Lower overall weight and better handling combined with maximum power equals the ultimate supercar. Drag racing weight transfer would be very favorable, since less weight up front improves the traction at the rear tires.

Factory special cars used aluminum front end parts. This engine jumped right to the heart of the matter! Another great feature of the engine is that it dissipated heat quickly so that you could do back to back quarter-mile runs in a ZL1 and not lose power from overheating.

the dealership. Then on Friday night, Fred flew out to California for the weekend racing. Selling 50 Nova SS COPO cars in a blink of an eye at full price certainly helped justify the time, energy, and money pouring into racing.

As if these COPO 396 Nova SSs weren't potent enough, Dick Harrell took a few to his shop in the summer of 1968 and dropped in 427 engines. Those Gibb/Harrell special Novas were sold through various dealerships. The 427 Novas would run a quarter-mile in nearly 12 flat. It is estimated that approximately 15 or 20 of these crazy beasts were pumped out of Dick's shop.

This was also a turning point for Dick Harrell. He connected with other dealerships that distributed his cars in a similar fashion to Yenko but on a smaller scale.

Fred Gibb continued to run his 1967 Camaro *Little Hoss* at the track. It was posting ridiculously low times for a small 302. For instance, in August 1968, the Gibb Camaro cut a 11.832 at 116.98 mph. His winning time for stock eliminator was a bit slower but still impressive at World Series of Drag Racing with 12.162 at 110.27 mph.

COPO ZL1 Camaro Concept

With the success of the racing program and the performance parts department and the ease with which he sold out COPO orders (back in the day with the "taxis" and now with the performance Nova SS cars), Fred confidently discussed an ultimate Camaro COPO plan with Dick Harrell.

Dick and Fred set their sights on the ZL1 427 all-aluminum engine. Vince Piggins had Fred worked up about the potential of the ZL1. Putting that lightweight powerhouse in a Camaro body would create a real winner. Dick and Fred were stoked. They needed 50 cars out there to make them legal for the AHRA opener held in Phoenix, Arizona, in January 1969.

The ZL1 Camaro

Fred consulted with Pete Estes on the template for the new COPO ZL1 Camaro package. The aluminum ZL1 engine was augmented with cowl-induction hood, K66 transistorized ignition system, and four-core radiator. To handle that much power, the Camaro received F70x14 Raised White Letter tires combined with power front disc brakes, a heavy-duty suspension, and a special 4.10:1 Posi-Traction unit. Larger heat-treated pinion and axle gears earned this tougher axle a new code (BE) instead of the established 4.10 Camaro axle code BV.

Fred's COPO Nova SS cars had paved the way for automatics being attached to monster motors. The COPO ZL1s were ordered as either an automatic TH400 or Muncie 4-speed. Fred Gibb's COPO color choice was limited to Dusk

Helen Gibb designed this ad, building anticipation for the new ZL1 Camaro influx. The Gibb Sports Center logo incorporates a drag racing "Christmas Tree." Quaker State Oil sponsored Gibb, which explains its presence in this ad. Fred avoided wearing the Quaker State jacket with green stripes due to the racing taboo of bad luck green. (Photo Courtesy Nancy Gibb)

Blue, LeMans Blue, Fathom Green, Cortez Silver, and Hugger Orange. The cars were all radio delete with the black standard interior. The automatic cars were column shifted.

Combining all these special items in one package for a run of 50 cars created COPO 9560. AMA specifications underrated horsepower at 430. Factory dyno tests recorded ZL1 real numbers around 550 to 575 hp (still capped with manifolds). The shipping weight was around 3,300 pounds, which equaled that of a small-block Camaro. This car was a true monster.

The ZL1s were emissions certified and, unlike the COPO Nova SS cars that were only guaranteed for 90 days by General Motors, the ZL1 received the standard GM car warranty.

AHRA Deadline Approaches with No ZL1

Because production ZL1 engines were intended for Corvette installation, there were several issues that thwarted a direct bolt-in to the Camaro. The K66 transistorized ignition system had to be adapted to the Camaro wiring harness, and the oil pan and water pump from the Corvette didn't work on the Camaro. Dick Harrell and the GM engineers consulted on these issues. A new aluminum water pump specifically

Fred Gibb and Jim Tice (president of the AHRA) pose at the dealership. Tice bought all the AHRA staff cars from Gibb Chevrolet, including his personal Corvette driver. Aside from 427-equipped Caprice station wagons, the fleet included an Impala convertible used as a parade car and by the ladies who worked in the timing towers. (Photo Courtesy Nancy Gibb)

Fred and Helen Gibb hosted the AHRA staff when they came to buy the AHRA staff cars in 1968. Jim Tice and his staff arrived with their wives. Helen Gibb served a buffet for 40 people at the Gibb home. The cars were then driven back to the AHRA Headquarters in Kansas City, Missouri. (Photo Courtesy Nancy Gibb)

intended for the ZL1 Camaro experienced reliability issues and was scrapped.

Once more, a Fred Gibb COPO order established precedents for future performance vehicles. The solutions to the oil pan and water pump issues translated to greater ease in building iron-block COPO L72 427 Camaros.

Other details snagged up progress. The COPO ZL1 cars were built using a basic L78 396 car as a starting point, but the 396 used an 11-inch clutch while the ZL1 used a smaller 10.34-inch clutch, so the L78 starter couldn't be used.

The AMA specification book detailed an 850-cfm Holley model #4296 carburetor. Low supply on the production line caused the factory to substitute a 780-cfm Holley model #4346 carburetor just to get the car built. This proved to be a hassle at tech inspection for Dick with the #1 COPO ZL1 Camaro.

Meanwhile, the end of the year was hurtling forward, leaving no prep time before the AHRA opener. The new 1969 Camaro was so popular that factories couldn't keep up. Production schedules indicated that the soonest a ZL1 car could be produced was mid-January 1969. So, Fred made some calls.

It pays to be friends with the president of General Motors and the head of Chevrolet! The first two ZL1s made it to Fred Gibb Chevrolet at the end of the year. On the bottom of one Body Broadcast (dated December 19, 1968, with "BA" indicating an automatic TH400) was a typed all-caps admonition: 9560BA SHIP 1230 ESTES REQUEST RED HOT PILOT 427 ENGINE OPT 9560BA

When Pete Estes tells you to get it done, it gets done!

1969 ZL1 COPO Camaro Disaster

The first two Fred Gibb Super Camaros were painted Dusk Blue. They arrived at Gibb's dealership on December 31, 1968, in −22°F weather, which ensured neither car would start. Fred had to get the company wrecker to pull the cars off the transport truck. Fred Gibb's hassles with the ZL1s were just beginning.

Car #1 underwent racing prep in three weeks of frenzied work in Dick Harrell's shop. Once Dick got to the track in Phoenix, Arizona, he couldn't run because #1 ZL1 failed tech inspection! Chevrolet used whatever carburetor was available on the line to finish the car. Chevrolet made good on this mess by dispatching a Chevrolet engineer immediately to Phoenix with the correct carburetor.

Car #2 was a demonstrator and then sold to a Gibb customer, which was a miracle not to be repeated too often in the ZL1 scenario.

Fred Gibb poses with the 1969 Camaro ZL1 painted up for race duty. (Photo Courtesy Nancy Gibb)

The wild plexiglass scoop showcases the dual quads on the Gibb ZL1 for a Carter Carburetor photo shoot in Detroit, Michigan. Helen and Fred Gibb lead with fill in driver Larry Sheperd to Fred's right. Far right is Gibb's body shop painter Glen Wright. Glen soon advanced to Gibb Service Manager. (Photo Courtesy Nancy Gibb)

The ZL1 performance lived up to expectations. On street tires, a stock Gibb ZL1 Super Camaro torched the quarter-mile in 13.16 seconds at 110.21 mph. With Dick Harrell supertuning, headers, and slicks, the times sunk to 12.11 seconds at 118.35 mph.

Where COPO Camaro ZL1s exceeded expectations was price. When ordering the COPO 9560 cars, Fred Gibb operated on GM's estimate that the entire option would run about $2,000 more than a normal Camaro's invoice. Chevrolet changed the policy after the order went through. Instead of absorbing development costs on specialty racing equipment as in the past, now Chevy was trying to redeem some, if not all, of its costs back on special options. This, of course, changed the price of COPO 9560. The ZL1 aluminum engine on its own cost $4,160.50. The ZL1 engine cost more than a car!

The base 1969 Camaro cost $2,786.50. Adding power front disc brakes ($64.25) and RWL Tires ($63.05) brought the final price for a Gibb manual transmission ZL1 up to $7,269.35. The extra cost of a TH400 ($290.40) raised the price of an automatic ZL1 to $7,364.70.

Having one white elephant on your lot is tough, but the panic Fred Gibb experienced was profound. He had 50 cars coming that were impossible to sell. All his business projections and cost estimates were thrown into total chaos.

Despite his very desperate circumstances, Fred was very particular about who he sold those ZL1s to. Money issues were hanging over him, but he was still concerned about what the car was actually going to be used for. He wanted them to be raced on a drag strip, not wrapped around a telephone pole in a gruesome headline.

Despite the occasional encouraging sale of a car, Gibb's problems with the ZL1 cars weren't over yet. Word was out that a fleet of special Camaros was sprawled all over the Gibb lot. Overnight in April 1969 six or seven ZL1s had their carburetors stolen. The staff had to cram 40 ZL1s into the dealership every night and pull them out the next morning. Fred built a 10-foot barbed wire fence to protect the cars.

Gibb Return Cars

As far as GM corporate was concerned, the only reason the 50 COPO Camaro ZL1s were even built was by special request of Fred Gibb. Now he wanted to back out of the deal. No one cared that it was GM's fault for repricing these cars out of the stratosphere. You bought it, now deal with it. Luckily, Fred had friendships within the organization that superseded officiousness.

In a totally unheard of move, Ed Cole allowed Fred to send the cars back! Fred was grateful for the save but still did his best. He sold as many ZL1s as possible, including wholesaling

Ken Barnhart's COPO ZL1

Ken Barnhart was an Elgin, Illinois, Standard Service gas station owner and long-time racer. Ken had read about the ZL1, but none of the Chicago-area dealers he spoke to knew anything about it. So, Ken decided to buy a 1969 Camaro 396 from Berger Chevrolet. Berger was a high-performance dealer with massive performance inventory.

Ken figured he could build his own ZL1 using the ample goodies from Berger's parts counter. Then he saw an ad in *Drag News* stating that Fred Gibb had ZL1s.

Ken immediately made a call and discovered his quest wasn't quite over yet. Fred questioned Ken for almost two hours on the long-distance call. He wanted to be sure that Ken intended to run the car on the strip and not the street. After Ken passed Fred's test, he went to look over the ZL1s. He had his choice of color and transmission. Ken chose a 4-speed Hugger Orange car (ZL1 #16), which he bought in early April 1969.

Ken put in a crate ZL1 engine that he blueprinted, did up the chassis, and started racing. He still has the original ZL1 with about 1.7 miles on it! Hassles of switching a car to accommodate rule changes convinced Ken to discontinue racing in the 1970s.

Ken Barnhart still owns the Hugger Orange 1969 COPO Camaro ZL1 that he bought on April 8, 1969, from Fred Gibb. Ken's 4-speed COPO cost $6,709 with tax lifting the total to $7,129.50. Ken's COPO has been in "Day Two" status (as seen in this photo) since 1969. (Photo Courtesy Ken Barnhart)

Ken's other issue was that he was a superfast shifter and liked to go full on. He couldn't handle muzzling his car or driving talents in the whole bracket racket. Ken left his car in "Day Two" condition. Today, he shows the car and engages in some fun nostalgia racing.

Here is Ken Barnhart's 1969 COPO Camaro ZL1 on the trailer being brought home to Elgin, Illinois, from Fred Gibb Chevrolet. Before Fred Gibb would sell the potent COPO to Ken, he subjected him to a two-hour phone interview to ensure the car was going to be on the racetrack and not the streets. Note that the car was factory built with steelies and dog dish hubcaps. (Photo Courtesy Ken Barnhart)

Ken Barnhart's 1969 COPO Camaro ZL1 looks great with Cragars in the NHRA Winner's Circle. Ken continued to race the car into the 1970s and still runs the car on the strip for fun in car shows. (Photo Courtesy Ken Barnhart)

Mark Hassett owns this green 1969 COPO Camaro ZL1 that was one of the Gibb return cars. Chevrolet flogged the return cars to known high-performance dealerships. This ZL1 was redistributed to Sutliffe Chevrolet at 1251 Paxton Street, Harrisburg, Pennsylvania.

This Sutliffe Fred Gibb return 1969 Camaro ZL1 has no paint on the aluminum intake and engine block. A turn of the ignition key results in total exhilaration. Savage waves of energy pulse out of the ZL1 at idle, promising total mayhem when the throttle opens. The car is light and easy handling. It doesn't plow into corners like iron big-blocks do.

The green Gibb return ZL1 Camaro retains its all-original no-nonsense black interior with no console, no radio, and a two-spoke steering wheel. This ZL1 was never cut up, never rusty, and retains all its original sheet metal. Mark Hassett picked up this pristine ZL1 in 1998 with only 8,184 original miles.

Sutliffe attempted to generate interest in this very expensive Gibb return ZL1 Camaro by having Bruce Larsen take it to the track for a run. Still no sale. Eventually, the dealership added spoilers and Rally wheels and replaced the rear tires that were burned to cords from various test pilots taking the car out for demo drives. In February 1971, the ZL1 finally sold.

cars directly to other dealers. In May 1969, Fred Gibb Chevrolet started shipping 37 unsold Camaro ZL1s back to Norwood, Ohio. These cars are famously referred to now as "Gibb return cars."

GM redistributed the cars to other dealerships. The Gibb redistribution reads as a who's who of performance dealerships. The ZL1s were hawked to dealers with strong Corvette sales as a duo; take two or none. Eventually, when desperation hit, Chevy was willing to ship a single car. Then Chevy increased the Corvette allotment if a dealer would take a ZL1.

Even when a dealer accepted a single ZL1, it still ran into the price roadblock and was generally unable to sell it. Some dealers removed and sold the ZL1 engines to racers then dumped in iron 396 or 427s, adding stripes and mag wheels to get them out the door.

Many of the return cars wound up cruising and street racing as the ultimate street sleepers! With Fred out of the picture, the other dealers were free to sell them to whoever wanted them for whatever purposes.

Dennis Cumby made the deal on his black 1970 Chevelle SS 454 LS6 while standing on a drag strip. Dennis, Fred Gibb, and Herb Fox were all at the Whitehall Dragway in Illinois when they discussed the order for this black LS6.

Dennis traded in his 1968 Chevelle SS 396 325-hp 4-speed. Because the LS6 was actually going to be a daily driver for him and his wife, he went for a bench column shift automatic. Of course, total price was a consideration in the option choices. The main go-fast part of this car was present: the King Kong LS6!

Racing the ZL1 and Funny Car Camaro

Dick Harrell and Herb Fox both drove the ZL1, posting low 10s and trap speeds over 130. Fox ended up mainly driving it because Dick was campaigning the Camaro Funny Car. Herb grew to hate the ZL1 and complained that it never ran right. He also said the aluminum engine was problematic. The Gibb-sponsored ZL1 was also driven by Dick Harrell team member Ray Sullins.

Fred Gibb also sponsored Dick's 1969 Camaro AA/Fuel Funny Car, which was painted to match the ZL1's race color.

The Legend of the ZL1

The COPO 9560 Camaros began as a run of 50 cars for Fred Gibb Chevrolet. That exclusivity eroded slightly when other high-performance dealers wanted in on the COPO Camaro ZL1. The extra orders inflated the total build to 69 ZL1 cars. Some of these cars had more optional equipment, but no one else ordered 50 of these cars at once!

Hot Rod magazine released an article on the ZL1 engine. A color image of the engine running on a stand adorned the cover of the December 1968 issue. Once the ZL1 engine was actually installed in Camaros, *Super Stock* magazine profiled Dick Harrell's #1 ZL1 setup for the strip plus one of the "regular" Fred Gibb cars for May 1969. The street Gibb car turned 11.64 at 122 mph with open headers and slicks. Dick's race car ran 10.29 at 132 mph.

Hi-Performance Cars tested the #3 ZL1 and managed a stock run of 13.16 at 110 mph without slicks. It was riding on E70x15s and capped exhaust with the AIR pump hooked up. This yellow car was the Berger Chevrolet car.

Dennis Cumby's 1970 Chevelle SS 454 LS6 retains the factory equipment. It ran so well there was no need to mess with it. All the 454 cars had the domed hood but the cowl induction was an extra cost item. The non-cowl-induction automatics received this chrome dual snorkel closed lid air cleaner. The 4-speed cars received an open element air cleaner. Cowl-induction cars added a foam sealer around an open element air cleaner. Note the A.I.R. injectors on the exhaust manifolds. The LS6 was Holley equipped and had to use the air injection system.

Fred Gibb gave away promotional racing jackets with the Gibb badge sewn on the left lapel. Note that Dennis Cumby's all-original 32,194-mile Chevelle SS 454 is just as pristine as the jacket.

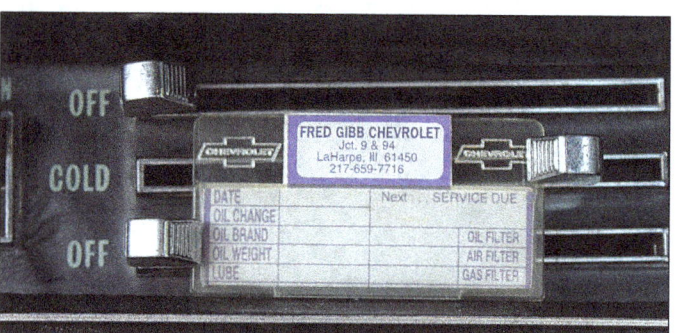

Fred Gibb also distributed these free maintenance reminders with plastic holders. Dennis Cumby keeps his held up by the heater control buttons on his 1970 Chevelle SS 454 LS6.

Dick's cars were bright Candy Apple Red (luckily the blue #1 ZL1 came with a black interior and not a matching blue interior!). Long-time Harrell shop member John "Oop" Fensom painted the cars. The pair of cars made a statement at the strip.

By this time, Fred Gibb was able to travel with the team. In the early days of racing, Fred had to stay on top of dealership matters and flew to the track on weekends. Fred's wife, Helen, had been the bedrock of the racing program in the early days. She went with the trucks and oversaw operations on the road for the first year of two of racing. Now that the dealership seemed on solid ground, Fred could travel with the team, towing the cars to races and taking some of the load off Helen.

Fred Gibb financed the racing operations. Chevrolet was officially out of racing and couldn't overtly do much other than direct the activities and ensure the right parts got to the right people whenever possible. Fred Gibb and Dick Harrell continued to race the ZL1 and forwarded progress reports to Chevy. There was still corporate interest but not rabid enthusiasm for the project anymore.

1970 COPO Super Camaro

Back at Fred Gibb Chevrolet, there were other ways besides the COPO system to get big-block power into a customer's car. Gibb's performance mechanics executed many good old-fashioned engine swaps. The small-town dealership attracted a lot of out-of-town action by maintaining a healthy stock of 427 crate motors and heavy inventory of high-performance cars.

Fred Gibb and Dick Harrell proposed a plan to build 50 LS7-powered 1970½ Super Camaros, but the project fizzled through the Chevy ranks. Chevy's engineers were preoccupied with emissions and safety tests, and John DeLorean was

Changes at Chevrolet

In February 1969, famous maverick and performance man John DeLorean became had of Chevrolet. John is famously nicknamed "the father of the GTO" because his engineering team had invented the car and pushed it through in defiance of corporate rules. Later, as Pontiac Motor Division manager, John adhered to a powerful performance philosophy. He blatantly ignored corporate culture and did whatever he wanted while releasing sales winners.

Expectations were that John would carry on in the same vein at Chevrolet, but he didn't. John was a person who focused on a particular goal to the exclusion of other factors. At Pontiac, it had been innovation (hidden windshield antenna, flexible rope driveshaft, etc.) and performance. When he was promoted to Chevrolet, John was tasked with a mission to tighten up the division. As much as he was a fan of fast cars, John went to work on his assigned priorities, and with Pete Estes gone from Chevrolet, the racing program became less urgent.

The highest factory horsepower-rated engine up to that time was released through Chevrolet under John DeLorean's watch when the 1970 Chevelle SS 454 LS6 was rated 450 hp. But John also upped the basic content in Corvettes to increase the profit from each unit. Hardcore performance buyers didn't dig the idea of Corvettes with standard power windows!

John DeLorean was trying to tame the sprawling Chevrolet division that was drowning in bureaucracy and total lack of communication. Performance engineers were diverted away to deadlines on bumper safety standards and emission work. Then the muscle car market collapsed on top of all that internal priority shifting.

trying to make Chevy's right hand know what the left was doing. On top of all that, the United Auto Workers strike nearly halted all production lines, which delayed the new Camaro's debut.

Rather than wait for the factory to get interested, Dick Harrell built the LS7 Camaro concept himself, free of the delays of factory red tape. Baldwin-Motion also made a few of these monstrous Camaros.

Dick Harrell's Hemi

For the 1970 season, Gibb sponsored Dick Harrell once again. Dick was campaigning a 1970 Camaro Funny Car. His reputation as "Mr. Chevrolet" was based on his persistence and inventiveness in sticking with Chevrolet power when the factory absented itself from racing. For the entire 1960s, Dick kept Chevrolet competitive and stayed on top of intense, highly professional racing. But in 1970, he had pushed the Chevrolet engine as far as anyone could possibly take it.

The decision to put a Chrysler Hemi in his Camaro Funny Car for 1971 was a tough one to make. It was either step back from the field as an undisputed winner and retire or go to a Hemi to stay current. Dick *needed* to race and couldn't sit out the action.

His decision to go to a Hemi incensed some fans. There was rabid brand loyalty to the point of near mania. Luckily, the majority of Dick's fan base was strongly loyal to him beyond brand issues. Dick was an approachable, charismatic person. Those who had been touched in personal encounters with Dick accepted the brand switch as a necessary evil.

Dick never stopped wrenching on his own cars, even when he was a top driver. Similarly, he could never be a crew chief or owner of a race team watching the action. He had to directly involve himself. And if he was driving, he had to win. And no one could win anymore without the Hemi.

This new phase of fuel Funny Cars was a deadly turning point. Now that Funny Cars were able to break 200 mph at the finish line, the front tires were failing. Most Funny Car tires were rated at maximum 140 mph and could withstand 200 mph for a brief instant but not more than 200 mph. At that point, tires came apart, cars went out of control, and drivers died.

On September 12, 1971, in Toronto International Speedway, Ontario, Canada, one of Dick Harrell's front tires exploded. His car hit a light pole and he died as a result.

Gibb's 1971 Bittersweet Win

For the 1971 season, Fred Gibb revived the 1969 COPO Camaro with Jim Hayter behind the driver's wheel. When the NHRA and AHRA instituted the Pro Stock Eliminator class, the first Fred Gibb Super Camaro was converted to suit the new rules. The Gibb car was set up with a tunnel ram, a dual-quad intake, a fiberglass hood, and fiberglass front fenders. The Gibb ZL1 won the 1971 AHRA Pro Stock Championship.

That #1 ZL1 was sold at the end of the 1971 season. Gibb had seen it through, but it was hard to celebrate the team's success after Dick's tragic death.

Larry Shepard campaigned a 1970½ big-block Camaro in AHRA Super Stock and Pro Stock under Gibb sponsorship. This was the plan that Dick and Fred had hatched and tried to interest the factory in.

Gibb sold his last new 1969 ZL1 Camaro in 1972. In order to get it out the door, he had to sweeten the deal with a $1,000 rebate from Chevrolet. The car came back on the lot like a boomerang when it was repossessed in 1973.

Fred Gibb allowed the muscle car movement to slide into memory as his dealership ceased racing activities and phased down the high-performance angle. This coincided with the crash of the muscle car era.

Fred Gibb (left) and new Gibb's new driver Jim Hayter (right) celebrate their 1971 AHRA World Championship win. Note the 1972 banner for the new model year cars in the dealership window. (Photo Courtesy Nancy Gibb)

Small-Town Dealership Once More

Fred Gibb Chevrolet returned to being a small-town dealership catering to standard car buyers. Herb Fox continued to work at the Gibb dealership until 1982.

Fred Gibb Jr. retired in 1984 when he sold the dealership. Fred was aware of the return of interest in the muscle car era, but a lifetime of smoking limited his ability to do much. He died on July 13, 1993, at age 74 from emphysema.

Fred's wife, Helen, carried his memory forth by attending car shows and contributing to research on the supercars that passed through the dealership. Helen had paperwork that helped owners verify cars. She bought back some of the historic vehicles from the dealership and traveled the country displaying the cars until her death at age 91 on April 20, 2014.

The city of La Harpe, Illinois, hosts an annual car show in honor of Fred Gibb. The show draws in some terrific cars and heavy attendance.

In 2002, a tribute ZL1 car was built in honor of Fred Gibb. The new car was based on a 2002 Camaro platform. There were 69 copies (to duplicate the original ZL1 production numbers) made of the 600-hp beasts. GMMG of Marietta, Georgia, did the conversions.

Today, the Fred Gibbs Chevrolet building still stands. It is the home of Clover Tires.

This October 1969 closeup view of the angled support posts of the Gibb sign reveals the cutting-edge architectural style for the era. A red 1970 Monte Carlo sits prominently in the showroom. (Photo Courtesy Nancy Gibb)

CHAPTER 14
ROYAL PONTIAC

Royal Pontiac
Location: Royal Oak, Michigan
Years in Operation: 1950s–1970
Founder(s): Asa Wilson Sr.
Current Status: Condominiums

This is what Royal Pontiac at 400 North Main Street in the Detroit suburb of Royal Oak, Michigan, looked like about 1959 when owner Asa "Ace" Wilson Jr. accepted Jim Wanger's proposal to specialize in performance. The small, modern, glass dealership was unchanged through the exciting 1960s muscle car era. Mechanic Milt Schornack recalls a deluge of hot cars overfilling the lot and parked all around the block awaiting Bobcat conversion packages.

On July 1, 1956, Semon "Bunkie" Knudsen was put in charge of Pontiac Motor Division. His mission: save the division! Pontiac sales were lost in the shuffle between the successful GM divisions Chevrolet and Oldsmobile. Although product and marketing was in place at Pontiac, there was a disconnect between traditional Pontiac dealerships and the new high-performance parts and cars that were on offer.

Jim Wangers was one of the advertising men working on the Pontiac account. He suggested to Bunkie that seminars educating dealerships could fill the gap between customers wanting to order a hot Pontiac or hop one up from the parts counter and the clueless dealers. Bunkie proposed an experiment instead. He tasked Jim with finding one dealership to specialize in Pontiac performance and see how it worked out. Enter Royal Pontiac.

Finding Royal Pontiac

In September 1959, Jim approached Packer Pontiac's Bill Packer Jr. with Bunkie's performance dealership concept. Packer Pontiac was the biggest Pontiac agency in town and would be an ideal location for this high-performance concept. Bill requested time to think it over.

The license frame on Jim Wanger's GTO is an original Royal Pontiac frame. The GTO was plated in Michigan, which is Royal's home state. Later, as sales boomed, the dealer name was modified to incorporate the owner's name: Ace Wilson's Royal Pontiac.

Semon "Bunkie" Knudsen

Semon "Bunkie" Knudsen was born on October 2, 1912, in Buffalo, New York. He was the son of a former president of General Motors. During his career, Bunkie revamped Pontiac's reliable "Old Lady" image by chasing the youth performance market. He released the 1957 fuel-injected elite convertible Bonneville in conjunction with some styling updates to the full Pontiac lineup.

Bunkie also ignored the American Manufacturers Association (AMA) ban on racing involvement from car factories. Pontiacs tore up the racetracks while "Wide Track" styling (wheels pushed out to the corners of the car) coupled with good performing 389 engines brought street Pontiacs back into the public eye.

Jim also ran the idea past a smaller dealership named Royal Pontiac located at 400 North Main Street, Royal Oak, Michigan. Royal Oak was a Detroit suburb midway between the cities of Pontiac and Detroit. Owner Asa "Ace" Wilson Jr. was so thrilled at the performance prospect that he insisted on embarking on the mission immediately.

Meanwhile giant Packer Pontiac became one of the great what-ifs in the performance world. If Pontiac had funneled its high-performance concepts through a monster dealership that also had satellite dealerships, imagine how many more high-performance Pontiacs would have been roaming the streets! Packer did get on board with some racing in the early 1960s, but not to the saturation level that Royal Pontiac did.

Jim Wangers

Jim Wangers was a performance nut almost from the moment of his birth in Chicago, Illinois, on June 26, 1926. He was street racing in his off time while working on various car ad accounts. When Jim was at the ad agency servicing Chevrolet, he hyped the Pikes Peak Chevrolet run made by Zora Arkus-Duntov ("father of the Corvette"). Later, Jim worked directly for Plymouth during the exciting 1957 Plymouth Fury unveiling.

Despite never being directly employed by Pontiac, Jim is the personification of Pontiac Performance. Fanatical devotion to the Pontiac image made him into a symbol of those glory years of the 1960s. He was in the exact right place working the Pontiac account as Pontiac ascended the performance ladder.

Asa "Ace" Wilson Jr.

Ace was the firstborn and only son of Asa Wilson Sr. and Doris Wilson. He was born in Michigan about 1928 and had two younger sisters.

Ace wasn't accepted in the dairy business that his grandfather Ira Wilson had established. In the late 1950s, Ace's father bought Royal Pontiac for Ace, when his uncle barred him from the family business. Ace's interest in the dealership was scant until Jim Wangers provided a concrete program of excitement that Ace could latch onto. Restless Ace had finally found something to capture his attention.

Building Royal High Performance

Jim Wangers immersed himself in the process of building Royal into a performance specialist. First came high-performance parts inventory, high-performance demo cars, and knowledgeable salesmen. Next came racing sponsorship to bring the dealership to the attention of performance fans. Jim's years of street racing experience and connections to drag strips and the Petersen magazine staff (*Hot Rod*, *Motor Trend*, and *Car Craft*) ensured that he would get the message out there.

Several of Royal Pontiac's staff responded favorably to Jim's input. Sam Frontera in parts got into the groove with the factory performance parts that quickly translated to increased sales at Royal Pontiac. Royal didn't just make money off retail customers. Other dealerships in the area eventually learned to call Sam for special high-performance parts.

Royal Pontiac salesman Dick Jesse enthusiastically embraced the dealership's new direction. Dick was deeply

Jim Wangers was still vibrant in his 80s. Here he poses with his 1969 Carousel Red GTO Judge in his Oceanside, California, garage. Jim had a good collection of cars and memorabilia but had to thin it down when age caught up to him in his 90s.

passionate about performance and enjoyed the lion's share of performance customers. The service department had capable mechanics who knew how to performance tune a Pontiac.

Royal Pontiac became a beard for Pontiac Motor Division to indulge in excessive muscle car mania while blaming it on a group of enthusiasts at a lone dealership. They could claim Pontiac Motor Division wasn't actually racing cars at the drag strip; a bunch of gearheads at a local dealership were!

Royal Racing

Jim Wangers got Royal into drag racing, which raised the Pontiac profile as well as Royal's visibility. Royal's racing exploits brought performance-hungry drivers to the dealership that was now stocked with parts, cars, and knowledgeable staff when they arrived. It all worked like clockwork.

The first Royal racing car was a red 1959 Pontiac Catalina with a "three on the tree" manual shift. It ran well using a 389-ci engine fitted with a solid cam and other NHRA-approved factory hop-up parts. The NRHA didn't let you run non-factory parts, so the Royal team had to deal with the clunky 3-speed column-shift setup.

When selling to a young market, you can also expect some youthful folly to encroach into things. Jim Wangers had to clean up one huge disaster involving his young driver Bill Sidwell. Sidwell was Royal's number-one drag strip driver, but he got fired when he had an accident on public roads showing off the 1959 Royal drag car to friends.

Royal cleared up the bad publicity and the legal aspects of the situation, but now it had no driver. Jim Wangers stepped forward to try his hand. The novelty of an ad man driving the car combined with a better-running car worked out really well. The Royal drag racer Jim campaigned was a huge improvement over prior Pontiacs. Jim's red 1960 Catalina race car had a 4-speed floor shifter, which had finally become factory available. The Catalina had an aluminum front bumper and a blueprinted engine built by top-notch performance mechanic Frank Rediker.

This 1963 Catalina ran in B/FX under Royal sponsorship and was owned and tuned by Pete Seaton Enterprises. Pete was the son of a GM executive with access to Super Duty parts. Precarious health frequently confined Pete in the Henry Ford Hospital. Pete's driver, Neil "Pappy" Ellis, sometimes snuck Pete out of the hospital to the drag strip! (Photo Courtesy Dr. Eric M. Schiffer)

Jim drove the 4-speed Royal-sponsored *Hot Chief #1* to an NHRA Super Stock win at the Nationals in Detroit held over Labor Day 1960. He ran the quarter-mile in 13.89 seconds and 102.67 mph. Royal Pontiac salesman Dick Jesse drove Royal's white 1960 automatic Catalina *Hot Chief #2*, coming in second to Al "the Lawman" Eckstrand, who won in a 1960 Plymouth Fury. *Hot Chief #3* was the old 1959 Catalina Royal racer from the prior year. Even with the lousy shifter, it went pretty far up the ranks of competition as driven by Clarence Walters.

Royal had an unofficial fourth car in the finals when Pete Seaton's blue 1960 Catalina Super Duty added a Royal endorsement to the side (Royal paid him a fee). That car ended up squaring off against Jim Wangers in the Top Stock Eliminator, which Jim won. Having two Royal cars at the pinnacle position certainly shone a light on Pontiac Motor Division and Ace Wilson's dealership.

High-performance salesman Dick Jesse pilots the Royal Pontiac 1963 Tempest station wagon down the strip. The Tempest combined a 421 Super Duty engine while retaining Pontiac's revolutionary rope drive hooked up to a rear transaxle, which placed plenty of weight over the rear wheels. (Photo Courtesy Dr. Eric M. Schiffer)

Chapter 14: Royal Pontiac 147

John DeLorean

John DeLorean blazed forth into the world in Detroit, Michigan, at noon on January 6, 1925. He was the firstborn son; hardworking and very competitive. He drove himself forward relentlessly from a humble beginning as the son of an alcoholic foundry worker to an executive in the largest car company in the world at the time.

John was a maverick who ignored the rules. These irreverent traits were the magic formula for catapulting Pontiac Motor Division upward in a dizzying rush through the 1960s. John took the powerful rule-breaking head start initiated by Bunkie Knudsen and later perpetuated by Pete Estes to its outer limits in his quest to win the muscle car race.

In 1973, John wasn't willing to sit pat. He wanted to quit General Motors to strike out on his own and create his own car company. DeLorean's relentless need for accomplishment and challenge was boundless.

An Unqualified Success

Jim's dealership experiment was an unqualified success. He was treated to lunch at the Pontiac headquarters, where he met chief engineer Pete Estes and John DeLorean.

John was working 18-hour days, obsessively forging his way up through the engineering ranks and racking up an impressive array of patents. He was seemingly shy, abrupt, and quiet until Jim started talking performance. Then he came alive and seemed to see Jim for the first time.

It was more than just a meeting of performance buffs. The all-consuming passion for their work was something that set both Jim Wangers and John DeLorean apart, even among the incredibly hardworking, dedicated people around them. Both men can be described as fanatics wholly consumed by their mission to exalt Pontiac Motor Division to the peaks. Both also rubbed many people the wrong way by charging headfirst into projects their own way without regard for diplomacy.

John DeLorean liked Jim and helped him with the copywriting for performance catalogs. The two kept in touch from that point forward, exchanging ideas.

Wangers Uses DeLorean

Jim marveled at how extraordinary his DeLorean relationship was by pointing out that when he was an actual employee at Plymouth, he was kept out of the action. Contrast that to Pontiac. Jim didn't even work for Pontiac!

Jim worked for an ad agency that had an account with Pontiac. Despite his supposed outsider status in the mid-1960s, Jim could brashly walk into John DeLorean's office anytime and ask for almost anything and get it.

This "anything goes" attitude flowed through Jim Wangers to Royal Pontiac, which burst forth with performance and excitement. Royal showcased all the new developments in high performance that Pontiac was pumping out. Royal also had a direct pipeline to parts. All the enthusiast magazine articles based on Royal started to create a mystique around the dealership. Royal was becoming a password among young street racers as well as hard-running drag strip warriors.

Van Seymore's Unofficial Sponsorship

One of the drag strip warriors was Van Seymore. Van was born on September 22, 1935, near Kennett, Missouri. He started work at General Motors in 1955 and eventually became involved in experimental parts for exciting Chevy projects such as the original Mark II "Mystery Engine."

Van enjoyed success campaigning his family Fords at the local Michigan drag strips. He requested one of the new factory lightweight Galaxies with fiberglass front end but Ford was giving him the runaround, doubtlessly because he was employed by Chevrolet. Ford evasions forced Van to seek alternatives, which is when Royal Pontiac performance salesman Dick Jesse crossed his path.

Van thought a used 1962 Super Duty would suit his needs. Dick Jesse had other ideas. Dick arranged for Van to get a car from the Pontiac Engineering Building on Joslyn Avenue near the final assembly plant in Pontiac, Michigan.

Van received a Nocturne Blue 1963 Catalina Super Duty converted over the counter into an HO car so it could run B stock with aluminum fenders, hood, and deck. The doors, rad support, inner fenders, and bumper brackets were steel. It had a regular production ("non–Swiss cheese") frame. The "Bobcat" appearance package paint scheme was complemented by color-keyed eight-lug aluminum wheels and wide whitewalls.

For $3,100, Van drove home in a brand-new Pontiac race car that was immediately pressed into daily driver status and racing. Although Van held the registration and title, Royal had inserted a manufacturer's lien on the title. This had shocking consequences for Van. One day, Royal Pontiac took the car back with no warning or refund!

What happened was the Jim Wangers racer had gotten dinged up while being towed. Royal didn't have replacement aluminum fenders on hand and Van's car happened to be at Royal awaiting service. Royal repossessed Van's car to allow the crew to cannibalize it for the aluminum fenders. Van was stunned by this turn of events and dashed into Dick's office in a frenzy. Dick smoothed it out, "Van, I want you to settle down. You are all set; your new GTO is here."

Dick handed Van the keys to a new red 1964 GTO. It was the fall of 1963 and the GTO bombshell hadn't hit yet, but it was coming. Van performed his own Royal Bobcat supertune job on the car, which provided undefeated status in B/S class competition. Van amassed so many wins he made a deal with the local track owners to bypass a trophy or cash for his wins in exchange for free admission the next weekend.

Bobcat Overflow Work

Van worked second shift at General Motors, which gave him time to hang out at Royal Pontiac, attending press events and test sessions. Van also helped the Royal crew pump out the popular customer street Bobcat packages. Van took Tri-Powers home in batches of five or six and re-jetted and performed other Bobcat procedures. He returned them to Royal ready for Frank Rediker or Charlie Brumfield to install. Van also converted wide-ratio 4-speeds into close-ratio 4-speeds in batches of five or six.

Van's assistance at Royal didn't pass unnoticed. Nothing was official outside of the Royal license plate frames, but Van was given a Shell credit card to pay for fuel and enjoyed access to an open account for race car parts. Royal shipped Van's parts via Greyhound to the Flint, Michigan, bus station for pickup. Van's parts frequently had red paint on them, indicating they were scrap. Those crafty Pontiac men sent Van enough "scrap" parts to remain undefeated in B/S competition. Van held the NHRA B/S record of 13.42 until Art Noey of Shaker Engineering took it to the next level.

Van allowed Royal Pontiac to put his 1964 GTO on display at the Fairground for the Michigan State Fair. A Royal salesman mistakenly sold Van's red 1964 GTO to an enthusiastic showgoer. It was shipped back East to the new owner at the end of the show. Van arrived at Royal Pontiac and found that once again his car was gone. Having his cars vaporize was becoming an annual tradition!

Royal not only sold the 1964 GTO but all of the hours of skilled hard work Van built into performance upgrades. The GTO was loaded with parts, including headers, tow bar brackets, and slicks mounted on wheels that were still in the trunk. Van was furious. Dick Jesse was perfectly calm and merely recycled his solution from when Van's Catalina vanished the year prior. He said, "Van, I want you to settle down. Your new '65 is here."

Van's 1965 GTO Lightweight

Dick Jesse took Van over to the Pontiac Engineering Building just as he had with the Catalina. Behind the building sat five white 1965 GTOs. These were serious cars with no radios, undersized radiators, heater delete, red or blue vinyl interiors, steel wheels, and dog dish hubcaps. They were ready for quarter-mile action with Tri-Power, manual transmissions, manual steering, and manual brakes.

Dick explained that these were engineering vehicles built with thin-gauge die tryout material to shave off some weight. Dick asked him, "So, which one would you like?"

"None of 'em. I can't drive that. It looks like a taxi cab!"

Van wanted a black GTO. Dick wasn't sure there was enough thin-gauge material left to build one more lightweight GTO. Phone calls revealed that there was enough material to build one more lightweight car. An order was placed.

Dick Jesse took one of the five white GTOs for himself and altered the wheelbase to create the *Mr. Unswitchable* Funny Car. Dick was definitely in hot water for that stunt, but he managed to talk his way out of the trouble.

Van's Black 1965 GTO

Van's GTO followed the standard pattern used on a typical Royal Pontiac order submitted by Dick Jesse. The correct

Royal Pontiac salesman Dick Jesse campaigned this 1965 GTO, which was one of five engineering special Tri-Power 4-speed GTOs built with lightweight thin-gauge metal bodies. Weight savings continued with radio and heater delete, undersized radiator, manual steering, and brakes. Dick turned it into an altered wheelbase car, which didn't sit well with Pontiac! (Photo Courtesy Dr. Eric M. Schiffer)

performance options were included (389 Tri-Power, 4-speed, 3.90 Safe-T-Track axle) along with some race-ready touches: battery installed in the trunk and a hood precut for use with a primitive prototype ram air pan. This was a very early version of the soon to be famous Ram Air series of scoops available from the factory for GTOs.

Van's GTO had red pinstripes matched to redline tires mounted on Rally I wheels. Quite a few options were loaded onto this car: tinted glass, backup lights, door edge guards, AM radio with reverb (although the reverb was nonfunctional; it was packed with lead for ballast), and floor mats. In what seemed to be a strange oversight, the GTO lacked the tachometer or rally cluster. The GTO was intended to have the tach and rally cluster, but because it was ordered late in the summer of 1964 the body was built the first week of September. Royal Pontiac had arranged for Van to appear at various Pontiac Motor Division Days events at local racetracks. Royal pressed the factory to get that car built right away.

The early build cars are often slipshod, but in this case the build of this GTO had been even more hurried. The job was expedited to prevent the completed car from getting trapped on the property if and when an anticipated UAW strike occurred. The haste of build was apparent when the car showed up with mismatched tires and a 3-speed installed in the car with the specified 4-speed loose in the trunk. The paint was rough, and the fit and finished were sloppy.

The official build date listed on the build sheet is September 18, 1964. The GTO was invoiced on Monday, September 21, 1964, which happened to be the official introduction date for the 1965 GTOs.

Van paid nothing. He was still riding on his now two-year-old $3,100 Catalina purchase. The black GTO was delivered without paperwork (no window sticker or build documentation). A penciled note on the owners' manual envelope succinctly stated "No COD," meaning no cash on delivery is due.

1966 LeMans Sprint Drag Racer

John DeLorean had high hopes for his new 1966 LeMans Sprint OHC 6-cylinder car and arranged for testers to drive the car in Europe as well as supplying high-profile dealerships, such as Knafel Pontiac, with copies of the car. In 1966, Royal Pontiac supplied an overhead cam 6-cylinder 1966 Pontiac LeMans Sprint to Van. Van continued to run his personal 1965 GTO until 1974, when rheumatoid arthritis prevented him from driving a stick shift.

Van's black 1965 GTO was registered in his name until the day of his death on November 12, 2005, at age 70. The Lightweight GTO remains in the Seymore family with Van's son Keith.

Royal Pontiac Celebrity Status

Jim Wangers recalls out-of-town street racers driving to Royal to get a performance tune-up early in the morning then

This 1965 GTO returned to the scene of the crime at the former Royal Pontiac dealership. Note the two tow tabs protruding from the front bumper with the Royal Pontiac license frames. Van Seymore ran in the 12s with this GTO while receiving unofficial support from Royal Pontiac for parts. (Keith Seymore Photo Courtesy of Al Rogers)

Keith Seymore now owns his father Van Seymour's 1965 GTO, which was special ordered by Royal Pontiac's Dick Jesse for race duty. This was the third of four cars that Royal supplied to Van for drag racing purposes. (Keith Seymore Photo Courtesy of Al Rogers)

What Does Your Name Mean?

Jim Wangers has made many forceful pronouncements about car dealerships over the years. During a visit with him, I was driving him across San Diego, California, and stopped to photograph a dealership. Jim groused, "Why bother taking a picture of this place? A dealership that doesn't have the name of the owner on the sign is going to be a nothing shop."

He explained that putting your name on your dealership puts you on the line. The next step is to delineate what your name means to customers. Just as Pontiac Motor Division meant a whole line of exciting cars in the 1960s, the name Ace Wilson's Royal Pontiac meant "a step beyond" the rest of the already powerful Pontiacs on the prowl out there. The name implied an extra half second in the quarter or a car length over the other guy in a street race.

Royal's rarely seen early 1964 GTO race car named *Royal's Tuff Lil' Gee Tee Ooh!* is seen launching at Detroit Dragway running in B/S class. Driving duties were shared between Jim Wangers and performance salesman Dick Jesse. (Photo Courtesy Dr. Eric M. Schiffer)

Popular drag racer Shirley Shahan the "Drag-On-Lady" was sponsored by Chrysler throughout the mid-1960s. For a lark, Shirley took part in an exhibition run at the 1966 Indy Nationals in the white 1966 Royal Pontiac *GeeToTIGER*. Royal's "Mystery Tiger" driver in the Tiger suit won the run with the black Royal car. The mechanics frequently tuned the cars to give the Royal driver an advantage over the other car. (Photo Courtesy Dr. Eric M. Schiffer)

street racing on Woodward Avenue before heading back to their hometown. Jim himself was out almost every night in the latest Royal Pontiac creations, street racing and building up word of mouth for Royal with the street crowd.

With Jim out terrorizing Woodward every night and drag strip racing wins stimulating plenty of walk-in traffic at Royal, it was easy to sell hot cars to those who wanted to win at the street stoplight. Expanding the theme further, some dealer special cars were developed to capture the interest of potential customers.

The Royal Bobcat Kit

A 1961 Catalina served as the basis of the first "Royal Bobcat." This car set a precedent for performance dealership special editions. High-performance tweaks plus unique paint, eight-lug wheels, and the Bobcat name resulted in a complete package.

The Bobcat name was quickly pressed into use again when Royal came up with a kit that was sold as an add-on option. Unlike the first Bobcat car, which had the Catalina nameplate completely removed to emphasize the new Bobcat identity, later cars were "Bobcatted" versions of existing cars. You could buy a GTO or a Catalina or a Grand Prix with a Royal Bobcat package added to it. A Royal Bobcat badge was added to the rear roof pillar resulting in a "GTO Bobcat" or a "Grand Prix Bobcat."

Eventually, the Royal Bobcat badges and performance kit could be bought from the dealership through mail order. The kit was very popular because it was an inexpensive, straightforward, proven way to significantly improve performance. The Bobcat kit supplied thin head gaskets to increase compression, heat riser blockers to ensure a cold dense intake charge, locknuts for the lifters to avoid pump up at high RPM, a mechanical linkage for the Tri-Power setup, equalized carb

Once a customer's car received the Royal Bobcat treatment, this emblem was attached to the rear roof C-pillar as a badge of honor or a warning to competitors. The badge was included in the mail order Royal Bobcat kits, too.

Car and Driver GTO Road Test

In his 1998 memoir, after years of rumors, Jim Wangers finally admitted that he went further than just a Bobcat package with the most famous Pontiac test car given to a magazine. The road test that "made" the Pontiac GTO appeared in the March 1964 issue of Car & Driver. The editors of the magazine were looking for a way to change its image from elite foreign sports car focus to general enthusiast magazine, and the Pontiac GTO served that purpose perfectly.

Decades after the muscle era was over, Jim Wangers shared that the 1964 Pontiac GTO used in the March 1964 Car & Driver acceleration tests was not equipped with a 389. It was a ringer with a 421 HO. The hype that poured forth from that article did a lot to bolster the GTO and started the entire muscle car era.

The red 1964 GTO "ringer" test car was built on November 11, 1963, with a 389 Tri-Power engine. The 389 was replaced with an externally identical 421 HO Tri-Power. As if that wasn't enough, the 421 was also treated to the Bobcat kit. The insanely fast test statistics made the Pontiac GTO into a must-have car.

The fact that Car & Driver dared compare the curvaceous, legitimate racer Ferrari GTO with a crass, boxy Pontiac sparked off a great deal of controversy. Purist readers were enraged by the accolades given to the Pontiac and dropped their subscriptions to Car & Driver, which went on to pick up domestic car fans as readers.

The controversy goes further: the test Pontiac GTO produced mind-blowing performance figures. Tests recorded in Florida on December 29, 1963, used handheld timing watches. The unsophisticated equipment helped blur the final specs in favor of the GTO. A later Car & Driver test of a 1965 Pontiac 2+2 also produced mind-blowing numbers, but these were legitimate numbers. The GTO numbers were not. The GTO was a fake!

After the test was over, Jim Wangers raced the red GTO 421 test car on the street for a spell until he replaced it with a new 1965 GTO. A local police officer bought the 1964 test car. Tenney Fairchild bought the GTO decades later. Tenney particularly wanted this car because as a young child he'd enjoyed a hair-raising ride in that exact car with Jim Wangers at the wheel. After restoration by Scott Tiemann of Supercar Specialties it was displayed at the 2009 GTO Nationals convention as well as the 50th Anniversary of the Pontiac GTO.

jets, and recalibrated ignition.

A typical ad for the kit, such as the one placed in the July 1965 issue of Car Craft magazine, garnered huge mail order response. Royal sold 1,000 kits through the mail every year during the peak of the muscle car era plus a like number installed at the dealership. A healthy number of these cars prowling the streets in the muscle car era boosted the Pontiac image.

Most press cars provided to magazine testers were Royal Bobcat cars. Jim Wangers wanted the writers to get the hottest, best-performing cars. John DeLorean, as head of Pontiac, was able to make certain that Jim had whatever he wanted. John typically ignored policy and simply misused the engineering budget to provide a fleet of hot cars permanently at the ready in the Royal Pontiac dealership.

Royal Pontiac Personnel

The Royal dealership relied on expert mechanics and drivers on the staff as well as highly qualified performance salesman and the undying relentless force of Jim Wangers driving the concept forward.

Milt Schornack

Milt Schornack was one of the Royal mechanics. Milt was born on July 8, 1935, in Detroit, Michigan. After considerable street racing experience and great success prepping cars, he worked for George DeLorean who had a race shop. George's older brother John DeLorean was the fast rising star of Pontiac.

Milt began at Royal Pontiac in October 1963, which was the same month the GTO option was announced. He tinkered and improved upon on the Royal Bobcat package, which is generally credited as being pioneered by mechanics Chuck Brumfield and Bud Conrad.

Milt also raced the Royal Bobcat cars on weekends, showcasing them at drag strips. Milt and the team traveled long distances to tracks on weekends then clocked in early Monday morning to start their days at Royal again. Milt also worked after hours on performance enhancements for Pontiacs. Many of his ideas flowed into the Bobcat packages and were directly incorporated into prep work for magazine test cars.

Dick Jesse

Dick Jesse was Royal's premier performance salesman and known on drag strips as "Mr. Royal Pontiac." In 1967, he was driving a 421-ci supercharged GTO *Mr. Unswitchable* Funny Car.

His main contribution to Royal was education by example. Jim Wangers encountered resistance among the diehard salesmen when he tried to transform Royal into a performance paradise. Once Dick Jesse absorbed every last atom of information about high-performance Pontiacs, he was able to talk to the drivers on their level. Jim said, "He could out-product the kids on Pontiac parts and tricks!"

The other salesmen watched Dick sell cars all day long. He even had a lineup of buyers waiting to order a car from him. The other salesmen began to warm up to high performance and made a serious attempt to learn the lingo of the new gold mine that suddenly appeared in the Royal Pontiac dealership.

GeeTOTiger Exhibition Racers

After making a splash initially as serious drag strip winners, the Royal racing program couldn't withstand the battering that Chrysler was giving to all the contenders as the 1960s unfolded. In 1965 and 1966, Royal shifted primarily to exhibition and entertainment as a way to demonstrate Pontiac performance. At this time in the mid-1960s, nothing was too over the top for Pontiac. Royal continued to delve into serious racing on occasion but mostly ran the exhibition cars.

Pontiac Motor Division ads were exciting and dripped with disdain for ordinary bland motoring. Until the end of 1966, Pontiac promotion was tied to the Tiger theme, which resonated well with the all-out promotion of youth, irreverence, and speed.

Royal's GeeTOTiger exhibition race cars played on the Tiger theme used in Pontiac advertising and also connected with the circus-like wrestling atmosphere of the drag strip. Examples of caricature and exaggeration abounded at the strip. Scantily clad Miss Golden Shifter Linda Vaughn wowed the crowds with her beauty alongside a replica Hurst shifter that was taller than she was. The Dodge *Little Red Wagon* derived its crowd appeal via a tailgate-sparking wheelie run for the whole length of the quarter-mile.

Funny Cars were just starting at this time and often included mock feuds between drivers. Cars had dual engines or four engines. Wild paint schemes and amusing names were the norm on dragstrip cars.

The *GeeTOTiger* cars provided entertainment between serious runs. The two Royal cars were Iris Mist and White in 1965 with paw prints painted across the hoods. In 1966, both cars were Tiger Gold but trimmed differently. One had a black top while the other had white. The cars were very fast with blueprinted 421 HO engines, Tri-Power carburetors, close-ratio 4-speeds, and 3.90:1 axles.

The gimmick was that the two cars raced against each other. Various drag racers wore a full tiger suit and played the role of the "Mystery Tiger," who raced randomly selected audience members. The Mystery Tiger hammed things up like the "bad" wrestlers getting crowd boos for being unsporting. The Royal team made sure that some of the guest challengers won the races. The Mystery Tiger would eventually challenge all comers to a race. With a bit of tweaking, the Royal cars could break into the high 12s, which left a lasting impression about Pontiac potential.

Although the Mystery Tiger was actually several different drivers throughout the program, a contest was created that challenged contestants to guess the identity of the Mystery Tiger. George Hurst of the Hurst shifter company played along and donned the Tiger suit for the final shows. He allowed himself to be unmasked as the Mystery Tiger.

The two 1966 GeeToTiger GTO drag racers have tow bars attached and are ready to hit the strip. Royal's midnight street racer John Politzer is wearing the full MysteryTiger suit with head piece on. The tall dealership sign replaces the old art deco–style sign that used "Indian head" logo and didn't include Ace Wilson's name. The new signage is cleaner and more in step with the simple 1960s' style. (Photo Courtesy Dr. Eric M. Schiffer)

The test runs reported in the March 1969 issue of Super Stock & Drag Illustrated proved that a 350 HO Firebird could fly. The Royal Pontiac–sponsored 1969 Firebird 350 used 400 heads and carb and a new cam to break into the 12s. With the air cleaner off the car, it ran low 11.90s. Milt Schornack's eagerness to tear down assured the writers on hand that this was a real 350 and not a "ringer." Milt took the car to Pomona later, but it was quickly factored out as non-production. Leader Automotive picked up the sponsorship briefly after Royal Pontiac closed down. (Photo Courtesy Robert Carrothers)

Image Issues at Royal Pontiac

Toward the middle of the 1960s, Asa Wilson Sr. was present at the Royal Pontiac dealership more than his errant son. Asa was known to be indifferent to the performance side of the dealership but didn't actively block the activities still bubbling through the building.

Although Ace was the owner of Royal Pontiac and he enthusiastically embraced the Jim Wangers template for a performance dealership, he blew it. His reputation as a wild character with a penchant for fast cars and women soon passed over the tipping point from youthful excitement and fun partying to chronic irresponsibility.

Jim laments that Ace missed opportunities to expand what they had built to even higher levels and create new connections. Jim said the business tie-ins open to Ace would not have been available to him if not for the performance publicity the dealership was generating.

Ace became merely symbolic. The concept of Ace was an icon to rally around but no longer the motivating force of Royal Pontiac. Ace became as mythical as the Mystery Tiger.

Royal in Magazines

Royal was heavily active in cutting-edge Pontiac engineering testing. A very interesting test came out of a collaborative effort between Royal Pontiac and supercar conversion partners Baldwin-Motion. CARS magazine reported on Milt Schornack and Dave Warren's prep of the 1967 GTO Ram Air 360-hp car. After ccing the top end, adding headers, and installing a Royal Bobcat kit, the ignition was reworked.

The dealership demonstrated the effectiveness of the functional "bathtub" ram air system that made the fake hood scoops functional. The basic system was devised by Milt Schornack, who kicks himself to this day for not patenting his work.

Royal took some cars to the drag strip to prove that the new 1967 400 4-barrel GTO could hold its own against the 1966 389 with Tri-Power. This test was an attempt to get back on steady ground following the GM ban on multiple carburetors (only the Corvette was exempt).

Royal demonstrated the first 1968½ model year GTO Ram Air II with Milt doing drag strip driving duties for a magazine article. That car was brutal and fast. The Ram Air II was the direct precursor to the famed Ram Air IV.

Royal's Pontiac's 1967 Ram Air Bobcatted GTO crosses the scales at Westhampton Raceway, Long Island, New York. Baseline performance figures were recorded by Marty Schorr and his cohorts from CARS magazine before the GTO was lettered up as a test car. Note the hood tach and Royal license frames. (Photo Courtesy Marty Schorr)

Royal also built the first prototype 1969 GTO Judge. Normally, prototype cars are factory builds. The involvement of Royal demonstrates how closely linked the dealership was to product development at Pontiac Motor Division. The first 1969 GTO Judge concept began when a new green 1969 GTO Ram Air IV was repainted at Royal Pontiac. After acquiring a Chevrolet Hugger Orange paint job (renamed Carousel Red for Pontiac use), Royal added spoilers and Dayglow pop art graphics and removed the ball shifter handle in favor of a Hurst T-shifter.

Jim Wangers was involved in the development of The Judge and still owns a 1969 Carousel GTO Judge to this day. He felt that it was a one hit wonder, totally in tune with the passing hip moment and refocused attention on the aging GTO concept. Journalists overwhelmingly felt the car was a caricature, but Jim said that was the whole point. Because it sold so well, Pontiac released the Judge for two more model years, which Jim felt was a mistake.

Drag Race Dealer Program

Royal Pontiac was one of the participants in Pontiac's Drag Race Dealer Program. Dealers who sponsored and raced a 1969 Pontiac GTO Judge received a second free backup drivetrain and could turn in worn parts for replacements. Dealers had a choice of Ram Air III 400 engine or Ram Air IV 400 engine and could specify a 4-speed or automatic.

The one condition Pontiac required of the 100 or so dealerships participating was that the Judges had to be painted Carousel Red. The first 2,000 of the new production line 1969 Pontiac GTO Judges were painted Carousel Red to create a strong impact. By insisting that all the drag strip Judges were the same color, Pontiac created a visual continuity with the advertisements and cars initially hitting the street.

Royal Pontiac continued to showcase exciting engineering developments, such as the tunnel port program, which was intended to be used on various cubic inch displacement racing engines. These Tunnel Port heads never saw any Trans Am racing action. The Ram Air V heads flowed too much to have any bottom end torque on the Pontiac 303. Racers did put Firebirds into Trans Am without Pontiac support by citing the fact that Canadian-built Pontiacs used Chevrolet engines. Racers exploited this fact to justify putting Chevy 302 engines into Firebirds for Trans Am racing. No one dug deep enough to realize that Firebirds weren't built in Canada at the time!

Royal Pontiac Firebirds

Royal Pontiac's GeeTOTigers were its best-known exhibition cars, but for a change of pace, Royal was given a pair of Firebirds to campaign named "Mystery Firebirds." Royal also prepped new 1967 model year Firebirds for press road testing.

Milt Schornack feels that the lighter Firebirds had more street potential than GTOs, and I have to agree, although I prefer the looks of the GTO. Firebirds have less frontal area and a lower roofline, which aids top end at the end of the quarter-mile. General Motors underrated Firebirds carrying the same engines as the GTO partly to adhere to the corporate pounds per weight dictum and also to avoid stealing the GTO's fire.

A 1968½ Royal Firebird 400 RA II was set up for the strip and magazine testing. It ran a 12-flat quarter-mile with only basic prep work. Royal also prepped a racer for Towne Pontiac Buick Cadillac located in Winnipeg, Manitoba. Raymond R. DuBois was president of the company in the 1960s.

Ray ordered a Firebird set up by Milt. Milt also purchased a trailer and set up the Buick station wagon tow car. Towne campaigned its 1968 Ram Air Firebird named *Ram-Bunctious* at the Keystone drag strip. A few months later, Milt received a call from Ray stating that the Firebird wasn't running as expected. Ray intervened with Ace Wilson and arranged to have Milt flown into Winnipeg.

Milt went through the Firebird and found that Ray's son had a Chevy pal who had tried to incorporate some Chevy tuning tricks to the car, which backfired and slowed it down. Milt got the car set up again then took Ray's son through some driving lessons at the strip.

Ray wanted Milt to hang around for an NRHA Points meet to drive the car, but Milt's wife was pregnant at the time and he had to get back home. Ray's son drove the car and won class.

Milt became very interested in the concept of a 350 HO Firebird, and the factory set him up with a red 1969 Firebird. The Royal crew used 400 heads and surprised themselves with how well the car ran. This was the final Royal race car. It still had *Royal* painted on the side after Royal Pontiac was sold but *Leader Automotive* was added at the top of the doors to reflect the new sponsorship.

Ram Air V GTO

When Pontiac lost interest in re-entering NASCAR, the only venue left for the Ram Air V heads was to bolt them onto a 400 and try drag racing. The Royal Pontiac crew brought a Ram Air IV GTO down to Miami, Florida, in January 1969 for testing by *Hi-Performance Cars* magazine and then switched in the Ram Air V engine.

Milt Schornack and Dave Warren of Royal Pontiac set up the RA IV and V GTO with a Bobcat kit, headers, and a new Schiefer clutch. The Ram Air IV ran great but the full

The Royal Ram Air V Crystal Blue Turquoise 1969 Pontiac GTO was thrashed on Michigan and Florida strips for magazine articles and then thumped on the streets of Detroit, Michigan, in Jim Wanger's stable of press fleet cars before street racers bought and sold it. Bill Schultz rescued it and restored it to its CARS magazine test status.

Note the 428 badge on the rad support of the *Boss Man* GTO. Before the engine was swapped into the car, Arnie Beswick bolted a set of preproduction round-port Ram Air II heads to the 428. The March 1968 cover of *Popular Hot Rodding* featured Royal mechanics Dave Warren and Milt Schornack lowering the 428 into place. Mike Guarise brought both men in to reproduce the feat during the final stages of his restoration of the GTO. When this car was street raced back in the day, it had headers installed. (Photo Courtesy Mecum Auctions)

First owner Mike Rutherford ordered his *Boss Man* 428 GTO as a street racer, but wanted to shut down the competition in comfort. The AM radio with power antenna is backed up by an 8-track tape player. The 4-speed is housed in a console, which was often eschewed by racers because of weight. Mike shaved weight with the absence of power assist for the steering or brakes. The factory gauges and tach are valuable additions. Mike street raced the GTO and hit the drag strip on occasion during 7,000 miles of hard roaming from 1968 until the beginning of the 1970s. (Photo Courtesy Mecum Auctions)

Once original owner Mike had exhausted the competition on the streets in sleeper status, he lettered his GTO *Boss Man*. What really ended all hope of getting a run was the fender letters proclaiming to the world that the GTO was tuned and maintained by legendary Pontiac drag racer Arnie Beswick. Arnie was famous beyond Pontiac circles. (Photo Courtesy Mecum Auctions)

Note that on the *Boss Man* 1968 GTO, the Royal Bobcat Badge is placed on the door and not the rear roof pillar, as often seen in 1964 through 1967 GTOs. Seeing just the Bobcat emblem and no Royal plates indicated a home installation job. An astute street racer would assess this GTO with apprehension. The combination of Royal license frames plus the Bobcat emblem indicates that this car had been tuned at the Royal dealership by experts. (Photo Courtesy Mecum Auctions)

Royal Pontiac Days Are Numbered

In February 1969, John DeLorean departed Pontiac for Chevrolet. As soon as John was out of Pontiac, the press cars and experimental factory cars ceased to flow into Royal Pontiac from Pontiac Motor Division. John wanted to take Jim Wangers with him, despite Jim being employed at a freelance advertising agency.

Jim was suddenly a nonentity at Pontiac and needed to find a new path. He receded from the Royal Pontiac milieu and sadly watched everything built up in the 1960s dribble away. By this time, Ace Wilson was perpetually missing in action and his father Asa was forced to stand in for him to deal with the daily operations. Performance days were numbered at Royal.

A ray of hope appeared when Royal Pontiac was sold to George DeLorean in May 1969. George was John DeLorean's younger brother and was a drag racer running a race shop named Leader Automotive. George was a serious case. Consider this: George Delorean received one of the four 427 SOHC-powered factory A/FX cars produced in 1965. The others went to "Dyno" Don Nicholson, Arnie "the Farmer"

potential of the Ram Air V was not revealed because the engine spun a bearing in testing.

Royal's blue Bobcat Ram Air V Florida test car later ran blistering fast 11.70s at Detroit Dragway. It was street driven then rescued by Bill Schultz, who restored it. A second Ram Air V was built through Royal and its Espresso Brown paint job featured the same "Bobcat" white accents used on the blue car. Both the Royal RA V cars miraculously survived through the years and were on display at the 2009 GTO Convention in Dayton, Ohio.

It is known some other Ram Air V cars were put together using parts that were available through service centers, but the Royal cars were the ones that actually reached the public mind via the magazine stories.

Beswick, and Hayden Proffitt. George's *Chargin' Cyclone* was sponsored by Stu Evans Lincoln-Mercury.

George's hard-core racing perfectionist personality prevented him from making the transition to building streetable compromise cars. Old faithful Royal mechanics Milt Schornack and Dave Warren had to move on and set up their own businesses that catered to the needs of street racers.

Royal Pontiac Sold

Royal was sold and renamed Bob Schaffo Pontiac in 1970. Bob Shaffo was a Denver, Colorado, Chevrolet dealer. The dealership quickly changed hands once more and became Jim Fresard Pontiac, expanding to include Buick and GMC franchises. Fresard occupied the old Royal location until 2008.

Ace Wilson Jr. died of throat cancer on March 18, 1984. His father, Asa Wilson Sr., was still alive and well to see the revival of interest in the muscle car years. Despite his peripheral involvement in the dealership back in the 1960s and lack of performance interest, he was amenable to attending Pontiac car shows to share memories with fans of the dealership. Asa died on September 3, 1995, at age 95.

Jim Wangers maintains a collection of hot Pontiacs at his retirement headquarters in Oceanside, California. Jim's version of retirement revolves around a major travel schedule with heavy participation in Pontiac car shows, interviews, a revival of the GeeTOTiger, and various other projects.

Jim's collection of cars includes a formerly white (repainted red) 1965 Pontiac GTO Tri-Power cloned into a Bobcat with authentic Royal license plate frames and functional Ram Air. Jim also owns an Oshawa, Ontario, Carousel Red 1969 GTO Judge. He lamented that he didn't keep any of the dozens of cars that passed through his hands during the Royal Pontiac days of the 1960s. As he explained to me, "Pontiac kept coming out with newer and more exciting cars all the time. I kept upgrading and never kept anything!"

Mike Rutherford ordered this 1968 GTO through Royal Pontiac. Mike's friend, drag racing legend Arnie Beswick, didn't have time to swap in a 428 425-hp engine. Luckily, Royal was up to the task! After extensive street racing in sleeper status, Mike had the "Boss Man" and "Tuned by Arnie Beswick" lettering applied to the car. Collector Mike Guarise bought the car in 1999. His restoration reproduced the "post sleeper" lettering. (Photo Courtesy Mecum Auctions)

CHAPTER 15
BILL KNAFEL PONTIAC

Bill Knafel Pontiac
Location: Akron, Ohio
Years in Operation: 1959–1975
Founder(s): William John "Bill" Knafel
Current Status: Occupied

The Bill Knafel Pontiac dealership in the mid-1960s has a line of the stacked headlight Pontiacs lining the street. Pontiac's headlight design was copied by Ford. Note the "Indian head" side profile logos, which represents Chief Pontiac for whom the division is named. (Photo Courtesy Knafel Family Archives)

Bill Knafel Pontiac Inc. was located on 956 South Main Street, Akron, Ohio. The Knafel dealership originated as Conn Pontiac. Knafel Pontiac became one of the largest volume Pontiac dealerships and placed within the top 10 percent of Pontiac dealerships for more than 20 years.

Conn Pontiac

The Conn family set up some solid dealerships. Conn Ford in Cuyahoga Falls was still in business under that name in the 1960s. John D. Anderson was born about 1895 and worked his way up to vice president and general manager of Conn Pontiac during the 1940s. In August 1949, John bought the business, which was well supplied with up-to-date equipment and parts.

John kept the Anderson Pontiac location up to date, and it was thriving when he retired. After his retirement, the Anderson dealership became even bigger and much more famous under the ownership of Bill Knafel.

William John "Bill" Knafel was born on August 3, 1926. After serving in the US Navy during World War II, he embarked on a busy career spawning many dealerships, a racing team, and various other businesses. He also wrote a training manual for salesmen. Somehow, he found time to get married to Janet Bolin in 1952 and start a family during this whirlwind of activity.

Knafel Anderson Pontiac

When Bill bought the successful Pontiac dealership, he at first retained the name for continuity sake. On August 27, 1959, he incorporated as Bill Knafel Pontiac Oldsmobile Inc. This corporation was cancelled in 1963. The dealership became publicly known as Knafel's Anderson Pontiac in 1963 to ease customers into the transition. On September 15, 1964, the dealership was officially renamed Bill Knafel Pontiac Inc.

Bill Knafel was friends with Pontiac's general manager Elliott M. "Pete" Estes in the early 1960s. When John DeLorean rose to general manager, he also got to know Bill. Bill's dealership was always a high-volume place, but what really made Pontiac executives take notice was his comprehensive racing team and strong promotion powers.

Arlen Vanke piloted the Knafel Pontiac *Tin Indian III* 1963 Catalina on May 5, 1963, at Quaker City Dragway. Arlen won the day with a best run of 12.26 seconds at 115.68 mph. Arlen predicted 11s and 120 mph on faster tracks. Note the stock front wheel tire combo and utilitarian paint job. Soon Knafel cars would be known for their dazzling paint jobs and matched mags.

The Royal Ram Air V Crystal Blue Turquoise 1969 Pontiac GTO was thrashed on Michigan and Florida strips for magazine articles and then thumped on the streets of Detroit, Michigan, in Jim Wanger's stable of press fleet cars before street racers bought and sold it. Bill Schultz rescued it and restored it to its *CARS* magazine test status.

Bill Knafel saw a good publicity angle for the dealership and offered Arlen Vanke and Bill Abraham a nice package deal: Arlen got a job as a service manager and Bill was in charge of the Performance Sales Division at the dealership. The big part of the deal was heavy sponsorship and promotion of their racing activities. In 1962, the famous name *Tin Indian* was adopted for a series of Knafel-sponsored Pontiacs.

Bill Knafel Pontiac Racing

Bill's Pontiac racing sponsorship began in 1959 with a Catalina station wagon. Things got exciting when Arlen Vanke joined the team. Bill was in his office when he overheard local racer Arlen Vanke inquiring about a 421 Super Duty sitting on an engine stand near the parts department in Knafel Pontiac. Bill roped Arlen into his office and convinced him to order a Red 1962 Pontiac Super Duty Catalina.

Arlen was a gifted mechanic. When his 1962 Catalina arrived at Knafel's, he quickly prepped it and got racing in partnership with Bill Abraham. Bill Knafel followed Arlen's and Bill's progress at the strip and was impressed.

Bill Knafel retained the Anderson name for his dealership until 1964. Knafel placed this ad on November 5, 1963, to promote the new 1964 model GTO. Pontiac had just printed up promotional pictures of the GTO. Knafel was one of the first dealers to jump on this exciting forerunner of the mass muscle car explosion to come.

Arlen Vanke

Arlen Louis Vanke was born in 1936 in Barberton, Ohio, to Louis and Vilge Vanke. Arlen's racing started just like all racers usually did: by sneaking his mom's car to the track. In Arlen's case, he destroyed the transmission in his mom's brand-new car at the track. Arlen's old man was pretty blasé: "It's Tuesday, your mother don't need the car 'til Friday."

Arlen Vanke and Bill Abraham campaigned the 1962 Super Duty Catalina and a cool-looking 1962 Catalina convertible named *Black Whirlwind*. In 1963, Arlen drove a silver 1963 Super Duty Catalina named *Tin Indian III*.

Bill Knafel was serious about selling hot cars, and his performance division stocked supertuned Pontiacs. The 1964 Pontiac GTO option had barely been out for any time at all (most estimates place release date in mid-October 1963) and was a bit of an "invisible option" deliberately omitted from the sales catalogs. Already on November 5, 1963, Knafel had GTOs in stock and was pushing the "first muscle car" hard.

Bill went heavy on everything. He didn't soft pedal his performance sales manager, promoting Bill Abraham as "Mr. National Champion and Mid-American Record Holder." When Arlen drove *The Papoose I*, which was a Tempest station wagon, Bill Knafel wasn't shy about declaring the team's winnings to the world. He took out an advertisement when Arlen set a new AFX record on September 29, 1963, at the NHRA meet in Alton, Illinois. The Knafel Tempest ran the quarter-mile in 11.81 seconds at 125.50 mph.

Arlen Vanke left Knafel Pontiac in 1963 for various reasons. He didn't like the racing configurations in the Tempests and he was intrigued by the strong factory sponsorship coming from Plymouth. He figured he could set himself up with some winning Plymouths and rope in sponsorship just like he did when he ran his Catalina and drew in the Knafel sponsorship.

Next, Knafel Pontiac sponsored Arnie Beswick in the *Grocery Getter* 1963 Tempest wagon. Arnie set a new NASCAR record at Daytona Beach in March 1964 with a 11.41-second quarter-mile run at 124.5 mph.

Bill Knafel wasn't afraid to spend on racing. He was a big picture kind of guy and had to be the best at anything he did. This desire to dazzle was also reflected in his personal style. As soon as the dealership was humming, Bill wore a 1959 Bulova Beau Brummel 23-jewel 14-karat wristwatch. Bill was often pictured in tailored safari suits.

Just as Bill put across a statement with his personal style, he similarly wanted his cars to be the flashiest and his team to stand out. In contrast to the early Knafel entries, which had rudimentary lettering, the later race cars were custom painted and created a sensational effect. The team eventually had two transport trucks, three airplanes, and a motor home. Of course, the dealership was completely equipped with cutting-edge engine, body, and chassis shops. Bill personally loved publicity, but he was also savvy at business and translated that huge cash outlay into to a very successful bottom line.

Knafel Racing Clinics and TV Show

In the early days, Bill Knafel continued to fully finance his program from his own pocket. He was running multiple cars each season and predictably winning a few Stock class championships most years. Never a man to do something halfway, Bill already had a 1964 Pontiac GTO being prepped for stock class in March 1964, before the real mania had hit across the country. He was ahead of his time with latest trends.

Bill bolstered his racing team's exposure with performance clinics in the dealership, despite General Motors strictly withholding any money from anything related to performance. Knafel picked up the bill for all these performance-oriented promotions.

Bill sponsored "Bill Knafel Day" at Dragway 42, giving out prizes to top eliminators (helmets, jackets, racing oil, ignition kits, etc.) in addition to the regular cash prizes being

The Vanke Way

Arlen preferred prepping his cars using a big car axle and 421 Super Duty with 4-speed. Arlen used this setup for his *Running Bear* Tempest, which he ran as an independent. His Tempest racer started life as a 326 and dispensed with the rope drive and transaxle. Vanke used an aluminum front end and plexiglass windows to lighten the load. Vanke did it his way and Bill Knafel did it his way, running a transaxle under the dealer sponsorship.

Arlen Vanke admitted that although he clashed with Bill Knafel, the fact is that Knafel's huge personality translated into massive spending on racing. Knafel's gigantic budgets allowed Arlen to do things he couldn't otherwise have done on his own. The two men were equally hardheaded about things, which resulted in Vanke doing his own thing for a few years.

The crux of their disagreements also flowed from differing basic perspectives. Bill was a showman, and although he loved competition for its own sake (he also sponsored sports teams), he never failed to grasp the importance of promotion. Arlen was a purist racer. Each was correct in his approach for what he wanted to do, but neither would bend to the other.

Arlen Vanke went on to make a mark with Max Wedge and Hemi Plymouths. He was so good at tuning that his name became slang in Mopar circles. A Hemi tweaked right was "Vanked."

awarded by the strip. Dragway 42 was located 1 mile north of West Salem, Ohio, on Route 42. This was the local strip where Bill Knafel ran so many of his cars.

Bill also got his message out there with his own local TV show called *Knafel Pontiac at Dragway 42*. In his ads, Bill asserts that "GM is completely out of racing and does not build racing components. Ford and Chrysler are spending millions in order to obtain the performance image. Bill Knafel's Anderson Pontiac Inc. Racing Team is self-financed and engineered."

This was absolutely true at the time. Pontiac was ordered by General Motors to cease with its Super Duty parts and pretty much went underground with its performance program, channeling it into street machines for dealership floor plans.

Knafel Versus Royal

The closest rival to Knafel was the factory-fed Royal Pontiac in Michigan, which also had a race program. With Jim Wangers at the helm, Royal enjoyed a continuous stream of magazine coverage through his media connections. Royal Pontiac served as the factory test bed for performance pieces often reported in magazines touting the latest developments coming through Pontiac engineering (or from the dealership mechanical whiz kids).

The great exposure Royal received was rumored to have stung the Knafel organization, which felt left out of the loop. Being in personal and geographic proximity to the Pontiac Motor Division also gave Royal an edge despite Ace Wilson's reputation for meager racing investment.

Bill Knafel was a guy who made his mark and he did become well known to upper executives in Pontiac. An early Knafel collaboration with Pontiac occurred when Bill was tapped by the Pontiac division to help raise visibility of John DeLorean's labor of love: the Tempest Sprint Six OHC. In later years, Bill enjoyed access to engineering prototype equipment such as the Ram Air V parts that went into the Knafel 1970 Judge drag car.

Mystery Tornado II

Bill Knafel's *Mystery Tornado II* race car is a mostly forgotten overhead cam straight 6-cylinder 1966 Tempest. Bill campaigned the OHC as a favor to John DeLorean, who was head of Pontiac Motor Division. The OHC 6 was an unjustly overlooked DeLorean pet project. The race car did well but was overshadowed by the tremendous fame descending on the 1966 Bill Knafel *Tin Indian V* GTO that year.

The *Mystery Tornado II* was enlisted to help Pontiac sell the public on its new fiberglass-reinforced, neoprene-impregnated nylon fabric timing belt. If it could stand up to full throttle race action, that would really show how tough it was.

The Knafel-sponsored 1966 LeMans Convertible Sprint Six won NHRA Winternationals. Knafel's GTO drag strip season in 1966 was spectacular and overshadowed the Sprint Six. Even today, the OHC 6 Sprint Six cars are still unfortunately fairly obscure, despite a small dedicated group of owners who promote and preserve these very cool cult cars.

1966 Tin Indian V

When Arlen Vanke was offered a couple of GTOs to race in late 1965 by Bill Knafel, he came back to the Knafel team. *Tin Indian V* was a Cameo Ivory 1966 GTO hardtop with black interior. The car was ordered with 389 Tri-Power, heavy-duty cooling, close-ratio 4-speed, 4.33:1 Safe-T-Track axle, metallic brakes, ride and handling package, Rally gauges, radio and heater delete, custom sport steering wheel, and tinted windshield.

Arlen ran as low as 12.22 in his blueprinted 389 GTO, which competed in C/Stock in NHRA and BB/Stock in NASCAR. In an ironic moment, Arlen came head to head with his old car and teammate Bill Abraham in the 1963 Plymouth wagon at the NASCAR Winternationals at Daytona. Arlen beat his old car and teammate in his new GTO.

Bill Knafel Pontiac displayed two of its race cars in conjunction with its sponsor Quaker State. The Pontiac GTO and the Acadian in the background were part of Knafel/Quaker State "Beat the Champion" exhibition racing, and campaigned by "Doc" Dixon. This GTO has a black body and a white roof, which reverses the paint scheme of the famous winning 1966 GTO run by Knafel. This GTO was the backup car known as the *Tin Indian Twin*. (Photo Courtesy Todd R Wingerter)

Knafel wanted to cover as many classes as possible and hence ran a Canadian-built 1967 Pontiac Acadian that was a Canadian exclusive version of the Chevy II. The great success of Knafel's GTO overshadowed this interesting niche car that features modifications such as a Chevy 427, hood scoop, hood pins, and tow bars. Canadian Pontiacs used Chevrolet drivetrains, which made the 427 "legal" or at least "correct" for this car. (Photo Courtesy Todd R Wingerter)

The *Tin Indian* GTO won 27 trophies in 1966, but Arlen Vanke went his own way once again in late summer 1966. He was put off by Knafel's new deal with Quaker State. Bill Knafel already had Hurst and Firestone as sponsors. When Bill brokered a sponsorship deal with Quaker State for exhibition-style racing, the program didn't appeal to Arlen. Arlen was also offered a factory sponsorship from Plymouth and decided to go back to Plymouth and "real" racing. Quaker State featured the Knafel *Tin Indian* racer in its ads, which was a typical Bill Knafel "win-win" outcome.

At this point, Royal Pontiac was also doing mainly exhibition racing with its GeeTO Tigers, which pitted the Mystery Tiger driver against local audience members. Exhibition racing accomplished great promotional work for both Royal and Knafel, but for a hardcore racer like Arlen, it was just fluff.

Larry "Doc" Dixon Drives for Knafel and Quaker State

Larry "Doc" Dixon became the new Knafel driver for the *Tin Indian V*. Larry drove for about a dozen Quaker State–sponsored events. Al Pierce from Pontiac put on a "Beat the Champion" promotion with Quaker State. Knafel took two cars on the road. Each racetrack chose a local driver to compete against Doc. He had the phrase, "You've Just Been

Saved and restored back to exhibition racing status, the 1966 Pontiac GTO as run by Larry "Doc" Dixon features a typical Knafel Pontiac elaborate paint job. Note the matching Keystone mags that give the car a finished look. Many utilitarian racers mixed mags or used plain steelies. Bill Knafel was just as concerned with presentation as performance. (Photo Courtesy Don Keefe)

Quaker State ads were everywhere in car magazines of the day. This Knafel *Tin Indian* ad appeared on page 2 of *Car and Driver* in July 1967. The ad copy is attributed to Bill Knafel, and based on its enthusiastic synopsis of Knafel racing action, it sounds like Bill's authentic voice.

Bill Knafel Pontiac ran so many cars under the "Tin Indian" banner that Bill humorously named this 1968 Firebird 400 Another Tin Indian, seen here at Dragway 42 in West Salem, Ohio. Knafel ran this car on the strip in SS/E before taking a hiatus from racing for a while. Note the signature Bill Knafel style: matched Keystone mag wheels and the mylar reflective Knafel lettering. Aside from creating a great image, the consistency of the Knafel cars presented a united front in the public's eye. (Photo Courtesy Todd R Wingerter)

Doc-Tored" painted on the rear decklid to ensure those who got beaten by Larry "Doc" Dixon remembered who showed them the taillights.

Doc drove for Knafel Pontiac from 1966 to 1968 until the Knafel team quit for a year and a half. He returned to running Mopars when Knafel shut down the racing. Knafel racer Bill Abraham was killed in a car accident. This tragedy took the wind out of everyone's sails.

The most successful and best known racer in Knafel history, the *Tin Indian V* GTO, was found and restored by collector Merle Green Jr.

Knafel's Golden Sabre RA V GTO

The Golden Sabre RAV GTO was a special dealership car reportedly built by Knafel in model year 1969. It is possible that only a prototype was built with no other cars produced because of cost. There were supposed to be 12 built; however, none have appeared after all these years. The cars could have existed and simply been destroyed by the road salt of Ohio and vanished into junkyards.

Knafel 1970 Magnum 400

Knafel's second dealership specialty car was a minor local hit. Bill named his dealer creation the Magnum 400. Bill's Magnum 400 was a 1970 Tempest aimed at the Plymouth Road Runner strippo concept. In a sense, this car is also Bill's version of a COPO car since he got the factory to build at least 50 copies of a performance car that was not officially available.

To this day, none of the original Knafel Magnum 400 cars have appeared. Both Bill Knafel's Magnum 400 and the later release of the GT-37 from Pontiac were essentially a revival of the Pontiac engineering *ET* concept car. ET is short for elapsed time, which is the amount of time it takes to run a car down the dragstrip. Pontiac engineering created the ET as a low-budget 1968 Tempest 350 HO supercar answer to the Road Runner. Pontiac division head John DeLorean shot down the ET concept because it lacked a 400 motor.

The ET Carousel Red Pontiac concept car morphed from a bare-bones econo 350 car into the top-level expensive GTO with spoilers and a Ram Air III 400 engine as standard equipment. John DeLorean renamed it The Judge.

Pontiac T-37 Spawns GT-37

When DeLorean was promoted to Chevrolet in 1970, Pontiac was quick to implement some ideas that DeLorean forbade during his reign, including the reappearance of budget cars. DeLorean was a firm believer in positioning Pontiac above Chevrolet as an upscale and exciting performance-oriented division. Soon after DeLorean was gone, his carefully established hierarchy experienced a shakeup with the 1970 Pontiac budget entry named T-37 becoming briefly one of the cheapest GM intermediates on the market.

The T-37 became the basis for the performance-oriented GT-37 announced on May 15, 1970. It was a good platform for the launch of a new budget supercar. Lacking the GTO heavy Endura front end, the T-37 was a lighter starting point than the plush GTO platform. And the GT-37 was cheap.

The 1970½ GT-37 was a decent platform for budget people to work with. GT-37s came with a Hurst 3-speed heavy-duty floor shift, G70-14 white letter tires on Rally II wheels, stripes, hood pins, ride and handling package, and dual exhaust routed through rear valance. All you had to do was add an engine.

The 1970½ Pontiac GT-37 came standard with a 350 2-barrel 255-hp engine, which forced buyers to option out a bigger engine. The optional 400 4-barrel 345-hp engine was top dog for the first version of the GT-37.

T-37

T stands for "Tempest," which was the base intermediate Pontiac model of the time. The 37 is the Pontiac internal code for hardtop. Small items were stripped out of the T-37 to drop the price. But stripping also reduces weight, which is great for performance.

Bill Knafel previewed his dealer-special Magnum 400 on December 18–20, 1969. Look close and you can make out the "Magnum 400" lettering on the leading edge of the fender. Note that the Magnum is built on the two-door post platform for lower cost and lighter weight. Bill added enticement to the preview by featuring his sponsored driver Norm Tanner.

Magnum Surpasses GT-37

Bill Knafel beat the factory to the econo supercar punch—and he had a better car, too. Knafel's 1970 Magnums were released December 18, 1969, a full five months before Pontiac released the GT-37. The Knafel Magnum 400 was true to Pontiac's original Road Runner fighting ET concept but with the big engine already in place. Knafel not only had cubic inches but also had big valves and high-lift camshaft because his 400 was actually the GTO 400, not the 345-hp LeMans engine that was the option ceiling for a GT-37.

Bill Knafel held a three-day preview of the Magnum at his dealership from December 18 through 20. He was quoted as boasting that he sold 37 of the 50 cars in one night. Despite other sources quoting $3,200, Knafel stated in every ad from October 1969 through the following summer of 1970 that the Magnum cars sold for a super budget price of $2,995.

The Bill Knafel touch is evident in the wonderful hype he wrote about his new creation: "Magum 400 means a super lightweight 3,200-pound high-performance package of explosives.... Load your shotgun with our Magnum 400 and you'll be able to bag those asphalt animals such as the Mustang pony or the screaming Cougar..."

The Magnum 400 "Motion Machines" had supertuned GTO 400s with chromed air cleaner and valve covers. The Magnum was based on the inexpensive 1970 Tempest platform that was not available with the GTO 400. Bill convinced the factory to build him Tempests with a 400 4-barrel 350-hp GTO base engine.

The Magnum's base engine beat the best the GT-37 could do in 1970. Bill Knafel played this up by exclaiming that his Magnum 400 was "specially built for Knafel Pontiac." Bill hooked the Magnum 400 up to a Hurst-shifted M21 close-ratio 4-speed with a heavy-duty clutch, and Safe-T-Track 3.90:1 rear axle. The base Hurst-shifted transmission in the GT-37 was a 3-speed.

The Magnum package included a heavy-duty radiator, GTO ride and handling package, and raised white letter Uniroyal tires on Rally II wheels. To jazz it up, Knafel applied a 1969 Judge stripe combined with its own color-matched decal on the front fenders that announced this was a Magnum 400.

Inside the Magnum was a bargain-basement bench seat and no frills. There were 50 made. Of course, Knafel's Performance Department could hop up your Magnum with factory or aftermarket parts all the way up to an RA V. Bill's "March Auto Show" at the dealership represented the Magnum 400 alongside the new Firebirds, which were midyear 1970½ releases.

On September 3, 1970, Bill was still selling his Magnum 400 for his prior year price of $2,995, which indicates he didn't build in any margin on that car's budget price when he ordered the run. He dropped the prices on other cars significantly in the traditional blowout before the new model year cars were delivered.

In 1971, Pontiac got with it by allowing the full line of Pontiac engines to be optioned in a GT-37. Pontiac trumped everyone that year by making a 455 HO available in a 1971 GT-37 at a time when a Sizzler topped out at 318 and the Comet GT was a 302 2-barrel. Pontiac's improved engine options for GT-37 in 1971 may have contributed to Knafel's decision to not do another run of his Magnum for 1971.

Knafel 1970 GTO Judge

On January 19, 1970, Bill Knafel took out a large ad for two high-performance salesmen. Bill was a salesman's salesman. He carefully outlined the plan then provided concrete numbers and examples to bolster the argument that you were going to be fully supported by a million-dollar advertising budget plus multiple magazine coverage!

In 1970, Bill Knafel called old racing team member Arlen Vanke for advice on how to beat a 1966 Dart holding the AHRA national record. The Dart owner challenged Knafel to a best-of-three match race at Dragway 42. Vanke suggested running in three classes with the 1970 GTO Judge that Knafel was getting ready to run. Switching between blasts from 2-barrel, 4-barrel, and Tri-Power would blow people's minds. Norm "Sonny" Tanner was the Knafel driver in the three-classes-one-car trick. After Knafel set some national records in all three classes, the Dodge Dart driver dropped out of sight with his mind apparently blown.

NEW CAR SALESMEN READ THIS:

If you are performance oriented and have experience or are interested in new car performance sales, then read on.

The "tin Indian" performance div. of Knafel Pontiac has been reactivated after 1 ½ years layoff. The tin Indian racing cars have tacked up one of the most impressive national and world renown records of any team.

The need for the return of the Pontiac performance image on a national level is uppermost.

After thoroughly testing the new 1970 Pontiacs and more new products to come in conjunction with engineering we have not only reactivated the "tin Indians," but have begun a national program with three new 1970 tin Indian racing cars going to Florida for testing write ups which will be featured in three national magazines including Motor Trend. Then on to Phoenix, Arizona, and Pomona, California.

Arrangements have been made with most national magazines and news medias to cover the "tin Indians" and all the new Magnum 400 designed by Knafel Pontiac which has been premiered in Akron and selling at only $2995.00

The sale of this new motion machine and the super-tuned GTO's, Judges and Firebirds will be advertised and sold nationally by us.

A model kit replica of our new 1970 Firebird 400 Tin Indian will be on the market in two months by the M.P.C. Model Kit Co. The sale of these kits will be world wide and expected to do over 2 million sales.

Nationally known sponsors of the tin Indians will be: Champion Spark Plug Co., Hurst Schiefer, MPC, Quaker State Oil, Keystone Wheel Co., Hooker Headers, who will also advertise the Tin Indians throughout the world in many medias.

On a local level an all new performance products department, in conjunction with our parts department, will open soon.

With all this going we must hire two new car salesmen who are experienced or interested in performance sales. You will have millions of dollars of advertising going for you plus continuous showroom promotions.

Our pay schedule: Salary plus Commission plus Bonus plus Demo
See Bill Knafel or Joe Fleber now.

Bill KNAFEL PONTIAC, Inc.
956 S. Main St. • Phone 762-9021

Supersalesman Bill Knafel sells car salesmen on coming to work for Knafel Pontiac in this January 19, 1970, advertisement. All the publicity and magazine coverage he envisioned was going to be generated through Knafel Pontiac's return to sponsored drag racing.

The Vanke/Tanner 1970 GTO Judge that Knafel sponsored had extra behind-the-scenes help. This *Tin Indian* benefitted from a Pontiac engineering concept engine intended to be named "400 Super Duty." The 400 SD joined an RA V block to RA IV heads. Air Flow Research modified the heads to convert to an angle-plug design to enhance flow. The Trans Am profile camshaft adapts to the RA V crank while maintaining the RA IV firing order. Bolted on top of this monster

Norm Tanner (left) and Bill Knafel celebrate an AHRA class win at the Pro Am Nationals. The Knafel 1970 GTO Judge *Tin Indian* drag car turned a 12.04-second quarter-mile at 113.49 mph.

After a two-year absence from sponsorship, Bill Knafel Pontiac returned to racing with this highly successful 1970 GTO Judge. The factory RA IV TH 400 car was a radio/heater/seam sealer/insulation delete lightweight. Prep for racing included some trick Pontiac engineering engine pieces and a fiberglass front nose. The rear wing was left in place to enhance rear wheel loading. The car was later rediscovered by Knafel alumni Arlen Vanke. Mike Gaurise pounced on the car and commissioned a restoration. (Photo Courtesy Todd R. Wingerter)

Bill Knafel Pontiac's 1970 Firebird race car was overshadowed by its highly successful 1970 GTO Judge racer. Instead of a Trans Am, the lesser-known Formula 400 was chosen as the basis for this race car. The original format of the Formula included the Knafel-signature Keystone mags. This later version of the Formula (shown) deviates from the Knafel "theme" by running a multicolor paint job and featuring polished slot mags. (Photo Courtesy Todd R. Wingerter)

motor was a prototype aluminum intake fed by a ridiculously huge 1,050-cfm 4-barrel Carter Thermoquad. Power went through a Hurst Dual Gate automatic and 4.56:1 axle. It's best run was a scorching 11.61 at 119 mph in 4-barrel form. It ran in the 13s with a 2-barrel!

Knafel could never just run one car. He also campaigned another *Tin Indian* 1970 Firebird 400. Bill had gathered together an impressive roster of sponsors: Champion spark plugs, Hurst, Schiefer, MPC, Quaker State oil, Keystone Wheel Co, and Hooker Headers.

Bill continued his tradition of taking out ads extolling the records the car set every time it won at the track and tying that in with high-performance inventory on the lot.

Bill Knafel "Mr. Pontiac"

In July 1970, Bill Knafel billed himself as "Mr. Pontiac" and celebrated his GTO Judge *Tin Indian* race car setting a second world speed record with a huge ad. He took the opportunity to blow out a rack of new 1970 GTOs and Judges at great prices. Bill gave each buyer a round-trip ticket to Vegas on top of the discounted prices. A fully equipped 1970 GTO Judge was discounted from $4,369 down to $3,992.

The 1970 GTOs were blown out for as low as $3,558. By August, the prices were even better: 1970 GTO 4-speed, heavy-duty radiator, disc brakes, Safe-T-Track at $3,210 and a 1970 GTO Judge RA, 4-speed, Safe-T-Track at $3,525.

Similar to other high-performance dealerships, such as Mr. Norm's Grand Spaulding Dodge in Chicago and Bonanza Rambler in Los Angeles, Knafel had police fleet contracts. Knafel supplied Catalinas to the sheriff's department. If you buy a cop car from a dealership with a fully set up racing shop, you know it's going to run right in a high-speed chase.

As 1970 turned to 1971, trouble started for Bill Knafel. The high-performance formula wasn't working because of high insurance rates applied to muscle cars. Bill's high-performance parts department was slowing down, too. Bill followed Pontiac's lead and advertised that you could buy a Pontiac for "Chevy prices" and highlighted the new T-37. Bill didn't advertise the GT-37 likely because it would compete with the remaining Magnum 400s on his lot.

Knafel Closes

January 21, 1971, marked the end of the *Tin Indian* era. The 1970 GTO Judge race car was put up for sale. Despite having more than $9,000 into the car, Bill was blowing it out for $4,395. Bill stated that it would only be sold to a qualified driver.

Starting in 1972, Bill was using a backward K in his ads for his last name, perhaps after seeing the Nickey Chevrolet logo.

He also began carrying an International truck franchise in an attempt to keep volume flowing as Pontiac's market position eroded in the early 1970s.

In 1975, the Knafel dealership closed. Bill was still in business with Knafel Leasing, Knafel Finance Corp, a boating store, and a gun store. In September 1979, Bill Knafel invited his old customers down to a used lot named Bill Knafel Motors at 61 E. Waterloo, near South Main. He trucked in salt-free used cars from Southern states. He still had his usual big broad perspective when he stated that in his 20 years as a Pontiac and Olds dealer he sold more than 21,000 cars. Bill soon renamed his lot Tin Indian Motors.

Bill Knafel died February 1, 2006, at age 79. Bill's son John Knafel became curator of the Tin Indian archives, preserving the history of the era. In a surprising tally of his dealerships over the years, despite his Pontiac fame, Bill Knafel owned six Ford franchises.

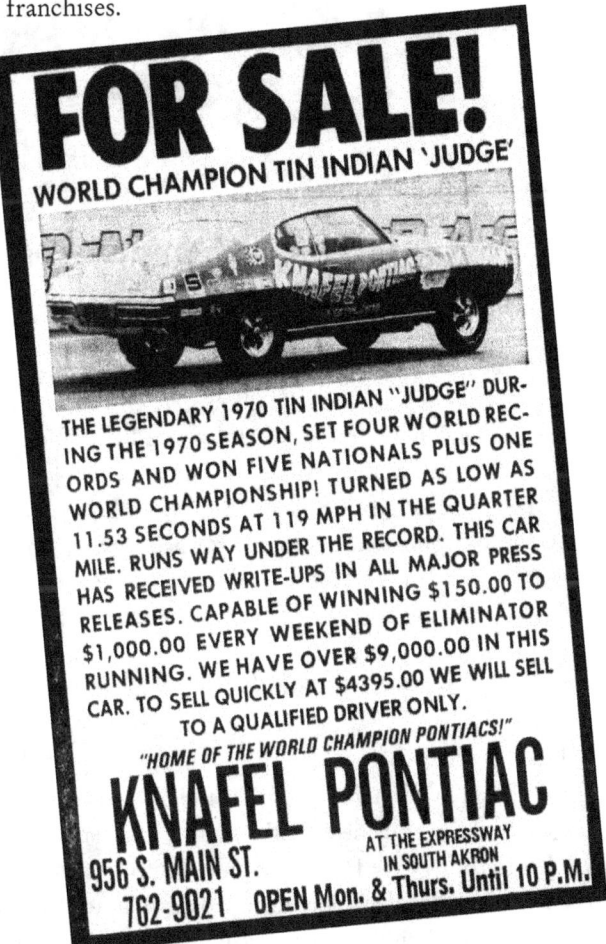

The end of a great run of Knafel sponsorship hit on January 21, 1971, when Bill Knafel blew out his 1970 GTO Judge drag car for half his investment. Note that it is almost one year to the day after Bill placed his ad for salesmen and extolling the coming boom times at Knafel. If the muscle car era hadn't been killed, Bill's grand vision for Knafel Pontiac would have continued for many more years.

CHAPTER 16
BILL ALLEN CHEVROLET

Bill Allen Chevrolet
Location: Kansas City, Missouri
Years in Operation: 1933–1988
Founder(s): William "Bill" Russell Allen Sr.
Current Status: Vacant

This original postcard image of the Bill Allen dealership shows the distinct shape of the building, which is easily recognized today despite being painted and re-signed. (Photo Courtesy Bob Allen)

Bill Allen Chevrolet Inc. was located at 101 Armour Road, North Kansas City, Missouri. The dealership was established in 1933 by William "Bill" Russell Allen Sr. Bill's dealership took some interesting performance twists and turns. When he expanded his Chevy dealership in 1945 with a new building, he had the Midwest's largest inventory of Chevy parts.

The Beginning of Bill Allen Chevrolet

Bill Allen Sr. was born on July 31, 1898, in Brookfield, Missouri. Bill sold musical items in Independence, Missouri, before getting into the car business. Bill's younger brother Alva Franklin Allen Sr. (born June 19, 1900) was also into cars and Chevys. He owned Alva Allen Chevrolet Co. in Clinton, Missouri. Alva's son Alva Franklin Jr. (born August 16, 1935) worked his whole life in the family Chevy business.

Bill Allen Sr.'s son William "Bill" Russell Allen Jr. was born February 12, 1921, in Independence, Missouri. After graduation from North Kansas City High School and a stint at the University of Kansas, Bill Jr. served as a lieutenant in the US Navy. He was a naval aviator and flying instructor during World War II. He returned to Missouri and was vice president of the family dealership; at only 22 years old he became president. Bill Sr. turned daily operations over to his son in 1953.

As the new president, Bill Jr. renamed the dealership Bill Allen Jr. Chevrolet Company. He expanded the scope of the business in the summer of 1953. Bill Jr. also plunged into a strong selling mode, hiring more salesmen. He soon simply referred to the dealership as Bill Allen Chevrolet Co., just like it used to be named in his father's era.

Bill Allen Features Muscle Cars

In the 1960s, the dealership was named Bill Allen Chevrolet Inc. As the 1960s muscle era descended, even small towns in Kansas heated up. Farming highways provided perfect opportunities for some high-speed runs beyond the typical quarter-mile blasts. Allen increased his stock of Corvair Monzas, Chevelle SS, Corvette, and Impala Super Sport 4-speeds.

Bill Allen Chevy added a used car lot at Antioch Shopping center. In March 1966, there were a few 1966 Chevelle SS factory official cars for sale at the used lot on 2646 Vivion Road, Kansas City. Bill Allen Jeep sales were also in full swing down at Allen's truck center at 1900 Armour Road. Things were

The old Bill Allen Chevrolet location at 101 Armour Road, North Kansas City, Missouri, has survived various tenants over the years since closure in 1988. Through all the years, the old Allen sign still remains as a reminder of the building's heritage. (Photo Courtesy Shirley Parsons)

Bill Allen Jr., seen here in a 1950s photograph, was a young man running a small-town dealership. Dick Harrell was racing without recognition at this time, but soon their paths would cross and monster muscle machines would be the result!

Note the subtle star pattern on the floor and luxurious leather chairs in the Bill Allen Chevrolet showroom at 101 Armour Road, North Kansas City, Missouri. A display on the left wall demonstrates some of the optional accessories available for new cars. Visible through the window are a Conoco gas station and the Kansas Flour Mills Company across the street. (Photo Courtesy State Historical Society of Missouri)

Bill Allen stands to the left, posing with his sales team and the 1958 models in his showroom at 101 Armour Road. Bill and his crew stand at the double doors, which are adjacent to the oval display windows that bubble out behind them, providing pedestrians a full view of the feature cars. (Photo Courtesy State Historical Society of Missouri)

Chapter 16: Bill Allen Chevrolet

Bill Allen Chevrolet produced many elaborate window displays. This display channels the Tiki craze that originated in 1930s Los Angeles with South Pacific–themed restaurants and bars. The two mannequins wear leis and are carting water skis. The Impala convertible doesn't have the 396 base on the front fender crossed flags. It appears to have a 327 callout above the flags. (Photo Courtesy State Historical Society of Missouri)

going well, but the action suddenly kicked into overdrive when Dick Harrell set up shop in the area.

Dick Harrell Drops the 427 Bomb

Bill Allen Chevrolet received the ultimate infusion of excitement when neighboring supercar creator Dick Harrell began working with Bill Jr. to produce 427 Super Camaros. Dick was best known as a highly popular drag racer who persevered in the face of intense competition without any factory support. This dedication to his brand led to his nickname as "Mr. Chevrolet."

Dick had fanned the flames of the muscle car era in various dealerships by marketing his 427 Camaros as the next logical step that the factory wouldn't take. Dick not only did 427 engine swaps but also supertuned the engine and chassis to make his cars live up to the name Super Camaro. Dick street drove his own Super Camaro, which showed his faith in these cars.

Dick's creations enhanced the image of Nickey Chevrolet in Chicago, Dana Chevrolet in Los Angeles, Yenko Chevrolet from Cannonsburg, and Fred Gibb Chevrolet. His new shop was temporarily set up in East St. Louis, and he was aiming to pump out 92 Super Camaros for Yenko distribution in 1967. Once Dick got a new work space set up at a proposed shop location in St. Louis International Raceway, his goal was to produce 300 Super Camaros for 1968.

After Don Yenko and Dick had a falling out, he worked closely with Fred Gibb Chevrolet. However, because of his proximity to Bill Allen Chevrolet, Dick's magic beasts were flowing through that dealership as well.

Bill Allen Exclusive Dick Harrell Super Camaros

Bill Allen distributed some Dick Harrell 427 Camaros and Chevelles but mainly promoted the Camaros. In a September 25, 1967, advertisement, Bill Allen Chevrolet demonstrated the dealership's eagerness to embrace the exciting muscle car era with a Yenko Super Camaro 427 for sale as "a Bill Allen exclusive." An ad run February 1968, dropped the

The original bill of sale for Roger Day's 1969 Monaco Orange 1969 COPO Chevelle SS with 427 and Dick Harrell modifications. Note that Roger's trade-in was the 1966 Chevelle SS he was driving to work when he spotted the COPO Chevelle on Bill Allen's lot. (Photo Courtesy Roger Day)

Roger Day received a full warranty from Bill Allen Chevrolet when he purchased his 1969 COPO Chevelle 427 with speed tweaks performed by Dick Harrell's Performance shop. If Roger had tried to engine swap or modify this car himself, he would have voided the GM warranty. (Photo Courtesy Roger Day)

Roger Day bought this fantastic-looking Monaco Orange 1969 Chevelle SS off the Bill Allen lot brand new. The color caught Roger's eye, but the car's COPO status plus Dick Harrell modifications to the L72 427 engine sealed the deal. (Photo Courtesy Roger Day)

Yenko name but again emphasized that the Harrell cars were built expressly for them

Bill Allen was instrumental in ordering COPO cars from the factory for Dick Harrell's work on the 1969 Camaros. Fred Gibb Chevrolet had ordered a big run of COPO Novas and the incredible COPO ZL1 Camaros in conjunction with Dick. When Fred Gibb and Dick parted ways, Dick needed a new factory connection. The established relationship with Bill Allen made the dealer the obvious choice to keep the COPOs flowing.

Dick received 1969 COPO 427 Camaros and Chevelles from Bill Allen with the L72 big-block 427 engines already factory installed. If the cars were destined for other dealership inventory, Dick had to leave the factory restrictive exhaust system intact, but he was able to do some supertuning by fiddling with valve lash, carburetor jetting, and timing to get the car up to an honest 450 hp. Harrell and his crew would also degree the harmonic balancer and work the distributor advances. Cars that were processed directly to a customer who asserted that the car was for "off-road use" (i.e., drag racing) could be tweaked further. Smog equipment was ditched and headers were added to bring these engines to full potential.

Most Harrell cars were also outfitted with Ansen mag wheels, a Sun tachometer, and Stewart Warner gauges. Once traction bars, badging, and stripes were added, the cars were ready for the street or strip!

John "Oop" Fensom was Harrell's in-house painter. He often spruced cars up with visual touches, putting contrasting paint on the cars. If there was more time and budget, Dick would ask Oop to repaint some of them. Some of Dick's COPO cars were ordered with special paint. One of the Harrell Performance Center 1969 COPO Chevelles came through with Monaco Orange special paint (Harrell approved!). This Chevelle was sold through Bill Allen to Roger Day on August 19, 1969. The L72 427 ran through a column-shifted super tough TH400 and 4.10:1 Posi-Traction 12-bolt axle.

Bill Allen Winds Down

Although performance died down in the 1970s, Bill Allen continued to highlight muscle cars. Allen prominently advertised Corvettes, Camaros, and the new European-themed Laguna with larger type ads in newspaper listings than the regular cars on his lot. Allen's used lot at 1900 Armour had impressive stock in 1971, such as a 1970 GTO Judge 4-speed for $2,295.

Bill owned and operated Bill Allen Chevrolet in North Kansas City for 35 years until his retirement and sale of the dealership in 1988. Bill Allen Sr. died a few years before this on July 4, 1984. In 1993, Bill Allen Jr. moved to Stuart, Florida, where he died on November 11, 2007, at age 86.

The Bill Allen Chevrolet building still stands and has served as home to several businesses, including Jim's Discount Tire and Brake and Johnny's Backyard.

A decade after the muscle car era fizzled out, the Corvette was still providing performance and fun for the last holdouts in the new world of emissions, bumpers, and expensive gas and insurance. Bill Allen displayed three Corvettes in its showroom as a nod to its past performance bias. Two of the Vettes have the T-tops removed to enhance the "convertible" feel of the cars. (Photo Courtesy State Historical Society of Missouri)

Bill Allen Dick Harrell COPO Camaro

Another color Dick Harrell approved of was Hugger Orange. This COPO Camaro found its first owner because Dick was in the Bill Allen dealership at the right time. Dave Richardson visited Bill Allen Chevy prepared to buy a new Camaro Z28. The dealership was sold out of Z28s and didn't expect a new batch until the new model year. Dick suggested Dave try a test drive in one of his prepped 427 monster Camaros instead.

The Hugger Orange 427 Camaro had Harrell-specific black stripes complimented with a black interior. The 427 was hooked to an M21 4-speed and 12-bolt Posi-Traction axle. Dave was sold on it after his test drive!

Dave added headers and ACCEL ignition and bigger tires to run in A/Stock Optional class at Kansas City International Raceway. He also drove it on the street. A blown transmission was fixed by Bill Allen under warranty. With a growing family and a marginal back seat, Dave traded the COPO back to Bill Allen.

Second owner Joe Stidham had worked with both Bill Allen Jr. and Dick Harrell, which gave him an insider's first shot at owning the COPO trade-in. Just as Dave had done, Joe took the Camaro to Kansas City International Raceway, where the car continued its winning ways. Joe's brother Gerry Stidham inherited the car when Joe died at a young age in 1977. Gerry rebuilt the engine and raced it a bit on street and strip. When the brakes went out, he parked the car but didn't want to sell it because of its sentimental value.

When his health declined, Gerry sold the car to super-car collector Dave Beem in 2018. Beem did only necessary mechanical work and kept the paint, interior, and engine compartment original, despite some wear and fade. In 2018 at Beech Bend Raceway, despite plunging through broiling-hot molasses-thick humid air, the car was in the mid-11s through the quarter-mile on 28x9-inch M/T racing slicks. The car had undergone some basic mechanical work to bring it back to life after sitting for many years but was basically "as is" from when Gerry last drove it.

This original paint Hugger Orange 1969 COPO Camaro 427 was a coproduction of Bill Allen Chevrolet and Dick Harrell's Performance shop. Orders were placed through Bill Allen Chevrolet on behalf of Dick Harrell, who then took the killer cars and found ways to make them even faster! Hugger Orange with black interior was one of Dick's favored color combinations.

After this Hugger Orange COPO Camaro 427 was prepped by Dick Harrell, it received Harrell badging on the fenders. Note that Dick's badge is inspired by the Yenko design.

The Hugger Orange Dick Harrell Camaro 427 is not only original paint but the engine bay retains its original status after receiving the Dick Harrell Performance Center touch. The 427 has headers, cowl induction, and original Dick Harrell stickers on the weathered chrome valve covers.

In the 1960s, Bill Allen Chevrolet found a way to use the factory badges to simplify the dealership emblem. By placing the Bill Allen script to the left of the factory-installed Chevrolet logo, the complete name "Bill Allen Chevrolet" was created.

The original Dick Harrell sticker on the front driver-side valve cover of the 427 is still legible. A Dick Harrell sticker was also applied to the chrome air cleaner lid. Look at the left of the photo: a chain is bolted to the corner of the engine block to prevent twisting from the enormous forces of torque generated by the 427 when the clutch is dumped.

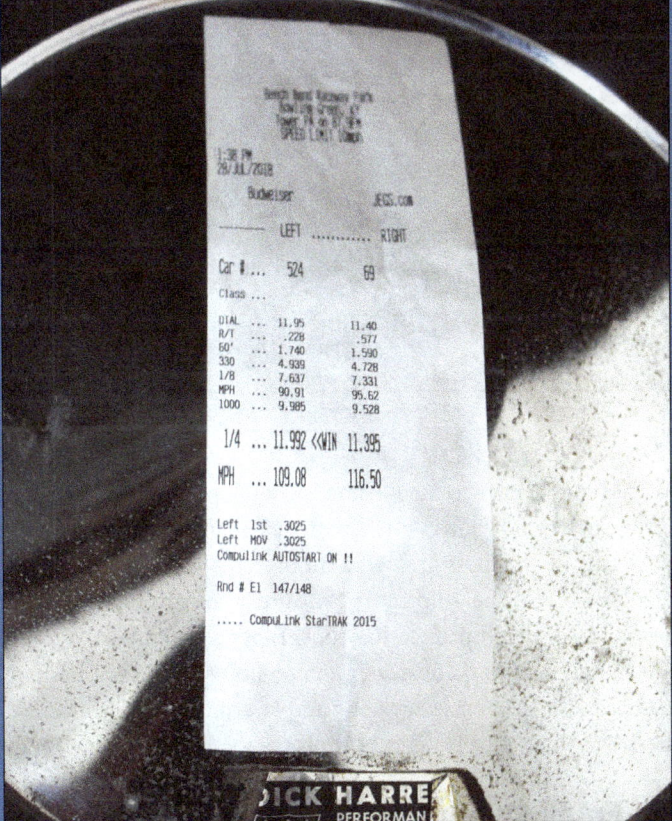

Here's the answer to how good a Dick Harrell COPO Camaro 427 runs: Dave Beem kept this car original except fluid change and plug change and other essential items and posted mid-11s in 2018 at Beech Bend Raceway running on 28x9-inch M/T racing slicks.

CHAPTER 17
Yenko Chevrolet

Yenko Chevrolet
Location: Canonsburg, Pennsylvania
Years in Operation: 1949–1982
Founder(s): Frank Yenko
Current Status: Private Motorcycle Storage

This location of Yenko Chevrolet at 575 West Pike Street, Canonsburg, Pennsylvania, opened in 1949. Don Yenko stands in front of a truck on the lot with his distinctive body posture: Don was always in a hurry to do the next thing! The Camaro SS sandwiched between the trucks perfectly illustrates the dichotomy in approach between Frank Yenko, who sold trucks to small-town customers, and his son Don, who sold excitement all over the country. (Photo Courtesy Bob McClurg)

Frank Yenko created a small-town Chevrolet dealership in Pennsylvania. His insistence that his son join him in the business created a monster he wasn't expecting! Frank's quiet dealership morphed into a hugely famous performance dealership once his son Don was involved. Yenko Chevrolet is famous for dealer conversion supercars, but also made a mark in sports car racing and later fielded some under-the-radar insurance beaters as well.

Frank Yenko's Small-Town Dealership

Frank Yenko was born in Presto near Bridgeville, Pennsylvania, on November 19, 1900. He "adjusted" his age in the 1940 census, where he is listed as being 36 years old and his wife as 32. His wife Martha Elizabeth (nee Campbell) was born on May 23, 1903, and was a teacher.

If only the walls could talk! A private owner now uses the former Yenko Chevrolet dealership as a storage facility for his motorcycles. Fifty years ago, Yenko 427 Camaros, Novas, and Chevelles used to reside inside. (Photo Courtesy Michelle Roberts)

Part of the Don Yenko package involved marketing. Aside from various stripes and the "SYC" logos on head restraints, the Yenko cars were badged with these metal emblems. Normally they were attached with metal pins, but in some instances they were held on with adhesive.

In 1925, Frank and a partner made the jump into the auto business by selling Durant autos. After the Durant franchise suffered a bankruptcy, Frank set up the Central Garage at 210 E. Main Street as a solo operation. In 1934, he augmented that business when he received the Chevrolet franchise for Bentleyville, Pennsylvania. Martha quit teaching and kept the books for their dealership.

Frank did well and expanded his dealership in 1947. The second location rented a building in Canonsburg, Pennsylvania. He left his top salesman, Bruno Bogdewic, in charge of the Bentleyville spot. In 1958, Bruno bought out Frank and renamed the dealership B Bogdewic Chevrolet.

Yenko Pike Street

Canonsburg proved lucrative enough for Frank Yenko to buy land and build a new dealership. Frank opened the doors at 575 West Pike Street, Canonsburg, Pennsylvania, on January 21, 1949. He displayed a 1920 Chevrolet in the dealership as a curiosity item to enhance the opening day. Frank's dealership was zone 13, dealer #898.

Don Yenko Shakes Things Up at Yenko

Frank's son Donald Frank Yenko was born on May 27, 1927, in Monongahela Hospital, Pennsylvania. Don grew up hanging out at his father's Bentleyville Chevy dealership. His adventurous side emerged early. Don began flying planes at age 15, which inspired him to enlist in the US Air Force. World War II was winding down, so the air force found a job for Don as a meteorologist.

After the air force, Don suffered through a poverty-stricken stay in New York while trying to establish himself as a jazz pianist. His father made him come home and train to run the family business. Don may have capitulated in the 1950s, but his zest for excitement and fun would soon distort his father's regular auto business into something totally unrecognizable.

Don attended Penn State, where he met his future wife, Hope, who was studying to be a teacher. Vivian Hope Meloy and Don Yenko married in 1952. Like Don's mother, Hope also worked in the dealership doing the books prior to starting a family with Don.

Don Yenko was going through the motions to please his father with his dealership activities. Fun-loving Don was well liked by other dealers, and he was a popular figure at Chevrolet official functions. When Don met fellow dealership owner Ben Moore, the entire trajectory of Yenko Chevrolet was changed. Ben Moore's Chevrolet dealership in Bethlehem, Pennsylvania, sponsored Roger Penske in a sports car race at the Cumberland, Maryland, airport. When Ben invited Don and Hope to watch the race, he ignited Don's obsession with car racing.

Don Begins Racing

Don bluffed his way into a race in 1957 at New Smyrna Beach Racetrack in Florida using a made-up competition driver number. He placed very well, driving a Corvette despite literally finishing the race in flames. On the final lap, Don was in fourth place when his differential exploded from being superheated by his straight-through exhaust pipes that were pointed right at it. He also destroyed his gearbox, having not mastered the downshift yet. After a haphazard start, Don consistently finished high in races.

Don Yenko (left) and his father Frank Yenko (right) were accompanied by their wives to break new ground for their final and largest Chevrolet location, which thrived during the 1970s. (Photo Courtesy Bob McClurg)

Don Yenko and Ed Lowther codrove this Corvette in the 1962 12 Hours of Sebring. The missing chunk of fiberglass on the front end is a direct result of GM's new fade-proof brake pads. The pads got harder and harder and eventually didn't stop the car. Immovable objects always win when you have a fiberglass car! (Photo Courtesy Douglas Morton)

On March 24, 1962, Don Yenko and Ed Lowther hammered this Vette through 12 Hours of Sebring and finished the event placing 19th overall. Only 37 cars finished out of the 65 cars that started this grueling race. (Photo Courtesy Douglas Morton)

Don Yenko's new racing mania quickly transformed the dealership. Don immediately advertised Yenko as a Corvette specialist. Yenko Chevrolet suddenly had meaning to Don, who quickly distorted the Yenko image to reflect his interests. Advertising for Yenko switched from selling transportation to selling excitement!

Frank kept a steady hand on daily business while exuberant son Don hijacked the image of the dealership overnight. But Frank couldn't argue against the bottom-line evidence. Don generated exposure for the dealership via his racing exploits and performance operations.

Yenko Sports Cars

Yenko Sports Cars was formed as a subsidiary of the dealership to sell roll bars and other equipment aimed at Corvette owners. Yenko also began prepping race cars. All this action translated to sales of Corvettes and parts, which Frank admitted was increasing the customer base and sales. Frank did grouse about the cash outlay of racing and wondered if the whole concept was self-cancelling insofar as money in and money out.

In 1962 and 1963, Don won SCCA B Production while racing Corvettes. Yenko was the largest Corvette dealership in Pennsylvania by the mid-1960s. Out-of-state and even out-of-country buyers displayed their Yenko license frame as a sign of being "in the know."

An ad Don placed in March 1966 didn't refer to Yenko Chevrolet but rather "Yenko's Corvette Center." The ad listed nine used Corvettes for sale with the list topped by a 427 Corvette. Each car synopsis listed horsepower rating, gears, and transmission. Another "Yenko's Corvette Center'" ad placed on June 26 emphasized: "We buy Corvettes!"

Don Yenko was well known enough to be name dropped on the East Coast in an advertisement run in December 1966 by Ken Wilson Chevrolet in Vestal, New York. They were selling a 1965 Corvette with a race-prepped 396 engine. The fact the car was prepped by Don Yenko gave the car "cred." It included an SCCA roll bar, racing tires, and suspension.

Yenko Manufactures Corvair Stingers

The official line as to why Don Yenko built high-performance Corvairs is that he was sick of Chevrolet Corvettes gaining weight every year. Don liked to win and Chevys were starting to lose. Many sources believe Yenko developed the Corvair into a race car because it was lighter than the Corvette. Simple as that. However, Don's Corvair was competing primarily with foreign cars in D Production; he continued to race Corvettes in B Production.

The Yenko dealership took a big plunge when Don Yenko committed to building 100 copies of his 1966 Yenko Stinger based on the Corvair Corsa. In order to qualify the Stingers in Production class racing Yenko had to produce 100 copies. Yenko Sports Cars Inc. became a "manufacturer" of Corvair Stingers in the eyes of the racing sanctioning bodies. Don used the argument that producing a high-performance Corvair would allow the dealership to remain competitive in sports car racing circuits. Is it worth building 100 cars just to get a blurb in the paper? Frank Yenko probably didn't think so, but he completely supported Don in his latest venture, which turned into a gargantuan task.

Edwin J. Myers was brought in to help. Edwin was the president of E. A. Myers and Sons (a hearing aid company) and put his production experience into action as production manager of the Stinger project.

A company named Span Inc. (which was essentially just a guy working out of a rented office space) was a Lotus distributor and added Yenko to the roster to become the official distributor of Stingers to other car dealers. Since Span was a Chicago-based company, it was only natural that 25 Stingers found their way to supercar dealer Nickey Chevrolet. Yenko's packaging and distributorship of his Stinger most definitely ignited some ideas at Nickey.

The scope of what Don took on was immense and to make it more hectic, he was on a time crunch as well. Inspector Claude C. Cardwell of the SCCA visited the Yenko dealership on December 28, 1965, and counted 96 Stingers on-site. Four Stingers had already been shipped out. Yenko received approval, having built his 100 Stingers before the end of 1965.

Using the COPO System

One of the tricks Don employed to cut through the maze of issues facing him was to farm out work. Local body shops painted the stripes and affixed parts. Don even found a way to get the Stingers put together with help from General Motors.

The GM Central Office Production Order (COPO) saved Don's hide. The COPO system was typically used to produce identical runs of fleet cars, such as police cars or taxis, but Don used it to crank out Corvairs with heavy-duty suspension, upgraded steering, and M21 4-speed transmissions. The COPO system relied on bulk unit orders adhering to the same pattern. All 100 Stingers were white with black interiors.

Once the COPO Corvairs arrived at Yenko's dealership, his mechanics switched the cars to 3.89:1 Posi-Traction axles and dual master brake cylinders. A local body shop applied racing stripes. The Stingers were available as Stage I, II, or III, depending on whether the buyer wanted to street drive the car or race in SCCA competition. Yenko also offered an ultimate performer that exceeded the Stage III, but this wasn't legal for Production racing.

After building 100 Corsa Stingers by the end of 1965, a new batch of 25 were built later using Monzas as the base starting point. The first competition to see Stingers in action had Don Yenko in the pits while the Stinger was copiloted by Russ MacGrotty Jr. (a Flushing, Long Island, Chevy dealer) and Art Riley.

Miss Think Pink and the Racing Dentist

One of Don Yenko's more visible race drivers was Donna Mae Mims of Bethel Park. Donna Mae was popularly known as "Miss Think Pink." She was a bombshell blonde who dyed her hair pink. She wore all pink clothing and raced pink cars.

Donna Mae Warnock was born on July 1, 1927, in Pittsburg, Pennsylvania, to George and Margaret Warnock. In the 1950s, Donna Mae was a secretary at the Yenko dealership and married Mike Mims. She divorced her husband around 1960 and delved further into racing. She created a stir when she won the 1963 American Road Race of Champions in a Sprite. This was in a time period where few women competed in racing let alone won a championship.

Donna Mae handled promo for NASCAR as well as other accounts. Don was a fun-loving guy, and he liked her irreverent humorous style. He hired Donna to do promotion for Yenko Sportscars as well as racing the cars.

Attention was focused on Yenko's new car when a Stinger was placed on display in the March 11, 1966, Pittsburgh Auto Show in the Hunt Armory. At the May 1966 SCCA races "The Racing Dentist" Dr. Dick Thompson won two classes: first in a Ford GT40 and later in a Stinger on the Virginia International Raceway.

Two Stingers were entered in the 12-hour Grand Prix of endurance at Sebring, Florida. During the race on March 26, 1966, Donna Mae Mims and codriver John Luke of Morgantown, West Virginia, were sidelined by a blown piston. The other Stinger was piloted by Russ MacGrotty Jr. and Art Riley.

Yenko's performance image was flourishing and performance sales were mounting. One might wonder why Don Yenko wasn't piloting one of the Stingers. That is because Don primarily raced Corvettes. By July 1966, Don Yenko was points leader in the SCCA Class B racing driving a Corvette.

This is one of "Miss Think Pink" Donna Mae Mims' race cars. A couple of individuals are working on her car, looking very incongruous with the feminine color scheme on her Yenko-built and -tuned Stinger. Donna was not ladylike when she got behind the wheel, however. She was the first female to win an SCCA championship when she beat everyone in 1963 Class H. (Photo Courtesy Douglas Morton)

Don and his codriver Bob Johnson of Columbus, Ohio, finished second in the Glen 500 (Watkins Glen, New York) on August 21, 1966.

A Stinger won Class D-E at Elkhart Lake, Wisconsin, driven by Jerry Thompson of Clawson, Michigan. Some Stingers were also entered in the GLEN 500 race, which covers 500 km (310 miles). One of the cars had Miss Think Pink codriving with T. Dale Moss of Uniontown, Pennsylvania. By the end of the season, Stingers had won five Class D championships, which had formerly been the sole domain of Triumphs and other foreign cars.

The success that Yenko had selling the Stingers off his lot and through other dealers went beyond people buying these vehicles as quick street cars. For instance, a June 25, 1966, advertisement from Bob Gates Chevytown promised quick delivery of Yenko Stinger Stage II competition-ready Corvairs for $3,850. No mention of street cars at all. The Stingers were credible race cars in Stage II and Stage III and completely legal in most race classes. Don created a race car manufacturing reputation in one year.

Yenko's home lot was doing well enough to become the only dealership with three salesmen at the top in a sales contest run by Chevrolet zone manager B. G. Stevens. With that much revenue coming through, Don was able to supply parts and help to anyone campaigning a Stinger. He wasn't able to throw around money, but he did get out there and support his Stingers as much as he could.

Sunray DX 1967 Corvette L88

While the Stingers were gaining traction, Don Yenko was racing a Sunray DX–sponsored 1967 Corvette L88 in the 12 Hours of Sebring. Don and codriver David Morgan came in first in the GT Category.

Don Yenko had cemented his Corvette image so well that Sunray DX's racing coordinator, Ralph Morrison, hired Don to source, prep, and drive its car for 1967. Ralph was a communications supervisor at Sunray, which was a Southwest oil company. Ralph suggested some racing sponsorship in 1965. It went over so well that he soon had a big enough budget to hire Don to go all out at Sebring.

Don Yenko was able to score the first 1967 L88 Corvette built. The coupe was Ermine White with a red interior. Don's codriver for Sebring, David Morgan, drove the L88 all the way from St. Louis final assembly to Yenko's dealership on March 9, 1967, in the heart of winter.

Don Yenko and his crew prepped the car with red and blue stripes and a Sunray logo. Firestone Goldline tires and American Racing Torque Thrust wheels were added. Bodywork included removal of bumpers, crafting larger air extractors on the front fenders, and adding fender flares to clear the fat rear tires. A roll bar was installed and some interior bits were taken out to save weight. Don's insider status is evident in some of the specific parts he managed to source. Don got a 2.60:1 differential ratio axle and L88-specific headers and pipes produced by Chevrolet Engineering. Sunray was delighted with the program and came to Don again in 1968 when it wanted a new race car.

Pike Street Problems

One forgotten dark side of the muscle car era is the frequency of Corvette thefts in particular and muscle car theft in general. When rising insurance rates are mentioned at the end of the muscle car era, it's usually discussed in terms of accidents, but insurance companies were feeling the pinch because of muscle car thefts as well.

Aside from outright theft, the muscle car era was plagued by car strippers. They were ripping off mag wheels, headers, intakes, etc. Yenko's Pike Street dealership was targeted by car strippers who used the stream behind the dealership to paddle down to strip cars.

Yenko Camaro Stormers and Stompers

The year of the Camaro for Yenko and the turning point toward legendary muscle car action at the dealership happened in 1967 when Don Yenko introduced a road racing version of the potent Camaro Z28 called the Stormer. It was quickly eclipsed by the street fighting/drag racing 427 Yenko Stomper Camaros that were inspired by the success of 427 Camaros built through Dana Chevrolet and Nickey Chevrolet.

Stormer

On May 14, 1967, the new Yenko version of a Camaro Z28 was seen for the first time in Maryland when Don Yenko raced his "Yenko Z28 Camaro Stormer" in Cumberland Class A Sedan race. It was Don's first time behind the wheel of a Z28 taking on Mustangs, Cougars, and Barracudas. Yenko had won prior Cumberland Class B races in Corvettes.

Don advertised his Stormers as FIA ready-to-race lightweight beasts with 400 hp. Span Inc. was geared up to distribute the Stormers just as it had with the Stingers but without the need to homologate. A few of the Camaro Stormers were built, but all interest in a small-block racer vaporized once the Yenko 427 Camaros caught on. Bud Gates Chevrolet took delivery of a Stormer and it is believed a Hollywood, California, dealer bought the second one. The third Stormer was never completed, and the Z28 platform car intended to become a Stormer became a normal sale off the lot.

Don Yenko was a Corvette-fevered sport car–racing enthusiast when he entered the muscle car market with this potent Camaro in 1967. Dick Harrell is credited with engineering this 427 Super Camaro. Dick's drag racing experience and popularity as "Mr. Chevrolet" helped launch Yenko's dealer-special 427 engined monster.

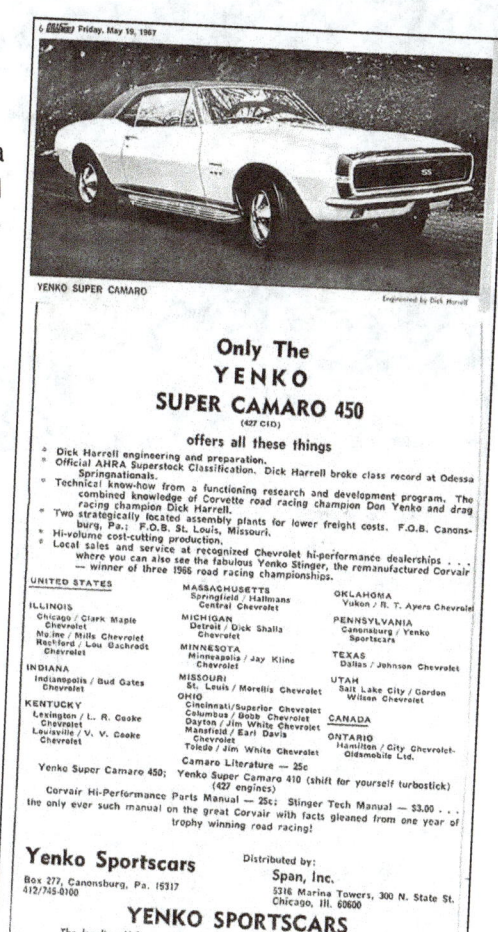

Stompers

A May 14, 1967, Yenko Corvette Center ad boasts that Yenko had the only 400-hp chassis dynamometer for the public use in the East. The same ad also urged drivers to test drive a 475-hp Yenko 427 Camaro Stomper. These were brutal muscle cars that could also take a corner.

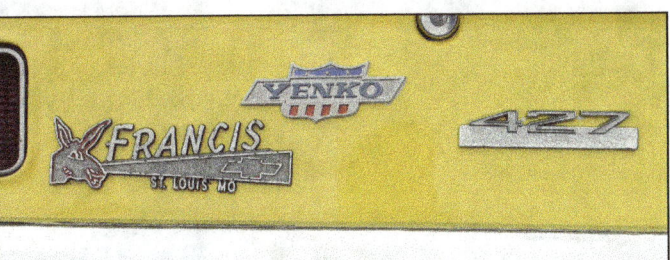

Note the proliferation of dealer badges adorning the back of Tom and Rob's COPO Camaro! Don Yenko placed his badge on this car plus a 427 badge. What is a mule doing on the back of a Yenko? Francis Chevrolet president Les Francis tied his name in with the "Francis the talking mule" movies to create a memorable advertising gimmick. Francis Chevrolet kept a mule at the dealership as the mascot.

Yenko Stompers transplanted 427 425-hp engines into Camaros along with fiberglass Stinger hoods, heavy-duty suspension, and a 4.10:1 Posi-Traction axle. SYC first meant Yenko Stomper Camaro and later it was taken to refer to a Super Camaro. When Chevelles (and later Novas) were converted by Yenko, the headrest logo SYC meant Yenko Super Chevelle or Yenko Super Car.

Don Yenko Legend

Don Yenko Chevrolet means a big-block Camaro to most collectors today. Back in the day, Don raced Corvettes and was a Vette fanatic from the 1950s right through the 1960s. Yenko was associated with monster big-block Camaros but the man behind the machines was Corvette crazed.

For more than a decade, Don tried to brand his sporty arm of the Yenko dealership as the "Yenko Corvette Center." Despite racing the Vettes himself and pushing Corvette prep and parts, the simple fact is that Corvettes were not a mass-market car like the Camaro.

This spectacular Yenko COPO 427 Camaro was sold through Francis Chevrolet in St. Louis, Missouri. The car looks great in a light yellow with rarely seen white stripes. Most yellow Yenko cars typically received black stripes. The car is owned by Tom and Rob Clary.

Left: Don Yenko's artistic tendencies are evident in his design of these hood stripes, which emphasize and flow along the cowl-induction hood. The 427 chrome badges were added to either side of the hood bulge. SYC stands for Yenko Sports Cars. The same logo easily matches Yenko Super Camaro or could be reinterpreted to mean Yenko Super Car if applied to a Nova. Right: The rear side view of this Yenko COPO 427 Camaro illustrates the way the stripes flow and blend into the spoiler. Unlike some COPO cars that were delivered with plain bodies, dog dish hubcaps, and steelies, this Camaro has spoilers, Rally wheels, and raised white letter wide ovals.

In the 1960s, the Corvettes were a "halo" car for Chevrolet, bestowing excitement and interest across the dealership base countrywide. Most dealerships had a token Vette in the showroom for drivers to drool over and have a two-minute fantasy about before buying a station wagon or perhaps boldly get an Impala SS.

Young drivers buying muscle machines reached their spending limit right at the Camaro or Mustang, which is why so many were sold. If a buyer had a little more to spend, he or she could get a righteous machine from a Camaro with 427. The other issue that made the Vette "not a muscle car" to some in the 1960s was it was usually too impractical even for hot rod–crazed drivers.

The muscle car masses had limited money to spend. Their muscle machine needed to do double duty as work or school transportation in addition to cruising with pals or gals. The four seats plus trunk of the typical muscle car along with lower entry price made them the volume sellers.

The Camaro was a much less practical car than a Chevelle SS but still doable. A Camaro rear seat was a joke, but at least it had one, unlike the Vette that only had two seats. The Camaro trunk was also ridiculous, but it trumped Corvettes that had virtually zero luggage area.

The Camaro was not Don's choice of car, but it was a better option for those needing a multipurpose, less-expensive rocket ship. A race-prepped Corvette destined for a road racing course is the perfect symbol for Don Yenko the Man. But today, when Don Yenko the Legend is mentioned, the immediate image we conjure is a 427 Camaro or perhaps a 427 Chevelle or Nova.

Don Yenko was a competitive racer and pilot. Don's take-no-prisoners cars reflected his hard, no-nonsense, get-it-done approach. Don built his 427 Camaros to address a trend, not to enable his own racing efforts. Don Yenko didn't compete at the drag strip, and his first big-block Camaros don't particularly reference his niche interests the way his forgotten Stormer Z28 Camaro did. The Don Yenko influence began to permeate later Yenko 427 cars; but the first run of cars were not uniquely his.

"Mr. Chevrolet" Dick Harrell

Don's first venture into muscle car waters was with another legend: Dana Chevrolet. The ads for a Dana/Yenko Super Camaro prove their intention to collaborate but is not absolute confirmation that they built cars together. Whatever transpired between the two super dealers ended before much could be accomplished.

A residual effect of the Yenko and Dana team up is Yenko's use of Bill Thomas parts. Dana Chevrolet and Nickey Chevrolet had used the assistance of Bill Thomas expertise to build 427 Camaros. Bill was an experienced ready-made supplier to Yenko for 427 Camaro–specific headers and traction bars needed to make the conversions. Bill Thomas was also hooked in with the Dana Chevrolet guys and would have been in some way a part of the brief connection between Dana and Yenko.

Don Yenko's exciting early batch of Super Camaros were built to rule the streets but had a hint of racecourse heritage in them. Don tapped drag racer Dick Harrell to develop his 427 Camaros. Straight-line launches require a different setup than a racer destined to cover 300 or 500 laps. It's all over in an instant in a street race. The engineering of a drag race car is specific and targeted. Dick Harrell played a crucial role in the 427 Camaro program. Early Yenko Camaro ads acknowledge this fact when they say: "Engineered by Dick Harrell."

Nickey Chevrolet in Chicago was possibly the first dealership to officially produce a branded package dealership 427 Camaro. The earliest printed evidence of a dealer-converted 427 Camaro is a November 1966 newspaper listing from Nickey Chevrolet. Dick Harrell built the Nickey Camaro 427 when he was Nickey's service manager.

It is very likely that Bill Thomas was nudged by Vince Piggins of Chevy on an unofficial basis to do the exact same thing at the exact same time. Bill entered an agreement to become the West Coast builder of Nickey 427 Camaros. Bill and Dick had slight differences in their approaches to building 427 Camaros.

Dana Chevrolet swapped in a 427 and produced its own dealer-branded Camaro around the same time. Magazine articles of the era place 427 Camaro development for Dana and Nickey in roughly the same time frame. A magazine article has lead in time and publishing dates are not the same as the cover date. Only that dated newspaper ad reflects the first provable date that a car was completed. For official purposes, Dick Harrell won the "who was first" debate for a dealer-special package 427 Camaro in the fall of 1966.

Don didn't get into the big-block 427 Camaro game until after Nickey had its program up and running. Dick Harrell ended his performance manager stint at Nickey when an argument between Bill Thomas and Nickey management in early 1967 spelled the de-escalation of the racing program. Dick's main purpose for being at Nickey was to race.

Dick ending up back at his own shop, converting Camaros under his own brand. Things really came together for Don once Dick Harrell was free of his Nickey contract. Don Yenko had the finances to supply plenty of raw material for conversions and a bigger market to get them out there to buyers. Dick had a ready-made product with his racing reputation to back it up. By rebranding the 427 Camaros into Yenko Super Camaros, they had a winning combination.

Don and Dick Build Super Camaro 427s

Don scooped up Dick Harrell to engineer the 427 Camaros in the spring of 1967. In accordance with Dick's conversion approach, Don paid his mechanics at the Yenko shop a flat rate to swap out engines for East Coast Camaro 427 production. All of the Southern and West Coast production of 427 Camaros would be handled by Dick Harrell.

Advertising featuring Dick and Don at events specifically mentioned that the Super Camaro benefits from each man's different racing experiences. A drag strip Camaro need only make it to 110 or 120 mph for a brief instant before shutting down again. Both Bill Thomas and Dick Harrell treated the drivetrain in ways to make it bulletproof and reinforced weak spots in the axle as well as devising traction assist methods to get the power to the ground. Don Yenko's touch is seen on the 427 Super Camaro in relation to steering and suspension.

Don had acquired parts from RST Engineering to replace the stock Camaro steering components in the Stormer with durable parts able to withstand g-forces through 100s of miles of full-out running on curved tracks. Those parts made their way into some early Yenko 427 Camaros. That philosophy also continued in later iterations of the Yenko supercars.

The early Yenko/Harrell Camaros were also similar to Baldwin-Motion's early Camaros, where an abundance of speed equipment and experience enabled a customer to have a one-of-a-kind car built. Early Yenkos were available with Corvette side pipes, L88 engines, fiberglass hoods and rear decklids, dual quads, and other goodies. Later Yenko cars were more of a production-line consistent package.

A July 16, 1967, newspaper announcement stated that the new Yenko Super Camaro 427s were underway at Dick's shop. Four cars were in progress and 32 others were on railway cars awaiting conversion. Dick was producing Super Camaros from his shop in a vacant gas station at 9th and St. Clair, East St. Louis. Harrell Speed Center was due to open in October 1967 at the St. Louis International Raceway, which would provide a handy place to test completed cars. Dick built a 16-car garage where Interstate 70 met Route 203 in East St. Louis. Aside from building cars for Yenko, Dick intended to stock his new location with speed parts and offer his own parts catalog.

The Yenko Stingers were still being made at Yenko's headquarters in Pennsylvania. Both the Stingers and the Harrell-built Yenko Camaros were slated for distribution in the St. Louis area by performance dealership Barford Chevrolet at 8500 Maryland Avenue in Clayton.

Don and Dick Promote the Super Camaros

Dick Harrell built Yenko 427 Camaros in 1967 for retail sales as well as creating a "halo" Camaro Funny Car to attract further attention to the dealership Camaros. Dick was all about racing, and he didn't need to do much to convince racing fanatic Don Yenko about the value of competition-proved publicity.

A 1967 "Super Camaro" Funny Car relied on the usual tubular frame and fiberglass body (with steel rear to resist torque twist), but Dick Harrell sat in the normal production car driver's position. On July 16, Harrell beat Tasca Ford's car three times in a row with his best quarter-mile run being 8.19 seconds and his best speed 170.83 mph.

Earl Davis Chevrolet in Mansfield, Ohio, was a Yenko distributor and displayed the Super Camaro in the dealership on July 18. Dick raced and showed the car as he worked his way toward Chicago and Detroit.

Yenko Distribution of the Super Camaros

Yenko went further than the other supercar dealers by increasing the scope of his sales via a network of dealers. Yenko initially had Span Inc. disperse his Stingers to other dealers to sell them after the purpose of getting 100 cars certified was accomplished. The disbursement of Stingers was more of a "clearing out" mission than anything else. But now having seen the possibilities of muscle car marketplace madness, 427 cars were built with the intention of marketing and selling them across the country.

The sales potential of dealer-special cars quickly became apparent to Don. This time he had a clear intention of expanding his influence across the country and dispatched salesmen to sign up other dealerships. Supercar dealers Nickey and Dana both stocked a healthy inventory of the Yenko Super Camaros despite doing their own cars in-house. You can't have too many 427 Camaros in one place! It took time to build these cars, and if Don Yenko could pump them out, then why not?

Returning to COPO

Things were going well, but Don and Dick parted ways toward the end of 1967 before they could work any magic on 1968 model year Camaros. Dick went on produce some very innovative and creative collaborations with Fred Gibb Chevrolet.

Don Yenko was back to square one, or so it seemed. Losing his main engine swapper would seem a big setback; but for Don Yenko it just turned into an opportunity to get even bigger. Yenko had the image out there, he had distribution, and now he wanted to increase production of his 427 Camaros. Don devised a way to get this done with shortcuts through a return to the COPO system.

Don had a small garage in his dealership with a single-chain winch engine hoist and no lifts or air tools. He simply wasn't set up to mass-produce a car that required engine swaps. Now that he didn't have Dick Harrell's shop to take up the slack, Don needed to find a new way to fill the hungry demand he had created for his 427 Camaros. So, he got the COPO system going again for his Camaros.

The 1968 car served as a stepping stone to not only Don

This 1968 Yenko Camaro (#YS-8021) was sold by high-performance dealership Francis Chevrolet in Bridgeton, Missouri. The fiberglass Yenko hood is held down with hood pins. Yenko included a block-off plate for the dual scoops during cold weather use. Yenko added his badge to the grille and specified front and rear spoilers. (Photo Courtesy Bob McClurg)

The 1968 Yenko Camaros used COPO 9373 Sports Car Conversion Package (big 427 carburetor, heavy-duty suspension, and 140-mph speedometer) to get the factory to build the car with the basics in place. Yenko's mechanics pulled the 396 block then substituted the 427 short-block, reusing most accessories. (Photo Courtesy Bob McClurg)

Yenko's ultimate vision of supercar production for 1969 but opened up the gates for other high-performance dealers to use his techniques. Don was a pioneer in engine swapping by seeking methods to mass-produce, mass-market, and mass-distribute his creations. Don went beyond the rest.

Don's process began with the basic starting point Dick Harrell and other conversion places began with. Conversion dealers reduced the cost of the engine swap by ordering the high-performance 396 375-hp Camaro as the base car to

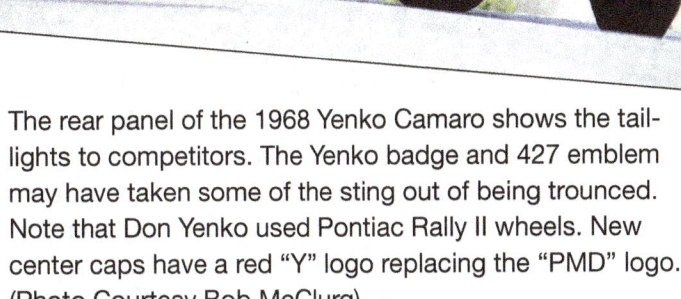

The 1968 Yenko Camaro (#YS- 8021) has an M21 4-speed and the SS three-spoke steering wheel. The car received the 140-mph speedometer due to the factory COPO order. The Stewart Warner gauges and glove box Yenko badge were added at the Yenko dealership. (Photo Courtesy Bob McClurg)

The rear panel of the 1968 Yenko Camaro shows the taillights to competitors. The Yenko badge and 427 emblem may have taken some of the sting out of being trounced. Note that Don Yenko used Pontiac Rally II wheels. New center caps have a red "Y" logo replacing the "PMD" logo. (Photo Courtesy Bob McClurg)

be converted. This way, heavy suspension, big radiator, and heavy driveline components were already in place. It was also reasonably easy to sell a 396 375-hp engine once it was yanked out. But this wasn't good enough for Don.

Don tried to get Chevrolet to build him a 396 375-hp Camaro with the 427 already factory installed through the COPO system. COPO had worked well for his Corvair Stinger project, but General Motors wasn't going to stick its neck out. Even under a Yenko smokescreen, the automaker refused to officially build a 427 Camaro, even if it was a special order dealership run.

Don didn't give up. He found ways to use COPO to cut time and costs for 1968. Instead of pulling the entire engine out, Don had COPO set up his cars so that all his mechanics had to do was switch out the 396 short-block (block, pistons, rods, and crank) and substitute in a 427 short-block.

In a typical swap, only some of the 396 goodies (alternator, starter, etc.) went back into the car. Don jumped past this issue by having the 396 goodies on his special COPO Camaros specced out as Yenko 427 goodies.

Don created Camaros using a COPO order that was code numbered 9737. It became known as "Sports Car Conversion." What got built under this order was a Camaro L78 396 with an MV engine code that was topped off not with the 396 375-hp carburetor but the 427 carburetor. Now when Yenko's technicians dropped in the 427 short-block, they simply bolted the provided carburetor back onto the short-block. Yenko didn't have to buy 427 carburetors, nor did he have to sell unneeded 396 375-hp carburetors.

Don's high-speed touring and racing touch was apparent in other parts of the package. COPO 9737 substituted a specially designed 140-mph speedometer in place of the factory 120 unit. A straight-line drag racer doesn't need a speedometer at all; but if the driver was curious to look down, the factory 120 mph is the outer limit of what could be expected in a quarter-mile run. This detail cost time and money but was important to Don.

COPO came in handy for suspension and steering upgrades. Sports Car Conversion allowed Yenko to bypass more dealership work by simply getting the cars set up by the factory. Yenko's road racing interest comes to the fore with the suspension specs: The heavy-duty springs and shocks are strategically set up in rear with bias-mounted shocks. Rear springs are four-leaf heavy-duty with heavy-duty bushings. The heavy-duty 3.73:1 ratio Posi-Traction axle included large-diameter axle shafts.

Now the Super Camaro was evolving away from a Yenko-badged Dick Harrell machine to a Don Yenko–influenced all-purpose machine. The 1 1/16-inch front stabilizer bar kept the car flat on turns. The Super Camaro was easily capable of using its power on turns or on rough roads. The Tuff-Trided spindles could handle the greater weight of the 427 as well as resist forces expected as the car was pushed through corners at great speed. The process uses a salt bath at high temperature to increase the hardness of metal, making it more resistant to fatigue and corrosion. The steering tie-rods, relay rods, arms, knuckles, and ball studs were all shot-peened for greater strength. This process blasts the metal at normal temperatures but creates a hardened, even surface to prevent cracking under stress.

Don's conversion package made no provision for wheels because he had an outside supplier in mind for this detail. The Super Camaro relied on 14-inch diameter "quad Yenko wheels" instead of 15-inch units. The Yenko Super Quad Sport wheels were really Pontiac Motor Division Rally II wheels with Yenko identification inserted into the hubs. A local Pontiac dealer supplied the wheels to Don. Don also experimented with having knock-off wheels cast by a local company, but they didn't work out very well.

The heart of the car is a 427 high-compression engine with mechanical lifters sucking fuel through a Holley 850-cfm carburetor and high-performance intake manifold. The 450-hp powerplant was coupled to a close-ratio Muncie transmission with heavy-duty clutch and pressure plate. A 410-hp unit was hooked up to an automatic. The 427 was dressed up with chrome air cleaner and valve covers and augmented by temperature-controlled fan and extra-capacity cooling system.

The Yenko Super Camaro had spoilers that were add-ons at first that were too troublesome and costly for the dealership to keep fooling with. Yenko later went to factory units. Stewart Warner gauges were added to the interior.

In 1968, Don Yenko changed his 427 Camaro hood to a dual scoop version reminiscent of the ones used on Dana Camaros. The resemblance between Dana hoods and Yenko hoods is likely a residual effect of their brief supercar collaborative effort.

Don was satisfied with the stripes and SYC headrest logos he had devised for 1967; so with a new hood the 1968 Yenko 427 Camaro seemed ready to carry on in the footsteps of the 1967 version. Visually, things were the same but (as detailed in the COPO process) the 1968 cars were pumped out much more quickly than the 1967 cars. About 64 of the cars were built.

An unanticipated fallout for Don Yenko (and boon to other high-performance dealerships) was that the COPO 9737 didn't belong to Don Yenko. It was developed and engineered by General Motors and the automaker could sell it to anyone it wanted. Just as some police fleet orders were often simple duplications of a large city police spec sheet, a high-performance dealer could reap the benefits of Don's pioneering and order COPO 9737.

Any savvy dealership who was part of Yenko's distributorship system could catch onto this fact. And some did! But for the 1968 model year, they were blissfully unaware of what Don was doing and proudly announced that they were the exclusive dealer in that area. This would ensure curious gawkers coming to the lot. Even if the gear heads couldn't afford the Yenkos, they may have bought a lesser-cost supercar based on that visit.

Yenko Chevrolet's New Dealership

A larger purpose-built dealership was constructed at 3663 Washington Road, McMurray, Pennsylvania. It was a few miles away from the Pike Street dealership. Floods and thefts inspired the move.

Once the Chevrolet franchise was fully operating in the new building, Don managed to weasel Frank into letting him open a Porsche franchise in the old Pike Street building.

The new modern Don Yenko Chevrolet building at Route 19 South was open as early as 1968 and remained open into the 1980s. It was described as being 5 miles south of South Hills Village Shopping Center, McMurray, Pennsylvania.

1969 COPO Yenkos

Yenko cultivated his "conversion" process even further in 1969 when he found a way to circumvent the whole process of switching engines at his dealership. Don used the COPO system to get his Camaros built with L72 427 engines directly out of the factory. Now he saved conversion cost and was also covered under warranty when someone blew up an engine.

The code for this new super Camaro was COPO 9561, which started with an L72 427 425-hp engine. Other goodies were the cowl-induction hood, which used a throttle-activated flapper at the base of the windshield instead of hood scoops. Don didn't have to fuss with his dual-scooped fiberglass hood as he had for 1968. The cowl induction was much more effective and factory made! Simple. The cowl induction migrated from COPO to become a popular Regular Production Option for Z28 and other Camaros in mid-1969 model year.

This Yenko ad correctly identifies its offerings as "the mean ones!" Note that Yenko was now offering 427 engines rated at 450 hp in the Camaro, the Chevelle, and the Nova.

Dennis Albaugh owns this Rally Green 1969 Yenko Nova 427 4-speed. Amazingly, Yenko pumped out 37 of these outrageous Nova 427s. Chevrolet refused to process Don's request for 427 COPO Novas, so he engine swapped them at his dealership. Don later expressed regret for building such crazy cars.

Rick and Anne Nelson of MuscleCar Restoration & Design in Pleasant Plains, Illinois, restored this 1969 Garnet Red Yenko COPO Chevelle in 2019. Originally sold through performance heavyweight dealer V. V. Cooke, the L72 427 engine is coupled with a close-ratio M21. The first owner parked the car at 18,000 miles in his Louisville, Kentucky, garage after a front end accident. (Photo Courtesy Anne and Rick Nelson)

Don's 427 COPO option also included heavy-duty cooling and the special heat-treated extra-strength 4.10:1 code BE axle. Power front disc brakes were considered essential by engineers to cope with the extra power and were included as a mandatory part of the package.

Don's 1969 Camaro 427s are nicknamed "Double-COPO" cars by modern collectors because he coupled the new COPO 9561 engine option with his old "Sports Car Conversion" COPO 9737 to add other goodies. As he did in 1968, Don's package added a 140-mph speedometer, and a 13/16-inch-diameter stabilizer bar.

The 1969 also included bigger wheels. The prior year Don's 427 Camaros used 14x6-inch Pontiac Rally II mag-styled wheels. In 1969, Don put bigger wheels right on from the factory with E70x15 Goodyear Wide Tread GT tires on 15x7-inch rally wheels. The Sports Car Conversion option expanded later in the year when it included a factory tachometer and gas gauge relocated to center position.

Yenko added his badge to the rear of the Nova so people would know whose car blew off their doors. The 427 badge explained why it happened! This Yenko Nova was originally sold through V. V. Cooke Chevrolet in Louisville, Kentucky. Cooke was a major high-performance dealership, racing sponsor, and Yenko distributor.

As shocking as a 427 Nova sounds, the engine actually fits in the engine bay quite nicely. Note that no attempt was made by Yenko to duct cold air to the engine or create hood scoops. In 1970, Don toyed with the concept of a hood scoop for the Yenko Nova Deuce cars.

Chapter 17: Yenko Chevrolet

The Yenko cars were tough. The manual transmission provided was the M22 heavy-duty rock crusher. If the automatic transmission was ordered, then the engine was downgraded from the solid lifters to hydraulic.

After a Double COPO car arrived at Don's dealership, the only conversion left to do was to apply the stripes and SYC logo to the headrests. Local teens, including his daughter, applied the stripes!

The COPO system also worked for Chevelles. Yenko produced some 427 Chevelle SS cars, too. The Chevelles lacked the 140-mph speedometer. The hassle of redesigning and printing a new face and recalibration was considered too excessive for the small run of cars envisioned. General Motors also refused to allow a COPO order for 427 Novas because they were too small and light for so much power.

Don Yenko simply returned to his old practice of yanking and replacing engines to produce the 427 Yenko Nova for 1969. In later interviews, Don mused that the Novas were probably a mistake, as they were dangerously overpowered for the chassis.

Don heard rumors the factory was finally going to allow 400+ cubic inches into pony car and intermediate muscle cars. If the rumor wasn't true, Don was poised to order a big batch of COPO big-blocks.

By the end of 1969, Don Yenko's vision for ever-expanding big-block COPOs was pierced as insurance rates skyrocketed on these cars. By the end of the 1969 model year, the widespread insurance agency surcharge hassle had begun. "Ordinary" big-block factory muscle cars were becoming uninsurable, which made the extra-special Yenko breed even more of a challenge to insure.

Don Yenko Loses Exclusivity

Insurance hassles weren't the only thing closing in on Don Yenko in 1969. Other dealerships figured out what he was doing and piggybacked off his COPO packages. Don's nicely put together COPO packages were appealing to other high-performance dealerships, such as Berger Chevrolet, which ordered a ton of COPO cars. Emmert Chevrolet got into the game early with COPO cars via Jim Mattison, who heard about the program and helped facilitate an order.

Jack Douglass of Jack Douglass Chevrolet found paperwork in one of his Yenko cars and used it to order his own COPO cars. When Don Yenko found out, they reached an agreement for Jack to apply Yenko stripes and brand the cars as Yenkos to ensure Don got his cut.

In 1968, Vince Piggins gave both Fred Gibb and Don Yenko the go ahead for 427 Camaro programs. Don got his green light in November, but because of the pressing need to have the racing aluminum-block 427 ready for Winternationals, racing development of that COPO option may have taken precedence over the iron-block street cars.

At this time, Dick Harrell was working with Fred Gibb. Dick was liaising with engineering in the development of Fred Gibb's legendary order of 50 1969 COPO ZL1 427 Camaros. Dick and Chevrolet engineers discussed mounting issues with the Corvette L72 427 using the Camaro chassis. Much of the development work done on that car was applicable to Don's iron-block 427 Camaros.

Fred Gibb Chevrolet received two copies of 1969 COPO ZL1 Camaros before the end of 1968. Don's iron-block 427 cars seem to have arrived a little later in winter. In a case of crossover, two copies of 1969 COPO ZL1 Camaros were ordered as "Double COPOs" with Don's 9737 Sports Car Conversion package added to the order!

Yenko's Insurable Nova Deuce

When insurance companies crushed the muscle car movement, Yenko was one of the few supercar conversion dealerships to quickly circumvent the hassle by creating a 1970 Yenko Deuce 350 Nova. That was the only special car Yenko offered in the peak ultimate watershed year of muscle mania.

In 1970, General Motors finally lifted its 400-ci restriction on intermediates and pony cars, rendering the need for a Yenko big-block conversion car superfluous. Chevelle SS 454 LS6 beasts were available at any dealership. Camaros with 396 engines were still the limit for the pony car, but

When insurance companies made big-block muscle machines virtually unaffordable, Don Yenko struck back with a stealth machine: the Yenko Deuce. How can a car with a Corvette LT1 350, hood stripes, and long body stripes that swoop up over the rear deck be a stealth machine? Because when you brought in the paperwork on this car, it appeared to be a basic Nova 350. The trick was not to let the insurance agent view the car!

The owner-added black integral tachometer and hood scoop was actually an AMC item. Don Yenko was contemplating this scoop as a regular part of the Deuce package but abandoned the idea. A new air cleaner to seal to intake would be needed and major metal cutting work was required to cut a hole in the hood to make the scoop functional.

Mick Price's 1970 Yenko Deuce was originally sold directly through Yenko. The Gobi Beige paint really highlights the great stripe pattern that Don came up for this model year. Note the way the black stripes widen for Yenko Deuce nomenclature cutouts on the rear quarters then sweep over the trunk.

insurance premiums were going through the roof for young buyers of muscle machines. Yenko had trouble moving the last of his 427 Camaros in 1969.

Yenko had the solution to insurance shock: a stealth Nova that he named the Deuce. The name refers back to the Nova's origin as a Chevy II. The Deuce was actually a 360-hp (the exact same engine is 370 hp in a Vette installation) car, but on paper it was innocuous. It was based on the lower bodystyle Nova to reduce cost.

Yenko ordered two COPO packages to create his Deuce: his usual Sports Car Conversion coupled with a COPO engine option for a 350 360-hp LT1 engine. The result was a superfast, good handling Nova that was a "mere" 350-ci car.

Don's Deuce was indistinguishable on the title paperwork from a pedestrian Nova 350 when an insurance agent processed the premiums. The Deuce flew under the insurance radar with ease. Don's plan started with an order of 125 base-model Novas to avoid triggering the insurance bombs.

The stripped Novas were ordered with RPO L65 350 250-hp engines with mandatory N10 dual exhaust; M20 4-speed or M35 automatic; G80 12-bolt 4.10:1 Posi-Traction rear axle; JL2 power front disc brakes; 731 black vinyl bench and rubber floormat; ZJ3 interior brightwork, dome light, and mirror; and U63 AM radio. That bare-bones start put some of the right stuff in place and kept the weight and cost out of the car.

COPO 9010 substituted the 350 360-hp LT1, and COPO 9737 Sports Car Conversion added heavy-duty F41 suspension with the same front 13/16-inch sway bar from on the Camaros back in the 1960s. It also added a rear sway bar, and, most crucially, the wide-ratio transmission was ditched for a M21 4-speed. If the auto M35 was in place, it was upgraded to a TH400. The 12-bolt rear received the sturdier heat-treated ring-and-pinion setup.

When the Novas arrived, all Yenko had to do was apply stripes and put on some nicer wheels to disguise the plain origins of these Novas. Yenko's crew pulled off the column shift

Mark Hassett bought this 1972 Hugger Orange Vega Stinger to complete his Yenko Hugger Orange set (Camaro, Nova, and Chevelle). Mark's Vega is an original car that was originally sold through high-performance dealership Colonial Chevrolet in Norfolk, Virginia.

The front nose of the Vega really evokes the Camaro. Adding spoilers and choosing an appropriate color made the Vega into a good looker.

lever and installed a floor shifted control for the automatic.

No matter how fast or cutting edge Don Yenko got, other guys caught on. In this case, there wasn't a landslide of people piggybacking off Don's Deuce. Central Chevrolet Oldsmobile in London, Ontario, tried to get 10 of these Novas and eventually received 2. They went out without any external clues to what was under the surface.

The Vega Stinger II

As the muscle car era died off, Don attempted to keep performance alive when he went full circle back to his initial Corvair compact performance concept. Don introduced the Stinger II, which was based on the new Chevrolet Vega.

Today, most have forgotten the introduction of the Vega because of the stigma of engine problems and crazy rust issues, but there was a lot of excitement when they were first released. They looked like mini Camaros and held a lot of promise for dreamers.

The 1972 Yenko Stinger augmented the internally beefed-up Vega engine with a bigger radiator to address overheating issues. Don Yenko used the same foundry that produced his wheels a few years prior to create this really nice-looking aluminum valve cover with the Yenko logo stamped into it.

The interior of the Yenko Stinger Vega used the Camaro steering wheel and front seats. The Vega GT–supplied 130-mph speedometer, tachometer, and fake wood accents take the driver away from the budget Vega image. Yenko specified a tough M20 transmission linked to the sporty 4-speed shifter.

The "mini Camaro" lines of the Vega are very evident in this side view. Note the Yenko Stinger identification using a cutout into the black side stripe with Yenko's name above it. The Yenko crest was also added to the front fender.

The mag wheels and raised white letter Goodyear tires are correct for the Yenko Stinger Vega and are actually new old stock items. Note the downturned exhaust that feeds from a traverse-mounted rear muffler.

Don saw the nice looks combined with lightweight body as a sure winner. His bias toward small, maneuverable sports cars jumped to the fore, and he was fired up to see the Vega on racetracks. Like his old Corvair program, all this car needed was some guts and it would be a viable racer, or so Don thought. The 1970s were a whole different ballgame than the 1960s.

Don was immediately buried with hassles from the EPA because the addition of a turbo to the engine required a 50,000-mile reliability test. Don was a persevering and determined character and had worn down General Motors in his quest to have big-block muscle cars built on the factory line. He had jumped through the hoops of racing sanctioning bodies to push cars into race categories. He had last-minute prepped Vettes for races. Don was used to getting his way and bending or redrafting rules, but the EPA was too much even for him to crack.

Soon the public relations nightmare with the Vega followed. At the time of introduction, the Vega's disastrous body and drivetrain issues hadn't shown their face yet. The initial excitement of owning a sporty-looking compact devolved pretty quickly. Most owners started having problems almost immediately, and soon the Vega was widely known as a lemon.

Don finally made the Vega available to customers by putting the turbo in the trunk for customer installation. Now Don's dealership was no longer modifying or tampering with any emission certification. Big performance dealerships jumped on Don's concept and offered decent rates for installing a turbo upon delivery. V. V. Cooke (a Yenko Distributor) offered turbo kits or inexpensive installation. Because Cooke didn't sell the turbo car as a branded package, it seemed to get away with it.

Yenko Chevrolet Moves and Expands

With business booming in 1974 and not enough space, Frank and Don opened a new dealership at 2939 Washington Road, South Hills, just a few miles away from the McMurray location. This provided the final Yenko Chevrolet location. This dealership was huge and could handle 1,400 cars per year turnover.

Don tried to get his performance dose from selling performance parts and some racing engineering projects. His hope that his Porsche dealership would provide some fun was dashed by poor sales in the blue collar milieu. He also inquired into the possibility of carrying a Bricklin franchise in 1974.

By 1978, Yenko was carrying Fiat, Subaru, Porsche, and more. Back at the high-volume Chevy dealership in 1978, Kim Mason was general manager and did an interview about leasing increasing in popularity. The interview touched on buyer enthusiasm for the Caprice. Don Yenko was not involved in this interview and was known to be withdrawing from the large, impersonal business that the dealership had become.

Last Shot

When the Porsche franchise fizzled, Don turned back to Chevy for one last kick at the performance can. He devised a new way to get a turbo onto a Chevrolet product with the 1981 Camaro Z28 as the basis for his Turbo Z. Very few sold and the dealer-special cars were allowed to fade away.

Without performance projects to motivate him, Don couldn't keep the fire alive for his Chevrolet dealership. Of course, all US dealerships were starting to feel the sales crunch by now. The large Yenko Chevy dealership was sold in 1982 to Dave Litzenburger and renamed Sun Chevrolet.

Don was chasing after a Jaguar franchise and still involved in racing activities, but his Chevrolet days were pretty much on the wane once the dealership was sold. On March 5, 1987, Don Yenko died when piloting his plane during a landing mishap in West Virginia. His ashes were put aboard a car in a 1988 IMSA Firehawk race, and he was listed as codriver. That gesture would have appealed to the fun-loving Don Yenko.

Don's parents remained active in the dealership, although in reduced capacity. Don's foresight regarding foreign cars and fuel economy paid off with a Honda franchise at the old McMurray building. Kim Mason eventually co-owned the Honda dealership with Don's daughters Lynn and Terri. The Honda dealership stayed in the Yenko family until 2008.

INDEX

A

Abraham, Bill 160–162, 164
Adams, Gene 6, 47, 49–52
Alan Green Chevrolet 43
Albertson Brothers Oldsmobile 5, 47–53
Albertson, Bruce 36, 39–41, 48, 53, 140
Albertson, Myron 47, 48, 96
Allen, William "Bill" Russell, Jr. 168, 170
Allen, William "Bill" Russell, Sr. 168, 171
American International Racers (A.I.R.) 14, 141
American Manufacturers Association (AMA) 136, 137, 146
American Motors Corporation (AMC) 9, 43, 69, 89, 187
Arlington Dragstrip 78
Armstrong, Dale 28

B

Baldwin-Motion 143, 154, 181
Baney Chrysler-Plymouth 45
Berger Chevrolet 9, 139, 141, 186
Berry Plasti-Glass 22, 23, 25, 29
Beswick, Arnie "the Farmer" 110, 156–158, 161
Bill Allen Chevrolet 5, 168–173
Bill Knafel Pontiac 5, 159–160, 162, 164, 166
Bill Murphy Buick 59
Bill Waters Ford 15
Bimbi, Stefano 129
Blocker, Dan 121, 122
Bondurant, Bob 28
Boulevard Buick 59
Brand Motors Ford City 37, 45
Bristow, Clifford David 5, 85–88, 92
Brown, Kelly 45
Brumfield, Charlie 149
Buick Motor Division 5, 9, 10, 19, 21, 54–64, 70, 71, 73–75, 77, 78, 80, 84, 85, 155, 158

C

Cahill, Bob 68
Camaro magazine 24
Car Craft magazine 96, 112, 124, 125, 146, 152
Car & Driver 24, 126, 152
Car Life magazine 24, 25, 95, 126
Carmichael, Michael 73, 74, 78–80, 84
CARS magazine 154–156, 160
Chrisman, Jack 39, 52
Christianson, Bob 102
Chrysler Company 8, 9, 18, 37–39, 41–45, 48, 52, 65, 68, 69, 76, 85, 95, 97–99, 103, 104, 112, 114, 117, 129, 133, 143, 151, 153, 162

Cliff Bristow Motors 5, 85–88
Clippinger Chevrolet 5, 10–18
Clippinger, Isaiah Hale 10, 11, 17
Clippinger, Norman H. 11, 17
Cole, Ed 131, 132, 138
Coletti Chrysler 43
Conn Pontiac 159
Conrad, Bud 152
Conroy Pontiac Buick 5, 6, 10, 70, 71, 73–84
Conroy, William F. "Bill" 70, 74, 79, 83, 84
COPO system 8, 25–27, 83, 89–92, 94, 130, 131, 133–143, 164, 170–173, 177, 179, 180, 182–187
Craig, Laurie 6, 70, 72–74, 79

D

Dale Chevrolet 5, 89–94
Dale, Elmer O. "Con" 89, 90, 94
Dale, William R. 90
Dana Chevrolet 5, 19–31, 68, 124, 126, 170, 178, 180–182, 184
Dana Chevrolet Hi-Performance Center 19, 28, 29, 31
Davis, Richard R. 11
Davis, Russell W. 11
Day, Roger 6, 170, 171
DeLorean, John 55, 81, 82, 92, 142, 148, 150, 152, 157, 159, 162, 164
Di Bari, Charles 65, 66, 68, 69, 149
Di Bari, James "Jim" 65, 66, 69
Dixon, Larry "Doc" 162–164
Downey Lincoln-Mercury 39
Drag Strip magazine 60
Dyer, Gary 105, 110, 111, 113, 115, 116

E

Eckstrand, Al "the Lawman" 147
Edison, Harry 12, 13
Emmert Chevrolet 186
Engel, Elwood 107
Estes, Elliot Marantette "Pete" 131, 136, 137, 142, 148

F

Farr, Don 49, 50, 53
Fensom, John "Oop" 142, 171
Ford Motor Company 5, 8–11, 14–18, 20–22, 24, 31, 37, 39, 44–46, 49, 54, 68, 69, 71, 76, 103, 105, 110, 111, 116, 117, 124, 133, 135, 147, 148, 159, 162, 167, 177, 182
Foulger Ford 46
Fox, Herb 131–133, 135, 141, 144
Fred Gibb Chevrolet 5, 6, 90–92, 130–144, 170, 171, 182, 186

Fred Gledhill Chevrolet 14
Frontera, Sam 146

G

Garner, James 14
General Motors Acceptance Corporation (GMAC) 17, 88
Gibb, Fred, Jr. 5, 91, 130–144, 170–171, 182, 186
Gibb, Helen 130, 133, 136, 137
Glowacki, Bill 6, 91, 92
Grant, Jerry 120
Great Lakes Dragaway 89, 111
Grove, Tommy 50, 65–68

H

Hanyan, Bill 42
Hardy, Phil 82
Harrell, "Mr. Chevrolet" Richard "Dick" 23, 27, 107, 122–126, 132–138, 141–143, 169–173, 179–183, 186
Harris, Leonard 47, 49–52
Hayter, Jim 143
Hi-Performance Cars 141, 155
Hirschbeck, Dennis 105
Holiday Oldsmobile 95, 96, 98
Holman-Moody 15
Hoover, Tom 102, 103
Hot Rod magazine 9, 14, 24, 28, 31, 34, 35, 41, 48, 54, 55, 57–60, 97, 100, 103, 125, 126, 129, 141, 146, 180
Hudson, Skip 120
Hurst Performance 113

I

Irwin, Dick 83, 84

J

Jack Douglass Chevrolet 186
Jeffords, Jim 119, 120
Jesse, Dick 146–153
Joe Cram Lincoln-Mercury 39
Johnston, Rollie 85
Jones, Parnelli 107

K

Kaplan, Ronnie 120, 129
Kennedy, "Pop" Lennie D. 55–64, 109, 110, 131, 155
Ken Wilson Chevrolet 176
Knafel Pontiac 5, 92, 150, 159–167
Knafel, William "Bill" 5, 159–167
Knudsen, Semon "Bunkie" 145, 146, 148
Kraus, Leonard 105, 117
Kraus, Norman "Mr. Norm" 5, 6, 8, 9, 18, 22, 30, 43, 44, 54, 105, 118, 120, 153, 165–167

L

Labarge, Gil 59
Lincoln-Mercury 9, 39, 158
Lionberger, Bob 132
Lions Drag Strip 26, 41, 43, 50, 111
Lorenzon, Fred 120
Luke, John 177
Lundberg, Myron 96
Lutz, Jim 96
Lynch, Tom 28

M

Macgrotty, Russ, Jr. 177
Mander Chevrolet Oldsmobile 5, 10, 70–74, 78–84, 92
Mander, James Orland 71, 83, 84
Marshall, Pierce 126
McCain, Don 22
McCurry, Robert B. "Bob", Jr. 112, 113, 117
McIntyre, Duke 79–81
McNabb, Phil 47, 50, 51
Mel Burns Ford Performance Center 22
Melrose Motors 5, 65–69
Milne Brothers' World of Wheels 42, 43
Milne, Cordy 42, 43
Milne, Jack 43
Mims, Donna Mae 177
Mission Raceway 72, 78, 82
Mobil Economy Runs 122
Moore, Ben 175
Morgan, Bruce 39, 41
Morgan, David 178
Moss, Stirling 72, 73
Motion Performance 45, 129, 165
Motor Trend magazine 24
Motschenbacher, Lothar 28
Mouldry, Rich 113
Mulligan, John 45
Murphy, Neil 79
Murphy, Skip 6, 98, 99, 104

N

National Dragster 60
Nicholson, "Dyno" Don 40, 157
Nickey Chevrolet 5, 19, 22–25, 107, 110, 119–129, 133, 167, 170, 177, 178, 180–182

P

Pacific Lincoln-Mercury 39
Packer, Bill, Jr. 145
Packer Pontiac 145, 146
Parson, Chuck 27
Paul Harvey Ford 16
Penske, Roger 22, 175
Perkl, Bert A. 95
Perkl, Jerry 95–104
Piggins, Vince 23, 124, 131, 132, 134–136, 181, 186
Pike, Joe 12, 174, 175, 178, 184
Pontiac Motor Division 5, 7, 10, 26, 40, 41, 49, 52, 54, 55, 57–59, 62, 64, 68–71, 73–82, 84–86, 89, 92, 97, 109, 111, 112, 131, 142, 145–167, 183–185
Powell, Don 6, 78
Prudhomme, Don "the Snake" 45

R

Ralph Williams Ford 37
Ray Andrews Ford 16, 17
Rediker, Frank 147, 149
Revson, Peter 28
Reynolds Buick 5, 9, 54–56, 59–61, 63, 64
Reynolds, Don 6, 54, 56–64
Reynolds, Irven Gibbs 55, 56, 64
Reynolds, Irven Gibbs "Pete", Jr. 55–57, 59–62, 64, 131, 132, 136, 137, 142, 147, 148, 159
Riley, Art 177
Road Test magazine 112, 114, 152
Ronda, Gaspar "Gas" 14–17, 68
Roote, T. F. 71
Rosen, Joel 6, 124
Royal Pontiac 5, 7, 54, 64, 84, 109, 112, 145–155, 157, 158, 162, 163
Russ Davis Ford 5, 10, 11, 14–18

S

Sachs & Sons 10, 32, 39
Savage, Dave 6, 85, 86, 88
Sawyer, Pam 123
Schifsky, Bill 102
Schornack, Milt 6, 145, 152, 154–156, 158
Schorr, Martyn L. 6, 154
Scow, Gary 103
Scrima, Ron 50, 52
Scritchfield, Dick 124
Seymore, Van 6, 43, 101, 103, 115, 117, 148–150
Shaker Engineering 149
Shelby American 19, 21, 22, 27, 28, 117
Shelby, Carroll 21, 22, 25, 28, 31, 45, 72
Shepard, Larry 143
Shrewsbury, Bill 39
South-Lyn Auto Repair 30
South-Lyn Auto Sales 30, 31
South-Lyn Honda Suzuki 30
Sox, Ronnie 39
Span Inc. 125, 177, 178, 182
Sports Car Graphic 121
Stedelbauer Chevrolet Oldsmobile 85
Stephani, Edward "Ed" Joseph 35, 40, 45, 61, 119, 120, 125–127, 131, 132, 138, 176
Stephani, John "Jack" F. 32, 35, 39, 42, 43, 48, 52, 119–122, 125, 127, 129, 186
St. Louis International Raceway 170, 181
Stroppe, Bill 39
Sullins, Ray 141
Super Stock magazine 15, 28, 38, 39, 41–43, 51, 66, 113, 125, 127, 141, 143, 147, 154
Swiatek, Don 122, 127, 129

T

Tanner, Norm "Sonny" 165, 166
Tasca Ford 8, 14, 16, 105, 182
Ted Baker Buick 59
Thomas, Bill 22–24, 41, 61, 74, 124–126, 180, 181
Thompson, Dick "the Racing Dentist" 177
Trevor, Bill W. 55, 58

U

Ubly Dragstrip 110
Union Grove Raceway 91

V

Vallerga, Dominick 65
Vallerga, Henry 65
Vanke, Arlen 160–163, 165, 166

W

Walters, Clarence 147
Wangers, Jim 6–8, 92, 109, 129, 145–148, 150–152, 154, 155, 157, 158, 162
Ward, Jim 44
Warren, Dave 154–156, 158
Washburn Chevrolet 14
Westwood Race Track 72
White Bear Dodge 5, 8, 90, 95–104
Willison, Clarence "Willie" 12, 18
Wilshire Oldsmobile 35–38
Wilson, Asa "Ace", Jr. 54, 84, 145–147, 151, 153–155, 157, 158, 162
Wilson, Asa, Sr. 145, 146, 154, 158
Wright, Ben 131

Y

Yeakel Brothers Cadillac 34, 36
Yeakel Plymouth Center 5, 6, 8, 10, 32–46
Yeakel, Robert "Bob" Arthur 8, 32–38, 40, 46
Yeakel, Stephen "Steve" Alan 6, 24, 40
Yenko Chevrolet 5, 25, 88, 90, 126, 133, 170, 174–176, 179, 184, 189
Yenko, Donald Frank 25–28, 125, 126, 135, 170, 174–184, 186–189
Yenko, Frank 174–176
Yother, Cecil 65, 68
Yunick, Smokey 131

ADDITIONAL BOOKS THAT MAY INTEREST YOU...

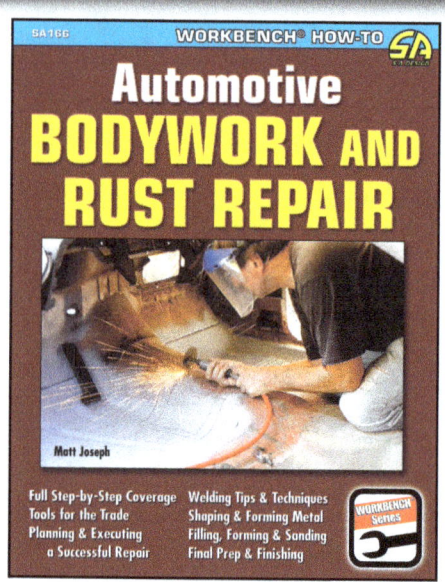

AUTOMOTIVE BODYWORK AND RUST REPAIR *by Matt Joseph* Author Matt Joseph shows you the ins and outs of tackling both simple and difficult rust and metalwork projects. He shows you how to select the proper tools for the job, common sense approaches to the task ahead of you, preparing and cleaning sheet metal, section fabrications and repair patches, welding options such as gas and electric, forming fitting and smoothing, cutting metal, final metal finishing including filling and sanding, the secrets of lead filling, making panels fit properly, and more. Softbound, 8.5 x 11 inches, 160 pages, 400 color photos. **Item # SA166**

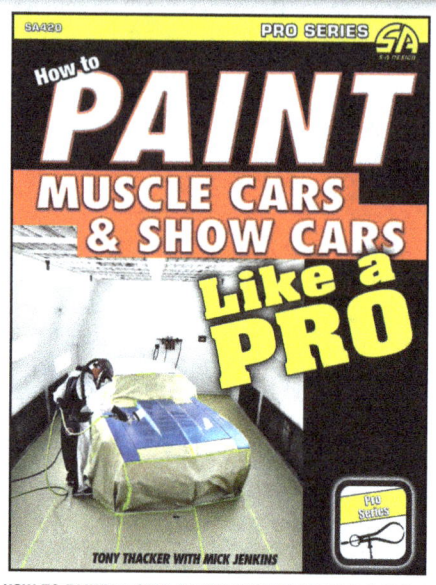

HOW TO PAINT MUSCLE CARS & SHOW CARS LIKE A PRO *by Tony Thacker with Mick Jenkins* Veteran author Tony Thacker teams up with LA-based award-winning painter extraordinaire Mick Jenkins to bring you this complete guide to show-quality painting. Included is all the information you need to create a show-quality finish, including chapters on making a plan, the tools needed for the job, complete disassembly information, repair versus replacement decisions, metal prep, the latest and best paint products, application, custom finishes, and more. Softbound, 8.5 x 11 inches, 144 pages, 527 color photos. **Item # SA420**

AUTOMOTIVE UPHOLSTERY AND INTERIOR RESTORATION *by Fred Mattson* Starting with a list of necessary tools, the author guides you through various tasks including seat restoration; door panel removal, patterning, assembly, and installation; headliner removal and installation; carpet cutting; and convertible top restoration. Softbound, 8.5 x 11 inches, 192 pages, 519 color photos. **Item # SA393**

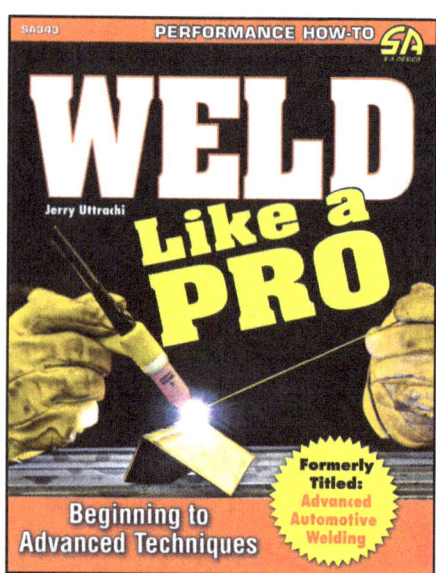

WELD LIKE A PRO Beginning to Advanced Techniques *by Jerry Uttrachi* In this revised edition of the previous title, *Advanced Automotive Welding*, Jerry Uttrachi, past president of the American Welding Society, shows you how to perform basic welding procedures with steel and cast iron. He also reveals advanced welding techniques and the use of aluminum, titanium, magnesium, stainless steel, and other specialty materials. TIG, oxyacetylene, arc, and wire-feed welding processes are detailed, with special coverage on stick and MIG processes. Welding butt and V-joints is explained as well as welding more complex joints, including J- and U-joints. Step-by-step instruction gives you the necessary information to tackle and complete almost any welding job. Softbound, 8.5 x 11 inches, 176 pages, 450 color photos. **Item # SA343**

Check out our website:

CarTechBooks.com

✓ Find our newest books before anyone else

✓ Get weekly tech tips from our experts

✓ Featuring a new deal each week!

Exclusive Promotions and Giveaways at www.CarTechBooks.com!

www.cartechbooks.com or 1-800-551-4754